The International Theological Commentary on the Holy Scripture of the Old and New Testaments

General Editors

Michael Allen
of Reformed Theological Seminary, USA

and

Scott R. Swain
of Reformed Theological Seminary, USA

Consulting Editors

Mark Gignilliat
of Beeson Divinity School, USA

Matthew Levering
of the University of St. Mary of the Lake, USA

C. Kavin Rowe
of Duke Divinity School, USA

Daniel J. Treier
of Wheaton College, USA

Micah

An International Theological Commentary

Mark S. Gignilliat

T&T CLARK

Bloomsbury Publishing Plc, 50 Bedford Square, London, WC1B 3DP, UK
Bloomsbury Publishing Inc, 1385 Broadway, New York, NY 10018, USA
Bloomsbury Publishing Ireland, 29 Earlsfort Terrace, Dublin 2, D02 AY28, Ireland

BLOOMSBURY, T&T CLARK and the T&T Clark logo are trademarks
of Bloomsbury Publishing Plc

First published in Great Britain 2019
This paperback edition published 2025

Copyright © Mark S. Gignilliat, 2019

Mark S. Gignilliat has asserted his right under the Copyright, Designs
and Patents Act, 1988, to be identified as Author of this work.

All rights reserved. No part of this publication may be: i) reproduced or transmitted in any form, electronic or mechanical, including photocopying, recording or by means of any information storage or retrieval system without prior permission in writing from the publishers; or ii) used or reproduced in any way for the training, development or operation of artificial intelligence (AI) technologies, including generative AI technologies. The rights holders expressly reserve this publication from the text and data mining exception as per Article 4(3) of the Digital Single Market Directive (EU) 2019/790.

Bloomsbury Publishing Plc does not have any control over, or responsibility for, any third-party websites referred to or in this book. All internet addresses given in this book were correct at the time of going to press. The author and publisher regret any inconvenience caused if addresses have changed or sites have ceased to exist, but can accept no responsibility for any such changes.

A catalogue record for this book is available from the British Library.

A catalog record for this book is available from the Library of Congress.

ISBN:	HB:	978-0-5671-9512-8
	PB:	978-0-5677-1660-6
	ePDF:	978-0-5676-8899-6
	ePub:	978-0-5676-8898-9

Typeset by Integra Software Services Pvt. Ltd.

For product safety related questions contact productsafety@bloomsbury.com.

To find out more about our authors and books visit www.bloomsbury.com
and sign up for our newsletters.

For Frank Limehouse
Pastor, Friend, and Lover of the Gospel

Contents

General Editors' Preface	viii
Preface	x
Micah Commentaries Bibliography	xii
A Theological Introduction to a Theological Commentary	1
Micah in Critical Dress: A Cursory Overview	33
Who Is a God Like You? Micah's Theological Witness in the Book of the Twelve: An Introductory Excurses	51
1 Micah 1:1—Prophetic Identities	71
2 Micah 2:1-5—Love Your Neighbor	101
3 Micah 3—Prophetic Recapitulation and Justification	127
4 Micah 4—Between Then and Now	149
5 Micah 5	173
6 Micah 6	193
7 Micah 7—Lamenting in Hope	213
Index	233
Scripture Index	247

General Editors' Preface

The T&T Clark International Theological Commentary Series aims to offer interpretation of the Bible that addresses its theological subject matter, gleaning from the best of the classical and the modern commentary traditions and showing the doctrinal development of scriptural truths. In so doing, it seeks to reconnect to the ecclesial tradition of biblical commentary as an effort in *ressourcement*, though not slavish repetition. Alert to tendencies toward atomism, historicism, and skepticism, the series seeks to offer a corrective to the widespread pathologies of academic study of the Bible in the modern era.

In contrast to modern study of the Bible as a collection of witnesses (fragmented and diverse) to ancient religious beliefs and practices, this series reflects upon Holy Scripture as a common witness from and of the triune God of the gospel. These interpretations will give priority to analysis of the scriptural text as such, reading any given passage not only in its most immediate context but also according to its canonical location, in light of what has historically been termed the *analogia scripturae*. In so doing, however, the series does not mandate any uniform approach to modern critical methods or to the appropriation of classical reading practices; the manner in which canonical reading occurs will follow the textual form and subject matter of the text rather than dictate them.

Whereas much modern biblical criticism has operated on the presumption that the doctrinal resources of the church are a hindrance to the exegetical and historical task, commentaries in this series will demonstrate a posture of dependence upon the creedal and confessional heritage of the church. As Zacharius Ursinus noted centuries ago, the catechetical and doctrinal resources of the church are meant to flow from and lead back unto a cogent reading of the biblical canon. In so doing, the reception history of the text will be viewed as a help and not merely an obstacle to understanding portions of Holy Scripture.

Without mandating a particular confessional position (whether Eastern or Western, Roman or Protestant), the volumes will be marked by a creedal and confessional alertness.

Finally, commentary serves to illumine the text to readers and, thus, does well to attend not only to the original horizon of the text but also to its target audience(s). Unfortunately, much biblical interpretation in the modern academy (from both its more liberal and conservative wings) operates as if a sharp divide should be drawn between the source horizon and the receptive horizon. This series, however, gestures toward contextual concerns regarding how the biblical literature impinges upon, comes into confrontation with, or aligns with contemporary questions. While the series does not do the work of homiletics, the commentator ought to exposit with an eye to that end and an ear to those concerns.

In seeking to honor these canonical, creedal, and contextual commitments, then, the T&T Clark International Theological Commentary Series will include sequential commentary on the totality of scriptural books, though the format of volumes will be shaped by the specific demands of the various biblical texts being expounded. Commentators will provide English translations or make use of widely known contemporary translations of varying sorts, but their exposition will be based ultimately upon the original language(s). Commentators will be selected for their capabilities as both exegetical and dogmatic theologians, demonstrated in linguistic and literary facility, creedal and confessional clarity, and an ability to relate the two analytic exercises of dogmatic reasoning and exegetical reasoning. Through its principles, format, and selective criteria for commentators, the series intends to further sketch and, in so doing, show the significance of a theological reading of Holy Scripture in the modern era.

Michael Allen and Scott Swain

Preface

This project took longer than I anticipated. I am also aware it could use more time. Like ships, commentaries need to be abandoned at times, especially given the richness of Scripture's material form and the infinite reach of its subject matter. In part, the challenge of this commentary was its seemingly limitless possibilities. The plane struggled to get off the runway, so to speak. I have little doubt this commentary may frustrate readers who inhabit the social space of a particular theological discipline. Bible scholars may take issue with lines of inquiry unexplored or left attenuated, with the expected interpretive hurdle of transgressing Micah's historical particularity. Theologians may wonder why a particular line of thought or figural extension received short shrift. I feel the force of these potential receptions as I abandon ship.

The form of the commentary follows a pattern established by Karl Barth's *Church Dogmatics*, though in reverse. The larger print follows the text's verbal character and literary logic, in light of Micah's theological subject matter. The small print explores figural or theological extensions of the text where such are deemed "organic" or in accord with the text's literal sense. The danger of this format is the suggestion that the small print is where theological reflection occurs, somewhat distanced by material form from the verbal and literary logic of Micah's prophetic text. "Now, let's do some theology *post facto*." Such is not the case. I understand the small and large print as inhabiting the same space provided by the text's verbal character and theological subject matter. I retain the distinction in font as an aid to the reading process, a tool to help the reader retain his or her orientation. At the same time, readers will discover the small and larger print bleeding into each other and not living up to a strict division or pattern.

I owe a debt of gratitude to Beeson Divinity School and Samford University for a sabbatical leave during the 2011–2012 academic year. I was awarded a faculty development grant from Samford that significantly aided my sabbatical travels. I remain grateful for this opportunity as much of the groundwork for this project took place during that time. I also extend my thanks to Professor Hermann Spieckermann of the University of Göttingen who hosted me during a six-month stay in Göttingen. For those who know Professor Spieckermann, it goes without saying that a kinder and more gracious host cannot be found. I also thank Nathan MacDonald and his family who also hosted us during our time in Göttingen. Nathan's productive research habits are exemplary, and I benefited much from my time with him.

My *Doktorvater* Christopher Seitz stands out as a consistent dialogue partner both in the real and in my head. His intellectual energies and capabilities loom large, and I am honored to stand in his shadow. My thanks go to Don Collett as well. Dr. Collett is a friend and thinker of the highest order. I owe much to him and his intellectual gifts. Former student and priest, David Tew read through the manuscript and offered substantial help along the way. My colleagues at Beeson Divinity School continue as fruitful and able interlocutors. I thank especially Dr. Carl Beckwith, though many others should be named. I would be remiss if I failed to mention my students at Beeson Divinity School and the parishioners of the Cathedral Church of the Advent. These friends in both places afforded me contexts for teaching and thinking through Micah. I've grown accustomed and grateful for the fruitful interaction of academy and church.

And finally, to my family. My parents, Bill and Martha Gignilliat, continue to support and encourage their middle-aged son. Their moving near us in Birmingham has brought innumerable blessings. My wife and I inhabit a domicile marked by the frenetic energy of four children, ranging in age from early adolescence to preschool. Needless to say, it is a wild ride, and I'm so glad and grateful to be on it with my wife, Naomi. Writing books like this one seem far removed from what appears to constitute my "normal" life. The aberrant pen marks found here or there in my books remind me of what's of enduring temporal and eternal value. Thank you, Mary Grace, for those indelible reminders.

Micah Commentaries Bibliography

Andersen, Francis I., and Freedman, David Noel, *Micah: A New Translation with Introduction and Commentary* (Anchor Bible; New Haven: Yale University Press, 2000).

Calvin, John, *The Commentaries of John Calvin on the Prophet Micah* (Calvin's Commentaries Volume XIV; trans. J. Owen; Grand Rapids: Baker Books, 2005).

Calvin, John, *Sermons on the Book of Micah* (trans. B.W. Farley; Phillipsburg: P&R Publishing, 2003).

Cyril of Alexandria, *Commentary on the Twelve Prophets, Volume 2* (The Fathers of the Church; trans. R. C. Hill; Washington: CUA Press, 2008).

Hillers, Delbert R, *Micah* (Hermeneia; Philadelphia: Fortress Press, 1984).

Jeremias, Jörg, *Die Propheten Joel, Obadja, Jona, Micha* (ATD 24, 3; Göttingen: Vandenhoeck & Ruprecht, 2007).

Luther, Martin, *Minor Prophets I: Hosea-Malachi* (AW 18; Saint Louis: Concordia Publishing House, 1975).

Mays, James Luther, *Micah* (Old Testament Library; Philadelphia: Westminster Press, 1976).

McKane, William, *Micah: Introduction and Commentary* (Edinburgh: T&T Clark, 1998).

Nogalski, James D., *The Book of the Twelve: Micah-Malachi* (Smyth and Helwys Bible Commentary; Macon: Smyth and Helwys, 2011).

Smith-Christopher, Daniel L., *Micah* (Old Testament Library; Louisville: WJK, 2015).

Smith, Ralph L., *Micah-Malachi* (Word Biblical Commentary; Nashville: Thomas Nelson, 1984).

Sweeney, Marvin A., *The Twelve Prophets, Volume 2* (Berit Olam: Studies in Hebrew Narrative & Poetry; Collegeville: The Liturgical Press, 2000).

Theodore of Mopsuestia, *Commentary on the Twelve Prophets* (The Fathers of the Church; trans. R. C. Hill; Washington: CUA Press, 2004).

Theodoret of Cyrus, *Commentaries on the Prophets, Volume 3: Commentary on the Twelve Prophets* (trans. R. C. Hill; Brookline: Holy Cross Orthodox Press, 2006).

Waltke, Bruce K., *A Commentary on Micah* (Grand Rapids: Eerdmans, 2007).

Wolff, Hans Walter, *Micah: A Commentary* (Continental Commentaries; trans. Gary Stansell; Minneapolis: Augsburg Fortress, 1990).

A Theological Introduction to a Theological Commentary

Character of a theological commentary

The genre of biblical commentary writing has a long and noble history. Its roots can be traced to the compositional history of the Old Testament itself where in a process of interpretive and reflective hearing of the biblical traditions the Bible comments on itself.[1] Various terms express this dynamic of self-referencing and interpretation: intertextuality, *relecture, Fortschreibung, Schriftgelehrte Prophetie*.[2] One of the more promising and interesting developments in recent Old Testament studies is the detailed and analytical treatment of the intertextual character of the biblical witness. The scholarly discussion on intertextuality ranges from the technical – What is the criterion used to identify intertextual allusions or quotations? How does one distinguish a redactor from a *Fortschreiber*? – to the larger meta-theological matters such as the social-religious underpinnings and

---

[1] I will refer to the first part of the Christian canon as the Old Testament for the sake of staking out clearly the interpretive stance from which this commentary is written, i.e., the Old Testament as the first of a two-part Christian canon. See Christopher Seitz, "Old Testament or Hebrew Bible? Some Theological Considerations," in *Word without End: The Old Testament as Abiding Theological Witness* (Grand Rapids: Eerdmans, 1998), 61–74.

[2] See, e.g., Jörg Jeremias, "Das Rätsel der Schriftprophetie," ZAW 125 (2013): 93–117; Konrad Schmid, *Schriftgelehrte Traditionsliteratur: Fallstudien zur innerbiblischen Schriftauslegung im Alten Testament* (FAT 77; Tübingen: Mohr Siebeck, 2011); Reinhard Gregor Kratz, *Prophetenstudien: Kleine Schriften II* (FAT 74; Tübingen: Mohr Siebeck, 2011), esp. chs 1–3.

motives for receiving and recalibrating biblical traditions from another time in Israel's religious history.³

In the body of this commentary, intertextual or cross-referencing associations will play an important role. Suffice it to say at this point, the force of the biblical traditions yields thoughtful theological reflection on the enduring character of the biblical witness even within the compositional history of the Old Testament itself. This internal textual dynamic has been presented in various ways: Gerhard von Rad's concept of *Vergegenwärtigung*, viz., a process of older traditions being made present in new moments of the divine economy; or Michael Fishbane's distinction between *traditio* and *traditum* in the tradition-building process; or Brevard Childs's understanding of a canon consciousness (*Kanonsbewusstein*) as embedded within the Old Testament's compositional history.⁴

Though the precise dating of the phenomenon is blurry, the Old Testament's compositional history elides into reception history. The

---

³ See especially the work of Bernard Levinson, e.g., *The Right Chorale: Studies in Biblical Law and Interpretation* (Winona Lake: Eisenbrauns, 2011) and *Legal Revision and Religious Renewal in Ancient Israel* (Cambridge: Cambridge University Press, 2008). Readers may find the annotated bibliography in the latter volume helpful even if there are disagreements over the thesis. See also Benjamin Sommer, *Revelation and Authority: Sinai in Jewish Scripture and Tradition* (New Haven: Yale University Press, 2015). Sommer affirms much of Levinson's reading of the legal revision taking place in the compositional history of Israel's Scriptures, though he differs on some crucial matters, viz., Levinson's notion of a "scribal sleight of hand" where the scribes gesture toward the legal traditions but only as a rhetorical trope to support their overturning of that tradition. Sommer understands the scribes as viewing their "innovations" as within the stream of previous legal traditions. Sommer makes a distinction between occasional *Gesetz* and divine *Gebot*. The latter is that which undergirds all of the *Gesetze* in Judaism. Sommer draws heavily from Franz Rosenzweig on this point and others (Sommer, *Revelation*, 241–51).

⁴ There are substantial differences between the various approaches listed above. In particular, Childs's approach works with necessary theological/ontological categories for coming to terms with the way Scripture's varied voices relate to each other on the level of a shared subject matter. As will become apparent, my own theological and interpretive sensibilities align with Childs on this matter. Von Rad and Fishbane, though different in their own respective approaches as Childs points out in a review of Fishbane (see below), view the intertextual character of Scripture as primarily a text-to-text phenomenon within an historicist frame of understanding. See Brevard Childs, "Review of Michael Fishbane's *Biblical Interpretation in Ancient Israel*," *JBL* 106 (1987): 511–13. The taxonomy, therefore, is not intended to attenuate these significant differences. Rather, it aims for a simple point: from various interpretive angles and intellectual/theological sensibilities, scholars see the phenomenon of Scripture listening to itself as a central component of its coming to be.

distinction between scribe and editor is not hard and fast but can be described by disposition toward the material. Once shaping, ordering, and editing ceases then the activity becomes one of preservation and transmission (Freedman, Micah, 29). In brief, composition of the texts becomes reception of them with an explicit and implicit notion of their anterior authority. The early efforts of reception are seen in the following: in many senses the LXX is an exercise in reception and resignification, the *pesharim* at Qumran, the New Testament documents, Rabbinic midrashim, patristic exegesis, and then on through the history of Jewish and Christian interpretation.

A word should be said here about the formal comparison of Rabbinic and Christian approaches; these comparisons have been observed for some time (Ellis et al.). For example, interpreters refer to Paul's reading of the Old Testament in 2 Cor 6:2 as pesher-like in quality or Matthew's hearing of the Old Testament is "midrashic." From one angle, the formal comparisons are helpful in situating the New Testament use of the Old Testament in its Jewish and historical context. The unfortunate side of these formal comparisons is the attenuation of the material differences between these approaches. The recognition of these material differences between New Testament reading of the Old Testament and *pesher* or *midrash* led Hans Hübner to describe the New Testament reading of the Old Testament as "sui generis."[5] Hübner's assessment makes a valid point and helps to highlight the unique character of Christian reception of the Old Testament, even when formal comparisons with other religious reading practices are identified.

While taking into account the material differences between Jewish and Christian reading practices, one shared outlook between these approaches is a commitment to the sacred character of the Old Testament/Hebrew Bible and the immediate proximity of the text's

---

[5] Hans Hübner, "New Testament Interpretation of the Old Testament," in *Hebrew Bible/ Old Testament: The History of Its Interpretation; Vol. I From Beginnings to the Middle Ages* (ed. Magne Saebø; Göttingen: Vandhenhoeck & Ruprecht, 1996), 237.

authorial voice, i.e., God is speaking now.⁶ For example, in a recent chapter by Benjamin Sommer entitled "Dating Pentateuchal Texts and the Perils of Pseudo-Historicism," Sommer calls a spade a spade when he says modern biblical scholars are copping out when they reduce texts to their historical genesis—"texts as reactions to historical, political, social, and/or economic factors"—without taking into account, in Sommer's terms, "religious intuitions that are essentially timeless."⁷ From a theological understanding of the canonical character of the Scriptures as *norma normans non normata*, these biblical texts are a divine word whose meaning and significance are not locked in their compositional genesis. They continue as a unique vehicle for divine self-disclosure.⁸

Admittedly, the language of "timeless" runs the danger of eviscerating the texts of their creaturely and historical character, so perhaps instead we might claim the following: *the biblical texts as*

---

⁶ Commenting on the significance of the Twelve at Qumran, Francis Watson comments, "Above all, text and interpretation both articulate what might be called an *oppositional ethos*. Hosea, Micah, Zephaniah and Malachi have no inhibitions about denouncing current religious and political power structures, and empower their commentators to do likewise. In that sense, the sect's oppositional ethos is a genuinely scriptural construct; in its interpretations, the prophetic voice from the past again becomes contemporary." Francis Watson, *Paul and the Hermeneutics of Faith* (London: T&T Clark, 2004), 111.

⁷ Benjamin Sommer, "Dating Pentateuchal Texts and the Danger of Pseudo-Historicism," in *The Pentateuch: International Perspectives on Current Research* (ed. T. B. Dozeman, K. Schmid, B. J. Schwarz; FAT 78; Tübingen: Mohr Siebeck, 2011), 107.

⁸ Dutch theologian Herman Bavinck provides the following account of Scripture's inspiration: "Scripture, accordingly, does not stand by itself. It may not be construed deistically. It is rooted in a centuries-long history and is the fruit of God's revelation among the people of Israel and in Christ. Still it is not a book of times long past, which only links us with persons and events of the past. Holy Scripture is not an arid story or ancient chronicle but the ever-living, eternally youthful Word, which God, now and always, issues to his people. It is the eternally ongoing speech of God to us. It does not just serve to give us historical information; it does not even have the intent to furnish us a historical story by the standard of reliability demanded in other realms of knowledge. Holy Scripture is tendentious: whatever was written in former days was written for our instruction, that by steadfastness and by the encouragement of the Scriptures we might have hope [Rom. 15:4]. Scripture was written by the Holy Spirit that it might serve him in guiding the church, in the perfecting of the saints, in building up the body of Christ. In it God daily comes to his people. In it he speaks to his people, not from afar but from nearby ... It is the living voice of God ... Divine inspiration, accordingly, is a permanent attribute of Holy Scripture. It was not only 'God-breathed' at the time it was written; it *is* 'God-breathing.'" Herman Bavinck, *Reformed Dogmatics, Vol. I: Prolegomena* (trans. John Vriend; Grand Rapids: Baker, 2003), 384–85.

products of time-conditioned realities may be illuminated by their time-conditioned status but their range of meaning and effects are not hemmed in by it.[9] The compositional history of the Old Testament documents themselves attests to this phenomenon as the sacred traditions of Israel are transmitted for the sake of the enduring nature of the legal, prophetic, and wise counsel of God for his people. "Write this down for a future generation," says Isaiah the prophet twice over to his disciples in the prophetic book that bears his name (Isa 8:16; 30:8). Similarly, Paul says in Rom 15:4 that what was written in the former days was written for *our* instruction.[10] The Christian Scriptures are "eternally youthful," in Herman Bavinck's felicitous turn of phrase, making themselves immediately present by means of the teaching and exhortative office of the Holy Spirit. Such a theological claim resides near the center of the Old Testament's own coming-to-be and its history of reception.

Uwe Becker traces the methodological move from form-critical approaches to the prophets—dominant until the 1970s—to tradition-historical approaches where the distinction between "authentic" (*Echt*) and "inauthentic" (*Unecht*) becomes brittle. By methodological instinct, the form-critical approach sought *"die prophetische Stimme"* and required a sifting through the layers of tradition built upon the *viva vox* of the historical prophet to find this authentic voice. Walther Zimmerli's monumental and celebrated commentary on Ezekiel drew attention to the problems of the form-critical approach because of the expansive or

---

[9] Commenting on the significance of the Cyrus Cylinder for interpreting Isaiah, Childs comments, "Regardless of this continuing debate, the importance of studying these parallels lies in providing a check against isolating the Hebrew prophet from his specific historical context as if his text represented timeless religious literature that floated above all historical particularity." Brevard S. Childs, *Isaiah* (The Old Testament Library; Louisville: Westminster/John Knox Press, 2001), 350.

[10] Commenting on the preserving of Isaiah's prophetic word, von Rad claims, "If his own generation had rejected it, then it must be put in writing for a future one. The very fact that Isaiah did write it down makes clear that in his eyes the prophetic message was far from being a dead letter even if it had failed." Gerhard von Rad, *Old Testament Theology, Volume II* (trans. D. M. G. Stalker; San Francisco: Harper & Row, 1965), 167. Von Rad elaborates on the tradition-historical implications of such "handing down" of the prophetic traditions when he describes them as a "living organism, speaking directly to later generations as it had done to its own, and able even of itself to give birth to new prophecy" (Von Rad, *OTT II*, 168).

"lively" (*Lebendigkeit*) character of the prophetic word via the prophetic schools attached to the prophets. As an aside, Zimmerli does not rule out the prophet's own involvement in these acts of prophetic editing and *Fortschreibungen*.[11] Zimmerli gave these so-called "secondary" passages a new valuation (*Bewertung*). "Mit den Kategorien Echt-Unecht ist diese Sekundärtradition nicht zu fassen. Vielmehr bezeugt sie die unmittelbare Lebendigkeit des Prophetenwortes in Schülerkreis. Deiser sucht die Worte in einem etwas späteren Zeitpunkte neu aus dem Ganzen des durch Ez hörbaren Otteswortes heraus zu verstehen."[12] Becker identifies the earlier thought of Gerhard von Rad as leaning in the same direction regarding the prophets. Von Rad claims, "Ohne Zweifel muss es unsere Prophetenexegese noch mehr lernen, diese langsame Anriecherung der prophetischen Überlieferung unter einem anderen Gesichtspunkt zu betrachten als dem der 'Unechtheit' und einer unerfreulichen Entstellung des Ursprünglichen. Ist dieser Prozess doch vielmehr ein Zeichen für die Lebendigkeit, mit der die alte Botschaft weitergegeben und neuen Situationen angepasst wurde."[13] The prophetic word as "Gotteswortes" is lively and fertile as it makes its force felt in new situations. Such a tradition-historical account of the prophetic books' coming-to-be teems with Christian theological vocabulary regarding the inspiration of Scripture and God's providential oversight of his own prophetic word.

The biblical documents witness beyond themselves to the God who has spoken and is speaking through them. This understanding of the character of the biblical witness shapes the exegesis of the text itself. More than this, however, is the ordering of our knowing and reading in light of the identity of the one God with whom we have to do, a God whose identity and name within Christian discourse is the Father, Son, and Holy Ghost. A theological commentary operates within this

---

[11] Walther Zimmerli, *Ezekiel 1–24* (BKAT XIII/1; Neukirchener Verlag, 1969), 111.
[12] Uwe Becker, "Die Wiederentdeckung des Prophetenbuches: Tendenzen und Aufgaben der gegenwärtigen Prophetenforschung," *BTZ* 21 (2004): 32.
[13] Ibid., 33.

interpretive tradition: the sacred character of the biblical witness is brought to the center of the exegetical task. In other words, theological commitments or confessions of faith regarding the character of the Old Testament in the divine economy are not viewed as exegetical trimmings on the table. They constitute the meal.

The "scientific" character of Christian theology, as Barth reminds, requires "criticism and correction" of the Church's talk about God. It engages this activity in accord with the "criterion of the Church's own principle."[14] The object of theology's inquiry necessitates a path of knowledge that is commensurate with theology's objects and is, therefore, not beholden to the standards of other scientific disciplines.[15] There are significant hermeneutical implications with such an account of theology's "scientific" character. With the history of the Christian, interpretive tradition—a tradition with which this commentary identifies itself—a commitment to the ontology of the Old Testament as a vehicle for divine self-disclosure is affirmed. Because these theological commitments are front-loaded and not "bracketed out," our exegetical approach needs to be constrained by this governing ontology of the text. Moreover, it is confessed on the front end of the exegetical task that God has disclosed himself as Father, Son, and Holy Spirit. This self-identification of God is constitutive of Old Testament reading and the identification of the subject matter with which we are dealing, or better, encountering. Colossians reminds us that "he [Christ] is before all things" (Col 1:17).[16] Such a claim relates materially to Christian reading practices of the Old Testament.

John Webster claims, "In Christian theological usage, Scripture is an ontological category; to speak of the Bible as Holy Scripture is to indicate what it *is*."[17] Webster presses the matter further. "To say

---

[14] Karl Barth, *Church Dogmatics I.1* (trans. G. W. Bromiley; ed. G. W. Bromiley and T. F. Torrance; Edinburgh: T&T Clark, 1975), 6.
[15] Ibid., 10.
[16] See the comments ad loc. in Christopher Seitz, *Colossians* (Brazos Theological Commentary on the Bible; Grand Rapids: Brazos, 2014).
[17] John Webster, "Resurrection and Scripture," in *Christology and Scripture: Interdisciplinary Perspectives* (ed. A. T. Lincoln, A. Paddison; London: T&T Clark, 2007), 144.

'Scripture' is to say 'revelation'—not just in the sense that these texts are to be handled *as if* they were bearers of divine revelation, but in the sense that revelation is fundamental to the texts' *being*."[18] If such a formal claim is made about Scripture's ontology, it follows naturally to speak of the ontological or metaphysical dimension attendant to the material character of Scripture, namely, language as shaped canonically in our two-testament canon.[19]

John Webster's sagacious contributions to the interface of biblical exegesis and Christian dogmatics remain an enduring and fruitful gift to the church and its theological community. One particular concern of Webster's later work on the subject matter is a proper theological/metaphysical account of Scripture's being (as indicated in the previous paragraph). Webster stresses that "bibliology is prior to hermeneutics."[20] As he further explains, "Theology talks of what the biblical text *is* and what the text *does* before talking of who we are and what we do with the text, and it talks about what the text is and does by talking of God as Scripture's author and illuminator."[21] These instincts relate to Webster's long and nurtured allergy to the fussiness of a term like *hermeneutics* in favor of a more modest category like *reading*.[22]

---

[18] Ibid., 144.

[19] The reciprocal relationship between literary semantics and Scripture's Trinitarian subject matter is especially evident in Luther's Old Testament exegesis. In her insightful examination of Luther's Trinitarian hermeneutic, Christine Helmer shows how Luther tethers himself to the Hebrew text and language itself as the "vehicle for Trinitarian knowledge" (Christine Helmer, "Luther's Trinitarian Hermeneutic and the Old Testament," *Modern Theology* 18 [2002]: 55). The Holy Spirit as teaching and authorial agent of Israel's Scriptures opens up the tangible and fixed character of the Hebrew text to the divine mystery. In Helmer's terms, "Hebrew is the language the Spirit uses to refer to a theological subject matter" (ibid., 55). Of significance here is Luther's close attention to the Hebrew text and the peculiarities of its syntactical/lexical idiom as "a first step in grasping the Trinitarian reality" (ibid., 55). She concludes, "With respect to the Trinity, the only material is the letter that points beyond itself, to a subject matter in eternity" (ibid., 65).

[20] John Webster, *The Domain of the Word: Scripture and Theological Reason* (London: T&T Clark, 2012), 4.

[21] Ibid., 4.

[22] John Webster, *Word and Church* (London: Continuum, 2002), 47–86.

Theological exegesis and modernity's challenge

Hermeneutical commitments shaped by the speculative theological tradition became strained in the period of modernity when the literal sense was identified with the historical sense simpliciter.[23] This is an oft-rehearsed narrative, and I run the risk of simplification. Nevertheless, the theological character of the Old Testament's witness on this account was either ignored or located in the safe and distant place of Israel's ancient and developing religious experience. The gracious and thunderous voice of Yhwh becomes the object of analytical and detached study of an ancient people: a tamed Bible and a tamed God.[24]

The rise of modernity and critical approaches to reading the Bible brought with it fresh challenges, new avenues of thought, and a sharpness to the critical questions posed to the biblical documents. The previous paragraphs run the danger of identifying the usual suspects of modernity with facile descriptors unable to do justice to the great achievements of this period. Despite how one interprets the evidence of the ancient Near East and the literary character of the biblical documents—and the evidence does demand interpretation and is not self-authenticating—the fruits of knowledge in comparative religion and philology, archaeology, paleography, scribal practices, literary history, and a host of other illuminating phenomenon from the ancient

---

[23] Brevard Childs, "The Sensus Literalis of Scripture: An Ancient and Modern Problem," in *Beiträge zur Alttestamentlichen Theologie: Festschrift für Walther Zimmerli zum 70 Geburtstag* (Göttingen: Vandenhoeck & Ruprecht, 1977), 80–93.

[24] Langdon Gilkey's 1961 shot over the starboard bow against the post–Second World War Biblical Theology movement retains its devastating force. Langdon Gilkey, "Cosmology, Ontology, and the Travail of Biblical Language," *Journal of Religion* 41 (1961): 194–205. Gilkey problematizes the relationship between a modern scientific cosmology and an orthodox faith: the two facets that the Biblical Theology movement sought to hold together. Gary Dorrien expresses Gilkey's thesis as follows: "Thus the Bible, as rendered by biblical theology, did not really describe the acts of God, but the faith of Hebrew religion. In the Bible, God was the subject of the verbs, but in biblical theology, Hebrew faith displaced God as the subject of the verbs." Gary Dorrien, *The Making of American Liberal Theology: Crisis, Irony, & Postmodernity 1950–2005* (Louisville: WJK, 2006), 277. Or in Gilkey's own terms, "For us, then, the Bible is a book of the acts Hebrews believed God might have done and the words he might have said had he done and said them—but of course we recognize he did not" (Gilkey, "Cosmology," 196–97). See also, Seitz, *Word without End*, 79.

world continue to fascinate and draw scholars down interesting avenues of discovery. These achievements notwithstanding, the conflation of the literal sense of Scripture with its historical sense creates a different kind of interpretive and scholarly goal for those in the discipline of Old Testament studies. The literal sense of Scripture, along lines set out by Benedict Spinoza, went the way of historical excavation of one kind or another while the spiritual or theological sense of the Scripture went the way of homileticians and church-persons.[25] The uneasy relationship, at times more acute than others, between modern, critical approaches and a commitment to the sacred character of the Bible is felt to this day.

The German historicist tradition entered the philosophical stage with force after the demise of Hegel's long reign in the German philosophical tradition. I lean heavily on Frederick Beiser's account of philosophy after Hegel in the second half of the nineteenth century. Beiser recounts a compelling narrative of philosophy's fight for existence in university life because of the dominant interest in the natural sciences. The natural sciences gave serious pause to the intelligentsia of the day as to the necessity of philosophy as a stand-alone discipline. Enter the materialist controversies. Enter Schopenhauer. And more germane to our subject matter, enter the historicist tradition.[26]

Historicism, as an intellectual movement, arose in response to the search for transcendent warrant for moral, political, and societal values. In other words, though the Enlightenment had rejected the classic Christian metaphysics where God and God's providential ordering of history toward his own ends played center court, it had not rejected metaphysics outright. Rather, it sought to ground metaphysics in universal principles of reason located in the rational and ordered inquiry of humanity. These universal principles are irrespective of

---

[25] Benedict Spinoza, *Theological-Political Treatise* (Cambridge Texts in the History of Philosophy; ed. J. Israel; Cambridge: Cambridge University Press, 2007), 3–12. On the broad-ranging influence of "Spinozism" c. 1650–1750, see Jonathan I. Israel, *Radical Enlightenment: Philosophy and the Making of Modernity 1650–1750* (Oxford: Oxford University Press, 2001), esp. ch. 24.

[26] Frederick C. Beiser, *After Hegel: German Philosophy, 1840–1900* (Princeton: Princeton University Press, 2014).

historically particular places, times, or cultures. Historicism rejects outright both Christian and Enlightenment metaphysics, resisting any account of the transcendent apart from the particularities of place, time, and culture.

Beiser points out in his insightful book, *The German Historicist Tradition*, that historicism as a philosophical movement operated with the intellectual orbit of their nominalist forbearers. Nominalism in its late medieval guise also rejected universals in favor of particulars. Or put in other terms, universals were concepts of the mind (thus "conceptualist") based on shared relations. But, according to Richard Cross, substance is numerically one and singular in Ockhamist nominalism.[27] Existence resides in the particular and concrete, not in the abstract or ideal. Forms *are* material things. As Beiser summarizes, "The meaning and purpose of a thought, intention, value or belief did not exist apart from the determinate context, actions and words that expressed or embodied it. Since these expressions and embodiments are so different, indeed incommensurable, there cannot be a single form of human nature, reason or value. To talk about reason, value or human nature in general, apart from their specific expressions or embodiments in a specific time and place, is to indulge in mere abstractions."[28] So to repeat what has been stated, historicism as an intellectual movement rejects metaphysics of both the Theistic/Christian type and the Enlightenment kind. As Beiser concludes, "The fundamental principle of historicism is that all human actions

---

[27] Richard Cross, *The Medieval Christian Philosophers: An Introduction* (New York: I. B. Tauris, 2014), 190. Radner makes a compelling case for the potential of figural reading from both participationist metaphysics and a metaphysics of omnipotence (Ockham). Ephraim Radner, *Time and the Word: Figural Reading of the Christian Scriptures* (Grand Rapids: Eerdmans, 2016), 160–61. It should be noted, according to Radner and others, that Ockham's understanding of the singularity of substance does not necessitate a strict literalist reading of Scripture. Ockham's metaphysics of omnipotence allows for figural reading (p. 152). In a similar and perhaps more accessible vein, see Matthew Levering, *Participatory Exegesis: A Theology of Biblical Interpretation* (South Bend: University of Notre Dame Press, 2008).

[28] Frederick C. Beiser, *The German Historicist Tradition* (Oxford: Oxford University Press, 2015), 5.

and ideas have to be explained historically according to their specific historical causes and contexts."[29]

Beiser's book is some five hundred plus pages of densely researched argument regarding the character, scope, and principal figures of the German historicist tradition: all the way from Chladenius and Herder through Humboldt and Dilthey to Max Weber. So it goes without saying that the surface is barely being picked. Nevertheless, enough of the picture is before us to begin to see the massive impact historicist modes of thinking have had on biblical studies in the academy and the church. I want to avoid reduction or a Whig interpretation of history. Modern biblical criticism is a rich and varied thing, whose results provide important avenues of inquiry and appreciation for Scripture's linguistic, poetic, and historical depth. But somewhere lurking in the shadows or perhaps dancing in full view is the historicist resistance to theological metaphysics as a critical tool for reading historical texts.

The achievements of modern, critical readings of the Old Testament need not be dispensed with in toto on this "theological" account of reading. In fact, this commentary in the hands of Calvin or Luther would strike them as odd simply because of its placement on the far side of modernity and the challenges needing to be negotiated because of this providential location. Certain kinds of questions related to the biblical documents were not as sharply anticipated by the premodern

---

[29] Ibid., 15. There are other approaches to this matter than the metaphysical (though I think from a Christian theological perspective this is the preferred track). Gadamer in *Truth and Method* speaks of the implicit problems of historicism and romantic psychological approaches in their sealing off texts from their reception and effects (*Wirkung*). Temporal distance, in Gadamer's terms, is not something that must be overcome (308). Gadamer links this notion with the "naïve assumption of historicism." Rather, temporal distance creates the necessary conditions because the "yawning abyss" is filled with the continuity of custom and tradition. In an important point, Gadamer claims the following: "The positive conditions of historical understanding include the relative closure of a historical event, which allows us to view it as a whole, and its distance from contemporary opinions concerning its import" (309). Gadamer's "fusion of horizons" is born out of these reflections. There seems to be compatibility in this view and Childs's privileging of the final form of the text. Where Gadamer's project suffers for theological exegesis is in its theological anemia. For Childs, the final form of the biblical text is itself an historical achievement of God's providence. Without such a theological understanding of God's ordering of creaturely affairs, the final form of the biblical text would not claim superiority in light of early literary layers and strata.

tradition—though even here one is surprised to find Calvin wrestling with issues such as the authorship of Joshua and 2 Peter. Modern criticism has brought the complexity of the Old Testament's literary history into acute focus along with attention to the creaturely character of the biblical documents. At the same time, modern, critical instincts, and judgments need to be placed in a proper dogmatic locale in order to be situated organically within a single act of reading, a reading that is unsettled when careful textual and exegetical work goes one way while "homileticians" and "theologians" go another.

The epistemic starting point of faith seeking understanding has a hermeneutical force to it. It shapes and alters what we mean by "meaning." Spinoza's early insistence on reading the literal sense of the text within the hermetically sealed world of its storied and compositional genesis has had a very long shelf life in Old Testament studies: whether in the vein of baldly historicist approaches (Vatke's "only as it really occurred") or more sensitive religious-historical ones like de Wette's or in time Gunkel's. Still, a theological account of "meaning" became more problematic with these approaches. Meaning became located in the reconstructed historical moment or religious experience as a more manageable or objective entity whose treasures could be unlocked with careful and rigorous philological analysis conjoined with religious-historical feeling and imagination. Meaning, however, was not framed within the epistemic contours of a Trinitarian faith or within the potential of the Christian Bible as a two-testament canon to recalibrate our understanding of the Old Testament's subject matter. "The Scriptures became a source not a witness," as recounted by Brevard Childs.[30] A theological commentary such as the one on offer here seeks to hear the Old Testament as an abiding theological witness whose authorial voice and governed deployment remain under the providential care our Triune God.

---

[30] Especially insightful on this point is Christopher R. Seitz, "Scripture Becomes Religion(s): The Theological Crisis of Serious Biblical Interpretation in the Twentieth Century," in *Figured Out: Typology and Providence in Christian Scripture* (Louisville: WJK, 2001), 13–34.

Before turning to the Trinitarian character of Scripture reading, a final word should be offered about the significance of the task of continued Old Testament exegesis. Early in the twentieth century, A. J. Gunneweg declared, "Indeed it would be no exaggeration to understand the hermeneutical problem of the Old Testament as the problem of Christian theology, and not just one problem among others, seeing that all the other questions of theology are affected in one way or another by its resolution."[31] Such a statement seems hyperbolic prima facie. But as the recent resurgence of interest in patristic exegesis has made manifest, the early church's struggle after the triune character of God was a battle waged on the battlefield of biblical exegesis, and more particularly, the exegesis of the Old Testament.[32]

The demise of a certain kind of confidence attached to methods that promised objective results has had the positive outcome of revealing the important and inescapable significance of the interpretive apparatus we bring to the task. Jon Levinson reminds Christian and Jewish readers of Scripture to avoid hiding behind the gossamer veil of "objectivity" while being more forthright about their religious location as scholars.[33] These positions influence our reading, and they should. With all the exegetical help offered from modern, critical readings of the Old Testament in tow, this commentary operates within a Trinitarian confession along with the hermeneutical implications of this confession. Such an approach is not necessarily "heavy-handed," forcing texts to bear more theological weight

---

[31] A. H. J. Gunneweg, *Understanding the Old Testament* (trans. J. Bowden; London: SCM Press, 1978), 2.

[32] See, e.g., Lewis Ayres, *Nicaea and Its Legacy: An Approach to Fourth-Century Trinitarian Theology* (Oxford: Oxford University Press, 2006). Ayres warns modern Hegelians about accepting fourth-century Trinitarian conclusions while denying the exegetical instincts leading to these conclusions (ibid., 388).

[33] Jon D. Levenson, "Teaching the Texts in Context," *Harvard Divinity Bulletin* 35:4 (2007): 19–21. Levenson makes a pointed comment about "secular" approaches to biblical studies in the face of the religious convictions making possible the broad influence of this field of study. "But quite a challenge awaits those secular students of the Bible when they find themselves teaching college students whose main motivation for pursuing the subject is deeply involved with their religious commitments. The more thoughtful of them may come to suspect that there is something parasitical about a field of scholarship that travels on the residual momentum of religious traditions that it studiously keeps out of view, or even disparages" (ibid., 20).

than they can or finding Jesus hidden behind textual rocks and trees. Rather, the Scripture's subject matters, shaped as it is by the totality of the biblical witness and theological confession, provide a broader frame of reference than the hermetically sealed world of the texts in the various historical contexts of their composition. Allow me to illustrate these hermeneutical instincts from the subject of this commentary, Micah.

The prophetic ministry of Micah the eighth-century prophet took place in one of Israel and Judah's most cataclysmic historical events. This was a period of great upheaval for both the Northern and Southern Kingdoms. After a period of decline, the Neo-Assyrian Empire renewed its expansive energies under the leadership of Tiglath-pileser III (744–727 BC). This expansion included Israel and Judah as part of Neo-Assyria's move into the Levant. Amélie Kuhrt suggests, "It is possible that the rapid succession of usurpations in Israel between 745 and 722 is to be explained by the internal instability within Israel created by conflicting attempts to cope with Assyrian demands."[34] Because of Israel's alliance with Damascus in the so-called Syro-Ephraimite war, Tiglath-pileser III reconfigured large portions of Israel in 732 BC, leaving Samaria diminished in comparison to its former self.[35] A decade later, Israel's alliance with Egypt brought with it the ire of Tiglath-pileser's son, Shalmaneser V. As is oft-repeated and well attested, Samaria fell in 722 BC, but Neo-Assyria's tyranny continued to haunt Judah in the South long past these finalizing events in the North.

Sargon II (721–705) and his forces brought with them the dread of a ruthless, imperial force. His successor, Sennacherib (704–681), invaded Judah during Hezekiah's reign (701/702 BC). Sennacherib's incursion into Judah wreaked havoc in the Shephelah region of Micah's hometown in Moresheth.[36] It is possible that the rough syntax of Mic

---

[34] Amélie Kuhrt, *The Ancient Near East: c. 3000–330 BC, Volume Two* (New York: Routledge, 1995), 496. See also the accessible and helpful description of these events in Marc Van De Mieroop, *A History of the Ancient Near East, ca. 3000–323 BC, Second Edition* (Blackwell History of the Ancient Near East; Oxford: Blackwell Publishing, 2007).

[35] Ibid., 469.

[36] James B. Pritchard (ed.), *The Ancient Near East: An Anthology of Texts and Pictured* (Princeton: Princeton University Press, 2010), 287–88.

1:10-16 reveals the horrific confusion of the time. The second greatest city of Judah, Lachish, fell in the onslaught of Sennacherib—as the famed Lachish reliefs tell in pictured form. For all intents and purposes, Judah's total demise was immanent, except for the intervening hand of Yhwh on their behalf. These are the moments in which Micah ministered; these moments set the prophetic trajectory for the literary composition of the book as we now have it.

At the same time, the book's ending tells us something about its canonical intention. The critical issues will be engaged later, though it is enough to mention now the possible redactional addition of Mic 7:18-20 during the period when the Book of the Twelve was being shaped as a literary whole. As will be discussed more fully later, this does not attenuate the canonical status of these "additions" within Micah's prophetic book. In fact, they may function as interpretive guides for helping the reader to understand the book's broad intent. In the case of Micah, the book ends with an intertextual appeal to Exodus 34 where the character of God is revealed. The canonical conclusion of Micah frames for subsequent readers the theological reception of the book. The historical accident of Micah's prophetic activity and subsequent prophetic reflection on his ministry are recorded and preserved to tell us something about the character of Yhwh, the character of the God who (a) would allow the Assyrians to do what they did and what the Babylonians would eventually do (the theonomy question) and (b) not allow these fatal moments to be God's final word—והיה באחרית הימים.

In Neil MacDonald's helpful phrase, the identity of Yhwh in the Old Testament is a judging, yet desisting and forbearing self.[37] The historical encounter between Yhwh and the kingdoms of Israel and Judah reveals the character of the one God of the two testaments. The internal dynamics at play in the book of Micah—sin, judgment, covenant infidelity, political and religious machinations devoid of faithfulness, the threat of other nations—are the redemptive stage of the divine

---

[37] Neil B. MacDonald, *Metaphysics and the God of Israel: Systematic Theology of the Old and New Testaments* (Grand Rapids: Baker Academic, 2006).

economy, now attested to in the canonical prophet and in association with other prophetic witnesses as Yhwh reveals his identity. Yhwh is a God who judges sin, does not allow his judgment to be the final word, and promises redemption on the far side. An attendance to the internal claims of Micah itself reveals the canonical force of the book as an enduring word that goes beyond the immediate circumstances that gave rise to the historical prophet and the book attached to his name. Indeed, "Who *is* a God like you?"[38] The canonical prophet Micah anticipates generations of readers who will raise the same inquisitive and hopeful question.

Trinitarian retinae or exegetical metaphysics

Let us return to the matter of a Trinitarian hermeneutic for reading the Old Testament. The claims about to be made here are straightforward from the perspective of the church's belief in the gospel—namely, belief in the triune God provides the epistemic grounding for all exegetical activities.[39] Nevertheless, their hermeneutical significance for reading the Old Testament creates unfortunate difficulties for those involved in rigorous engagement with the biblical text in an academic sense, who

---

[38] Gerhard von Rad makes much of the canonical afterlife of the prophetic word beyond the human *personae* in his *Old Testament Theology*. While Isaiah's prophetic words may have fallen on deaf ears in the eighth century and while, empirically speaking, the eighth-century hearers may not have observed the fulfillment of Isaiah's prophetic utterances, nevertheless, Isaiah's words remain true and necessary even if for subsequent generations. "If his [Isaiah's] own generation had rejected it, then it must be put in writing for a future one. The very fact that Isaiah did write it down makes clear that in his eyes the prophetic message was far from being a dead letter even if it had failed" (Gerhard von Rad, *Old Testament Theology, Volume II* [trans. D. M. G. Stalker; San Francisco: Harper & Row, 1965], 167).

[39] Bruce Marshall explains, "A more satisfying approach to truth as a theological problem, rather than taking the church's central beliefs as to be especially in need of epistemic support, will take the church's Trinitarian identification of God itself chiefly to confer epistemic right. In order plausibly to maintain that the Trinity and other distinctively Christian doctrines are true, without drastically altering the meaning the Christian community ascribes to them, these doctrines must be regarded as epistemically primary across the board, that is, as themselves the primary criterion of truth" (Bruce D. Marshall, *Trinity and Truth* [Cambridge Studies in Christian Doctrine; Cambridge: Cambridge University Press, 2000], 4).

at the same time regard the text as a sacred and treasured document properly located in the social context of the church. The situation is problematized on the far side of the Enlightenment Bible, a situation so polarized that Michael Legaspi concludes his book on Johann David Michaelis and the rise of biblical studies at the University of Göttingen with a less than sanguine outlook on the rapprochement between the academic bible and the church's bible.[40] Governing assumptions and interpretive goals are so markedly different between the two interpretive communities that a happy marriage is unlikely.

This divide is unfortunate, however. Perhaps on the far side of modernity's inflated claims and optimism, a resurgence of interest in the biblical texts, their creaturely character (the critical enterprise), and their sacred origin and role will come together as an academic, though churchly discipline whose *Wissenschaftliche* nature is shaped by the epistemic resources given by faith. Modern concerns of biblical exegesis should not be dismissed in order to gain a maximal hearing of the text's "sacred character." In other words, repristinating premodern interpretation as if modernity never occurred will not do. At the same time and moreover, even the modern concerns raised by biblical criticism cannot from a Christian confessional standpoint be engaged in an attempt at arriving at historical *bruta facta*—something the Bible itself is good at keeping at arm's distance—or the displacement of belief in order to secure the text as object.[41]

As mentioned earlier, the ascendancy of historicism in German universities of the nineteenth century breathes the anti-metaphysical air of their nominalist forebears of the Middle Ages. In this sense, historicist instincts seek to provide a rational and scientifically rigorous account of the past devoid of any operative metaphysic, religious or

---

[40] "I believe that the scriptural Bible and the academic Bible are fundamentally different creations oriented toward rival interpretive communities." Michael C. Legaspi, *The Death of Scripture and the Rise of Biblical Studies* (Oxford Studies in Historical Theology; Oxford: Oxford University Press, 2010), 169. See also Jonathan Sheehan, *The Enlightenment Bible: Translation, Scholarship, Culture* (Princeton: Princeton University Press, 2005).

[41] See John Barton on the "bracketing out" of theological assumptions and modern criticism, *The Nature of Biblical Criticism* (Louisville: WJK, 2007).

Enlightenment. The search for universals by which historical and social differences might be adjudicated, either by appeal to God/providence, natural law, or the constancy of human nature, comes undone by the historicist instinct to valorize the historically particular and the socially conditioned aspects of human history. Historicism aims to provide an intellectually rigorous account of human history by attendance to intellectual norms that differ from the primary concern of the Western intellectual tradition, namely, the "transcendent justification for social, political and moral values."[42] In lieu of the search for "transcendent justification," historicism recognizes that human belief and practice are more socially and historically conditioned according to "their specific historical causes and context."[43]

While the benefits of the historicist tradition for the social and historical understanding of the biblical texts remain indisputable, Christian exegesis sits uncomfortably to the reduction of the biblical material and its critical inquiry to historical and social particularities. A theological metaphysic of some sort will be operative in the exegetical and theological hearing and reading of Christianity's sacred text because Christian exegesis in all forms is a discipline whose context is *coram Deo*. When it is not, one can say with some level of confidence, or at least with the history of the church's interpretative tradition behind him or her, the text being read or interpreted is no longer Christian Scripture but something else.

This brings us to an important topic, namely, the relationship of the human character of Scripture to its divine authorship in God's redemptive economy and the proper dogmatic ordering of the two. The recognition of the human authorship of Scripture—which now on the far side of modernity highlights the authoring roles of tradents, editors, and scribes—is in accord with the history of Christian interpretation of the Bible. Even within American and British fundamentalism of the early twentieth century, the term "organic inspiration" was preserved over

---

[42] Frederick C. Beiser, *The German Historicist Tradition* (Oxford: Oxford University Press, 2011), 10.
[43] Ibid., 19.

against "dictation" models of inspiration. B. B. Warfield, for example, championed for such an understanding of inspiration in his work on the subject matter.[44] Even as inspired agents, the human instruments of Scripture are affirmed in all their humanity and particularity of outlook: Isaiah was not Jeremiah. The model of organic inspiration can quite easily expand to incorporate the concepts of tradents and editors of the biblical material as well.

A straw man can at times be created against theological exegesis when critics portray theological interpretation as disinterested in non-confessional exegesis.[45] The very basic matters of the Old Testament's language, Hebrew and Aramaic, its cultural and provincial setting within the ancient Near Eastern world, and its character as Israel's scriptures demand attention simply for gaining an understanding of "the way the words go." The relationship between the church's interpretive tradition and those outside it is not easily codified—for example, tensions existed in the Reformation period between those who valued the Rabbinic exegetical tradition and those who did not. Nevertheless, because of the creaturely character of the Old Testament, certain exegetical matters, especially on the philological level, necessitate attention.[46]

An exchange of letters between Karl Barth and Walther Baumgartner illustrates the tensions on the ground between biblical scholars and theologians. These two engaged in an amicable, though heated, exchange toward the middle of the twentieth century over this precise point.[47] Barth had immense respect for Baumgartner's abilities in Semitic and

---

[44] B. B. Warfield, "Inspiration," *The Presbyterian Review* 2 (1881): 228–32.

[45] Hugh Williamson raises these concerns in his review of Brevard Childs's *The Struggle to Understand Isaiah as Christian Scripture*.

[46] In an attempt to sort out mischaracterizations of the canonic approach, Brevard Childs makes the following claim: "The materials for theological reflection are not the events or experiences behind the text, or apart from the construal in scripture by a community of faith and practice. However, because the biblical text continually bears witness to events and reactions in the life of Israel, the literature cannot be isolated from its ostensive reference. In view of these factors alone it is a basic misunderstanding to try to describe a canonical approach simply as a form of structuralism (*contra* Barton)." Brevard Childs, *Old Testament Theology in a Canonical Context* (Philadelphia: Fortress Press, 1985), 6.

[47] "Karl Barth und Walther Baumgartner: Ein Briefwechsel über das Alte Testament," ed. R. Smend, *ZThK* 6 (1986): 240–71.

ancient Near Eastern studies, even if he did call Baumgartner's lectures "dry bread."[48] Barth's son eventually took his doctoral degree under Baumgartner, whose philological legacy can hardly be denied. No student of the biblical text can afford to dismiss his lexical work because it is "not confessional." Barth's complaint against Baumgartner had nothing to do with his great achievements in Old Testament exegesis and philology. In similar fashion, one observes Barth's dependence on Martin Noth's *Geschichte Israels* in his rehearsal of the history of the covenant in *CD IV.1*. Barth borrows Noth's language of amphictyonic league—a notion of Israel's early tribal leagues borrowed from Greek histories that has come undone in subsequent histories of Israel (see de Vaux, Lemche, Grabbe)—without any interference or clarifying comment. The simple point here is that confessional or theological exegesis does not turn a blind eye toward the guild of Hebrew Bible/Old Testament scholarship.

At the same time, Barth's complaint against Baumgartner, and as his preface to the second edition of the Romans attests, was for the historical-critic to be more critical, that is, critical of themselves and their governing assumptions. Moreover, Barth had real reservations about Old Testament scholars and their preparation of women and men for pastoral/preaching responsibilities. In fact, Barth was more sanguine about New Testament scholars on this account than Old Testament scholars. The real concern was over the subject matter of the text (*die Sache*). Barth did not deny the creaturely character of the Scriptures, a matter that has gotten him into hot water with some evangelical accounts of Barth's doctrine of Scripture. But he resisted the historicist reduction of the text's theological subject matter to the issues pertaining to its creaturely genesis and historical setting. As is well known, for Barth when one enters the world of the Bible, one enters the new world of God, and God's word is not locked in the historical accidents that gave rise to the Bible's literary witness.

---

[48] Eberhard Busch, *Karl Barth: His Life from Letters and Autobiographical Texts* (trans. J. Bowden; Grand Rapids: Eerdmans, 1975), 268.

The relationship of the divine author and human author is not coequal, each having an equally divided portion. Rather, the divine authorship of Scripture is dogmatically prior to the human authorship and governs our understanding of the latter—"the grass withers the flower fades but the word of our God stands forever" (Isa 40:8). The primacy of the divine word has a shaping influence on our reading strategies and allows us to look for the multi-perspectival yet unified voice of the Old Testament witness.

At the beginning of *Church Dogmatics IV.1*, Karl Barth speaks of Jesus Christ as the epistemological principle of Christian belief.[49] Barth's larger concern is to ward off the danger of treating the name Jesus Christ as materially insignificant to the church's beliefs and actions. On this account Jesus Christ is the one responsible for the affairs of the church, though he hovers somewhere in the distance when it comes to actual faith and life. Barth senses a great danger here, a danger where Jesus in effect becomes superfluous to the church's lived existence. Barth counters:

> But the Christian message does say something individual, new and substantial because it speaks concretely, not mythically, because it does not know and proclaim anything side by side with or apart from Jesus Christ, because it knows and proclaims all things only as His things. It does not know and proclaim Him, therefore, merely as the representative and exponent of something other. For it, there is no something other side by side with or apart from Him. For it, there is nothing worthy of mention that is not as such His. Everything that it knows and proclaims as worthy of mention, it does so as His.[50]

There is a theological force in these reflections of Barth that exerts itself on the hermeneutical task as well. The authorizing presence of Jesus Christ constrains our reading of the biblical text, and this constraining elicits from the reader of Scripture an affirming nod in

---

[49] Karl Barth, *Church Dogmatics IV.1* (trans. G. W. Bromiley; Edinburgh: T&T Clark, 1956), 21.
[50] Ibid., 21.

the direction of Jesus Christ's governing role in the exegesis of his word. "Everything that it knows and proclaims as worthy of mention, it does so as His." The compartmentalization of our exegetical work from the Lordship of Jesus Christ in all spheres of knowledge runs the real risk of disobedience.

The hermeneutical significance of Barth's Trinitarian vision is towering. In the naming of God as Father, Son, and Holy Spirit biblical "meaning" begins to take shape. Gerhard Sauter uses a memorable metaphor chosen in contrast to Calvin's famed "lenses." Sauter suggests faith functions more like retina than lenses.[51] Lenses bring matters into focus, whereas our retina allows us to see in the first place. The context of Sauter's metaphor is the Trinitarian center of Christian belief. "Christians are Trinitarians," says Sauter. As mentioned in the beginning of this section, such a claim is straightforward; it is the content of our gospel hope. But the governing role such content has in all spheres of Christian existence, including the art and practice of biblical exegesis, is not always so straightforwardly clear or received. Barth's earlier "epistemological" warnings hold true in the realm of biblical exegesis as well. Biblical exegetes in the church run the risk of going about their tasks with little to no reference to him.

This kind of epistemological disposition was at the heart of the fourth-century debates over the identity of God. Khaled Anatolios situates the Trinitarian debates of the fourth century within a pan-global epistemological effort. According to Anatolios, Kant considered Trinitarian doctrine nonsensical, while Schleiermacher dismissed the ontological relationship of Trinitarian doctrine to the actual divine being—the doctrine of the Trinity is an accommodation regarding God's interaction with the world as Son and Spirit.[52] Anatolios suggests a closer examination of these "nonsensical" propositions, along with a deeper appreciation of the significance Trinitarian doctrine held for

---

[51] Gerhard Sauter, *Protestant Theology at the Crossroads: How to Face the Crucial Tasks for Theology in the Twenty-First Century* (Grand Rapids: Eerdmans, 2007), 38.

[52] Khaled Anatolios, *Retrieving Nicaea: The Development and Meaning of Trinitarian Doctrine* (Grand Rapids: Baker Academic, 2011), 3.

those who formulated it. At the same time, he reminds readers that "we cannot directly perceive with the mind's eye what we are saying about God when we say that God is Trinity."[53] Nevertheless, it is important to retain the meaning and judgments registered by Athanasius, Gregory of Nyssa, and Augustine even if full comprehension is beyond the human purview.[54]

The main point I wish to draw from Anatolios is his understanding that despite the intellectual hurdles created by the doctrine of the Trinity, this doctrine was not one among others whose resolution relates to *an* aspect of Christian thought and life.[55] Anatolios counters, "Rather, orthodox Trinitarian doctrine emerged as a kind of meta-doctrine that involved a global interpretation of Christian life and faith and indeed evoked a global interpretation of reality."[56] Anatolios walks a careful line when he explicates this theological epistemology. On the one hand, a Trinitarian doctrine does not allow us "to encompass the being of God within the confines of human knowing."[57] On the other hand, it does allow us to order our thinking, praying, and living so as to relate all of life to the God who has revealed himself as Father, Son, and Holy Ghost. God's triune character is not a possession of the human mind nor is it an achievement of human cognition. God's triune character is an eschatological hope revealed by God in the Scriptures that orders our thinking, believing, and living in this period of eschatological hope.

If our thinking, praying, and living are formed within the Trinitarian contours of our Christian faith, then it follows quite naturally and necessarily that our biblical exegesis falls under this global theological epistemology as well. For the church fathers and the Christian interpretive tradition of which they are a founding part—whose

---

[53] Ibid., 7.
[54] Ibid.
[55] In the Evangelical orbit, D. A. Carson's "Yes, but" reaction to theological exegesis includes a dismissal of the foundational or central role Trinitarian doctrine plays in all Christian, theological discourse. D. A. Carson, "Theological Interpretation: Yes, But ...," in *Theological Commentary* (ed. M. Allen; London: T&T Clark, 2011), 204–05.
[56] Anatolios, *Retrieving*, 8.
[57] Ibid., 9.

hermeneutical instincts reside in the New Testament's own pioneering achievement of Scripture reading—any other kind of exegesis would be inconceivable. God's identity as Father, Son, and Holy Spirit provides the epistemic possibilities for all arenas of life, how much more so our reading of Holy Scripture.

Gilles Emery's impressive account of Thomas's Trinitarian theology makes much of the shared goal between Thomas's biblical commentary and speculative theology, namely, the elucidation of God's truth. Similar comments may be made about many of the best theological voices from the tradition, Roman Catholic and Protestant: Calvin and Barth come to mind as more well-known figures but lesser figures do so as well. Emery makes a significant point about Aquinas and the hermeneutical role speculative theology made in his engagement with the biblical text.

Aquinas's commentary on John provides Emery with the tools necessary to make the following claim. Thomas resists too material a distinction between Trinitarian theology of the biblical and speculative types. "It is the same theology," writes Emery.[58] The synthetic character of speculative theology and the close reading of the biblical text in commentary form both have the same purpose: "the reflective explanation of Scripture."[59] Emery's conclusion is worth repeating in full: "In every case, speculative theology is not superimposed on or juxtaposed with the biblical text, but is *part and parcel* of the biblical reading."[60]

I wish to highlight the terms "part and parcel" here because the substantive point of this collocation is straightforward. The literal sense of Scripture is not devoid of theological sensemaking, nor can the literal

---

[58] Gilles Emery, *The Trinitarian Theology of Saint Thomas Aquinas* (trans. F. A. Murphy; Oxford: Oxford University Press, 2007), 19.

[59] Ibid., 19. Emery comments on the means by which Aquinas brought the speculative work to bear on textual commentary, to wit, a deployment of Hugh of St. Victor's three levels of literal exposition: *Littera* (textual analysis with reference to grammar and linguistics, an overview of the words' meaning in their immediate context), the *sensus* (the analysis of the signification of each member), and the *sententia* (a genuine understanding of the text, which draws out its theological and philosophical meaning) (ibid., 20). The *sententia* allows speculative theology its hermeneutical role in establishing the text's letter.

[60] Ibid., 20.

sense of the text in its Christian, canonical form be established when verbal signs are disjointed from their theological subject matter. This hermeneutical instinct can be traced in practice to apostolic figures such as Paul which in time were given a formal character in works such as Augustine's *De Doctrina*. Aquinas's Augustinian hermeneutic is in full gear at this point with the necessary dialectic between sign and thing signified remaining intact.[61]

For Augustine, the *signa* of the text mediate divine instruction. Moreover, Christ, as the *res significans* of the Scriptural word, makes himself present via the *signa* of the Old Testament's verbal character.[62] As such, the words of Scripture are laden with metaphysical import when the subject matter, properly identified in the various and sundry voices of Scripture, is God's own self and expressed will to redeem. Words mean something given the formal character of language in its phonetic and syntactical arrangement. But, as George Steiner

---

[61] The use of analogical language, like *ousia* and *hypostasis*, by no means diminishes the mystery of the divine Godhead. This abstract language provides a rational account of God's triune identity (Emery refers to this as the "far-reaching goal") and more modestly, "the theologian carries out a contemplative exercise in order to grasp a droplet of the divine knowledge communicated by revelation, without losing sights of the limits of our knowledge" (Emery, *Trinitarian Theology*, 35). George Hunsinger distinguishes Barth's use of analogical reasoning from Aquinas's precisely at this point. For Aquinas, our analogical language breaks down regarding the knowledge of God *in se* with God's identity in himself remaining a mystery. Whereas for Barth, in line with the Reformed tradition, God's revelation of himself truly corresponds with God's actual identity and provides the epistemic possibility for real knowledge of God, accommodated as this revelation is. While at the same time, comprehensive knowledge of God's eternal identity remains beyond the purview of human knowledge, thus the linguistic appeal to analogy in opposition to univocal and equivocal: apprehensive knowledge versus comprehensive knowledge. George Hunsinger, *Disruptive Grace: Studies in the Theology of Karl Barth* (Grand Rapids: Eerdmans, 2001), 210–25.

[62] See especially Michael Cameron, "The Christological Substructure of Augustine's Figural Exegesis," in *Augustine and the Bible* (ed. and trans. P. Bright; South Bend: University of Notre Dame Press, 1999), 74–103. Cameron's conclusion bears repeating: "If Christ as the *res significans* of God had acted within history, and was not merely witnessed by history, then in principle every historical sign was open to bearing something of its *res*, either before or after his advent. This revision made the Old Testament into a bearer of New Testament grace, and opened prophecy to sacramental interpretation. Where Augustine had once thought the prophetic sign acted as the diaphanous and obsolescent pointer to the future reality, Christ was understood to have been present within the sign both to denote and to communicate his power. The ancient saints did not merely anticipate but actually partook of him" (Cameron, "Christological Substructure," 96).

claims, "a sentence always means more."⁶³ With his own Augustinian hermeneutical instincts engaged, Steiner warns, "the absolute decisive failing occurs when such approaches seek to formalize *meaning*, when they proceed upward from the phonetic, the lexical and the grammatic to the semantic and aesthetic."⁶⁴ Why, we might ask Steiner, is this a problem? He answers, "There is always, as Blake taught, 'excess' of the signified beyond the signifier."⁶⁵

When Steiner insists that "a sentence always means more," he clarifies the conditions for such a claim in the following: "The informing matrix or context of even a rudimentary, literal proposition ... moves outward from specific utterance or notation in ever-widening concentric and overlapping circles. These comprise the individual, subconsciously quickened language habits and *associative field-mappings* of the particular speaker or writer."⁶⁶ This expansive character of language reveals, in Steiner's terms, "the incommensurability of the semantic."⁶⁷

In a similar vein, Rowan Williams's Gifford Lectures remind us of the metaphysical realities of language. "We are always saying more

---

⁶³ George Steiner, *Real Presences* (Chicago: University of Chicago Press, 1991), 82.
⁶⁴ Ibid., 81.
⁶⁵ Ibid., 84. Steiner's metaphysical understanding of the semantic potential of words relates to Origen's understanding of figures in the Old Testament and the twofold potential of words. Words have their basic referent (the literal) but are also symbolic of some other referent—literal and allegorical. See Peter Martens's *Origen and Scripture: The Contours of the Exegetical Life* (OECS; Oxford: Oxford University Press, 2012), 66. See Erich Auerbach, "Figura," in *Selected Essays of Erich Auerbach: Time, History, and Literature* (ed. J. I. Porter; trans. J. O. Newman; Princeton: Princeton University Press, 2014), 88. "Even if Augustine decisively rejects abstract allegorical spiritualism and develops his entire interpretation of the Old Testament out of its concrete reality in worldly historical time, he nevertheless continues to endorse a kind of idealism that removes the concrete event from time as *figura*—even though it also remains entirely real—and places it into the perspective of timeless eternity. Such ideas were implicit in the very fact of the incarnation." John David Dawson identifies Origen's hermeneutic along anthropological lines as the letter of Scripture and its spirit relate to humanity's body and soul. The two are necessarily and organically fit to each other. Thus, the figural sense of Scripture is, in Dawson's terms, "not non-literal." John David Dawson, *Christian Figural Reading and the Formation of Christian Identity* (Berkeley: University of California Press, 2001), chs 1–3.
⁶⁶ Steiner, *Real Presences*, 82.
⁶⁷ Ibid., 83.

than we entirely grasp."⁶⁸ Williams's lectures provide a stunning and beautiful account of the ability of our language to describe and represent while remaining fully aware that these activities of language are never sealed off from the potential for representation or description via new modes and tropes of discourse. Williams speaks of the "unfinished character of language" and a "hinterland of significance" when our language necessarily turns to silence. We represent with our words and the task of representation is never once-for-all. Merleau-Ponty makes a similar claim about painting: "For painters, if any remain, the world will always be yet to be painted; even if it lasts millions of years ... it will all end without having been complete".⁶⁹

It should be noted that Williams is speaking of our normal discourse in the language games we play in communicating and sensemaking in our world. If we speak this way about human language and discourse in "ordinary language," to borrow from Stanley Cavell, how much more so do we understand the potential of biblical language to "say more." Aquinas appeals to the authority of Scripture's authorial intentionality, quickly clarifying who the author of Scripture is: God. Such a confession releases the philological clutch to allow words in their given morphological and syntactic form a fuller frame of referentiality when the associated field-mapping brought to bear in textual analysis is the God Christians confess as Triune.

Such an account seeks to do justice to the ability of biblical language to swell into the subject matter of Scripture's referent, namely, the Triune God's procession and mission: the theological field-map for the terrain of Scripture. It also resists an anemic linguistic approach to biblical language by minimizing their potential referent to the hermetic moment of original utterance or writing (the distinction

---

[68] Rowan Williams, *The Edge of Words: God and the Habits of Language* (London: Bloomsbury, 2014), 167.
[69] Maurice Merleau-Ponty, "Eye and Mind," in *The Merleau-Ponty Aesthetics Reader: Philosophy and Painting* (ed. G.A. Johnson; Evanston: Northwestern University Press, 1993), 148.

between the two itself is an interesting thought experiment about the canonical intentionality of language once embedded in particular books and quarters of the canon). This linguistic reduction cuts the chord that holds together sign and reality or Scriptural language with its divine subject matter. And wittingly or unwittingly it falls prey to Spinoza's hermeneutical legacy where biblical texts are relegated to their historical moment full stop. A Trinitarian hermeneutic resists a sclerotic tendency to leave language in the past, unencumbered by the metaphysical underpinnings of language in general and biblical language in particular.

Conclusion

The reading strategy presented here accords with the church's "ruled" approach to Scripture reading, to wit, the *regula fidei*. This ecclesial location for reading constrains and unleashes simultaneously. A Trinitarian hermeneutic is a ruled reading and thus locates the canon in the redemptive movement of God *ad extra*. This dogmatic location of Scripture within its soteric/christological context is the point of entry into Scripture's subject matter (*die Sache*), resisting an ontologically underdetermined text. The *regula* is not a fixed formula, easily identified in codified form. Rather, it orients the church toward the proper "hypothesis" for reading Scripture.[70] In this sense, the *regula* constrains.

Likewise, a ruled reading unleashes the text in an organic extension beyond the confines of its literary and historical fixity toward its subject matter. Modern, biblical criticism aids readers of Scripture in appreciating the literary and historical dynamics of the biblical texts in the particularity of their genesis and compositional history. To turn a blind eye away from these achievements as if they contribute nothing

---

[70] See especially, Christopher R. Seitz, *The Character of Christian Scripture* (Studies in Theological Interpretation; Grand Rapids: Baker, 2011), ch. 7, 195–98.

to the theological engagement with the biblical texts runs the dualistic risk of lionizing the text's soul over against its body. For all Origen's supposed fanciful allegorizing of texts, his attention to the letter resists bifurcating the text's body and spirit.[71]

The resistance, however, to a Spinozist hemming in of texts to the immediacy of their historical particularity—an identification only problematized by modern criticism's atomistic instincts—leans against the necessary conjoining of Word and Spirit. Theologically speaking, the written Word becomes an inert object of study without the recognition of the Spirit's material engagement with Scripture's continued life in the church.

Admittedly, a good deal of hermeneutical and theological throat clearing takes place in this introductory chapter. I did not pursue every line of thought to its end. Rather, a theological case is being made for the sake of clearing hermeneutical space for reading the biblical text closely in light of Scripture's authorizing subject matter. At the same time, the central role of Scriptural exegesis itself should not be obscured as if theology as a Christian, intellectual discipline hovers somewhere beyond the Scriptural text. Mark Elliott warns theological interpreters, enamored with the "ruled" reading of a figure like Irenaeus, against making too much of the *regula fidei*. Creeds, according to Elliott, complemented Scripture but were never intended to "work as a grid to be put over it."[72] Elliott makes use of helpful battle metaphors to clarify

---

[71] The necessary attendance to the body of the text does cause pause, for example, when R. R. Reno says in the preface of his Genesis commentary that Westermann's classic work on Genesis offered him no help given the questions he was asking of the text. Limited help would be understandable, but "no help" seems to miss the very basic elements of the interpretive assistance Westermann might offer: e.g., linguistic and structural limitations of the texts; philological analysis (the words matter); literary insights into the final form of a composite text, etc. Westermann's interests in the "body" of the text is surely limited given the intellectual context of his activity, but to claim "no help" is only to widen the wedge between biblical scholars (*confessional ones at that*) and theologians. R. R. Reno, *Genesis* (Brazos Theological Commentary on the Bible; Grand Rapids: Brazos Press, 2010), 24. In fairness to Reno, he does acknowledge finding von Rad's Genesis commentary "sometimes helpful" (ibid.).

[72] Mark Elliott, *The Heart of Biblical Theology: Providence Experienced* (Surrey: Ashgate, 2012), 6.

Introduction to a Theological Commentary   31

the relationship of the *regula fidei* to the exegesis of Scripture itself. The former functions as a *shield*, staving off bad interpretive instincts or "heavy ideological 'spin.'" The latter is a *sword*, where the constructive and material work of Christian theological reflection resides.[73] Elliott identifies Irenaeus's motto as follows: "Let the scriptures speak for themselves."[74] A better exegetical or theological strategy is difficult to conceive.

---

[73] Ibid., 6–7.
[74] Ibid., 7. See also, Anatolios, *Retrieving*, 282–84.

Micah in Critical Dress: A Cursory Overview

Bernard Stade's seminal study on Micah's redaction history left a long and lasting impact on studies of the book.[1] By means of a somewhat standard *tendenz* analysis that included the minimal portrait of Micah in Jer 26:18, Stade suggested Micah's authentic voice may only be found in chs 1–3.[2] The hopeful tones found throughout chs 4–6 clash with Jeremiah's portrayal of Micah, rendering them as most likely from a later hand. Following the selfsame pattern, Stade assumes the Messianic prophecy of 2:12-13 is from the exilic period, added to Micah's authentic corpus at a later period.[3] Based on a complex algorithm of identifying shared themes from other quarters of the prophetic literature—literature having been run through the same literary-critical mill, e.g., Second Isaiah—nothing after ch. 3 can be traced to the preexilic period. The real Micah is found only in chs 1–3.

Stade's study breathes the literary cum form-critical air of his day, setting out to distinguish the authentic prophetic material from its *Nachgeschichte*. The effects of such interpretive instincts are observed to this day in various attempts to locate Micah the prophet and the developing prophetic book in his/its most fitting social-historical context: from Micah the country decrier against the urban gentry to

---

[1] Bernard Stade, "Bemerkungen über das Buch Micha," *ZAW* 1 (1881): 161–72.
[2] Ibid., 165–66.
[3] "2,12-13 setzt voraus, dass Israel sich in der Zerstreeung, im Exile befindet" (Stade, "Bemerkungen," 164–65). Ewald, before Stade, blazed a redaction-critical trail in his literary analysis. Heinrich Ewald's understanding of Micah's "integrity" developed over the course of time. Initially he identified the entirety of the book as from Micah, save the superscription. In time, he identified chs 1–5 as Mican with 6–7 coming from the hands of another prophet.

Micah the antimilitary lowlander. The problem of such approaches, as Dillers pointed out some time ago, remains the insufficiency of evidence (Dillers, 4), not to mention the flat-footedness of reducing a prophet's voice to a singular register and subject matter, e.g., Stade's totalizing view of Micah the prophet based on Jeremiah's minimal portrayal. Dillers himself opted for a synchronic approach where the social location giving rise to Micah as a literary whole—a "revitalization" movement—resists reduction to any one given social-historical moment. Such a revitalization movement occurs in the eighth century as well as in subsequent moments again and again (Diller, 4).

In Jeremias's notable commentary on Micah, he identifies Micah 1-3 as the *Kernkapitel*, with earlier and later material shaped into a literary whole by "die exilischen Redaktoren" (Jeremias, 116). Less interested in sorting out the authentic from inauthentic Mican material for form-critical purposes, Jeremias attends to the diachronic structure of the book for the sake of coming to terms with the net effect of the final form. The *Kernkapiteln* give rise to a series of *Fortschreibungen* in *Teile II* and *III*, chs 4–5 and 6:1-7:7, respectively (Jeremias, 118–19). Chapters 4–5 assume the destruction of Jerusalem (*Zerstörung Jerusalems*) as a past event while attesting to the fact that, though deserved, the judgment of God on Samaria and Jerusalem "nicht das Ziel seiner Wege mit seinem Volk ist" (Jeremias, 119). *Teile II*, for Jeremias, contains a chiastic structure (*Ringkomposition*) framed around 4:9-5:5—A [4:1-5], B [4:6-8], C [4:9-5:3], B' [5:6ff], A' [5:9-13]. The forthcoming redemption of chs 4–5 centers on the promise of a coming king, as the *Ringkomposition* itself attests.

Surprisingly, according to Jeremias, *Teile III* of Micah (6:1-7:7) makes no significant linguistic or conceptual references to *Teile II* (4-5). This literary-compositional fact on the ground leads Jeremias to reject Kessler's theory that the compositional history of Micah mirrors that of Isaiah with its threefold form building upon the anterior chapters/form of the book—1-39 + 40-55 yielding Third Isaiah's 56-66.[4] Micah 1-3 + 4-5

---

[4] See, e.g., W. Lau, *Schriftgelehrte Prophetie in Jes 56–66: Eine Untersuchung zu den literarischen Bezugen in den letzten elf Kapiteln das Jesajabuches* (BZAW 225; Berlin: De Gruyter, 1994).

do not form the basis of *Teile III*'s prophetic *Fortschreibung*. Rather, Micah 1-3 yields "eine doppelte" *Fortschreibung* with 4-5 and 6:1-7:7 as the parallel results (Jeremias, 119–20).

The intertextual character of these respective *Fortschreibungen* of Micah 1-3 is marked by associative reference to different prophetic corpi. Micah 4-5, as long observed, is riddled with references (*Bezügen*) to Isaiah 1-12 (Mic 4:1-5//Isa 2:2-5; Mic 5:1//Isa 11:1; Mic 5:2//Isa 7:14; Mic 5:9-13//Isa 2:6-8). While Mic 6:1-7:7 emerges as a literary unit stamped by Jeremiah and the Deuteronomic tradition, the intertextual nature of these respective sections, both building upon the prophetic material of Micah 1-3, indicates their close association with the tradents of Isaianic and Jeremianic traditions, respectively.

Jeremias's reading of the diachronic history of Micah's composition lends credence to Brevard Childs's earlier claim regarding Micah's compositional history. Childs states, "The redactional process of editing the book of Micah within a theological framework shared by Isaiah points to the effect of a growing sense of a unified prophetic corpus within the canon of scripture."[5] This matter will become a more focused point of discussion in the next section. Suffice it to say at this point, the appeal to history and historical particularity when attending to biblical books begs questions regarding what kind of history is being sought. If Micah and Isaiah "debated" one another, as is sometimes claimed,

---

[5] Brevard S. Childs, *Introduction to the Old Testament as Scripture* (Minneapolis: Fortress Press, 1979), 438. Childs registers his misgivings about the redaction-critical readings of Mays, Jeremias, and Renaud, claiming their hypothesis is too refined given the evidence in Micah. It is not that Childs denies an editing process that takes place over some time. Rather, he denies the underlying assumption of the various hypothesis on offer, namely, the biblical traditions are being edited to address specific historical needs. He clarifies his own position in the following: "Rather, I would argue the case that the major force lying behind the redaction of Micah appears to have been the influence exerted upon its editors by the larger corpus of other prophetic material, particularly the oracles of Isaiah. The point is not to deny that later historical events influenced the redactors, but to contest a direct and intentional move on their part to adjust the tradition to each new historical situation" (ibid., 434). Childs continues, "Thus the effect of the changing historical situation was mediated through an interpretation of scripture and was only an indirect influence" (ibid.). See Odil Hannes Steck, *Der Abschluß der Prophetie im Alten Testament: Ein Versuch zur Frage der Vorgeschichte des Kanons* (Neukirchen-Vluyn: Neukirchener Verlag, 1991).

because one represents the concerns of the lowland worker and the other the concerns of the gentrified elite of Jerusalem, then this "debate" remains ensconced in the religious history of the eighth century. Such a claim is fair enough, even if and where such a theory remains contested.

The canonical history, however, tells a different story. Here, the tradents of Isaiah's prophetic legacy and Jeremiah's prophetic oeuvre in their acts of preservation and prophetic *Fortschreibungen* understand these prophetic books as mutually informing and, despite their differing theological tone or pitch, as in concert with one another.[6] Ronald Clements recognizes the theological forces at work at the editorial level of compositional analysis. He describes this "process of 'theologizing'" as follows: "These were that all the prophecies so brought together should be regarded as emanating from the same deity and that this deity should be regarded as possessing a completely consistent and unchanging nature."[7] The theological character of the material emerges from concerted efforts to preserve the divine word emanating from a single Being. Put simply, Micah and Isaiah may have debated their theological outlooks regarding Yhwh and his plan for Jerusalem in the religious history of a particular moment.[8] Nevertheless, their respective prophetic books exist not for the preservation of a religious-historical debate but for a unified, even if complex, witness for the sake of future generations regarding the character and will of Yhwh for his people and the nations.[9] While it is true that Israel's religious history

---

[6] See Rolf Rendtorff, *The Canonical Hebrew Bible: The Theology of the Old Testament* (Blandford Forum: Deo Publishing, 2005), 3.

[7] Ronald S. Clements, "Prophecy as Literature: A Re-Appraisal," in *The Hermeneutical Quest: Essays in Honor of James Luther Mays on his Sixty-Fifth Birthday* (ed. D. G. Miller; Allison Park: Pickwick Publications, 1986), 61.

[8] Clements claims that a necessary "de-politicizing" or "de-historicizing" was involved in the canonical process as individual sayings were shaped into larger scrolls or books. Ronald E. Clements, *Old Testament Prophecy: From Oracles to Canon* (Louisville: WJK, 1996), 5.

[9] Gerald T. Sheppard, "Canonization: Hearing the Voice of the Same God through Historically Dissimilar Traditions," *Int* 36 (1982): 21–33. A recognition of the canon's authorial and substantial unity does not necessitate a monotone account of unity. As Sheppard claims, "Canon conscious redactions do not succeed in harmonizing the diverse and even contradictory traditions within the Bible. However, they do enhance the presumption of biblical unity by creating interpretive contexts between books or

is the accident giving rise to its theological or canonical history, the distinction between the two remains valid for historical and canonical reasons. Prophetic traditions were preserved because the tradents of the material recognized them as the word of God, sought within them to discern the character and ways of God (Hos 14:9), and listened to the divergent canonical voices in light of this theological judgment.[10]

Though Calvin is not working with a tradition-critical analysis of the compositional history of the prophets, his canonical instincts are on full display when he identifies Micah and Isaiah as colleagues and friends. Calvin's historical imagination is at work when he describes them as such because this kind of historical information is not available to us. Calvin can make this claim, however, because these two prophets share so much in common and seem to borrow from each other freely.

> And we shall hereafter find that they adopted the very same words; but there was no emulation between them, so that one accused the other of theft, when he repeated what had been said. Nothing was more gratifying to each of them than to receive a testimony from his colleague; and what was committed to them by God they declared not only in the same sense and meaning, but also in the same words, and, as it were, with one mouth. (Calvin, 152)

Whatever the historical relation between Micah and Isaiah might have been, readers of the prophets recognize the overlap in material content even where the tone or register may differ between the two. Whether or not Micah and Isaiah were friends remains a theory with

---

group of books" (ibid., 25). In other words, the tradents of the biblical traditions create space for associative reading practices across the canon. Sheppard provides examples of these "interpretive contexts" by bringing Proverbs into conversation with Qoheleth, the worldly politics of David in Kings with his piety in the Psalms, or the differing perspectives on the day of the Lord in Joel and Amos.

[10] See Konrad Schmid, *Is There Theology in the Hebrew Bible* (CSHB 4; trans. P. Altmann; Winona Lake: Eisenbrauns, 2015), 63–64. Schmid refers to the work of Steck and his student Bosshard who recognize the redaction-history of the prophetic corpus as stemming from theological judgments regarding the "internal coherence" of Isaiah-Malachi or even the whole of the *Nebiim* (see the inclusio of Josh 1:7 and Mal. 3:22-24). ibid., 64.

no evidence, though there is little doubt as to whether or not Micah and Isaiah are canonical friends and colleagues.

Returning to Jeremias's understanding of Micah's structure, *Teile IV* (7:8-20) takes shape as a prophetic liturgy in response to the prophetic words of *Teile II* and *III*.[11] Jeremias resists the notion that 7:8-20 is simply subsumed under 6:1-7:7. Intertextual references to Mic 4-5 and 6:1-7:7 may be found in 7:8-20. The prophetic liturgy that brings Micah's corpus to its conclusions grounds itself on that which precedes it as an elaboration and actualization of the prophetic words of Micah's book.

In the commentary to follow, Jeremias will prove a signal interlocutor because his exegetical and redaction-critical concerns shed light on the theological effects of the text in its final form. For Jeremias, Micah as a prophetic book conceives of itself as the elaboration and fulfillment of the eighth-century prophet's prophetic word in associative relationship with a growing corpus of prophetic literature (*Mehrpropheten*). Admittedly, the redaction-critical specificity of Micah's compositional history may be challenged. Securing texts to the particular *tendenz* of a given moment in Judah's history is not a hard science, remaining provisional at best.[12]

---

[11] See Herman Gunkel, "The Close of Micah," in *What Remains of the Old Testament and Other Essays* (trans. A. K. Dallas; New York: The Macmillan Company, 1928), 115–50. McKane dismisses the liturgical unity of 7:8-20. He sees three separate and discontinuous Psalms that served as "congregational responses" to the book of Micah in public liturgical settings (McKane, 21).

[12] Building on Stade's earlier redaction-critical conclusions, Hans Walter Wolff's learned Micah commentary works with the kind of redaction-critical confidence where the redaction-history of the book is sorted out by locating literary seams, assigning them to particular religious-historical moments of Judah's existence, and tracing out the steps of the "school of tradents" responsible for this literary achievement (Wolff, 17–27). The four-part structure Jeremias identifies in Micah mirrors Wolff's. Jeremias's commentary does operate with a similar redaction-critical model as his *Doktorvater*, Wolff, though Jeremias is not as heavy-handed in assigning the redactional levels to particular moments in Judah's religious history. Jeremias also draws marked attention to the nature of *Fortschreibung* in Micah's compositional history. Mention should also be made of Jan A. Wagenaar's *Judgement and Salvation: The Composition and Redaction of Micah 2-5* (VTSupp 2001; Leiden: Brill, 2001). Wagenaar identifies five stages of compositional growth building from an early collection of Micah sayings, to the application of those sayings to the events surrounding the fall of Jerusalem (Jeremiah's school is suggested as the possible tradents), to a third stage where elements of hope are added (e.g., 2:12-13), then a fourth stage in the postexilic period where hope is expanded to include a

As mentioned in the previous chapter, Benjamin Sommer registers his own misgivings about the "pseudo-historicism"—an admittedly loaded term—biblical scholars often practice in their efforts to fix texts to particular moments in Israel's religious history. Though speaking specifically about Pentateuchal literary criticism, Sommer illustrates his larger point by appeal to Mic 4:1-5 and Isa 2:2-4, making his comments especially germane to the present work. Within critical scholarship, these two texts are postexilic or exilic at best. They illustrate the religious outlook of Judah after the *Zerstörung*, making little sense of the religious sensibility of the preexilic period. But Sommer asks why? Linking ideas to eras is perilous business. Moreover, what vitiates against the view that Micah or Isaiah, the eighth-century prophets, might have anticipated a future era of universal peace, *pace* Stade et al.? Sommer concludes,

> Even if it is surprising to suggest that an eighth-century thinker might have hoped for peace in Israel and among the nations, this would not make the suggestion impossible. Micah and especially Isaiah conceived of notions that were unexpected, even bizarre. Therein lies the genius of any original thinker. To deny that an idea could have been thought of in a given age is to deny the possibility of intellectual creativity. Such a denial is a very odd position for a scholar of the humanities.[13]

While good arguments can be made for identifying redaction-critical seams and providing a diachronic history of the text's literary development, attaching such literary blocks of tradition to particular historical moments is tenuous. "For centuries," Andersen and Freedman suggest, "biblical scholars have been trying to attach dates to these kinds of texts, to plug these texts into known history. It cannot be done" (Andersen and Freedman, 26). Recognizing a literary depth dimension to the prophetic books/prophetic corpus and the linking of redaction-critical levels to particular moments in Judah's history may seem prima

---

Völkerwahlfahrt to Zion (4:1-5), and finally to a fifth stage where the prophetic collection of Micah (1:2–5:14) is added to an anonymous prophet from Northern Israel (6-7). The brittleness of Wagenaar's conclusions stems from the brittle character of reading religious history off the back of redaction-critical conclusions of the literary type.

[13] Sommer, "Dating Pentateuchal Texts," 96.

facie as flip sides of the same coin, but, in fact, a distinction between the two remains requisite.

While on the subject of redaction-criticism, it is worth noting a distinction Brevard Childs makes between two related textual phenomena, namely, redaction-criticism and *Fortschreibung*. Childs understands redaction-criticism as an editorial activity attentive to the changing sociological forces of the present scribal moment. The scribe as redactor seeks to harmonize current viewpoints with original texts. Hugh Williamson further clarifies the distinction between redaction and various glosses (*Fortschreibung* included). The former is a wholesale rewriting of the inherited text.[14] Given the expense and difficulty of such scribal rewriting in the ancient world, full-scale redactions are not to be found at every juncture where glosses—additions, modifications, or clarifications—are suggested.[15] Williamson recognizes that the identification of various and sundry textual glosses does not necessitate a "redaction," and that the endless identification of redactional levels may in fact be textual glosses not on the level of full-scale redaction.

Fortschreibung, insofar as it differs from redaction, has as its aim the clarification of the original text by interpretive extension.[16] The two terms are often used interchangeably, though the distinction Childs and Williamson make remains important. For *Fortschreibung* as an editorial activity operates under the assumption of the anterior pressure and priority of the prophetic word for future reception. The prophetic word relates in dynamic fashion to future generations of hearers as a "living organism," to borrow from von Rad.[17]

---

[14] H. G. M. Williamson, "Redaction Criticism: The Vindication of Redaction Criticism," in *Biblical Interpretation and Method: Essays in Honour of John Barton* (ed. K. J. Dell and P. M. Joyce; Oxford: Oxford University Press, 2013), 31–34.

[15] Van der Toorn suggests that the scribal rewriting of biblical scrolls took place perhaps once a generation, and only valued texts would receive such labor-intensive efforts. Van der Toorn further claims that redactional activity of the rewriting kind most likely took place at these momentous junctures of scribal rewriting and was not a continuous scribal activity. Karel Van der Toorn, *Scribal Culture and the Making of the Hebrew Bible* (Cambridge: Harvard University Press, 2007), ch. 5.

[16] Brevard Childs, "Retrospective Reading of the Old Testament Prophets," *ZAW* 108 (1996): 365.

[17] Von Rad, *OTT II*, 168.

Childs also raises concerns about the governing norms for the method of redaction-criticism practiced by many on the Continent. He enters into an appreciative debate with two of Germany's leading redaction-critics, Odil Steck and his erstwhile student Reinhard Kratz. Redaction-critics such as Kratz insist on the empirical character of their redaction-critical analysis, primarily by means of the identification of conceptual incoherence at the level of the prophetic book's final form.[18] Childs illustrates his misgivings about a bald application of this principle in the work of Hermisson on Isaiah. Hermisson identifies a *qarob* redactional layer whose characteristics are immanent release from exile conditioned upon better conduct from Israel. The presentation of Isa 40:1ff, on the other hand, reveals the unconditional forgiveness of Yhwh for his people. The "conceptual incoherence" between these redactional layers indicates that the latter layer stems from Isaiah's disciples and not the prophet per se.

Childs warns, however, against hasty conclusions based on these supposed conceptual tensions for reasons on analogy to the problems Sommer identifies in dating sources/literary strands to particular moments in time. Modern interpreters should take caution when imposing our notions of conceptual incoherence on texts that are not operating within the selfsame epistemological space.[19] What may appear to a modern mind as conceptually incoherent may be perfectly compatible to authors and tradents of the biblical materials. In other words, care should be taken when identifying redaction-critical seams on the basis of modern epistemological instincts.

---

[18] In fairness to Kratz, he avoids the "pseudo-history" Sommer warns of because his diachronic interests do not necessitate the linking of redaction-critical units to particular moments of time. In fact, Kratz speaks of a "relative Chronologie" as his textual aim. Reinhard Gregor Kratz, "Die Redaktion der Prophetenbücher," in *Prophetenstudien: Kleine Schriften II* (FAT 74; Tübingen: Mohr Siebeck, 2011), 38. Still, Childs's criticism stands because Kratz's "relative Chronologie" builds off the internal incoherence Childs notes in the above. For critical interaction with Kratz's notion of Isaiah as primarily a *Heilsprophet* in the eighth century and only retrospectively assigned the role of *Gerichtsprophet* by the tradents of this material, see Jörg Jeremias, "Das Rätsel der Schriftprophetie," *ZAW* 125 (2013): 93–117, esp. 103–05. See also Kratz's rejoinder. Reinhard Gregor Kratz, "Das Rätsel der Schriftprophetie: Eine Replik," *ZAW* 125 (2013): 635–39.

[19] Childs, "Restrospective Reading," 368–69.

With the aforementioned warnings of redaction-criticism's potential overreach, a positive effect of redaction-criticism remains, namely, the priority given to the literary character of the prophetic books.[20] The search for the authentic prophetic material over against later prophetic accretions has given way to the valuing of the literary final form of the prophetic books for the sake of shedding light on the diachronic features or "depth dimension" leading to the text's final form. An appreciation for the text's "depth dimension" does not necessitate (1) a seemingly endless atomization of the prophetic book based on tenuous assumptions about either literary incoherence or differing literary *tendenz* attached to particular moments in time nor (2) a clearly reconstructed diachronic history of the prophetic traditions on their way to the final form.[21]

While it may be preferable to conceive of a text's redaction-history as a forward-moving project where one tradition gives rise to the next, the facts on the ground make such a tidy framework difficult to sustain, especially when cross-fertilization is more likely at the compositional level of the text en route to literary stabilization. The prophetic voices and traditions spawned by them cross-fertilize with each other in the canonical process of prophetic reception, ordering, and stabilization. Where such cross-fertilizing effects may be responsibly demonstrated

---

[20] See Kratz, "Redaktion," 34ff. The literary form of the prophetic books is the necessary ingredient for redaction-critical analysis. Or in Kratz's terms, "Die Diachronie ist nicht ohne Synchronie, die Syncrhonie aber auch nicht ohne Diachronice zu haben" (Krats, "Redaktion," 36).

[21] My sympathies lie with Roberts's measured account of the redaction-critical project. Speaking of Isaiah's redaction history, Roberts claims, "I am not convinced that the ancient Judean and Jewish audiences that hear or, in rarer cases, read the oracles in the Isaianic collection in whatever edition were as enthralled by elaborate book-length literary coherence as modern scholars and contemporary readers are, and I am amazed at the confidence with which biblical scholars can reconstruct the editorial growth of a biblical book over the centuries with the barest minimum of evidence. It is not that I consider this process unimportant or uninteresting; it is more that I consider the details of this process to be largely unrecoverable." Roberts continues, putting an edge on the matter, "The confidence with which many modern scholars, who lack any datable manuscripts earlier than the final form of Isaiah, reconstruct hypothetical redactors living at particular periods, who make particular editorial changes in the service of some equally hypothetically reconstructed theological interest, strikes me as extreme hubris." J. J. M. Roberts, *First Isaiah: A Commentary* (Hermeneia; Minneapolis: Fortress Press, 2015), 2–3.

by means of intertextual association of the linguistic and conceptual types—even when determining the direction of the intertextual reference remains elusive—then appreciation for the theological character of the prophetic witnesses is enhanced.

While this commentary will make judicious use of the insights gained by diachronic investigation, the focus of the commentary will be on the literary character of Micah's final form. From a certain vantage point, this commentary shares the outlook of Ehud Ben Zvi's *Micah*, a commentary whose hermeneutical outlook has much to commend it. Ben Zvi's focus is on the text as a literary product that assumes a readership competent to read it, and more importantly, to reread it. Ben Zvi clarifies,

> Moreover, the book of Micah was not produced to be read once and then put aside, but rather to be read and reread and meditated upon (cf. Josh 1:18; Hos 14:10 [NRSV 9]; see Sir 38:34-39:3). It is a book that claims to be and was composed to be treated as an authoritative writing for its readership, that is, as Scripture. (Ben Zvi, 5)

Ben Zvi assumes Micah's final literary form emerges in the setting of Yehud in the Achaemenid period with the religious and political outlook of the time reflected in Micah's final form.[22] So for Ben Zvi, the readership and rereadership of Micah are the historically conditioned social group under the purview of the prophetic book's intentionality (Ben Zvi, 6). As with most commentators, Ben Zvi does work within the constraints of the religious and social context of an identified historical setting—postexilic Yehud. Nevertheless, and perhaps going beyond the scope of Ben Zvi's historical constraints, the concept of rereader has much to commend it along canonical hermeneutical lines. For Ben

---

[22] Ben Zvi identifies five important postexilic themes: "(1) the story of postmonarchic Israel (i.e., the Jerusalemite-centered communities of the Achaemenid period) about itself, (2) those communities' self-understanding, (3) their understanding of the divine economy and their place in it, (4) their understanding of the attributes and past and future actions of YHWH, and (5) hope for a great and glorious future, in opposition to their actual position in worldly terms" (Ben Zvi, 5).

Zvi's form-critical concerns arise particularly from the *Sitz im Buch*, even as this is informed by the *Sitz im Leben* of postexilic Yehud.

For instance, Ben Zvi claims, "[R]ereaders, and particularly those who meditate on the text, are aware of the entire text even as they reread its first line. They may make connections between different units not only according to their sequence in the book but in multidirectional and cross-linked paths" (Ben Zvi, 5–6). In other words, the activity of rereading, especially in the theological context where the text read is assumed as divinely authoritative, is a continuous activity where individual units within the text are cross-associated with other texts in the selfsame prophetic book. Such literary cross-associations yield a combustive hermeneutical context for enriched and deep reading. Worth highlighting here are Ben Zvi's terms "multidirectional" and "cross-linked paths." His interpretive insight remains located at the level of the prophetic book, and understandably so. Nevertheless, if Childs, Steck, Bosshard-Nupestil, Jeremias, and others, are right about Micah's compositional history as inextricably linked with the growing prophetic corpus (*Mehrprophetenbuchen*), then the deep reading of the cross-associative kind Ben Zvi identifies need not be limited to the individual prophetic books alone. In fact, the textured reading of the cross-fertilizing kind called for in this commentary emerges at the level of the prophetic books own canonical intentionality.

Furthermore, Ben Zvi keeps the hermeneutical aim clear by identifying the rationale for Micah's preservation within the prophetic corpus:

> It is worth mentioning that no textually inscribed markers indicate that the readership of the book was asked to reread the book or any READING within it in a manner governed by their own awareness of either any proposed redactional history of the book, or by the place of the relevant READING in a text other than the present book of Micah, be it a hypothetical forerunner of Micah or any other text. Indeed, it is far more likely that communities of rereaders will continually reread a certain book that they accept as YHWH's word in a way that

is governed by the actual text of the book and its textually inscribed demands than by the text of an alternative—and hypothetical—book that they are not reading, rereading, copying, and studying. (Ben Zvi, 7–8)

As mentioned above, insights may be garnered from Micah's diachronic history where such may be responsibly reconstructed. However, this commentary does inhabit the interpretive space of Micah's original readers, rereaders, and the broad stream of Jewish and Christian interpretation spawned by them. Micah was preserved within the community of faith in its given canonical shape for the sake of a continued rereading of the book in order to hear the authoritative word of Yhwh. Such a hermeneutical claim is both theological and historical at the same time.[23]

Micah's canonical shape

Building on the assumptions of its literary-critical predecessor, the form-critical approach embraces the Romantic view of the individually inspired genius. Such a view lends itself to Gunkel's distinction between *Klassiker* and *Epigonen* when attending to the composite character of the prophetic literature.[24] Because the final form of prophetic books blend the *Klassiker* with the later and secondary *Epigonen* voices, the search for the authentic prophetic genius necessitates the identification and distinction between these two prophetic components. The classic form-critical ambition of identifying the original prophetic genius by means of sophisticated sorting through the complex literary layers has given way to approaches whose focus is the prophetic book itself. The ascendant view of the *Schriftgehlerte* nature of the prophetic books, along with the insight provided by this view into the character of

---

[23] Cf Sir 38:24-39:11.
[24] See Konrad Schmid, *Schriftgelehrte Traditionsliteratur: Fallstudien zur innerbiblischen Schriftauslegung im Alten Testament* (FAT 77; Tübingen: Mohr Siebeck, 2011), 9.

the compositional history of single prophetic books and a growing prophetic corpus, has challenged the "secondary" status of the original prophet's afterlife (*Nachinterpretationen*), whether in oracular or written form. The *Fortschreibungen* or extension of the prophetic words are activities governed by the providential oversight of the Holy Spirit. They are no less "prophetic" or "inspired" than the original oracular or written words of the named prophets. Isaiah 40:6-8 and Zech 1:1-6 intimate as much. By way of illustration and analogy, readers of red letter Bibles do well to remember that the red letters of Jesus in the fourfold gospels are not more inspired or authoritative than the black letters surrounding them.

It is increasingly recognized that the original prophetic word, as given in its form-critical specificity, resists easy identification. In other words, Micah the eighth-century prophet most certainly resides within the pages of his prophetic corpus.[25] But at the same time, Micah the eighth-century prophet is now identified with his prophetic book, a book whose shaping and reworking of Micah's *ipsissima vox*, as well as the *Fortschreibungen* of his prophetic oeuvre, make oracular reconstruction a nigh impossible task. In Christopher Seitz's clever description, canonical attentiveness to the prophetic literature must "allow the text to act like a man."[26]

Moreover, a Christian theological commitment to divine providence in the preserving, expanding, and shaping of the latter *Nebiim* makes such a quest misguided from the beginning. Micah's prophetic book is the canonical location of God's continued revelatory work in synagogue and church. This canonical location of Micah's prophetic word is not

---

[25] According to Jeremias, "Die *mündliche Verkündung* des Propheten Micha aus Juda kennen wir nicht bzw. Können wir nur noch in Umrissen aus den Texten, die für später lebende Leser gedacht waren, rekonstruieren" (Jeremias, 121). Jeremias continues, however, by providing this outline of Micah's preaching and prophetic concerns. Micah speaks for the people, identifying them as "mein Volk." Moreover, he suffers with his people in solidarity as he stands against the abuses of the House of Jacob, a house Micah no longer affirms.

[26] Christopher Seitz, "On Letting a Text 'Act Like a Man' The Book of the Twelve: New Horizons for Canonical Reading, with Hermeneutical Reflections," *SBET* 22 (2004): 151–72.

found in the reconstructed prophet of the lowlands from the eighth century per se. It is the prophetic book in its canonical form where the authorizing voice of the prophet is found. Such a claim does not intend to drive a wedge between the eighth-century prophet and the book that bears his name. Rather, the claim affirms the priority of the prophetic book's final form for our understanding of the eighth-century prophet's continued prophetic presence in the communal life of faithful readers. The prophet's original words have an afterlife that goes beyond the purview of his historical existence. And why would they not? The grass withers, the flower fades, all flesh is grass (including the prophets), but the word of the Lord stands forever (Isa 40:8).

With attention given to the literary character of the book in its final form, various suggestions for structural analysis have emerged. Willis's 1969 *ZAW* studies identified an A-B-A pattern, demarcated by the imperative "hear" (מעו) at critical junctures in the book's macrostructure (1:2; 3:1; 6:1).[27] Within each of these units there is a discernable pattern of doom leading into hope: Judgment (1:2-2:11)/ Salvation (2:12-13); Judgment (3:1-12)/Salvation (4-5); Judgment (6:1-7:6)/Salvation (7:7-20). Willis's account looms large in Mican studies with many commentators following suit: Allen, Mays, Smith, Waltke, Nogalski, to name a few of the more notable studies.

Others identify the book's literary structure as twofold—Micah 1-5 forming the first half and 6-7 the latter. Mignon Jacobs proposes such a macrostructure for the book with each section beginning with a summons to hear.[28] Both sections are concerned with the fate of Israel and begin with a dispute.[29] Yhwh's justice and mercy are the theological rubrics bringing conceptual coherence to the book in its more universal (1-5) and particularistic (6-7) sections. For Jacobs, this conceptual coherence is the product of intentional redaction. Those who opt for

---

[27] J. T. Willis, "The Structure of Micah 3-5 and the Function of Micah 5. 9-14 in the Book," *ZAW* 81 (1969): 191–214.

[28] Mignon R. Jacobs, "Bridging the Times: Trends in Micah Studies since 1985," *CBR* 4 (2006): 300–01. See also, Mignon R. Jacobs, *The Conceptual Coherence of the Book of Micah* (JSOTSupp 322; Sheffield: Sheffield Academic Press, 2001).

[29] Jacobs, *Conceptual Coherence*, ch. 3.

the twofold pattern over against the threefold do so because of the more balanced symmetry between the Judgment/Salvation pattern on offer in this literary schema.[30]

Hagstrom believes the two best options for the literary structure of Micah are 1-2/3-5/6-7 or 1-5/6-7.[31] The strength of the former rests on the attendance to the literary marker "hear." Its weakness is the difficult interpretive challenges posed by Mic 2:12-13. Hagstrom worries that 2:12-13 does not rise to the substantial level of the other two salvation subsections, not to mention 2:12-13 is a contested text regarding its sense. Is this text a word of hope or judgment? The threefold pattern certainly mitigates this interpretive hurdle, necessitating its sense as a word of hope. Hagstrom opts for the twofold pattern because of these stated weaknesses of the threefold, including his reservation about the different character of the summons to "hear" in 3:1 vis-à-vis the juridical context of 1:2 and 6:1.[32]

A word of caution is in order here. In their Anchor Bible Commentary, Freedman and Andersen warn against allowing one structural analysis or search for conceptual coherence a hegemonic place over against others (Freedman and Anderson, 23). "Attempts to fit everything," suggest Freedman and Anderson, "into such patterns are in danger of reaching a point where arguments have to be stretched and strained, and the results lose credibility" (ibid.). Hagstrom registers a similar proviso, despite his own preference for the twofold schema: 1-5/6-7. "However, despite the fact that I have signaled my own preference, from the analysis above no compelling reason emerges to prefer one of these two options over the other."[33] Both strategies for reading Micah present a prophetic movement from judgment to salvation or from doom to

---

[30] David Gerald Hagstrom, *The Coherence of the Book of Micah: A Literary Analysis* (SBLDiss 89; Atlanta: Scholars Press, 1988), 21.

[31] Hagstrom sketches the various structural options, suggesting that any division driving a wedge between chs 3 and 4 allows too much privilege for critical conclusions regarding Micah's composition in light of the obvious thematic links between chs 3 and 4 (Hagstrom, *Coherence*, 11–22).

[32] Hagstrom, *Coherence*, 15–24.

[33] Ibid., 21. Dillers registers similar reservations against the confidence Mays attaches to his structural analysis, an analysis riding the back of a redaction-critical schema (Dillers, 8).

hope. One advantage of the twofold pattern is that it does not rest on the contentious character of 2:12-13. Our attention will turn to this text ad loc. Nevertheless, the twofold and threefold options are both commendable.

Freedman and Andersen provide a helpful and modest set of interpretive instincts when they register their doubts about the priority of one structural pattern over against another. "Our critical method is not strong enough to decide whether such connections were worked out consciously by the editor(s) in order to achieve some overall unification of the material that came to his (their) hands, or whether they are just things that we are noticing" (Freedman and Andersen, 23). Despite our uncertainty about editorial intentionality, these features of the text remain as textual constituents. Whether the twofold pattern (1-5/6-7) is preferred with the first section divided between 1-3 and 4-5 or whether the threefold pattern (1-2/3-5/6-7) is favored, the book's theological coherence does not trade on one or the other pattern. For the sake of laying claim on some structural pattern, this commentary operates with the twofold pattern, with the first section divided between 1-3 and 4-5.[34] The rationale for this preference, slight as it is, stems from Jeremias's understanding of the book's compositional history (see above).

This commentary will lean on Jeremias's understanding of Micah's structure where a division is noted between chs 3 and 4. It should be stated, contra Hagstrom, that the recognition of a literary division does not necessitate a thematic division or fissure in thought. In point of fact, the critical juncture beginning at ch. 4 has to do precisely with this corpus of the material drawing on and expanding the prophetic material of 1-3 in an act of prophetic *Fortschreibung*. I do not wish to place Jeremias's proposal "over against" the Judgment/Salvation schema of the threefold and twofold patterns noted above. Nor do I wish to be beholden to a particular redaction-critical model steering the

---

[34] Freedman and Andersen identify 4-5 as a textual unit because of the repeated and strategic use of והיה throughout this section (Freedman and Andersen, 24).

interpretive ship. Rather, I lean on Jeremias because of his attendance to the intertextual character of Micah's prophecy and his drawing specific attention to the interaction of the Mican corpus with itself, the Twelve, and the larger prophetic corpus.[35]

Before turning to the commentary proper, we turn our focus to Micah's canonical location in the Twelve, with attention given to the specific theological contribution such a location offers. This excursus is suggestive in nature and does not attempt to give a complete *Stand der Forschung* on current developments in the Twelve research. Rather, it offers a modest attempt at a theological reading where the pressure for such a reader emerges from what might be properly called Micah's canonical intentionality.

---

[35] Bruce Waltke's commentary on Micah is magisterial by any account, providing exegetical, syntactical, and text-critical analysis that will aid interpreters for years to come. Nevertheless, Micah's intertextual character and diachronic history make little to no contribution to his understanding of the canonical intentionality of a book whose final form is itself the product of a larger prophetic conversation. One can appreciate Waltke's resistance to allowing matters of compositional history a significant place at the interpretive table, given the speculative character of many of these efforts. Nevertheless, the final form of the prophetic books signals enough in the direction of cross-fertilization in their compositional history that attention to these matters is more than warranted, despite our inability to provide a crystal clear reconstruction of the diachronic history of the prophetic corpus.

Who Is a God Like You? Micah's Theological Witness in the Book of the Twelve: An Introductory Excurses

Identifying the character of God in the Book of the Twelve requires the coalescing of several strains of thought on the biblical material: e.g., recent research on the Twelve; relating diachronic ordering with synchronic associative readings; clarifying conceptions regarding "monotheism" in light of Israel's religious history and normative history (and where these two differ). As becomes the case, identifying "God" is not a prima facie activity but requires a patient listening to the biblical material and the traditions they proffer. It may be suggested that the shaping of the Twelve by the tradents of the material intended this kind of effect on the reader, namely, an invitation to read and reread the voices of these prophetic witnesses in increasing relation to one another.[1] It may also be suggested that embedded within the canonical

---

A version of this chapter appeared in *Monotheism in Late Prophetic and Early Apocalyptic Literature* (FAT II/172; ed. N. MacDonald and K. Brown; Tübingen: Mohr Siebeck, 2014).

[1] Rolf Rendtorff claims, "Finally, I point out that in studying the Book of the Twelve as a whole there is no simple alternative between 'diachronic' and 'synchronic' reading. The diachronic features are not only obvious but are marked explicitly by the different datings of a number of writings. On the other hand, those who gave the writings their shape (whatever we call them) obviously wanted the reader to read the writings as a connected whole and to reflect on their different messages. I think it is a challenging and fascinating exegetical task to follow their advice." Rolf Rendtorff, "How to Read the Book of the Twelve as a Theological Unity," in *Reading and Hearing the Book of the Twelve* (ed. J. D. Nogalski and M. A. Sweeney; Atlanta: Society of Biblical Literature, 2000), 87. It is not entirely clear what "diachronic" means for Rendtorff in the above account. Even texts that are clearly dated have their own complex compositional history and cannot always be dated with ease in their given form. But the final point is worth heeding well,

shaping of the Twelve are the remnants of a struggle to identify the character of Yhwh in light of difficult historical exigencies and the constraining pressure of Judah's anterior traditions. I will not engage all the features mentioned above. Rather, a modest step forward will be taken by investigating the theologizing instincts present within the complex of Jonah, Micah, and Nahum.

Though the literature is continuing to expand, some account needs to be given for reading the corpus of the Masoretic Text (MT) from Hosea to Malachi as a multi yet unified literary voice. Within this relatively new field of research, even the preceding sentence needs careful argumentation as to why the Masoretic ordering may be preferable to alternate orderings, e.g., LXX or Qumran. Or whether the ordering we have in the MT on final analysis offers the kind of *intentional* associations some scholars have identified in the compositional history of the individual books and the corpus itself.[2] If the Twelve has been shaped by the tradents of the material to present a multivoiced choir whose harmonies and melody come together to form a single, if complex, libretto—an outlook affirmed here despite the complexity of providing a compelling account for the diachronic history of its shaping—then the whole is indeed more than the sum of its parts.[3] This

---

those who shaped the materials as a Scriptural/canonical deposit for a future generation of faithful readers intended a continued and associative reading and re-reading of this material. Ben Zvi frames the matter with the terms reading and rereading. Ben Zvi's attention is on the individual books themselves, though the extension of Ben Zvi's insight into the corpus as a whole is plausible: a move Ben Zvi himself might resist. B. Ben Zvi, *Micah (FOTL XXIB)* (Grand Rapids, 2000), 7.

[2] Schart makes the point well, "The main difficulty for all the different models is establishing controls about what is considered deliberate redactional shaping and what is only accidentally connected. Which features should be construed as important goals of the final text, and which should be viewed as less significant?" Aaron Schart, "Reconstructing the Redaction History of the Twelve Prophets," in *Reading and Hearing the Book of the Twelve* (ed. J. D. Nogalski and M. A. Sweeney; Atlanta: SBL Press, 2000), 42–43. From this point, Schart continues by stating that it is most plausible to begin with the so-called Book of the Four. Even this is not as plausible as Schart et al., suggests as evidenced by the recent work of Levin. Levin, "Das 'Vierprophetenbuch.'"

[3] The most recent attempt to provide a diachronic account of the Twelve's literary development is provided by Jakob Wöhrle, in both *Die frühen Sammlungen des Zwölfprophtenbuches* and *Der Abschluss des Zwölfprophetenbuches*. Building on the

sketch will move in the direction of Twelve research with attention given to the characterization of God in Jonah, Micah, and Nahum. Moreover, the strategic placement of Micah between Jonah and Nahum yields a portrait of Yhwh, particularly his relationship to the nations, not on offer in the presentation of the individual books themselves. Put in other terms, the complex of Jonah, Micah, and Nahum come together in a combustive dialectic of mutual interpretation and presentation of

previous work of Nogalski and Schart, Wöhrle seeks to provide a more thorough analysis of the redaction history of the Twelve by examining carefully the individual books within the corpus and how they were fitted and arranged within a growing corpus. Wöhrle recognizes a developing *Fremdvölker* corpus, with the later incorporation of Habakkuk, a further *Heils-für-die-Völker* corpus, a *Gnaden* corpus, followed by the ending of Malachi and a refitting of the book of Hosea. Wöhrle's project is concerned to allow the redaction-historical reconstruction of the Twelve a mirroring role of the various religious and social-historical debates taking place in the exilic, Persian, and early Hellenistic periods of Judah. Though impressive in breadth of learning and closeness of reading, Wöhrle's redaction-critical scheme has been challenged on several levels. Most recently, Christoph Levin has challenged the basic starting point of all redaction-critical studies of the Twelve, namely, the so-called Book of the Four (Hosea, Amos, Micah, and Zeph). Levin, "Das 'Vierprophetenbuch.'" Levin suggests another "book of the four": Isaiah, Hosea, Amos, and Micah, with special attention given to the shaping influence of Isaiah on the other three. The "Deuteronomistic" link between these four as well as the shared form of their superscriptions is thoroughly challenged by Levin. Also, Klaas Spronk wonders whether or not it is too crystalline to place the various intertextual appeals to Ex 34:6-7 within the same *Gnaden* level of redaction. Instead, Spronk suggests the antiquity of the tradition represented by Ex 34:6-7 certainly allows for different authors to appeal to it at different times. Spronk concludes, "The repeated use of Exodus 34:6-7 does not have to be ascribed to a separate layer, but is probably part of this process of one book reacting to the other." Klaas Spronk, Nahum, 9.

Moreover, a general danger in redaction-critical studies is the sometimes brittle assumption that ideas expressed within a text clearly reveal the time of writing or that certain theological viewpoints only fit within a particular segment of Judah's religious history. Returning to Benjamin Sommer's essay on the subject, he reminds of the perils facing biblical scholars when they link too narrowly particular texts to particular historical periods. He warns, "To deny that any idea could have been thought of in a given age is to deny the possibility of intellectual creativity. Such a denial is a very odd position for a scholar of the humanities." Sommer, "Dating Pentateuchal Texts," 96. In a related context and in conversation with Hermisson, Steck, and Kratz on II Isaiah, Brevard Childs warns, "However, is there not the same danger present which once afflicted source critical analysis? The assumption that conceptual tension always implies different literary strands results in the endless proliferation of redactions. Is it not possible that the tensions which Hermisson observes regarding divine salvation constitute the very uniqueness of II Isaiah's message and to posit a separate and alternative redactional layer pulls apart elements which closely cohere, even in tension?" Childs, "Retrospective Reading," 368.

the identity of Yhwh that enhances the single prophetic witness in a broader frame of reference.[4]

On canonical arrangement

Though the Twelve may be read in fruitful ways according to the LXX ordering, the logic of *lectio difficilior* does render a compelling case for the priority of the Masoretic ordering.[5] The grouping together of the eighth-century prophets in the LXX—Hosea, Amos, Micah—does appear to be a chronological smoothing out of the minor chronological

---

[4] Burkardt Zapff's earlier work on the redaction-critical history of the Jonah, Micah, Nahum complex is of particular importance, e.g., B. Zapff, "The Perspective on the Nations in the Book of Micah as 'Systematization' of the Nations' Role in Joel, Jonah and Nahum? Reflections on a Context-Oriented Exegesis in the Book of the Twelve," in *Thematic Threads in the Book of the Twelve* (BZAW 325) (ed. P. L Redditt and A. Schart; Berlin, 2003), 292–312. Zapff did much of the redaction-critical spadework on this corpus with specific attention given to the position of Micah between Jonah and Nahum. Zapff's redaction-critical study focuses primarily on the social and historical forces pressuring this redactional history with specific attention given to diachronic reconstruction. Zapff advances the notion that one must make a distinction between the origin of Jonah and its particular placement within the Twelve. Whoever was responsible for the latter is, according to Zapff, most likely the same figure responsible for the redactional insertions of Nah 1.2b.3a. Zapff, "The Perspective on the Nations," 301. This article places the redaction-critical emphasis on the theological effects such shaping has on implied readers who receive the text as a normative witness to the identity of God, rather than the religious-historical reconstruction of the various "debates" among differing tradents. Most recently, Zapff has made a compelling case for the theological centrality of Micah to the whole of the Twelve. Micah's sixth position among the Twelve in the Hebrew ordering is not a redactional happenchance but is indicative of its theologically central place to the larger thematic concerns of the Twelve's unified voice. Following Wöhrle, Zapff identifies the ending of Micah and its appeal to Ex 34.6-7 as ingredient to the grace layer of redaction (*Gnaden Korpus*) and thus provides the redaction-critical logic for Micah's theological centrality. Burkard M. Zapff, "The Book of Micah—the Theological Centre of the Book of the Twelve," in *Perspectives on the Formation of the Book of the Twelve: Methodological Foundations—Redactional Processes—Historical Insights* (ed. R. Albertz, J. D. Nogalksi, and J. Wöhrle, BZAW 433; Berlin: De Gruyter, 2012), 142–44.

[5] Despite claims to the contrary, I find Nogalski's initial claims regarding the priority of the MT ordering persuasive, James D. Nogalski, *Literary Precursors of the Book of the Twelve* (BZAW 217; Berlin: De Gruyter, 1993), 2–3. For the significance of the ordering of the Twelve in the primary textual witnesses of the LXX, see M. Sweeney, "Sequence and Interpretation in the Book of the Twelve," in *Reading and Hearing the Book of the Twelve* (ed. J. D. Nogalski and M. A. Sweeney; Atlanta 2000), 49–64. The identification of Jonah at the end of 4QXIIa has come under critical scrutiny by Guillaume. P. Guillaume, "The Unlikely Malachi-Jonah Sequence (4QXIIa)," *JHS* 7 (2007): 2–10.

difficulties present in the MT ordering. In other words, the move to the LXX makes good sense as to why the traditional ordering would be rearranged, whereas the reverse is not as conceivable. The placement of Micah in the middle of the collection and not with the identifiable eighth-century prophets at least piques interest in the direction of "why?"[6] A rough chronology remains in the MT Twelve because even though Joel is dated by most scholars as late, along with Jonah, their titles do not demand such readings. In fact, Jonah's appearance in 2 Ki 14:25 locates the prophet canonically within the eighth-century reign of Jeroboam II. Nevertheless, Micah is identified in its superscription with Hosea and Amos but is not placed next to them as it is in the LXX. This raises paradigmatic questions as to why it might be placed where it is in the Twelve. As mentioned above, it is suggested here that Micah is located between Jonah and Nahum to provide an internal guide for reading these two books in light of the revealed character of Yhwh and what it means to identify Yhwh as God.[7]

In his oft-cited chapter, Raymond van Leeuwen identified the prominent role of Ex 34:6-7 in the growing corpus of the Twelve. His arguments need not be repeated here in toto, but it is worth rehearsing the main line of his thought. The bipartite description of Yhwh in Ex 34:6-7, a description that can be described in short as his mercy and severity, provides a sapiential point of entry for the larger theme addressed in the Twelve, namely, the theodicy question in light of the cataclysmic events of 722 and 587 BC. Van Leeuwan makes his way

---

[6] See Zapff, "The Book of Micah," 130–42. The so-called Book of the Four thesis has gained ascendancy among Book of the Twelve researches (e.g., Albertz, Nogalski, Schart, and Wöhrle), namely, a Deuteronomistically edited collection of Hosea, Amos, Micah, and Zephaniah was the first collection (*Sammlungen*) in the expanding corpus of the Twelve during the exilic period: the latter two books joined to an earlier Hosea and Amos corpus. As mentioned above, Levin has brought this thesis under critical scrutiny. For sake of argument, however, if an original Book of the Four did exist, then both it and the ordering of the LXX reveal the mobility of Micah in the growing corpus of the Twelve and further raises the paradigmatic question of its placement in the Twelve. Why here?

[7] Raymond C. Van Leeuwen, "Scribal Wisdom and Theodicy in the Book of the Twelve," in *In Search of Wisdom: Essays in Memory of John G. Gammie*, ed. L. G. Perdue, B. S. Brandon, and W. J. Wiseman (Louisville: Westminster John Knox, 1993), 31–49. See also, Christopher Seitz, *Prophecy and Hermeneutics: Toward a New Introduction to the Prophets* (Grand Rapids: Baker Academic, 2007).

through the Twelve, identifying the key places where the thirteen *middot* of Ex 34:6-7 appear. He then teases out the import this had for an understanding of the Twelve as a whole. Though not all of van Leeuwan's findings may be persuasive in particular, the general effect of his work is to provide warrant and an identifiable handle on the unity of the Twelve. Van Leeuwan's initial work is also an invitation to press the matter more fully and this has been done with some measure of success in the work of House, Nogalski, Schart, and Wöhrle, to name a few.

Sorting out the diachronic history of these three books may at first glance appear straightforward: Micah, Nahum, then Jonah, most scholars agreeing that Jonah is one of the latter additions to the Twelve. And while this is true, the nature of intertextual cross-fertilization and the complexity of the compositional history of the individual books themselves make surefire reconstructions not so sure. It is quite likely the gradual growth of the Twelve involved editorial decisions with the individual books at every level of the Twelve's development, e.g., Wöhrle's *Gnaden Korpus* cutting across the grain of all these books. Nevertheless, the reality of the diachronic history of the Twelve and the evidence of shared thematic and linguistic links between books—despite how difficult it is to sort this out even in a relative chronology—provide sufficient justification for the reader of the Twelve to read these texts both as individual prophetic witnesses and in ever-increasing association with the other prophetic voices within the corpus. In this sense, the diachronic history of the Twelve's composition provides internal evidence for reading the Twelve as a unified, if complex, prophetic witness.[8]

The strategic intertextual use of Ex 34:6-7 is noteworthy in Jonah, Micah, and Nahum, where reference to the *middot* appears at key junctures in these respective books. In Jonah, the gracious character of Yhwh is a source of frustration for Jonah when he provides his rationale for why he fled to Tarshish in the first place. "[F]or I knew that you are a gracious God and merciful, slow to anger, and abounding in steadfast

---

[8] See Zapff's engagement with Ben Zvi on this point, Zapff, "The Perspective on the Nations," 296–97.

love, and read to relent from punishing" (Jon 4:2b). The book of Micah ends with the question that plays off the name of Micah, "Who is a God like you?" The answer to this liturgical question has its source in the *middot*.[9] At this juncture is one of the more identifiable catch-word links (*Stichwortverbindungen*) between books in the Twelve. Nahum 1:3 refers to the *middot* as well, creating a chain-link between the end of Micah and the beginning of Nahum. Whereas Jonah and Micah emphasize the merciful side of Yhwh in their appeal to Ex 34:6-7, in Nahum the chord is struck on the severity side of Yhwh's character: the Lord will by no means clear the guilty (Nah 1:3).

An aerial view of Jonah, Micah, and Nahum reveal the balance and direction of the *middot* in Ex 34.6-7. I am borrowing from Benno Jacob's classic commentary on Exodus. He identifies the thirteen *middot* from the Talmud (Rosch. hasch. 17b) as follows:

1. *God of mercy*
2. *Grace*
3. *Long of nose (patient)*
4. *Full of ḥesed*
5. *Faithful*
6. *Visiting ḥesed to the thousandth*
7. *Forgiving iniquity*
8. *Forgiving rebellion*
9. *Forgiving sin*
10. *Visiting sins of fathers to the sons*
11. *Sons sons*
12. *Visiting sins of the fathers to the third*
13. *Visiting sins of the fathers to the fourth.*

If the Talmudic *middoth* provide a helpful schema, then the exposition of the divine name in Ex 34:6-7 is a 9 to 4 ratio with the gracious

---

[9] The liturgical character of the ending of Micah was observed a century ago by Gunkel. See also, John T. Willis, "A Reapplied Prophetic Hope Oracle," in *Studies on Prophecy: A Collection of Twelve Papers* (Suppl VT XXVI; Leiden: Brill, 1974), 64–76.

character of Yhwh tipping the relational scales in their direction. In light of God's singularity and simplicity, his judgment and mercy are not played over against one another, as if his justice and judgment are more alien to his being than his mercy. All of Yhwh's attributes are of a single piece. Yet in God's relating to his people, as observed in the golden calf encounter, forgiveness and mercy are future possibilities even though Yhwh's claims of justice and judgment would remain perfectly within his remit.

The ratio of the *middoth* is similar in Jonah, Micah, and Nahum with the deployment of the *middot* in Jonah and Micah emphasizing Yhwh's gracious character with Nahum reminding readers of the Twelve that his patience is not limitless. God's mercy cannot be equated with the indulgence of a coddling parent. This aerial view of Jonah to Nahum reveals the similar balance and direction of the *middot* between Exodus and Jonah, Micah, and Nahum. Though the engagement will be limited, a brief look at the function of the *middot* in Exodus will aid our reading of Jonah, Micah, and Nahum.

Exodus 34:6-7: Yhwh merciful and severe

According to Donald Gowen, "The book of Exodus thus reaches its theological conclusion with chs 32–34, for they explain how it can be that the covenant relationship continues in spite of perennial sinfulness."[10] As is well known, the literary context of the *middot* is the golden calf episode of Exodus 32. The interchange between Moses and Yhwh on Mt. Sinai is brought to an abrupt halt as Yhwh informs Moses of the people's idolatry. The fury of Yhwh's jealousy is on full display in this text. With a key choice of words, he tells Moses to go down to *your people*.[11] The cleavage between Yhwh and his people in light of their

---

[10] D. Gowan, *Theology in Exodus: Biblical Theology in the Form of a Commentary* (Louisville, 1994), 218.
[11] A similar distancing of Yhwh is noted in the prophets: "go and tell this people" in Isa 6:9; *lo-ammi* in Hosea 1.

idolatry signals their impending doom. "Now let me alone, so that my wrath may burn hotly against them and I may consume them; and of you I will make a great nation" (Ex 32:10). Moses intercedes on their account, and Yhwh relents. The golden calf incident becomes an iconic representation of Israel's tendency to stray to other lovers and Yhwh's predilection toward gracious patience.

It is important to recognize the backdrop of the golden calf incident to the revelation of the divine name in Ex 34:6-7. On the far side of the golden calf encounter, Moses asks to see Yhwh's glory and understand his ways (Ex 33:13). What he receives is a divine exposition on the significance of the divine name, Yhwh. Though the syntax creates some difficulties, there is little doubt that the one proclaiming the name, "Yhwh," in 34:5 and crying out "Yhwh, Yhwh" in 34:6 is Yhwh himself. Moreover, the link between 34:5-7 and the revelation of the divine name in Exodus 3 should not be overlooked as well: 34:5-7 is an extension of ch. 3's divine unveiling.[12] This revelation of the name in Exodus is a revelation of Yhwh's divine identity, that is, his character or his "narrative identity" if I may borrow a helpful term from Paul Ricouer.[13] This is how one recognizes and "plots" Yhwh so as to identify him over against any other. The revelation of the divine name or identity is an explanation of his character and actions: the insoluble relationship between being and action in the divine. It provides a ballast for the people of God to respond to various divine actions with an understanding that such are in accord with Yhwh's own self-understanding and self-determination.

The burning anger of Ex 32:10 elides into the patient character of Yhwh in 34:6-7. Thomas Dozeman identifies a change in the character of Yhwh at this point in the unfolding of the divine name. Whereas in the Decalogue, Yhwh's response to fidelity or idolatry is presented in polar extremes, love/hate, obedience or punishment (Ex 20:4-6), Ex 34:6-7 provides a way forward for Yhwh's people after the sin of the

---

[12] See, Christopher Seitz, "The Call of Moses and the 'Revelation' of the Divine Name: Source-Critical Logic and Its Legacy," in *Theological Exegesis: Essays in Honor of Brevard S. Childs* (ed. C. Seitz and K. Greene-McCreight; Grand Rapids: Eerdmans, 1999), 145–61.

[13] P. Ricouer, *Oneself as Another* (trans. K. Blamey; Chicago, 1992).

golden calf.¹⁴ "Yhwh, the jealous God, now becomes Yhwh, the most merciful and gracious God."¹⁵ As the *middot* remind in their latter third, this is not a complete displacement of divine jealousy, but it provides the proportionality fit to the character of Yhwh's own self-disclosure: merciful and severe, with the latter open to the supervening grace of the former.¹⁶ Yhwh and the Scripture's bearing witness to him know nothing of *billige Gnade*. Yhwh's relational mode of being with Israel may alter in light of his propensity toward steadfast love. As in Jonah, repentance can lead to a divine reversal of fortunes. And like Jonah, the people of God should not be surprised, "It is just like Yhwh to act in this way."

With this brief look at Ex 34:6-7 in mind, we turn to Jonah, Micah, and Nahum to see how the severity and mercy of Yhwh are worked out in this canonical complex.

Jonah, Micah, Nahum: Eschatological potentialities

On the surface, Jonah and Nahum present a contradictory view of Yhwh's dealings with Nineveh. Rolf Rendtorff identifies the Nineveh in Jonah as a literary construct and not a real political power who threatened the existence of Israel and Judah.¹⁷ Nineveh represents a sinful Gentile city deserving of God's punishment. However, Yhwh extends a gracious hand to this sinful Gentile city in light of their repentance. As Jonah laments at the end of the narrative (Jon 4:2), it is just like Yhwh to act in accordance with his nature: slow to wrath and quick to mercy. Nahum, on the other hand, presents Nineveh in the real: the city known and feared by Israel and Judah who on final

---

[14] T. Dozeman, *Exodus (Eerdmans Critical Commentary)* (Grand Rapids, 2009), 737.
[15] Ibid.
[16] Benno Jacob emphasizes the enduring significance of the *middot* in Israel's religious life, "[I]mmer wenn Israel sündigt, sollen sie hiernach vor mir verfahren, und ich werde ihnen vergeben. Das will sagen: Diese Sätze sind ein Gebet, das gleichsam Gott selbst den Mose gelehrt hat." Jacob, *Das Buch Exodus*, 969–70.
[17] Rendtorff, "How to Read," 83.

analysis continue as a city of bloodshed without the enduring effects of the citywide repentance of Jonah.[18] What appears in Jonah as the ideal, with both the sailors at the beginning of the book and the city of Nineveh toward the end, is revealed in Nahum as life in real time. What appears prima facie as contradictory accounts on second glance reveal the possibilities extended to the nations by Israel's severe yet merciful God: potentialities offered but never in full received.

Micah's position between these two books provides an angle of repose on the stark contrast between Jonah and Nahum. In other words, Micah offers interpretive clues for how to negotiate such divergent views regarding the character of Yhwh and his posture vis-à-vis the nations. Micah might be seen as the second third of the *middot*, if the scope and balance of the *middot* can function in such a metaphorical fashion. The tensions felt between Jonah and Nahum are felt in Micah's corpus as well, especially in Micah 4-5.[19] By way of procedure, I will begin with an examination of a few key texts in Micah and their relationship to the surrounding literature.

The picture of Yhwh's relationship to the nations is acute in Micah 4. Micah 4:1-4 (5) promises a coming day where the nations stream to Zion to be taught *Torah* in an age of universal peace.[20] As the memorable images of 4:3 remind the reader, in that day weapons of war

---

[18] Rendtorff, "How to Read," 83–84. Schart lists three options for the tension between Jonah and Nahum. First, the historical solution is Nineveh's repentance did not last long. Second, Jeremias suggests Jonah represents God's final will, while Nahum represents his temporary will. Third, Jonah himself comes under critical scrutiny. Schart, Jonah-Narrative, 137–38. Rendtorff's canonical instincts offer a different view given the literature as continued testimony, namely, both Ninevehs are literary tropes witnessing to the different possible routes for the nations vis-à-vis their repentance toward Israel's God.

[19] My instincts are with Zapff over against Schart to view Micah 4-5 as a canonical text in its present form and not to sort out the tensions on final analysis by appealing to the contrastive theological viewpoints from various postexilic circles. The importance of the book of Isaiah framing Micah 4 and 5 is indicative of the intentional shaping of this material for an intended theological purpose, multiperspectival as it may be. Zapff, "The Book of Micah," 133–34.

[20] The eschatology presented in Micah 4.1-4 (5) and Isaiah 2.2-4 need not be understood as end of the world eschatology but as an event taking place in space and time in the future. Shemaryahu Talmon, "The Signification of אחרית and אחרית הימים in the Hebrew Bible," in *Emanuel: Studies in Hebrew Bible Septuagint and Dead Sea Scrolls in Honor of Emanuel Tov* (ed. S. M. Paul et al.; Leiden: Brill, 2003), 795–810.

are transformed into tools of the field as everyone sits under their own vine and fig tree. The phrase is particularly memorable because in Joel 4:10 a very different image of Yhwh's relationship to the nations is given, one in which plowshares and pruning hooks are turned into swords and spears. As one observes the tension between Jonah and Nahum on the relationship of God to the nations, so too does one observe the selfsame pattern between Micah 4 and Joel 4.

While resisting the tendency to flatten out the particularity of Joel and Micah into a tidy theological package, the reader on the level of the whole is invited to make some sense of the theological character of the books in relation to one another on the level of a shared subject matter. From a religious-historical perspective, it could be claimed that Joel as a postexilic book is expressing the frustrations one might expect from unfulfilled hopes and continued foreign domination in light of previous prophetic promises. Another kind of reading seeks after the substance of the witness as a unified whole and the effects this has on the implied reader in the community of faith. The distinction between the two texts in Joel and Micah may be on the same conceptual/theological field as the distinction between Jonah and Nahum. What Micah 4 presents as an eschatological promise for the future—a presentation of the nations making good on the claim that those who take refuge in Yhwh are blessed (Nah 1:7)—Joel and Nahum present the facts on the ground or in the real. The invitation to the nations in Mic 4:1-4 (5) is an eschatological hope promised but not yet actualized. In the idiom of Nahum's voice, "Why do you plot against the LORD? He will make an end; no adversary will rise up twice" (Nah 1:9). When Joel presents Yhwh as a roaring lion making judgment in the valley of Jehoshaphat, the force of the presentation in intertextual association with Micah 4 makes clear the nations have not sought refuge in Yhwh and continue in their plot against God.

What Jonah pictures as an ideal response of the nations may be considered a narrative account of the eschatological promise of Micah 4.[21] The editorial challenge of Mic 4:5 to walk in the name of

---

[21] In a similar vein, see Zapff, "The Perspective on the Nations," 304.

Yhwh forever while the nations continue to walk after their gods finds a possible linguistic link in Jon 1:4: "each one cried out to his God." The collective use of איש is deployed in each context. The phraseology in Mic 4:5 is, "each one walks in the name of his God." The nations of Mic 4:5 in this particular moment of the divine economy are much like the sailors at the beginning of Jonah 1; they continue on without taking refuge in him and in the trust of their own gods. By the end of Jonah 1, however, a major transition occurs. This transition takes place at a critical juncture as the sailors respond to and obey the prophetic word from Jonah: throw me into the water. At the end of Jonah 1, the sailors "call out to Yhwh" no longer Elohim (cf. 1:4). They address Yhwh in a vocative form: "Ah, Yhwh." In 1:16 the sailors greatly fear Yhwh and make sacrifices and vows to him.[22] Speculation regarding the narrative behind the narrative, i.e., did the sailors become Yahwists or did they go to the temple to fulfill these promises, misses the laconic point of the narrative. The pagan sailors turn their full attention to Yhwh in recognition of his identity as maker of heaven and earth. In brief, they repent.

In this light, the sailors and the Ninevites, as Rendtorff suggests, are literary tropes functioning as narrative portraits of what the promises of Micah 4 might look like in a real encounter between the gracious God of Israel and the surrounding nations. The presence of Nahum and Joel 4 provides a sharp challenge to understand this picture as an eschatological hope and not a present reality. The contextual and particular placement of Jonah within the Twelve provides sharp relief on the "eschatologizing" of the Jonah narrative.

The portrait of the nations in Micah 4 is caught in a similar dialectic. "Now many nations are assembled against you ... Arise and thresh, O daughter of Zion ... you shall beat in pieces many peoples" (Mic 4:11-13). The picture here is surely of a different order than the eschatological vision at the beginning of the chapter. But, again, the nations who will be "pulverized" are those who have set themselves against Yhwh

---

[22] See ZVI on Jonah and pagan sailors.

and his people (4:11). The character of Mic 4:11-13 makes historical identification difficult. Israel had many enemies of the past and more to come in the future. Who exactly are the "many nations" rising up against Yhwh? It does not seem necessary to thrust this text into the eschatological future.[23] Rather the text is indeterminate enough to catch all kinds of historical possibilities for Israel now and in her future. The nations who set themselves over against Yhwh both now and in the future will know Yhwh as a roaring lion. While those who take refuge in him will find an extended hand of mercy from a relenting God whose mercy can cede his severity.

As mentioned at the beginning of this section, for some time now scholars have noted the intertextual link between Joel, Jonah, the end of Micah, and the beginning of Nahum. The strategic placement of Ex 34:6-7 at key junctures in these books reveals the gracious character of Yhwh for his repentant people in Joel, for the repentant nations in Jonah, as a concluding promise in Micah, and as a warning in Nahum: Yhwh is patient but his patience is not limitless.[24] Micah's characterization of Yhwh in Mic 7:18-20 is preceded by an account of the nations that is more akin to Joel and Nahum than Micah 4 or Jonah. As in the days of old when Israel was led out of Egypt, so too will Yhwh act again on behalf of his people such that the nations can only respond with ritual shame and genuine fear in the face of Yhwh's marvelous acts (Mic 7:15).

The juxtaposition of Mic 7:11-17 and Mic 7:18-20 in the final literary form of the text again creates a field of possibilities for the nations with respect to Yhwh's identity. The presence of Ex 34:6-7 both at the end of Micah and on the lips of the king of Nineveh in Jonah 3 identifies God as one who responds graciously, who in fact is quick to respond with grace and slow to respond in anger for those who turn to him and take refuge in him. The nations who are placing their hands over their

---

[23] *Pace* Freedman and Anderson, ad loc.
[24] Nogalski identifies the redactional insertion of Ex 34.6-7 in Nah 1.3 because it breaks up the alleged acrostic present in Nah 1.2-8. James Nogalski, *Redactional Processes in the Book of the Twelve* (BZAW; Berlin: Walter de Gruyter, 1993), 106–07. See also, Zapff, "The Perspective on the Nations," 307.

mouths while exiting their fortresses in fear (Mic 7:11-17) also have the opportunity to encounter the mercy of God on the far side of his severity. Like the king of Nineveh in Jonah 3, they too can encounter Yhwh as one who is quick to mercy and slow to anger.

The intertextual placement of Ex 34:6-7 in Nah 1:3, however, has a sharper edge to it than its use in Joel 2, Jonah 3, and Micah 7. Indeed, Yhwh is slow to anger and great in power, but he will by no means clear the guilty. The chord is struck on the final half of the verse. The tight juxtaposition of severity and mercy in Nahum arrests the reader. Who can endure the heat of his anger (Nah 1:6)? The "heat of his anger" is precisely what the king of Nineveh hoped to avoid in his call for national repentance: from the greatest to the least (Jon 3:9). The Nineveh of Nahum, however, will not experience this because on final analysis they did not take refuge in Israel's God. Again, the portraits of Nineveh in Jonah and Nahum identify real future possibilities: the eschatological looking forward, the creating of literary tropes that exist as enduring promises and threats that flow from the identity of Yhwh. The canonical reader is able to see both the mercy and the severity of Yhwh: slow to anger, quick to forgive, yet by no means clearing the guilty. The nations may walk down the path of Jonah's Nineveh or Nahum's Nineveh. Both options are present and the eschatological hope of Micah 4 is that at some point in the future, the former will once again prevail. Yhwh's temporal "no" of judgment, though real, need not be final. The promise of Micah 4 and its effects are always on offer. Again, in Nahum's Psalm-like phrase, "He protects those who take refuge in him" (Nah 1:7b).

The dialectic of the severity and mercy of Yhwh with the nations is equally at play with his own people as well. The theophanic images at the beginning of Micah 1 and Nahum overlap in force of expression and shared imagery. In Nahum 1 the quaking mountains and melting hills are on display before the earth and its inhabitants. The nations are in view as the superscription indicates. Whereas in Micah, the fire of Yhwh's wrath is kindled because of the sins of Israel and Judah, the created order is called on as juridical witnesses in the divine court. He by no means clears the guilty irrespective of national identity. An assumed Zion theology with no repentance, no recognition of guilt, is thoroughly challenged by the prophetic word. Though the nations continue to walk in the name of their own gods, Judah is called on to walk in the name of Yhwh forever (Mic 4:5).[25] Heinz-Joseph Fabry suggests the redactional joining of Nahum to Habakkuk advances a creation theology (*Schöfungstheologie*) as rationale for God's actions with Nineveh. The hymn of Nah 1:2-8 enjoyed a literary independence before its deployment here in the context of the superscription's purview: Nineveh. The placement of the hymn in this context is not "seamless" (*nahtlos*) in Fabry's view but is made compatible with the oracle against Nineveh by the editor. The linking of this theological preamble to the forthcoming speeches against Nineveh provides a window into the identity of Yhwh, his lordship over creation (*Weltenherrscher*), and his sole power over history (*einzigen geschichtsmächtigkeit Gottes*).[26] The linking together of Micah 7 and Nahum 1 with the loan text (*Textanleihe*) from Ex 34:6-7 situates together the revenge of God with his patience. The feelings of those within Judah who desired God's vengeance on their behalf are warranted. Such sentiments flow from the character of Yhwh's own revealed self. "[D]ie gütige Seite Gottes auch in Vergeltungshandeln an den Feinden im Auge zu behalten und keener Verfinsterung des Gottesbildes zu verfallen."[27] The vengeance of Yhwh against the nations stems from his revealed identity in Ex 34:6-7 and his role as Creator: the whole world and all its nations are under his dominion and reign. The conclusion Fabry draws from the intertextual link between the end of Micah, the beginning of Nahum, and Ex 34:6-7 is especially insightful:

---

[25] This is a decidedly different reading of Mic 4.5 than offered by Sweeney and a host of scholars who have followed him, to wit, Mic 4.5 presents a religiously plural eschatology over against Isaiah's non-pluralistic view. M. Sweeney, "Micah's Debate with Isaiah," *JSOT* 93 (2001): 111–24. See the comments in the commentary proper.

[26] Fabry concurs with Schart and Kessler that the redactor who brought together the Psalm and the speeches in Nahum did so in connection with Habakkuk. They locate these texts in Jerusalem during the days of Habakkuk with the residence of Judah as the addressees. This substantiates, for Fabry, Schart's understanding of the redaction of the Twelve bringing together the Assyrian and Babylonian themes within the complex of theophany (*Theophanie-Motivkompmlex*). H. Fabry, *Nahum (HTKAT)* (Freiburg, 2006), 96–104.

[27] Fabry, *Nahum*, 92.

"Nicht die Feinde Israels generell sind der Vergeltung Gottes ausgesetzt, sondern nur die Fiende JHWHs; das aber können auch—auch wenn es nicht explizit gesagt wird—Israeliten/Judäer sein! Es sind genau diese Feinde, die von der Glut seines Zornes weggefegt warden (Nah 1,6a)."[28] The enemies of Yhwh can be found in all nations, Israel included—the oracles against the nations in Amos 1-2 culminating in Judah and Israel concur. Such an outlook may be observed in the description of Nineveh as a "city of blood" (עיר דמים; Nah 1:3) with Micah decrying against the leaders of Israel who build Zion with blood (בדמים; Mic 3:10). Those, on the other hand, who take refuge in him, including those from nations other than Israel, rest secured.

The revelation of the divine name on the far side of the golden calf episode creates possibilities of forgiveness and renewal. It is the character of Yhwh to be severe; his justice and judgment demand it. No saccharine view of Israel's God is available to readers of the Twelve. Yet Yhwh's severity and judgment against the rebellion of Israel and the nations is always open to a real future of mercy, forgiveness, and covenant restoration. The golden calf episode is an enduring witness to Yhwh's severe and merciful relation to his people.

For the generation of ancient Judah who received and shaped this literature, as well as for future generations, these texts witness to the necessity of forward-looking hope. Even when the effects of divine displeasure are experienced, the community of faith is called on to remember the identity of Yhwh and the significance of his name: merciful and severe, with the latter always capable of cessation in the light of Yhwh's mercy and human repentance. Israel's God is quick to run off the front porch to meet the returning prodigal. Moreover, the nations come into view as those who fall under the lordship of Judah's creator God. The gracious character of Yhwh extends to all who take refuge in him. Both the enemies of Yhwh and the friends of Yhwh are reconceived in such a way as to make categories such as universalism and particularism increasingly problematic or at least invite readers to a more nuanced account.

---

[28] Ibid.

Conclusion: Preliminary thoughts

Building on the work of previous scholarship, my aim in these reflections is to unlock the theologizing instincts of the various authorizing voices within Jonah, Micah, and Nahum. Such a reading is not offered for the sake of minimizing the integrity of the individual voices in the Twelve. In other words, Jonah, Micah, and Nahum can and should be read as discrete witnesses with their own theological integrity. The commentary to follow is an example of this effort, even when intertextual and canonical associations are explored. Nevertheless, the associative and intertextual reading on offer here brings these discrete voices into an internal and canonical conversation regarding a central concern of the Twelve, viz., Who is Israel's God and what are his ways?

"Who is a God like you?" is a rhetorical question whose function within Micah is similar to the sapiential invitation at the end of Hosea: "Let the wise discern the ways of the Lord?" There is a call to reflective discernment with a touchstone provided for such theological reflection in the revelation of the divine name in Ex 34.6-7. Sociopolitical and religious-historical crisis within the history of Israel and Judah are made sense of in light of the revelation of the divine name: gracious and severe. The anterior self-disclosure of the divine name in Ex 34.6-7 exerts a coercive pressure on the authors/tradents of these three books as they provide theological handles for identifying Yhwh in the complexities of a lived experience in God's presence. Karl Barth's "reading with the Bible in one hand and the newspaper in the other," though anachronistic, is a helpful metaphor.[29] The debates and struggles to come to terms with God's actions in Israel's and subsequently Judah's midst—a struggle whose residual tensions may be felt in the Twelve—

---

[29] The tendency to identify the various "tensions" within the prophetic literature as indicative of religious debates within exilic Judah and postexilic Yehud, though not denied, is framed rather differently by Brevard Childs in light of an understanding of the prophetic traditions preserving of the living voice of God. Childs clarifies,

are theological wranglings after the multifaceted character of the revealed name of Yhwh.

It is a perennial difficulty in the synagogue and the church to remain faithful to God in the midst of difficult historical circumstances. If I may draw from the Protestant tradition, the reader may recall Martin Luther's later admission that as a monk he did not love God. He hated God. Luther had no trouble with the severity of God; it was his basic theological category. In fact, it could be argued the Reformation took flight because of Luther's obsessive desire to find a God he could love. Taking the necessary changes into account, Judah also knew the severity of God. The effect of Jonah, Micah, and Nahum is not to attenuate the reality of Yhwh's severity but to put Yhwh's severity in the necessary dialectical relationship to his mercy. This characterization of Yhwh provides an enduring witness to God's identity in relationship to his people and the nations. In brief, Yhwh's severe "no" need never be his final word. Because this is the case, Judah is called to faithfulness in the current moment and to hope for the future reality of the ultimate triumph of Yhwh's mercy (Mic 4.1-5).

"Because the prophetic writings were soon treasured as authoritative Scripture, textual expansion occurred in the process of continual usage not toward the goal of correcting concepts deemed false—a concept quite unthinkable in Judaism—but in order to elucidate and confirm for its hearers the truth of a prophetic message which it was assumed to possess." Childs, "Retrospective Reading," 375. Similarly, Stephen Chapman encourages making the distinction between differing *ideals* and *ideologies* in the Law and the Prophets. S. Chapman, *The Law and the Prophets: A Study in Old Testament Canon Formation (FAT27)* (Tübingen, 2000), 283. Because the effect of the canonical process was to indict the self, Chapman says, "This means that a viewpoint finding expression within the canon has been recognized by the community as an insight leading to self-discipline and the good of the other, and not merely as a propagandistic effort on the part of the politically powerful to restrict or condemn those with whom they disagree." Chapman, *The Law and the Prophets*, 283.

1

Micah 1:1—Prophetic Identities

The word of the LORD that came to Micah of Moresheth in the days of Kings Jotham, Ahaz, and Hezekiah of Judah, which he saw concerning Samaria and Jerusalem.

On framing canonical expectations

Augustine's encounter with Ambrose, Bishop of Milan, stands as an enduring testimony to the hermeneutical complexity one encounters when coming to terms with the prophetic literature. After Ambrose directed Augustine to read Isaiah in preparation for his baptism, he concedes, "But I did not understand the first passage of the book, and thought the whole would be equally obscure. So I put it on one side to be resumed when I had more practice in *the Lord's style of language*."[1]

Augustine's framing of the complex world of the prophetic literature rings true for most readers of the prophets. Reading and making sense of the prophets is no mean task, much less coming to terms with their peculiar mode of discourse, structure, and theological outlook. Our particular location on the far side of modernity's critical inquiry into the biblical material only exacerbates the hermeneutical hurdles. Imagine if Augustine not only had to grapple with Isaiah but with a supposed First, Second, and Third Isaiah and the redactional layers embedded within these "discrete" literary units of the Isaianic corpus?

---

[1] Augustine, *Saint Augustine Confessions* (Oxford World Classics; trans. Henry Chadwick; Oxford: Oxford University Press, 2009), IX.13; Chadwick, 163.

On the far side of modern criticism's highlighting of the historical forces at work in Israel's religious history that gave rise to the biblical traditions across the canon, locating texts within their proper interpretive milieu, whether historically or literarily, remains a challenge. The challenges are not equally insurmountable, thus the proverbial baby with the bathwater should not be thrown out. Nevertheless, a canonical sensitivity to these challenges takes the final form of the prophetic book as its privileged form, even where lower-critical judgments are requisite for identifying it. Thus, the superscription of Micah's prophecy lays claim on the prophetic legacy of the eighth-century prophet as the material substance of the book to follow.

Micah's title or superscription tells us something of his social location as a prophet, his Judahite provenance, and the preexilic setting of his vocational activities. As the past few centuries of critical scholarship have made us aware, univocal associations between prophetic titles and the book's compositional history beg certain questions. Moreover, the application of post-Gutenberg notions of authorship onto the biblical material fails to take into account the priority of *auctor* (authority) accounts of authorship over against a facile linkage between prophetic titles and the sole authorship of the book by the prophet so named (a highlighting of prophetic *personae*). The prophetic word of the eighth-century prophet and the afterlife or *Nachinterpretationen* of those words in larger association with a growing corpus of prophetic literature need not be played over against each other in a providential account of canonization. The prophetic word is a "living organism" whose scope and reach remains under the oversight of the speaking God from whom the words originated. As observed in the introduction, good reasons exist for a certain amount of modesty when seeking to give a diachronic account of this textual history. Thus, overly rationalized accounts of inspiration where the details and mechanics of the compositional process are requisite need not be the cart pulling the horse. God's prophetic word is God's giving of his very self in acts of judging and redeeming communication. Whatever the details of the compositional process were, the claims of 2 Peter remain: "First of all, you must understand this, that no prophecy of Scripture is a matter of one's own interpretation. Because no prophecy ever came by human will, but holy men and women moved by the Holy Spirit spoke from God" (2 Pt. 1:20-21).

> John Webster makes use of the theological concept of "sanctification" when giving attention to the creaturely character of Scripture.[2] Readers of Christian theology might not initially see this move as theologically fitting because sanctification resides in the dogmatic location of salvation and its effects. Webster's theological move is a helpful one, however, in giving an ordered account of the human processes involved in the production and preservation of the Scriptural witness. God takes creaturely activities, activities taking place in the normal course of human affairs and actions, and sanctifies or sets them apart for his own unique, redemptive purposes. Far from shying away from the "creaturely" character of Scripture, Webster's account provides a helpful means by which the creaturely character of Scripture is affirmed and embraced.

The word of Yhwh comes to Micah

The expression *word of the Lord* (דבר יהוה; *dbr yhwh*) signals the character of the text. Readers are put on alert as to the expectations they bring to their hearing/reading along with the proper posture for reception of the material. Micah as a prophetic book is *dbr yhwh*. Jeremias notes the singular *dbr* rather than plural *dbrym* indicates the unity of the prophetic message in the entirety of Micah's corpus (Jeremias, 126). Micah's raison d'etre as a literary entity is described by this two-word Hebrew construct, highlighted and set apart as it is by the Masoretic disjunctive accents. This collocation clarifies the nature of the forthcoming material and the kind of readership it anticipates.

> Building on the assumption that prophetic superscriptions are the result of later editorial activity, many within the guild of Twelve scholarship have argued for a Book of the Four as the editorial building block of the Twelve's diachronic history: Hosea, Amos, Micah, and Zephaniah. Jeremias identified the intertextual/redactional relationship between Hosea and Amos, suggesting these two initially formed a single compositional unit. He observes the cross-fertilization of ideas/language between these two books with Hosea's intertextual presence at critical junctures of Amos. The latter observation led Jeremias to the conclusion

---

[2] John Webster, *Holy Scripture: A Dogmatic Sketch* (Current Issues in Theology; Cambridge: Cambridge University Press, 2003), 17–30.

of Hosea's more formative influence on Amos and thus its signal position in the Twelve.[3] Others have built on Jeremias's work in support of the Book of the Four theory, though he is less convinced by it. Jeremias understands the Book of the Four as a possibility (*möglicher*) but does not believe the overlap in superscriptions is sufficient ground (*zureichender Grund*) for the theory.[4]

James Nogalski pioneered the notion of the Book of the Four. These four books are "Deuteronomistic" in theological flavor and share a common feature in their superscription, namely, they all begin with *dbr yhwh*. Nogalski also drew attention to the parallel relationship between two Northern prophets (Hosea and Amos) and two Southern prophets (Micah and Zephaniah), with Micah linking Northern and Southern outlooks in Mic 1:2-9.[5]

Various challenges to the particularities of Nogalski's theory have arisen, though its basic contours are broadly received by scholars who see an intentional diachronic movement to a unified Book of the Twelve. Aaron Schart, in concert with Lohfink, believes the description of these exilic redactors as "deuteronomistic" is an inflated application of the term. Schart prefers to describe this corpus as a DK or D-Redaction which stands near deuteronomistic thought yet avoids a heavy hand in identifying the redactors as deuteronomistic. Schart is concerned to protect the specific language and thought of the Four.[6] Rainer Albertz refines the redaction-critical tools brought to the Book of the Four, calling for methodological clarity and offering his own diachronic reconstruction. He too builds off the "starting point for the theory" as the shared superscription: *dbr yhwh*.[7] Hosea, Micah, and Zephaniah all share the singular *dbr*, a "striking" phenomenon according to Albertz,[8] while Amos begins with the plural *dbrym* because, on Albertz's view, the book probably already had this superscription and the FPR (Four Prophets Redactor) could not alter it.[9] FPR demonstrates familiarity with the Deuteronomistic History and JerD (the deuteronomistic redaction of Jeremiah) and was most likely drafted after 550.[10] FPR also shows an internal knowledge of the four prophets and is influenced by the theology of Isaiah. Albertz's diachronic reconstruction serves the purpose of identifying the religious historical instincts of the exilic editors responsible for this corpus: a focus on Judah/Jerusalem, the parallel relationship of prophetic word and Torah, and a hostility toward the monarchy and elite upper classes. In brief, FPR belongs "to a more radical group of theologians, in solidarity with the lower classes."[11]

As is to be expected, several scholars have serious misgivings about the supposed Book of the Four. Ehud Ben Zvi makes a case against the dominant trend of Twelve scholarship that identifies an *intentional* editorial history where these books are brought together as a

---

[3] Joachim Jeremias, "Die Anfänge des Dodekapropheten: Hosea und Amos," in *Hosea und Amos: Studien zu den Anfängen des Dodekapropheten* (FAT 13; ed. J. Jeremias; Tübingen: Mohr Siebeck, 1996), 34–54. See Aaron Schart, "Reconstructing the Redaction History of the Twelve Prophets," in *Reading and Hearing the Book of the Twelve* (ed. J. D. Nogalski; M. A. Sweeney; Atlanta: SBL Press, 2000), 44.

[4] Jeremias, 121.

[5] James D. Nogalski, *Literary Precursors of the Book of the Twelve* (BZAW 217; Berlin: De Gruyter, 1993).

[6] Aaron Schart, *Die Enstehung des Zwölfprophetenbuchs: Neuarbeitungen von Amos in Rahmen schriftenübergreifender Redaktionprozesse* (BZAW 260; Berlin: De Gruyter, 1998), 46.

[7] Rainer Albertz, *Israel in Exile: The History and Literature of the Sixth Century B.C.E.* (Studies in Biblical Literature 3; trans. D. Green; Atlanta: SBL, 2003), 204–37 (209). For the particularities of Albertz's redaction-critical analysis, see the preceding.

[8] Ibid., 210.

[9] Ibid.

[10] Ibid., 236.

[11] Ibid., 237.

unified corpus by means of various catchwords and editorial linkages.[12] Christoph Levin expresses his reservations regarding the legitimacy of a Book of the Four in an article subtitled "An Exegetical Obituary" (*Nachruf*).[13] It is important to note that Levin does not deny the compositional growth of the Twelve as an editorial activity whereby an earlier corpus forms the basis for the growth and development of later books.[14] He affirms the linkages between Hosea and Amos that Jeremias identifies, along with other signs of intentional editorial activity. What he outright denies is the existence of a so-called Book of the Four: "Es hat zu keiner Zeit bestanden."[15] Levin denies the "deuteronomistic" influence on this corpus. According to Levin, it is *fraglos* (unquestionable) that these books are a running commentary on the theological implications of the preexilic period. But such could be said of Isaiah and Jeremiah too. In other words, what appears to some as an indication of "deuteronomistic" redactional activity may in fact be the prophets/editors imbibing a shared religious tradition and interpretive reception of the prophetic material. The linguistic and thematic links between these four prophets do not necessitate a collection identified as the Book of the Four. But others (e.g., Albertz and Schart) do not rest their arguments for a Book of the Four on deuteronomistic influences. The secured building block for the Book of the Four theory is the shared form of the prophetic superscriptions. But here too, Levin, along with Ben Zvi, resists the interpretive confidence afforded these titles as clear indications of an earlier collection of the four. For Levin, the deuteronomistic influence and the recognition of a shared superscription are necessarily related. Otherwise, what does one do with Joel, a prophetic book that also begins with *dbr yhwh*? Moreover, Zephaniah's "deuteronomistic" influence remains questionable. For Levin, the phraseology "the word of the Lord which came" has more to do with the shaping influence of Jeremiah on these prophetic books than their initial place in the Book of the Four. Levin also draws attention to the influence of Isaiah on Hosea, Amos, and Micah, noting that the relative clause "which he saw" found in Amos and Micah stems from the Isaianic traditions. According to Levin, if interpreters are to speak of a Book of the Four, it should be Isaiah, Hosea, Amos, and Micah. The dating of these texts in the frame of the eighth-century kings of Judah reveals the influence of Isaiah. Zephaniah parts company here.[16]

The shaping influence of the prophetic literature on the growing corpus of the prophetic literature is a phenomenon that can only be denied in the face of overwhelming textual indicators. But as stated in the introduction, charting this diachronic history and identifying the editorial origins of the prophetic titles remain a challenge. This commentary sits loosely to the so-called Book of the Four, remaining somewhat persuaded by Levin's challenges. The influence of Jeremiah and Isaiah on the coming to be of the Book of the Twelve has much to commend even when one does not attach a particular religious or

---

[12] Ehud Ben Zvi, "Twelve Prophetic Books or 'The Twelve': A Few Preliminary Considerations," in *Forming Prophetic Literature: Essays on Isaiah and the Twelve in Honor of John D. W. Watts* (JSOTSupp 235; ed. J. W. Watts and P. R. House; Sheffield: University of Sheffield Press, 1996), 125–57.

[13] Christoph Levin, "Das 'Vierpropheten Buch': Ein exegetischer Nachruf," *ZAW* 123 (2011): 221–35.

[14] Ibid., 221.

[15] Ibid., 222.

[16] Ibid., 233–34.

literary history to this "coming to be." Christopher Seitz offers a judicious judgment on this subject in his Joel commentary. "It could well be that the earliest prophets are those for whom coordination with the events of the Deuteronomistic History is simply a most obvious desideratum. That is, the four prophets Hosea, Amos, Micah, and Zephaniah are genuinely the first four to be active in Israel's history, however we are to judge the subsequent growth of their respective books."[17] He clarifies in a footnote, however, "It does not follow from this that they together circulated as the earliest precursor of the Twelve. That is speculation of a different order."[18]

The *persona* of the human prophet is a crucial feature of the prophetic record itself. The superscription identifies Micah as from the lowland region of *Moresheth*, with a prophetic ministry ranging from the reign of three Judahite kings: Jotham, Ahaz, and Hezekiah (739–699 BC). Micah's social location as a prophet in the Shephaleh region provided him a firsthand experience of the devastating effects of the judging hand of God against his people by means of a foreign invader. Micah's Moresheth experienced the war machine of the Neo-Assyrians near the end of the eighth century as Sennacherib's reign of terror moved south into this region. Something of the devastation of this moment may be on display in Mic 1:10-16.

While making the human agency of Micah a central feature of the text to follow, the superscription makes clear Micah's primary prophetic role as a servant of the *dbr yhwh*. The "word of the LORD" is that which comes (היה) to Micah. The language of "coming" or "becoming" is typical speech within the prophetic literature.[19] The "word of the LORD" stems from the sending agency of Yhwh toward his people and provides the authoritative warrant for the words spoken by the prophets. Commenting on John 1:18, Aquinas speaks of the Trinitarian implications of the Word coming to the prophets. "For in the past, the

---

[17] Christopher R. Seitz, *Joel* (The International Theological Commentary; London: Bloomsbury T&T Clark, 2016), 112.
[18] Ibid., 112, n. 4.
[19] *TLOT* claims that *hyh* "describes the intrusion of the word in the life of the prophet" (*TLOT 1*, 360).

only begotten Son revealed knowledge of God through the prophets, who made him known to the extent that they shared in the eternal Word. Hence they said things like, *the Word of the Lord came to me.*"[20] The personal agency of the Word as that which comes to the prophets in created form, namely word(s), adumbrates the unique moment in the divine economy when the Word "becomes flesh" (Jn 1:14). The giving of the Word in the creaturely medium of human language anticipates and witnesses to the singularity of that moment when in the fullness of time God takes on flesh in the incarnation (Heb 1:1). The prophetic word of the Old Testament as that which is sent and given, an extension of Yhwh's own revealed self, is fitted to the singularity of the divine being in tripersonal relation.

The *dbr yhwh* is not portrayed as that which emerges from the religious instinct of the prophet. It is an external phenomenon coming to the prophet *extra nos*. "[F]or he brought nothing of his own," claims Calvin, "but what the Lord commanded him to proclaim" (Calvin, 153). Such a "coming to be" of the prophetic word does not demand a euphoric or disembodied state, though such modes of reception need not be dismissed. The ordinary mixes with the extraordinary in God's providential ordering of his word and affairs. Nevertheless, the prophetic text makes clear the divine provenance of Micah's prophetic word. These words are no ordinary human words. These words are the very *dbr yhwh* whose sending extends the agency and presence of Yhwh.

Ben Zvi believes this linguistic feature of the prophetic expression is no accident. Rather than make use of a potential paranomasia where the verbal form of *dbr* is deployed—the *word* of the Lord which he *spoke* to—this typical prophetic expression predicates *dbr yhwh* with *hyh* not *dbr*. A distinction emerges between the Lord speaking (*dbr*) as direct communication and the character of the prophetic books described as the word of the Lord (*dbr yhwh*). He clarifies, "In other words, prophetic *books* were supposed to be considered 'YHWH's word,' that is, knowledge (or vision) that originates in the divine ..., or perhaps divine instruction, Torah (see Isa 2:3; Mic 4:2), but not a report of divine speech-acts (cf. Jer 1:2 with 1:4), though the latter may be (and often are) embedded in a prophetic book" (Ben Zvi, 15).

The opening words of Micah's prophecy, sharing much in common with typical language of other prophetic superscriptions, speak to the

---

[20] *Commentary on the Gospel of John Chapters 1–8* (Biblical Commentaries 35; Lander: The Aquinas Institute for the Study of Sacred Doctrine), C. 1 L. 11, 221.

kind of readership anticipated by the book. The community of faith emerges as the fitting and intended social location for the reception and reading of Micah. For the members of this community recognize the divine source and authority of this word, receiving at face value the enormous claim being made by the superscription.

In this light, there is much to commend in Ehud Ben Zvi's placement of Micah within a community of faith where the rereading of the prophet takes place. Because this "rereading" assumes a literary final form, Ben Zvi identifies the proper religious/social location for Micah's final form as Persian Yehud or post-monarchic Israel. In this sense, Ben Zvi maintains a historical and form-critical focus even when the monarchic setting of the book itself becomes the *Sitz im Buch* by which post-monarchic Judah "rereads" her own *Sitz im Leben* (Ben Zvi, 6, 9–11).

Furthermore, Ben Zvi notes how disinterested in historical particularity Micah appears. In other words, Micah's literary form resists mimetic linking of oracles to particular moments in Judah's religious history (Ben Zvi, 10–11).[21] Micah 2:1-5, for example, and its scrutinizing of communal injustice lack the specificity needed to link this text to one particular moment in time. In fact, these activities are descriptive of multiple times, opening them up to future readers who would come to understand their own moment in terms of the prophetic account on offer in Micah. In accord with form-critical and historical judgments, Ben Zvi limits his reader and rereaders to the "original" audience of post-monarchic Judah, that postexilic community seeking to make sense of their moment in the divine economy by the anterior

[21] Roy Melugin commends Ben Zvi's moving of the form-critical inquiry to the *Sitz im Buch*. Melugin registers his own misgivings about form-critical linking of prophetic oracles to particular moments, affirming Ben Zvi's claim that prophetic texts often resist mimetic correspondence to particular moments. Melugin clarifies Ben Zvi's approach as it pertains to Micah in the following: "Even though the world *within* the text (i.e., the world that the text presents) is portrayed within the monarchic world, especially because of the superscription (Mic 1:1), the actual readers of the book lived in the postexilic situation. Indeed, because they lived in a historical setting different from the world portrayed within the text, they would not have read the text mimetically, but rather as a text that they used to speak to their own situation—a situation that was markedly different from the monarchic world presented *within* the text." Roy F. Melugin, "Recent Form Criticism Revisited in an Age of Reader Response," in *The Changing Face of Form Criticism for the Twenty-First Century* (ed. M. A. Sweeney and E. Ben Zvi; Grand Rapids: Eerdmans, 2003), 59.

witness of a prophet removed in time and social location. There is little theological rationale, however, for limiting the category of "rereaders" to postexilic Israel, fruitful as such readings are. The enduring character of Micah as *dbr yhwh* exists with equal force for the first generation of readers down through the centuries to our current moment and such is the enduring character of the prophetic word as *the word of the Lord*. For acts of rereading becomes moments of reencounter with the One who maintains sole governance of his Word.

Martin Luther's preface to his Micah lectures intimates the kind of hermeneutical immediacy such a theological account of the prophetic literature suggests. The prophecy of Micah provides a figural pattern of God's goodness in his gracious acts of warning. "He calls us to repent, but just as they held all things in great contempt, so also do we" (Luther, 208). Luther understands Micah's warnings as a figural depiction of his own temporal moment in the gospel. "After all," he claims, "our princes rage against the Gospel and its preachers. They persecute its preachers, arrest them, throw them into prison, and kill them. Even bishops, whose responsibility it is to promote the Gospel, persecute them very much and confirm wickedness against the Word of God" (ibid.). Without much hermeneutical interference, Luther moves Micah's primary prophetic targets—political and religious leaders of the covenant community—into the current moment of Christian Europe. He continues, "So what happened to the Jews when they despised the Word is undoubtedly going to happen also to us when we despise it" (ibid.). The prophetic word as *dbr yhwh* shapes and patterns for faithful readers a proper understanding of their own moment by the figural pattern of Scripture. John Calvin's sermons on Micah (1550–1551) embrace Luther's hermeneutical instincts as Calvin also speaks of the immediacy of the prophetic word as a living word to sixteenth-century Geneva. "And since our world is no better now than it was in his time, our Lord willed that his sentences of condemnation, proclaimed first against the Jews, should remain in effect until the end of time" (Calvin, Micah Sermons, 4).[22] For Luther and Calvin, the Christian church in its various temporal moments and social locations acts as rereaders much in the same way Ben Zvi claims the original post-monarchic Judah reread: removed from the temporal and social world of Micah but making sense of their own moment by the enduring character of the prophetic word reaching forward in time to shape their place in it.

Which he saw concerning Samaria and Jerusalem

Both Mic 1:1 and Am 1:1 share a double relative clause in subordinate relation to *dbr yhwh*—"which he saw."[23] This peculiar feature of the

---

[22] See G. Sujin Pak, "Calving on the 'Shared Design' of the Old and New Testament Authors: The Case of the Minor Prophets," *WTJ* 73 (2011): 255–71.

[23] Brevard Childs understands the phrase "words which he saw" in Am 1:1 as an intentional move to relate visions and words under one prophetic umbrella. Both the "words" and the "visions" of Amos are included in the one prophetic book to follow. Childs, *Introduction to the Old Testament as Scripture*, 400.

superscriptions in Micah and Amos is an indicator for some interpreters of their complex history: the addition of the second relative clause, so they suggest, stems from editorial efforts to bring Micah and Amos into canonical proximity with Isaiah. Isaiah's prophecy makes use of the nominal and verbal forms of "to see" (חזה) in its superscription.[24] Whatever the particular literary history of these superscriptions might be, Isaiah's signal role on the shaping of Micah resists diminution as will be seen throughout the engagement with the book.

The semantic force of "to see" (חזה) relates to the revelatory source of Micah's prophetic words. Syntactically, חזה is relative to *dbr yhwh* thus extending the divine source of Micah's prophetic legacy. It is not necessary to limit the term חזה to a particular mode of reception or visionary experience. There is little reason to deny such modes of prophetic receptivity either, though the claim made here is a linguistic one about the semantic force of חזה. As observed in Isa 1:1, the nominal form of חזה modifies the entirety of Isaiah's corpus, a corpus that includes narratives which are not typically identified as an act of prophetic "seeing."[25] Thus, the semantic emphasis of חזה is primarily on the revelatory nature of the prophetic content to follow. At the same time, Andersen and Freedman do well to remind readers of the "plain meaning" of the term which suggests an "appreciation of the highly visual nature of the poetic imagery that suffuses the messages of the eighth-century prophets, including Micah"

---

[24] Levin, "Das 'Vierpropheten,'" 229–330. Williamson dates Isaiah's superscription late, suggesting that the editor(s) takes his cue from within the book—Isa 2:1 and 13:1—in conjunction with the forms of other prophetic superscriptions whose similarities it shares—Hosea, Amos, and Micah (Williamson, 17). Williamson quotes Tucker approvingly in the following: "While the superscriptions to the prophetic books do not represent the stage of canonization, they do reveal the decisive turning point when—at least for certain circles in Israel—the spoken prophetic words had become scripture" (op cit. Williamson, 17; see G. M. Tucker, "Prophetic Superscriptions and the Growth of a Canon," in *Canon and Authority: Essays in Old Testament Religion and Theology* [ed. G. W. Coats and B. O. Long; Philadelphia: Fortress Press, 1977], 70). What Williamson does not address (at least at this point in his commentary) are the peculiarities of the second relative clauses in Amos and Micah where Isaiah's particular language is deployed. If Tucker is correct, then the influence of Isaiah on Amos and Micah is an observable feature.

[25] See Williamson, 18–20, who challenges Goldingay's notion that the term *chzn* may only refer to a single revelatory experience. See also Willem A. M. Beuken, *Jesaja 1-12* (HThKAT; Freiburg: Herder, 2003), 57–58.

(Andersen and Freedman, 25). Put in other terms, Micah's prophetic legacy has the potential of making eyes out of ears or turning an act of hearing into a moment of seeing.

A peculiar feature of Micah's superscription is the scope of his prophetic vocation as including Samaria and Jerusalem. These two capital cities stand in a synecdochic relationship to their inhabitants, particularly those in religious and political leadership. The focus of Micah's ire in chs 1–3 makes the capital cities and the religious/political activities taking place therein a primary focus of his prophetic words. Admittedly, Samaria only makes a cameo appearance in the first chapter (1:2-7). Some suggest Samaria's presence in 1:2-7 led the editors to include Samaria as an object of Micah's seeing in the superscription.

Various other solutions are offered regarding the inclusion of Samaria in the superscription and its linkage with Jerusalem. Nogalski understands Samaria's role as a limited one, serving the purpose of warning Jerusalem and Judah. The incursion of Judah by Sennacherib in 701 BC and the destruction of Samaria in 722 BC link the judgment of Samaria with the judgment of Judah (Nogalski, 523–24). Something of this logic is at work in 1:2-9 where Samaria's destruction (1:6-7) leads to Micah's lamentation regarding the same wound making its way into Judah (1:8-9).[26]

Related to the preceding comments is a further feature of the "Jerusalem and Samaria" prepositional phrase. Typically, Hebrew grammar would repeat the preposition when two terms are governed logically by the same preposition.[27] Andersen and Freedman believe this grammatical peculiarity stems from a theological instinct whereby the absence of the second governing preposition indicates the unity of the two nouns, much like one observes in a similar construction in Isa 1:1—"Judah and Jerusalem" are governed by a

---

[26] Kessler understands the inclusion of Samaria in the superscription (a *Singulär* phenomenon) serving a twofold purpose: (1) It brings the scope of Micah's prophetic work into view, as observed in 1:2-9, and (2) the naming of Samaria in the superscription brings this particular theme of the Twelve to an end (*Abschluß*) (Kessler, 76).

[27] According to Joüon-Muraoka (JM), the double repetition of the preposition occurs 90 percent of the time (JM §132.g). JM identify this particular grammatical construction as more prevalent in Late Biblical Hebrew (ibid.).

single preposition (עֵל) mirroring Mic 1:1. The theological implication of this collocation is the scope of God's word as the whole people of God even in a divided monarchy. Jeremias makes a similar claim: "[D]as Gotteswort betrifft somit ganz Israel" (Jeremias, 126). Though Micah's prophetic provenance is Judah, the scope of his prophetic word is for all of Israel, Northern and Southern Kingdoms combined.[28] Micah's concern for both cities stems from his understanding of Yhwh's lordship over the whole of Israel, even when the redemptive promises for the whole are stamped by the centrality of Judah and Jerusalem. The superscription indicates this total view of Micah as expressed more fully in 1:2-7.

1:2-7: First table of the Law broken

Micah begins with a summons (שִׁמְעוּ) whose reach extends to the earth and its people/inhabitants.[29] The broad scope of Micah's first oracle

---

[28] A controversy in the current literature exists between those who believe the united monarchy was a myth of postexilic construction, with the language of "Jacob" or "Israel" when applied to Judah as stemming from this postexilic construct (e.g., Kratz), and those who understand the united monarchy and the liturgy of the First Temple (i.e., the Zion tradition, cf. Ps. 46) as having a residual theological presence with the prophets of the eighth century. The strongest critical arguments for the latter view are found with Williamson who cites Mic 3:9-10 as eighth-century evidence for his claims. In fact, Williamson believes Micah is often overlooked in this current scholarly debate. For Williamson, when Micah or Isaiah apply Israel language to southern Judah, they do so because of an "Israel inheritance" they received from a time before the exile. See R. G. Kratz, "Israel in the Book of Isaiah," *JSOT* 31 (2006): 103–28; H. G. M. Williamson, "Judah as Israel in Eighth-Century Prophecy," in *A God of Faithfulness: Essays in Honour of J. Gordon McConville on His 60th Birthday* (LHBOT 538; ed. J. A. Grant, A. Lo, and G. J. Wenham; London: T&T Clark, 2011), 81–95. See also, Ben C. Ollenburger, *Zion the City of the Great King: A Theological Symbol of the Jerusalem Cult* (JSOTSupp 41; Sheffield: Sheffield Academic Press, 1987), ch. 4; Nadav Na'aman, "Saul, Benjamin and the Emergence of 'Biblical Israel,'" *ZAW* 121 (2009): 211–24; 335–49. Na'aman argues for a preexilic setting for the application of the term "Israel" to the united monarchy. Rather than seeing the Saul and David episodes as indicative of Israel and Judah polemics, she understands Saul and David as both Judahite because of Benjamin's Judahite provenance.

[29] The first colon of v. 2 has what appears as an odd grammatical construction: שִׁמְעוּ עַמִּים כֻּלָּם. One might anticipate a second-person pronominal suffix after "peoples" (as one finds in the Syriac): "all of you." Nevertheless, the Hebrew syntax is somewhat typical as third-person pronominal suffixes (i.e., "them") are deployed after a vocative. W'OC, 4.7d.

remains consistent in 1:2-4 and its theophanic moment. The peoples (עַמִּים) and the earth (אֶרֶץ) stand in parallel relation to each other, along with "all of them" and "its fullness." When Yhwh Adonai in 1:3 comes forth as a witness against "you" (כֶּם), the antecedent of the pronoun is the peoples of 1:2.[30] Moreover, the lack of a definite article on "earth" leans against the proposal to understand "peoples" and "earth" as having Samaria and Jerusalem more narrowly in view, even though the focus in 1:5 turns toward these capital cities (Andersen and Freedman, 138).[31] Understanding the relation between 1:2-4 and 1:5 is a challenge because of the initial broad scope of Yhwh's judgment in 1:2-4 and then the more narrowly targeted reach in 1:5. With the turn of prophetic address to Samaria and Jerusalem in 1:5, interpreters have provided a broad array of literary critical suggestions to explain what appears to be an incongruity.[32]

Whatever the particular compositional history of this first oracle, the final form of the text presents a set of linkages that hold this unit together despite the immediate difficulty of sorting out the referential relationship between vv. 2-4 and v. 5. While vv. 2-4 keep the focus on the nations and the earth more broadly conceived, v. 5a identifies the rebellion of Jacob as the presenting cause of "all of this" (כָּל־זֹאת), with the antecedent of "this" as the theophanic moment of judgment in the preceding verses.

A major focal point of Micah emerges within this interpretive complex, linking Micah 1 with Micah 5. As mentioned in the introduction, the strategic use of judgment oracles beginning with "hear" marks the two major blocks of Micah's prophecy: 1:2 and 6:1.

---

[30] The summons of 1:2 differs from the summons at 6:1 where the "mountains," "hills," and "enduring foundations of the earth" are called on as witnesses of the divine indictment. For in 1:2, the "nations" and the "earth" are the focus of the divine judgment, not witnesses. See John T. Willis, "Some Suggestions on the Interpretation of Micah 1 2," *VT* 18 (1968): 377.

[31] Micah 4:13 is the only exception in Micah where the definite article is linked to "earth" when it is a cosmic referent (Cf. 1:2, 3; 5:3; 6:2; 7:17 for cosmic references and 6:4; 7:15; 5:5; 5:4, 5, 10; 7:2, 13 for particular references to land, i.e., Land of Egypt).

[32] E.g., A postexilic redactor brings Micah's more narrow historical focus into a broader cosmic linkage (so Mays, 40), cf. Albertz, *Israel in Exile*, 212-14. See Willis for the scope of interpretive problems and suggested solutions ("Suggestions," 372-79).

The inclusio relation of Mic 5:14 MT (5:15 New Revised Standard Version, NRSV) with Mic 1:2-5 provides further evidence for these structuring effects. Micah 5:14 brings chs 1–5 to a thematic conclusion before another summons to "hear" in 6:1. Micah 5:14 catches the reader off guard because the second-person address of Mic 5:9-13 MT is Jacob under judgment, now identified in 5:14 as part of the *goyim* who did not listen (שמע). Again, one observes the linguistic association between 1:2 and 5:14, with the latter as a resumptive rehearsal of the claims of 1:2 where the text begins with a summons to the nations "to listen." The latter text identifies the cause of Jacob's judgment as a failure "to listen." Perhaps the relation between 1:2 and 5:14, along with the rather surprising identification of Jacob with the *goyim* (relating *goyim* with *'mim* in 1:2), provides an interpretive handle for relating 1:2-4 with 1:5-7. Distinguishing between Jacob/Judah and the nations becomes difficult if not impossible when God descends in an act of judgment. The movements and logic of Amos 1-2 run a similar course, with the nation's 3+4 offenses and rebellion against God enfolding Judah and Israel into the mix of nations without discrimination. As Fabry in the context of Nahum reminds, the question about who are the enemies and friends of God is not quickly answered along national lines of demarcation.[33] Jonah's sailors and Assyrian king provide a figural example of how the prophets make such neat and tight categories like "universalism" or "particularism" quite problematic. Samaria and Jerusalem are part and parcel of the "peoples" or "nations" in a moment of Yhwh's nondiscriminatory judgment.

> Ephraim Radner's ecclesiology is shaped by a broad reading of Scripture and its capacity to figure the church's existence in time. Radner leans against what might be loosely called Platonic notions of the church where the Church as Church is demarcated from the Church as church, that is, the church in its *simul iustus et peccator* status in time. In other words, Radner believes Scripture and its range of figures by which the Church comes to understand herself in time will not allow a distinction to be made between "sins of the Church's

---

[33] "Nicht die Feinde Israels generell sind der Vergeltung Gottes ausgesetzt, sondern nur die Fiende JHWHs; das aber können auch—auch wenn es nicht explizit gesagt wird—Israeliten/Judäer sein! Es sind genau diese Feinde, die von der Glut seines Zornes weggefegt warden (Nah 1,6a)." H. Fabry, *Nahum* (HTKAT; Freiburg: Herder, 2006), 92.

members" and "sins of the Church."³⁴ According to Radner, the church's historical existence "cannot be sloughed off but represents the very order of her life as she lives in the world."³⁵ Because the Church cannot transcend her *simul* status as *iustus* and *peccator*, the Church recognizes in retrospect and prospect that she is "deformable and transformable."³⁶ Why? Because Scripture's figures, particularly that of ancient Israel, pattern a mode of existence where the community of faith before God is deformable and transformable. As Israel forgot its Maker (Hos 8:14), so too can the Church forget. Only God can forgive, taking "whoring" Israel unto himself. Repentance remains a matter of continual necessity in the Church's existence, as God's disciplining, yet loving, judgment for the sake of renewal is an ever present possibility (cf. Revelation 2-3). The thunderous claims of Mic 1:2-7 are a continued warning to the Church in time and cannot be left in the historical mist of Israel's ancient past.

A further word should be said about the nature of the Church's repentance. The figural patterns of Scripture are, in Irenaeus's terms, recapitulated in the person and work of Jesus Christ.³⁷ Adam, Israel, David, etc., are taken up and fulfilled in Him.³⁸ The Church's very existence stems from Christ taking her to himself—itself a figural pattern of Israel's prophets (e.g., Hosea; Ez 16). Therefore, the judgment and mercy of God in the figural landscape of Israel's narrative and prophetic history are Christologically shaped. The Church's relation to these figural patterns stems organically from our union with Christ. Put in other terms, the figural pattern of the prophets as a living word to the Church is framed by a covenant ontology whereby our continued repentance is shaped by a renewal toward what the Church and its members already are *en Christo*. The deforming and transforming moments of the Church's existence take place in respect to the Church's affirming or denying her existence in Christ.

Micah 1:2b portrays Yhwh Adonai coming from his holy temple as a witness against the *peoples* or the *nations*.³⁹ The literary setting does not necessitate a prophetic lawsuit genre.⁴⁰ Whether or not such a genre exists, the nations and earth are not called on as witnesses in any kind of trilateral judicial setting. Rather, Yhwh is the witness against his people, standing in judgment against them from that space properly belonging to him alone: his holy temple. Yhwh's identity as witness is found elsewhere in the prophets, all within the same context of divine

---

³⁴ Ephraim Radner, *A Brutal Unity: The Spiritual Politics of the Christian Church* (Baylor: Baylor University Press, 2012), 159. For Radner's figural hermeneutic, see *Time and the Word: Figural Reading of the Christian Scriptures* (Grand Rapids: Eerdmans, 2016). *Time and the Word* is a theological and creative force for theological hermeneutics.

³⁵ Ibid., 155.

³⁶ Ibid., 160.

³⁷ St. Irenaeus of Lyon, *On the Apostolic Preaching* (trans. J. Behr; Crestwood: St. Vladimir's Press, 1997), I.6.

³⁸ Ibid., 162.

³⁹ The LXX does not have אדני in the first colon of line 2. Some suggest a possible dittography because of the repeated אדני in colon b. Cf. Am 3:8 for a parallel construction of the divine name.

⁴⁰ See Ben Zvi, ad loc.; Dwight R. Daniels, "Is There a 'Prophetic Lawsuit' Genre?" *ZAW* 99 (1987): 339-60.

judgment. In Jer 29:23, Yhwh's role as witness against his people stems from his divine knowledge. Yhwh's omniscience provides the irrefutable warrant for his role as witness and judge (cf. Jer 42:5; Zeph 3:8).[41] Micah 1:2b anticipates the unfolding theophany of 1:3-4.[42]

The theophany of vv. 3-4 contains, according to Jeremias, the stock and trade imagery of the genre: the coming of Yhwh and the effects upon nature his coming produces (cf. Ps 68:7-8; Judg 4:4-5).[43] In v. 3, Yhwh comes down and treads on the "high places" (במות) of the earth.[44] His appearing in v. 3 is met with pronounced effects upon the natural order: mountains melting and valleys splitting open. The metaphoric imagery of melting wax and poured out water provides a heightened sense of the moment's gravity. It is worth noting by comparison the antipodal picture in Isa 40:4 where Yhwh's redemption and forgiveness of sins yield an overturning of the natural effects of his judgment.

Readers should also be aware of a possible double entendre associated with the location of Yhwh's treading. Yhwh comes down and treads upon "the high places of the earth" (במותי ארץ). While the appearing of Yhwh often takes place on a mountain—one recalls the Sinai narratives of the Pentateuch—the particular use of במה here is suggestive. The "high places" were open-air sanctuaries typically located outside the city center on mountains (cf. 2 Sam 21:9).[45] With the centralization of the cult at Jerusalem, the במה became permanently associated with irregular and idolatrous worshipping practices. Thus, the term also functions as a trope for the covenant infidelity of Yhwh's people. The

---

[41] Moses's song in Deuteronomy 32 functions as a "witness" against the people's future infidelity. The linguistic complex of "witness" (עד) and "whoring" (זנה) of Deuteronomy 31 (31:16, 21, 26) resembles the thematic and linguistic outlook of Mic 1:2-7 with or without intentional intertextual activity.

[42] Cf. Ps 50:1-7 where theophanic imagery and the witnessing of God against his people function together (see Hans-Joachim Kraus, *Psalms 1-59* [Continental Commentary; trans. H. C. Oswald; Minneapolis: Fortress Press, 1993], 49–51).

[43] Jörg Jeremias, *Theophanie: Die Geschichte Einer Alttestamentlichen Gattung* (WMANT 10; Neukirchen-Vluyn: Neukirchener, 1965), 11–12.

[44] The tower of Babel episode of Genesis 11 characterizes Yhwh "coming down" (11:5, 7) as the precursor to his act of judgment.

[45] See Rainer Albertz, *A History of Israelite Religion in the Old Testament Period; Volume I: From the Beginnings to the End of the Monarchy* (trans. J. Bowden; Louisville: WJK, 1994), 84–85.

fact that Yhwh places the foot of his judgment on the "high places" comes as little surprise given the unfolding of Micah's first prophetic oracle. The catalyst for Yhwh's judgment is Samaria and Jerusalem's idolatry (cf. 1:7).

Debates over the atonement in Christian theology range across the centuries of Christian thought. While reference to the Old Testament's sacrificial system is often rehearsed with varying degrees of success, the pressure of the prophets on a Christian theology of the atonement is not as prevalent. The theophanic imagery of Micah is a case in point of where such a forward-leaning pressure may serve the subject. The appearing of God in an act of judgment is followed by an attendant rupture in the natural order. The Gospels narrate the crucifixion with imagery of the selfsame theophanic character of judgment. The cosmic order is disturbed during and immediately after Christ's passion on Good Friday. The setting of the passion inhabits the theophanic space figured by the Old Testament.

Colin Gunton's noteworthy work on the atonement makes a compelling case for how multiple metaphors are requisite when coming to terms with the multifaceted reality of God's reconciling sinners to himself in the person and work of Jesus Christ.[46] Gunton warns against confining our understanding of the atonement to one metaphor, absent the contributing presence of others. A certain strand of modern theology has grown allergic to penal theories of the atonement where the cross is understood as a pouring out of God's wrath on Jesus Christ in an act of judgment. While heeding Gunton's warning against reductionism, the Old Testament's imagery of judgment as seen here in Micah 1 resists a dismissal of judgment motifs at the cross. The theophanic imagery of Micah 1 and the passion narratives of the Gospels are inextricably linked with divine judgment or divine punishment. Conceptualizing and fitting the nature of this judgment within a proper Trinitarian and relational frame remains of some consequence.[47] The substitutional character of Jesus's atoning work cannot be reduced to the *persona privata* Jesus Christ alone but should be fitted into a Trinitarian frame where the work of the cross, including the divine judgment taking place therein, is understood as the loving and self-giving action of our Triune God for us. Still, this loving and self-giving action involves the bearing of judgment in an act of place taking. Eberhard Jüngel rightly reminds us that judgment and grace are not alternatives.[48] Rather, "We need to learn that in the very act of judging God shows himself to be gracious. Only an ungracious God would allow injustice to run its course."[49]

In Barth's majestic account of the atonement in *Church Dogmatics IV.1* he makes a similar claim about the pressure of Isaiah 53 on a dogmatic account of the atonement. When the Judge is judged in our place (*Stellvertretung*), his place-taking is indeed a bearing of our punishment. Jesus Christ as Son of God bears the place of Israel as the one Israelite. In doing so, this one Israelite takes "the place of this disobedient son this faithless people and its

---

[46] Colin Gunton, *The Actuality of the Atonement: A Study of Metaphor, Rationality, and the Christian Tradition* (Bloomsbury: T&T Clark, 2003).

[47] See Dalferth's threefold context for a dogmatic account of atonement as relates to the person and work of Christ: (1) the context of Jesus's life (Jesus's embodied relation to the history of Israel and humanity); (2) the context of the life of God (a proper Trinitarian account of the salvific character of Jesus's sacrificial death); and (3) the context of our lives. Ingolf U. Dalferth, *Crucified and Resurrected: Restructuring the Grammar of Christology* (trans. J. Bennet; Grand Rapids: Baker, 2015), 302–03. See also Torrance's understanding of wrath as a *via* rather than a *terminus* in Thomas F. Torrance, *Incarnation: The Person and Work of Christ* (ed. R. T. Walker; Downers Grove: IVP, 2015), 54.

[48] Eberhard Jüngel, *Justification: The Heart of the Christian Faith* (trans. J. Webster; Edinburgh: T&T Clark, 2001), 85.

[49] Ibid.

faithless priests and kings."⁵⁰ Barth claims that punishment and judgment are not prevalent or even present themes in the New Testament. Despite whether Barth's reading of the New Testament is judicious at this point, it is his following comment that bears materially on the matter at hand: "But it cannot be completely rejected or evaded on this account."⁵¹ In other words, Isaiah 53 and its understanding of place-taking as an act of judgment bears pressures on a Christian account of the atonement whether the New Testament follows suit or not. Barth models a Biblical Theological instinct where "reading forward" from the Old Testament to Christian thought plays its own constitutive role. Rather than prioritizing either the Old Testament as received in the new (*vetus testamentum in novo receptum*) or the Old Testament as "read backward" from the New Testament, Barth allows the Old Testament's discrete character to play its own constructive role in the shaping of Christian thought. The theophanic imagery of Mic 1:2-7 serves as a modest example of a similar kind.

The theophanic moment of judgment remains somewhat abstract in vv. 2-4 with the presenting cause left unclarified. This abstraction becomes concrete in vv. 5-7 as the judging focus on the nations and the earth is more targeted now on Samaria and Jerusalem. As mentioned above, the antecedent of "all of this" (כל־זאת) in 1:5a is the theophany of judgment in 1:2-4. Calvin rightly associates the prophetic concern of Micah 1 with the breaking of the first table of the Law—"You shall have no other gods before me." The particularity of Israel's and Judah's sin relates to the covenant breach of the Law's first table. As the prophetic book unfolds, Calvin understands Micah 2 speaking to the breach of the second table of the Law—You shall love your neighbor as yourself (Calvin, 184).⁵² Calvin's framing of Micah 1 and 2 around the two tables of the Law is a helpful interpretive handle.

The three lines of 1:5 are broken down as follows: 1:5a—the transgressions (פשע) of Jacob and the sins (חטאות) of the house of Israel clarify the immediate cause of God's judgment; 1:5b—the rebellion of Jacob is formally tied to Samaria, the capital city of Israel; 1:5c—the high places of Judah, a metaphoric elaboration on the sins (האטות) of 1:5a, are associated with Jerusalem, the capital of the Southern Kingdom. These three verses, 1:5-7, reflect an A-B-A pattern with v. 5 identifying Israel/Judah's sin (A) as the divine rationale for God's judgment in v. 6 (B), leading to a fuller elaboration on the character of Samaria/Jerusalem's sin in v. 7 (A).

---

⁵⁰ Karl Barth, *Church Dogmatics IV.1* (trans. G. W. Bromiley; Edinburgh: T&T Clark, 1956), 171.
⁵¹ Ibid., 253.
⁵² See also Jeremias, 136.

The terms for *sin* in 1:5 are in parallel relation to each other. "Transgressions" or "crimes" (פֶּשַׁע) and "sins" (חַטֹּאות) become the focal point of vv. 5-7. Knierim resists defining פֶּשַׁע as "rebellion." He states, "Whoever commits *peša'* does not merely rebel or protest against Yahweh but breaks with him, takes away what is his, robs, embezzles, misappropriates it."[53] Knierim relates the two terms as follows: חַטֹּאות misses a goal, passing by the thing, and פֶּשַׁע breaks with, disengaging from a political or social partner.[54] Sweeney draws attention to the fact that פֶּשַׁע often refers to political revolt of one nation against another (cf. Am 1:3) or revolt against God (cf. Isa 58:1; Am 5:12).[55] The bringing together of these two terms in 1:5a highlights the moral-ethical character of Israel's transgressions and sins in relation to Yhwh and neighbor.

The second and third lines of 1:5 play with Hebrew grammar. All English translations begin both lines with the interrogative "what," and rightly so. The Hebrew interrogative particle, however, is not מָה ("what") as we would expect. It is מִי ("who"), the personal interrogative pronoun. The turn of phrase is not typical as מִי rarely refers to a thing.[56] A literal gloss of 1:5b might go as follows: "Who are the transgressions of Jacob, is it not Samaria?" The use of "who" underscores the metonymic relation of Samaria and Jerusalem with the political and religious leaders of these capital cities. Samaria and Jerusalem as places become personified as the people represented therein. These two cities also stand in for the totality of Israel and Judah's sin because their infidelity stems from these religious and political centers.[57]

---

[53] TWOT 1, 1036.
[54] Ibid.
[55] Sweeney, 351.
[56] JM §144b; WO'C, 18.2d.
[57] There seems little reason to doubt that Mic 1:5-7 has Samaria and the Northern Kingdom in view (see Sweeney, ad loc.). The influence of Hosea's imagery is stark and suggestive on this front. At the same time, there is a fluidity of language in Micah when reference is made to Israel and Jacob. As Jepsen observed some time ago, Jacob and Israel are almost exclusively predicated on the Southern Kingdom in the whole of Micah's book. A. Jepsen, "Kleine Beiträge zum Zwölfprophetenbuch I," *ZAW* 56 (1938): 99. See the discussion above between Kratz and Williamson on the origins of "Israel" as applied to "Judah."

The divine judgment of v. 6 is the "logical succession" of the conditions expressed in v. 5.[58] The transgressions and sins of Samaria and Jerusalem, fitted as these two entities are around a shared covenantal heritage, set the stage for the eventual razing of Samaria. While Samaria is the object of destruction in these verses, interpreters often point to Mic 3:12 where similar imagery paints the picture of Jerusalem's eventual fall. The imagery attendant to the destruction in v. 6 is straightforward. What was once a thriving city will in time become a heap of stones, exposed foundations, and flat, open surfaces. The quietness of a vineyard replaces the bustling of urban life. Put in modern terms, what will be left of Samaria are external indicators for a potential archaeological dig.

Another possible understanding of the relation between a heap of ruins and the positive imagery of a vineyard is to read 1:6 in association with Isaiah's song of the vineyard (5:1-7).[59] Isaiah 5:1-3 presents Yhwh as a vintner removing stones for the sake of clearing fertile ground for his choice vineyard. Isaiah's vineyard is Jerusalem, not Samaria, and this vineyard also becomes a wasteland as the song and its interpretation unfold. The literary association between Micah and Isaiah at this point would be subtle, if present at all. Nevertheless, the overall destructive sense of v. 6 should not be attenuated. Moreover, the language of "stripping bear" or "exposing" in v. 6b (אגלה, cf. 1:16b) is suggestive of the prostitution imagery of the following verse (cf. Hos 2:12).

As noted above, the A-B-A pattern of vv. 5-7 enclose the scene of destruction in v. 6 with causal explanations for the judging action of God. Borrowing from Kugel's description of poetic parallelism as the relation between A and "what is more A" in the second half of the parallel, a similar feature is found in the second A of vv. 5-7.[60] The transgressions and sins of v. 5 are made more concrete and vivid,

---

[58] See WO'C, 32.2, on the logical and temporal relation of the *weqatal* to a preceding condition.

[59] See Andersen and Freedman, 177.

[60] James L. Kugel, *The Idea of Biblical Poetry: Parallelism and Its History* (Baltimore: John Hopkins University Press, 1981).

providing textual evidence for Calvin's understanding of Micah 1 as centered on the breach of the first table of the Law (see Jeremias, 136). Samaria pursued other gods. And Yhwh, the first-person speaker in vv. 6-7, prepares for their destruction. Yhwh takes into his own hand the faithful actions Samaria should have taken herself (cf. Deut 7:5).[61]

Both terms for "idols" in v. 7 (פסילי and עצבי) intimate their physical nature as carved or shaped things. These two nouns are also in the plural suggesting that Micah does not have any particular god(s) in mind (cf. Hosea 1-3). Rather, Micah casts his net widely with a broad range of carved images in view. The collocation of these two terms are present in Isa 10:10-11, sharing much in common with Mic 1:7 linguistically and thematically. The destruction of Samaria in the Isaianic text serves as a warning and prediction to Jerusalem. A similar logic is at work in Micah, especially in the first chapter. The destruction of Samaria and Jerusalem, separated as they are in time and circumstance, shares in the same theological nexus of cause and effect.

The semantic parallel of the two terms for idol comes with few surprises. These are stock terms that, according to Ben Zvi, "point to sinful cultic behavior, as considered from the usual perspective informing the HB/OT" (Ben Zvi, 32). The parallel relationship between "idols" (פסילי) and "prostitute fees" (אתנן), however, does cause the reader pause. What is the semantic link between "images" and "prostitution fees"? Jeremias, and others, makes a compelling case for the fitting together of Micah's prophetic address against idolatry with the imagery of Hosea (Jeremias, 136). Much earlier, Jepsen had already identified the linguistic relation between Mic 1:7 and Hosea. He observed the three terms "prostitution fees" (אתנן), "prostitute" (זנה), and "images" (עצבי) as stemming from Hosea (Hos 4:14; 8:4; 9:1; 13:2; 14:9).[62] Samaria's idolatry is portrayed in the familiar terms of prostitution from Hosea's oeuvre.

---

[61] See Andersen and Freedman, 180.
[62] Jepsen, "Kleine Beiträge," 97.

The final line of v. 7 is obscure. A literal gloss goes something like the following: "for from the fee of a harlot you were gathered and unto the harlot's fee you will return." The obscurity stems from the unclear referent of "harlot's fee." Mays suggests there are political undertones to the passage. The acceptance of foreign gods aided Samaria in their political relations with them, only in time to be carried away by one of those nations (Mays, 48).[63] Waltke sees the text as a case of what goes around comes around. As Samaria had exploited courtesans for their own advantage, in time Samaria would be exploited by others (Waltke, 55). Ben Zvi draws attention to the collection of lexical terms in 6-7 associated with judgment ("strip," "gather," and "return"). Hillers recognizes the vague character of the line and opts to leave it vague. "Perhaps it is best, then, to leave the sense vague: as the precious things were gained, so they will be lost, the end will be like the beginning" (Hillers, 21). Whatever the exact sense of this obscure phrase, a few matters are worth noting. One, political and religious fidelity are flip sides of the same coin in the theological landscape of Micah. While the institutions may be distinct, their religious character is not. Second, the last phrase, obscure as it is, identifies Samaria's idolatry and political avarice as an example of sin doing exactly what sin does. Sin breeds and rebreeds with the final consequences latent in the first acts of covenant infidelity.[64] If left unchecked with prophetic warnings unheeded, sin moves toward its natural end: judgment and destruction.

The character of sin as transgression, missing the mark, and more pointedly, revolt against the divine, lends credence to Barth's understanding of sin as fundamentally pride.[65] Barth does not deny the broader definitions of sin as "disobedience" and "unbelief," recognizing that defining sin as pride is not exhaustive.[66] Nevertheless, he remains unsatisfied with the broader definitions because they run the risk of abstraction. (As a brief aside, Micah's logic in 1:2-7 resembles Barth's in its resistance to abstract definitions of "transgressions" and "sins": note the conceptual movement in 1:5-7.) Israel's election aimed toward the redemptive and gracious claims of Yhwh on his people, and Yhwh's insistence

---

[63] Smith follows a similar line (Smith, 61).
[64] Kierkegaard's category "state of sin" relates to the substance of sin's breeding and rebreeding. Søren Kierkegaard, *The Sickness Unto Death: A Christian Psychological Exposition for Upbuilding and Awakening* (trans./ed. H. V. Hong and E. H. Hong; Princeton: Princeton University Press, 1980), 106–09.
[65] Barth, *CD IV.1*, 413 ff.
[66] Ibid., 413.

that this relationship be founded on a loyal allegiance to Him and Him alone (cf. Deut 6:4ff). When in the torturous history of Israel and Judah's covenantal history they turn away from Yhwh's gracious election and Yhwh's claims of exclusive loyal love flowing from that election, human pride is on full display. Idolatry *is* pride in the sense that humanity has taken to its own self-sufficient and self-reliant means for the achieving of religious or political salvation or any redemptive action absent God's gracious and electing initiative. The history of Israel's idolatry is the history of humanity's pride. Our attempts to become like God or to reverse the *imago Dei* by our creating gods in our image are neutralized by God's self-determination to become man. In other words, humanity's pride and tendency toward idolatry is obliterated by the humility of God.[67]

1:8-9: Prophetic suffering and solidarity

The first-person address of vv. 6-7 continues into vv. 8-9. The referent of the first-person address is unstated in both sections. Given the judging context of vv. 6-7, it follows that the first-person speaking voice is Yhwh. Still, the ambiguity of referent continues into vv. 8-9. The lamentation of these verses has a bridging or Janus character as the text looks backwards and forwards.[68] Verse 8 begins with "concerning this" (על־זאת) and links the prophet's lamentation to the theophany and announcement of judgment in the preceding verses. The identification of "my people" (עמי) as the cause of the prophet's sorrow (v. 9) brings the specificity of 1:10-16 in view. It follows, therefore, to identify the first-person voice of the lamentation as the prophet. With that said, however, the ambiguity regarding the referent causes some pause as the lamentation expressed in vv. 8-9 could be placed on the lips of Yhwh, continuing the first-person address of vv. 6-7. Or put in other terms, the lamentation of the prophet may in a very real sense be indistinguishable from the lamentation of Yhwh. From this perspective, Micah's lamentation is a prophetic symbol witnessing to the action and perspective of Israel's God.

---

[67] Ibid., 423. See Anthony C. Thiselton, *The Hermeneutics of Doctrine* (Grand Rapids: Eerdmans, 2007), ch. 13. Thiselton states, "In linguistic terms *pride* as a catchword seems both too broad and too narrow. In theological terms, however, Barth shows in a masterly way that this term provides a key for unlocking the multiform dimensions of human sin especially in relation to the grace of God" (ibid., 299). See also Thiselton's helpful interaction with Pannenberg's retrieval of Augustine's understanding of sin as misplaced desire. For Pannenberg, pride generates perverted desires (ibid., 307–08). See also, Dalferth, *Crucified and Resurrected*, 42–44.
[68] Jeremias, 137; Ben Zvi, 33.

Jeremias distinguishes the kind of lamentation we observe in this section from the kind of intercessory lamentation we find elsewhere (cf. Am 7:1-6; Jer 15:11, 17:16, 18:20).[69] The prophet does not intercede for his people in order to assuage the plan of God just announced.[70] Rather, the prophet engages in acts of ritual lamentation as a fellow-sufferer, as one whose identity is inextricably linked with his people.[71] Three verbs (cohortatives) indicate the action of the prophet: lamenting (אספדה), wailing (אילילה), and going barefoot and naked (אילכה, cf. Ez 24:17-23; Isa 20:2).[72] All these activities indicate embodied rituals of mourning. Attendant metaphors provide a heightened sense of the mourning: lamenting like a jackel and mourning like the daughters of an ostrich or owl (cf. Job 30:29; Lam 4:3; Isa 13:21-22). The exact species of the last metaphor is debated, though the force of the similes do not require such specifications.[73]

> John Calvin's understanding of the threefold office of Christ as prophet, priest, and king is a testament to the constructive role of the Old Testament in his Christology. Admittedly, Calvin gives short shrift to the figural function of the prophetic office, remaining content to focus on the teaching side of the office. "And the prophetic dignity in Christ leads us to know that in the sum of doctrine as he has given it to us all parts of perfect wisdom are contained."[74] The figural scope of the prophetic office goes beyond Calvin's limited reading, however. The suffering of the prophet in solidarity with and as a representative of his people is in figural relation to Christ's prophetic office. Christ's suffering is bound to his identification with humanity (Phil 2) and his bearing of the burden of his own announcement of judgment. Barth's narrative reading of the gospels as the move from Judge

---

[69] Jeremias, 137.

[70] The lack of intercession may lend support for the suggestion that the first-person speaking voice is intentionally ambiguous at this point.

[71] Sweeney references Isa 7:20; 20:1-6 where the imagery of "barefoot and naked" refers to prisoners of war rather than mere mourning.

[72] The grammatical form of the final cohortative is not typical for I-yod verbs (GKC 69.b, n. 1). The BHS notes that multiple mss have the more typical, non-plene form. The most likely explanation for the grammatical oddity is the playing with grammatical forms for the sake of creating an alliterative relation between אילילה and אילכה.

[73] See Waltke, 66–67.

[74] John Calvin, *Institutes of Christian Religion* 1 (trans. F. L. Battles; ed. J. T. McNeill; Philadelphia: The Westminster Press, 1960), 496. See Jon Balserak, *John Calvin as Sixteenth-Century Prophet* (Oxford: Oxford University Press, 2014). As Balserak narrates, Calvin does see a figural extension of the Old Testament prophetic call and persona in his own call and person. The preface to the Psalms commentary, along with his reading of the prophets, attests to Calvin's intimate and mimetic reading of the prophetic office as it pertains to Calvin's office. As the prophets of old explained and applied the Scriptures to their particular moment in time, so too did Calvin fight the idolatry of his moment by the interpretation and application of Holy Scripture (ibid., 179).

to Judge judged in our place bears materially on Christ's prophetic office. Christ is the very prophetic Word of God, and, at the same time, He bears the suffering of judgment attendant to that selfsame word as both place-taker and representative.

The lamenting of the prophet in v. 8 leans into v. 9 with the latter clarifying the cause of the prophet's grief. There are several interpretive challenges with v. 9. The antecedent of "her" on "her wounds" is unclear. The exact nature of the "wound" that has made its way into Judah has no immediate referent. The verbs change tense in line two from a feminine "it enters/comes" (באה) to a masculine "it strikes" (נגע).[75] Needless to say, v. 9 is a challenge. If v. 8 refers back to the preceding material as the grammar suggests, then it follows that the antecedent of "her" in the current literary context of Micah 1 is still Samaria.[76] The lexeme "wound" (מכה) often refers to a blow received from God in an act of judgment.[77] And the "wound" of judgment that strikes Samaria is an incurable wound whose effects are total and finalizing. But questions remain. Why would a Southern prophet from Judah lament with such grief over Samaria? The answer to this question appears twofold. First, Micah's grief over the destruction of the Northern Kingdom is genuine. Kessler reminds us that Samaria had a history with Yhwh and because of this shared religious and theological heritage, the destruction of the Northern Kingdom was no cause for rejoicing in Judah—and this despite the often-strained political relation between the two.

Second, the judgment of God on Samaria stands as a material warning to Judah. Facts are on the ground, so to speak, as an indicator of a potential path for Judah. Such is the prophetic logic of Isa 10:11. Similar sentiments are found in v. 9 as Samaria's "wounds" become the grounds for the prophet's continued lamenting and forthcoming prophetic warnings and promises to Jerusalem. As it looks backwards and forwards, the literary context of v. 9 clarifies the nature of the "wound" making its way into Judah. For the "wound" as metaphor entails

---

[75] See Andersen and Freedman, 195. The lack of a *waw* conjunction before נגע suggests, according to Anderson and Freedman, a break in theme from Samaria to Judah.

[76] Sweeney recognizes the unclear antecedent but associates "her" with the Daughter of Zion who makes her first appearance in 1:13 (Sweeney, 353).

[77] Cf. Dt 28:59; Isa 30:26; Nah 3:19. Jeremiah speaks of his own prophetic burden as a "wound," cf. Jer 10:19, 15:18.

both the judgment of God and the causes leading to that judgment as explicated in 1:5-7. "Wound" has a broad connotative reach, and Judah is warned on the basis of Samaria's history with Yhwh (again, cf. Isa 10:11). At the same time, the "wound" looks forward because the horrific description in 1:10-16 of the sufferings in Micah's Shephelite region are aftereffects of Samaria's "wound" that have made their real presence known in Judah. The threat for a "wound" to Judah is real and for Micah and his people (עמי), experienced. Nevertheless, the wound is not incurable for Judah, reaching to the gates of the city but not yet overtaking it.[78] Yhwh's dealings with Judah are still active and probing.

1:10-16: Disruptive intimations

It goes without saying that this section of Micah's prophecy is the most challenging of the book. The place names of vv. 10-12 remain a mystery.[79] The syntax is a jumble. Textual difficulties loom around almost every corner as the ancient translations often go their own way. Modern readers should take some comfort from this textual-critical phenomenon. We are not the first readers to find this section difficult. When Jerome came to this section of Micah's prophecy, he identified the unit as marked by textual difficulties. Then he cried out for help from the Holy Spirit. Jerome reminds his readers that interpreters of Scripture always need the help of the Holy Spirit, but they especially need the Spirit when working through this section (*ut si quando indiguimus spiritu Dei, semper autem in exponendis scripturis sanctis illius indigemus aduentu, nunc vel maxime eum adesse cupiamus* ...).[80]

The devil is in the details in this unit of Micah's prophecy, though the overall sense is not lost when the details become opaque. The cities in the region of Micah's hometown, viz. the Shephaleh, are

---

[78] Kessler, 94. On the "gates of the city" as a metonym for Jerusalem, cf. Ob 13; Ruth 3:11.
[79] See especially Andersen and Freedman for the various theoretical accounts of these cities and their location (207–12).
[80] Jerome, 430.

experiencing Samaria's wound. The logic of Micah's prophetic warning in the preceding verses becomes an experienced event (cf. the "gate of Jerusalem" in 1:9 and 1:12). It is a possibility that the rough syntax and disordered nature of the section may be a literary device indicative of the chaos of the moment. The unit is marked by wordplays, and perhaps the literary play extends to the syntactical level as well? A few matters necessitate our attention. The first is the play on words in this section.

For all the difficulties of this section, the rhetorical play on words is impressive and not without success. Literary devices such as paronomasia and alliteration along with semantic plays on words serve the rhetorical force of the unit. Often linked to the quip *nomen est omen*, the wordplays are as follows:

1. 1:10a—*Gath* and the verb *taggîdû* are related sounds either by inversion or by the alliterative relation of the same sounds *gath* and *tag*.[81]
2. 1:10b—*Beth-leaphrah* or "dust town" is told to roll around in the *'phr* (dust).
3. 1:11A—*Shaphir* is contested as some link it to *shophar* or *horn* (Mays; Andersen and Freedman). More recent work relates *Shaphir* to "graceful" or "beautiful" based on a comparative philological judgment with Aramaic, *šāpîr* (Waltke, 74). The pun is as follows: O Beauty Town, walk around in nakedness and shame; or O Graceful Town, walk around in nakedness and shame (cf. 1:8).
4. 1:11Ba: *Zaanan* and the verb *ytzh* ("go out") share similar sounds.
5. 1:11Bb: Perhaps the most difficult phrases of the unit. Various emendations of the text are on offer (see Hillers, Waltke). The play on words appears to be one of lexical semantics. *Beth-ezel* relates to a rare verb *'ṣl* meaning "to remove or withdraw." The following verb, *lqḥ* "to take away," relates semantically to the place the name.

---

[81] Nogalski, 531; Sweeney, 355.

6. 1:12: *Maroth* or "bitterness" awaits for "good" (*tōb*) but receives only "evil" (*r'*). The reference to the "gate of Jerusalem" turns an eye back to 1:9.
7. 1:13: *Lachish* relates phonetically with "to the steeds" (*lrcsh*). The importance of Lachish as a fortress town or military stronghold for Judah should be highlighted. The historical referent for the claim that Israel's transgressions first began or had their first fruits there, resulting in their deleterious influence on the Daughter of Zion remains opaque. Some read these statements as an indication of Micah's antimilitary sentiment (see Smith-Christopher, 74–75).
8. 1:14a: The "parting gifts" may be a semantic play on the town *Moresheth*. The place name relates to the verb *'rš*, "to be betrothed." The "parting gifts" are gifts a father gives when sending away his daughter, i.e., a dowry (1 Ki 9:16) or when a husband sends away a wife (Ex 18:2).
9. 1:14b: *Achzib* means "deception" as *Achzib* is given to *achzib*.
10. 1:15: The participle *yrsh* ("conqueror") relates to the phonetic character of the city, *Mareshah*.

The wordplays (*Wortspiele*) mark the rhetorical nature of this difficult section. Other features of this unit bear discussion. "Tell it not in Gath" begins the section with a command not to weep following it. Prima facie, v. 10 appears disjointed from the unit leading some to suggest it is a later addition (Mays). The LXX differs from the MT regarding the first verb. Instead of "do not report" (אל־תגידו) the LXX reads "do not exult" (*megalunesthe*). S follows suit. The *Biblia Hebraica Stuttgartensia* (BHS) editors suggest emending the text to תגילו ("do not rejoice"). They also suggest replacing the negative particle (אל) of colon B with "yet, indeed" (אף). There is no textual evidence for the latter, though the possibility of a scribal error is not beyond the pale (see Hillers).

The text as it stands, however, provides an important intertextual link to 2 Sam 1:20. There David published his sentiments regarding the death of Saul and Jonathan and the same phrase is used: "tell it not in Gath." The summons not to report the deaths in Gath stems from Gath's proximity to Philistia and the avoidance of national derision. The precise meaning of the allusion in Micah remains somewhat elusive, though the reference to Adullam in v. 15 may be of aid. There a reference is made to the glory of Israel coming to Adullam. "Glory" (כבוד) may refer to many things: Israel's wealth, might, army, or even Yhwh (Ben Zvi, 36). If, however, the subtle allusion in 1:15 is to the narratives where David fled for safety to the caves of Adullam (1 Sam 22:1; 2 Sam 23:13), then the "glory of Israel" coming to Adullam may be in metonymic relation to Judah's king (cf. Isa 5:13). Thus, Davidic allusions at 1:10 and 1:15 create an inclusio. The effect of the Davidic allusion may relate specifically to the throne and/or the metonymic relation between the throne and the people represented therein. As David fled to Adullam, so too will his people flee from dangerous threats. Foreign incursion, national derision, fleeing for safety, and exile are the themes of 1:10-16. The Davidic allusions at 1:10 and 1:15 provide further thematic evidence.

In v. 13 the term "daughter of Zion" appears for the first time in the Twelve. Ancient cities were portrayed as the female consorts of the city's god, though this background is contested and an unlikely referent in Micah.[82] Williamson believes the metaphor, at least by Isaiah's day, was a "conceptual" or "dead" metaphor. In other words, the image was so much a part of the cultural discourse that its background or metaphoric origins were of no consequence.[83] Dead metaphors, according to Williamson, can come back to life in new prophetic contexts, thus requiring attentive examination of the particular use.[84]

---

[82] Williamson, 69.
[83] Ibid.
[84] Mark Boda believes the Daughter of Zion metaphor is an apt image for the vulnerability of Judah, especially in settings of judgment and lamentation. The metaphor entails the pain of loss as well as the anticipation of salvation. See Mark J. Boda, *The Book of Zechariah* (NICOT; Grand Rapids: Eerdmans, 2016), 563. See the essays in *Daughter Zion: Her Portrait, Her Response* (ed. M. J. Boda, C. J. Dempsey and L. S. Flesher; Atlanta: SBL Press, 2012).

We have already seen Samaria portrayed as a prostitute in 1:7, drawing from the imagery of Hosea. Gomer is the daughter of Diblaim (Hos 1:3). The Daughter of Zion in 1:10-16 is marked by sin and transgressions, engulfed in the wound of her prostitute sister to the north. The feminine imperatives of v. 16 are directed at the Daughter of Zion introduced in v. 13: shave the head, make bald, enlarge your (feminine pronominal suffix) shaved head (cf. the feminine imperatives in 4:10, 13). For the Daughter of Zion will see her own "children of delight" or "pampered children" go into exile. The fall of Samaria and the experiences of the Shephaleh region of Judah, separated as they are in time, are fitted together in the same drama of election and rejection, marriage and infidelity, promise and loss. "Thou shalt have no other gods before me," ranges over and makes claims upon the entirety of the Northern and Southern Kingdoms who share in a similar history with Yhwh.

It seems plausible, if not probable, to identify the invasion of Sennacherib in 701 as the historical moment giving rise to Micah's lamentation (1:8-9) and the events described in 1:10-16. The text itself, however, does not identify its historical setting, creating space for several theories of origin. For Ben Zvi, the lack of clear historical markers is telling and allows for multiple historical referents to be associated with Micah's lamentation: 701, 586, or any another analogous event. The text remains "open" to the future on this account (Ben Zvi, 34-35). As mentioned above, Ben Zvi tends to limit the text's openness to postexilic Yehud as the intended readership. Brevard Childs has a broader understanding of the prophetic texts' openness to the future. Oracles emerging from various and sundry historical moments are refitted into an eschatological pattern of judgment and salvation in the future hope of the coming kingdom of God.[85] While much of the focus of modern interpretation centers on identifying the originating historical setting, the canonical shaping of the prophetic literature intimates a differing set of interpretive concerns. Historical settings indicate God's judging and redemptive actions in time, yet the prophetic texts as texts are not hermetically sealed in those various and sundry moments. Rather, they pattern a set of hopes and beliefs about God's future actions and forthcoming kingdom. This eschatological patterning is part and parcel of Micah's canonical shape and final form.

---

[85] Brevard Childs, "The Canonical Shape of the Prophetic Literature," *Int* 32 (1978): 46–55 (52).

2

Micah 2:1-5—Love Your Neighbor

Introduction

John Calvin portrays Micah 1 as a prophetic witness against those in breach of the first table of the Law. Micah 2 then moves seamlessly to those breaking the Law's second table: love your neighbor as yourself. Martin Luther's oft-quoted phrase that God does not need our good works but our neighbors do presses into the dynamic at hand. For sin, as human pride and inward turning, may also be defined in Eberhard Jüngel's terms as "making myself my own neighbor."[1] The self-giving of God's own righteousness to others is the very opposite of a "divine selfishness" where God reserves his own benefits for himself.[2] As mentioned in the previous chapter, the pride of humanity is dealt a death blow by the humility and self-giving of God. The antipode of God's self-giving is *sin*, defined again by Jüngel as "the urge to pursue one's own right at the expense of others and thus to make oneself into one's own neighbor."[3]

The second table of the Law focuses on the relationships of the covenant community. When the Pharisees press Jesus to clarify the greatest commandment, He answers as any faithful Jew would, with the *Shema*: Love the Lord your God with all your heart, soul, and might (Deut 6:4). What sometimes escapes unnoticed in this theological banter between Jesus and the Pharisees is the extent of Jesus's response. They did not ask about the second commandment, but Jesus felt it incumbent

---

[1] Jüngel, *Justification: The Heart of the Christian Faith*, 86.
[2] Ibid.
[3] Ibid.

upon himself to provide the answer to the second question they should have asked. "And the second *is like unto it*, thou shalt love thy neighbor as thyself" (Mk 12:28-31). For Jesus, loving God and loving neighbor are in an ordered relation the one to the other, with love of God as primary yet the second is *like unto it*. As Jesus frames the matter, in accord with the prophetic legacy of Israel's Scriptures, you cannot have the first table of the Law without the second. You cannot have love of God without love of neighbor. The canonical shape of Micah's first two chapters concurs with this ordered and related account of love of God and love of neighbor. This theme is a leitmotif weaving its way through the whole of Micah's corpus.

2:1-5

The depiction in vv. 1-2 leaves little doubt regarding the presenting cause of the woe oracle. The powerful landowners are preying on the weaker landowners for their own advantage.[4] They are making themselves their own neighbor. "Woe" (הוי) is leveled against the "devisers" or "schemers" (חשב) who are making evil plans on their bed in order to actualize them when the sun appears on the morrow.[5] The effect of v. 1 is a merism

---

[4] Hillers argues against Alt's limiting the nobles to the Jerusalem elite with the oppressed as peasants from the countryside (Hillers, 33). The text does not suggest this limited scope and the force of Micah's prophetic word reaches to local land magnates as well. See also Jeremias, 148.

[5] "Woe" is most often followed by a participial form functioning as the vocative of the address, cf. Isa 5:8,11,18,20. Andersen and Freedman believe Micah is intentionally fiddling with the participles in 2:1a. What does it mean for the wicked "to do" (פעל) evil on their beds? And why does Micah invert the typical phraseology of "devising harm" (און) and doing evil (רע), cf. Jer 18:11. Andersen and Freedman suggest the unconventional use of these terms by Micah is a poetic play emphasizing the move from thought to deed (Andersen and Freedman, 263–64). The effect of the two participles is the bringing together of thought and deed as flip sides of the same coin. Even though the evil deeds are not expressly done while in bed, the thought and planning for the evil deed already entails the doing of it on the morrow. See Hillers on the common switch from third person to second person after the initial vocative of the *woe* (Mic 2:1-3 is a case in point). These grammatical features raise form-critical questions for Hillers, particularly his reticence to tie the *woe* oracles to a funeral rite. Rather, these *woe* oracles fit more naturally with the "hear ye" (שמאו) forms of address (cf. Mic 1:2). Delbert R. Hillers, "*Hôy* and *Hôy*-Oracles: A Neglected Syntactic Aspect," in *The Word of the Lord Shall Go Forth: Essays in Honor of David Noel Freedman in Celebration of His Sixtieth Birthday* (ed. C. L. Meyers and M. O'Connor; Winona Lake: Eisenbrauns, 1983), 185–88.

of sorts where the whole of the perpetrators' existence is given to the devising and enacting of their evil deeds. These evil deeds (און) speak to the misfortune and calamity inherent in and brought about by the deed. Unlike רע (the second noun for "evil" or "calamity" in 2:1a), God's deeds are never identified as און.[6] Acts of "wickedness" (און) are the very opposite of righteousness, justice, and Torah, and their effects are always harmful on the community.

These anti-righteous schemers give their total energies to these evil plans because they have the power to do it. In an arresting turn of phrase, the Hebrew text says, "for there is god in their hand" or, if, with Andersen and Freedman, the phrase does not denote existence but possession, "because their hand belongs to God" (כי יש־לאל ידם).[7] The exact origin of the phrase and its religious character are lost to us, though McKane suggests the idiom stems from a time when the hand was understood to have its own power because a god energized it (McKane, 60). From a synchronic perspective, the idiomatic force of the phrase may in fact be "they have the power in their hand" as observed in all English translations (cf. Gen 31:29; Deut 28:32; Pr 3:27). On this account "might is right." At the same time, the lexical character of the idiom opens other connotative possibilities, especially given the character of the actions about to take place the next morning: the power expressed by the force of their hand is their god; they execute their power as demigods, taking the place properly belonging to God alone; or the deeds of their hands are the only divine oversight of their actions.[8] Whatever the full range of the idiom, the wickedly wanton of v. 1 exercise their power under the governance of their own untoward desires (v. 2).

Calvin's tethering of Micah 2 to the second table of the Law is not a freewheeling association of the rhetorical kind. The text itself

---

[6] TLOT 1, 62.
[7] Andersen and Freedman, 267–68.
[8] Kessler believes the context of 2:1 gives the language of the phrase a "tiefere Bedeutung" (Kessler, 115). He continues, "Die Gewalttäter stezen sich an die Stelle Gottes" (ibid.); see Sweeney, 359.

intimates this linkage in v. 2 where the wicked schemes and actions of v.1 are concretized.[9] "They covet" (חמד).[10] The allusion to the tenth commandment comes to the fore with its focus on disordered desire (Ex 20:17). The term "covet" (חמד) has *desire* as its basic semantic sense. Absent a literary context the lexeme has no particular moral value attached to it. The term may be used in positive ways to indicate properly ordered desires. In Ps 19:10 the ordinances of the Lord are more to be desired (participial form of חמד) than gold (cf. Gen 2:9). Equally, the term may reflect disordered or inordinate desires as depicted in the Achan narrative (Josh 7:21). Therefore, the objects of desire often clarify the agent's motive. The tenth commandment speaks against the desiring of a neighbor's "house" in 20:17a with 20:17b filling out the material content of that abstract category: wife, servants, animals, or anything.[11]

A lexical argument centers on the question of whether "desire" (חמד) as a term connotes action more than emotion.[12] Durham makes a compelling case for why the term itself does not entail the twin action of "covet *and* seize" (*contra* Hermann). For every use of "desire" (חמד) in the Old Testament that leads to the actual possession of something is followed by an object. If the action were an ingredient aspect of the

---

[9] Waltke describes v. 2 as epexegetical to v. 1 and not chronological (Waltke, 95).

[10] Waltke understands the *weqatalti* forms, וחמדו and וגזלו, as protasis and apodosis, respectively (Waltke, 95; WO'C 32.2.3). When this, then that. Andersen and Freedman recognize the oddity of these forms, forms normally depicting future conditions. Yet, the conditions here do not appear as future events but events having already occurred, thus the prophetic ire. They conclude that the *weqatalti* forms are "archaic constative aspectual" references (Andersen and Freedman, 274). In other words, the verbal forms expose typical or constative actions that entail the past, present, and future unless stopped (ibid.). The term "steal" or "tearing away" (גזל) in v. 2 appears in the haunting metaphor of 3:2: "who tear the skin off my people."

[11] The numbering of the ten commandments or ten words is a matter of continued dispute among various ecclesial constituencies. Lutheran and Catholic interpreters view the tenth commandment as two commandments because of the repeated use of the term "covet" in 20:17a and 20:17b (a unique feature in the Decalogue). The former denotes the subjective emotion of the offender and the latter the objective action according to this reading. See Brevard S. Childs, *The Book of Exodus* (OTL; Philadelphia: The Westminster Press, 1974), 425 (393–401).

[12] See the classic commentary on Exodus by Benno Jacob, e.g., The lexical arguments may be traced more fully in the commentaries by Childs, Dozeman, and Durham.

verbal sense, then a stated object would be unnecessary in every usage.¹³ While in general agreement with Durham's lexical sensibilities, Childs understands the lexical term "desire" (חמד) to highlight an emotion that tends toward action.¹⁴ Such is certainly the case in Mic 2:2. The *desire* for fields and houses leads to "stealing" (גזל) and "taking" (נשא). The disordered desire becomes the gateway for the deed such that the desire and deed are related as cause and effect in a single horizon of action.¹⁵ The parallel grammatical structure of the verbs in v. 2 underscores the point.

A quick glance at the literature on v. 2 brings the story of Naboth and his vineyard into view. Some even suggest that v. 2 is a commentary on the Naboth narrative (cf. 1 Ki 21).¹⁶ *Fields, house,* and *households* are the inheritance of God's people given by God alone who is the sole landowner in Israel (Lev 25:23; cf. Isa 5:8; Deut 5:21). According to Sweeney, even if Naboth had sold his vineyard to Ahab and received a better vineyard elsewhere, there was no guarantee that the next vineyard would be in the territory of Issachar. The power move by Ahab threatened the whole of the tribal system of ancient Israel, and Naboth's response is in accord with this concern.¹⁷ "The Lord forbid

---

¹³ Durham, 298.
¹⁴ Much of the lexical discussion stems from the semantic distinction between the terms חמד and אוה. Deuteronomy 5:21 uses both terms in the tenth commandment with אוה coming after the former. Exodus only uses חמד. Childs shows how the two terms are used interchangeably in the Zion traditions (cf. Pss 68:19, 132:13f). Thus, a sharp semantic distinction between חמד as "action" and אוה as "emotion" is untenable. Still, Childs does see a semantic distinction between the two terms as the latter does highlight the emotion itself, while the former term "falls on an emotion which often leads to commensurate action" (Childs, *Exodus*, 427).
¹⁵ Durham offers a suggestive reading of the tenth commandment in relation to first commandment. Both are in signal positions as they pertain to the two tables of the Law. Durham believes the tenth commandment comes last because it is the most comprehensive of commandments, a gateway commandment of sorts with its focus on an attitude rather than action as observed in the other commandments. Coveting as an attitude can lead to the actions of stealing, adultery, dishonesty, and the mistreatment of parents (Durham, 298-99). For example, coveting led to the breach of the 9th and 6th commandments in the Naboth narrative (cf. 1 Ki 21), while lust or inordinate desire led to the breaking of the 7th, 8th, and 6th commandments in the story of David and Bathsheba (1 Sam 11).
¹⁶ See Wolff, ad loc.
¹⁷ Marvin A. Sweeney, *I & II Kings* (OTL; Louisville: WJK, 2007).

that I should give you my ancestral inheritance" (1 Ki 21:4).[18] To take such inheritances or to give them away remains in the threshold of Yhwh's provision for his people. To sell or to seize are both offensive to Yhwh's prerogative and oversight: a view Naboth understood and Ahab dismissed.

There is little to suggest in this verse that the poor per se are preyed upon. A man (איש) and a householder or citizen (גבר) are oppressed by those who have the power to do so.[19] A hierarchical system of social order, stemming from a Zion theology where Yhwh as divine king rests at the apex of this order, undergirds the sentiments of this and the next chapter.[20] Those in positions of strength vis-à-vis those whose place is not equal to theirs are, within Yhwh's social ordering, agents of protection and benefaction. Such an ordering relates analogously to Yhwh's own beneficence to Zion. It is a basic assumption of their position's privilege that a beneficent posture toward those "below" them is in order. "Listen you heads of Jacob and you rulers of the house of Israel, should you not know justice?" (Mic 3:1). The description of events here in Micah 2 and 3 represents a gross perversion of Zion theology where Yhwh's own merciful character as divine king serves as an exemplar for those in positions of social privilege.[21]

---

[18] "The economic and social ideal of ancient Israel was of a nation of free landholders—not debt-slaves, share-croppers, or hired workers—secure in possession, as a grant from Yahweh, of enough land to keep their families" (Hillers, 33). Hillers is stressing that the situation is not mere greed but a very attack on the basic social structures of God's people. "Each under his own vine and fig tree" is presented as the eschatological ideal in Mic 4:4.

[19] See the lexical discussion in Andersen and Freedman, 272–73.

[20] See H. G. M. Williamson, *He Has Shown You What Is Good: Old Testament Justice Here and Now* (Eugene: Wipf & Stock, 2012), 72. It is a curiosity that Micah 2 does not contribute to Williamson's larger thesis that social justice in the prophets is not based on received Torah or revelation per se but on what is instinctively perceived as socially right. While Williamson makes a strong case for the overall picture he paints, the place of the Torah in Mic 2 as an adjudicatory force is striking: "thou shalt not covet." The theology of the land as inheritance also stems from Priestly and Deuteronomistic traditions, and while such views from the perspective of the Near East might be instinctive, their judicial character in these contexts has a revelatory force behind them as well.

[21] Jeremias, 117.

It appears fitting to speak of Augustine's distinction between *enjoyment* and *use* in the conceptual space created by "desire" and its consequence in Mic 2:1-2. The proper ordering of desire in the shaping of our love toward God and neighbor is a central concern of Micah in particular and the prophets in general. In his *De Doctrina Christiana*, Augustine raises questions pertaining to "happiness" in terms that are familiar to those versed in Aristotle's *Nichomachean Ethics* and the Stoic distinction between *goods* and *preferables*. Goods bring *eudaimonia* which can be enjoyed by the habitual practices of moral virtue. Preferables, like wealth and health, are certainly to be preferred but do not make one "happy." Aristotle, as I understand him, is more nuanced than the Stoics on this account. In fact, Aristotle satirizes a Stoic sentiment in Book VII of the *Ethics*, "Those who say that the victim on the rack or the man who falls into great misfortune is happy if he is good, are, whether they mean to or not, talking nonsense" (Book VII.13). I believe we can agree.

Augustine, while drawing on these categories as borrowed capital, frames the matter differently. "So, then," Augustine suggests, "there are some things which are meant to be enjoyed, others are meant to be used, yet others which do both the enjoying and the using. Things that are to be enjoyed make us happy; things which are to be used help us on our way to happiness, providing us, so to say, with crutches and props for reaching the things that will make us happy, and enabling us to keep them" (*De Doctrina*, I.3). If things to be enjoyed, rather than merely used, make for genuine happiness, what exactly is "enjoyment" and what is thing to be "enjoyed"?

Augustine answers, "Enjoyment, after all, consists in clinging to something lovely for its own sake, while use consists in referring what has come your way to what your love aims at obtaining, provided, that is, it deserves to be loved." It *deserves* to be loved. What is deserving of love? What brings true happiness and is the end of all our pursuit, all our desire, all our longing? Augustine answers, "The things therefore that are to be enjoyed are the Father and the Son and the Holy Spirit, in fact the Trinity, one supreme thing, and one which is shared in common by all who enjoy it."[22]

What I find especially compelling about Augustine's case is the place of enjoyment and desire in the fundamental make-up of our humanity. What does it mean to be a person, a human, Saint Augustine? He does not give a purely rationalist account of what it means for humans to be persons, a version of Descartes's perceiving-self as the foundation for all that is. Rather, we are primarily marked by desire. We hunger. Such hungering is not abstracted from our cognitive faculties, our ability to reason and think; we are not purely animal in this regard—Augustine is clear on this matter as well. But the pursuit of *eudaimonia*, or happiness, for that which is to be enjoyed is woven into the very fabric of our existence.

The desire, the hunger, that lurks underneath our sternums and the pursuit of enjoyment that marks a sensual culture are Exhibit A of what Augustine believes to be the case about human nature. See, you can hear Augustine say, see that young person there or there rushing headlong into the ocean of pleasure, whether that pleasure is a virtue or a vice: glory, honor, prestige, success, sexual indulgence (Augustine knew something of this one), reckless ambition; that person is on to something. The pursuit of enjoyment or happiness is

---

[22] O'Donovan believes Augustine in his more mature thought escapes some of the problems attendant to his relating of God and neighbor by the categories of *use* and *enjoyment*. The criticism speaks to the arbitrariness of putting a neighbor in the category of a means to an end as an instrument of human will (so Kant). "Means" and "ends" both relate to human planning and devising. O'Donovan, however, understands Augustine's distinctions to emerge from the neighbor's ontology as a creature of God rather than from an imposed and extrinsic category from outside. Therefore, instead of seeing "use" and "end" as instrumental categories of human manipulation, Augustine properly read understand "love of neighbor" as an object for the sake of enjoyment of God. Love of neighbor depends on love for God. Oliver O'Donovan, *Resurrection and Moral Order: An Outline for Evangelical Ethics, Second Edition* (Grand Rapids: Eerdmans, 1994), 235–36.

ingredient to their nature. But the ordering of their love, of their enjoyment, is all wrong. It is misdirected; it is misshaped; it is skewed. In the language of the prophets, it is idolatrous, replacing creature for Creator. Those momentary pleasures that flee and then leave one in a state of existential emptiness are pale shadows, or in Augustine's terms, forgotten memories of a love ordered rightly for the sake of true *eudaimonia*—like trying to slake our thirst by licking a salt block. What is enjoyed, what is loved for its own sake? Where is true water for the thirsty, hungry soul? Augustine is unequivocal in his answer: God, whose name is Father, Son, and Holy Spirit. The love of neighbor exists for the sake of the ultimate good, loving God. Yet, as Micah warns, when desires become disordered, when *uses* become ends, sin and revolt of all kinds abound.

With the cause of the judgment speech stated in vv. 1-2, the consequences follow in vv. 3-5. The particle "therefore" (לכן) introduces the consequent outcomes, linking them to the verses that precede. Because those in positions of privilege, wherever such positions are located along the hierarchical chain, are marked by inordinate desires and actions, the divine response to the guilty mirrors their own scheming. Now Yhwh is scheming and devising (חשב) a calamity (רעה) of his own. In Jonah, readers note the lexical importance of "evil/calamity" (רעה) throughout the book. Nineveh's "evil" arose before Yhwh (1:2), leading to Jonah's prophetic commission. After Jonah's adventurous and circuitous journey, the Ninevites hear the prophetic word of judgment and embrace en masse the religious rituals of repentance. In a crucial verse of Jonah's rising and falling narrative, God relents from his "evil/calamity" (רעה) because the Ninevites had repented of their "evil" (3:10) (רעה).

The object of his calamitous planning is "this family" or "this clan" (המשפחה הזות).[23] The family or clan language moves the scope of judgment to the whole of Israel (cf. Am 3:2; Jer 8:3). Given the preceding two verses, this move comes as a bit of a surprise. The effect of the text as it stands is the expansive nature of the guilt of a few and its deleterious implications for the whole. This particular complex of guilt and judgment encompasses and effects the whole of Israel.

---

[23] The BHS editors suggest this clause is a later edition because it breaks the person of its literary surroundings. Wolff affirms the phrase as a later interpolation because it separates the participle "devising" from its object "calamity" (Wolff, 69). There is no textual evidence to support the notion, though several follow it (cf. Mays, 65). See also the discussion in Andersen and Freedman. They suggest the choice of this unusual term intends to make a play on the term "on their beds" (משכבותם) in v. 1 (Andersen and Freedman, 275–76).

Moreover, the use of the demonstrative pronoun "these" only highlights the relational distancing between Yhwh and "his" people (cf. Isa 6:10; Hos 1:9). These acts of disordered desire rupture the whole of Israel's social order and covenant relationship with their God. The covenant formula "I will be *your* God and you will be *my* people" only highlights the disruptive force of such a small part of speech: *this* family.

There are two effects of the calamity Yhwh is devising. First, they ("you," 2nd plural) will not be able to remove it from their necks. This is a curious phrase whose referent is not immediately clear. Ben Zvi believes the unusual term (plural, "necks" צוארת) forms a relation of assonance to "these" (זאת) with the shared *ōt* endings (Ben Zvi, 46). If this is the case, then the pairing of the sounds reinforces the distance between Yhwh and "this" people. Whether or not Micah is speaking metaphorically remains an open question as well. Jeremiah put a yoke on his neck as an act of prophetic symbolism for the political yoke Babylon would bring (Jeremiah 27). Or the yoke imagery could portend actual slavery.[24] Whatever the case, "this family" will be unable by an act of national will or might to remove the oncoming judgment of Yhwh in whatever form it comes.

Second, they will be unable to "rise up" or "walk haughtily" as in the NRSV. The term "walk haughtily" (רומה) is a *hapax legomenon*, though its relation to רום terminology is assumed. As observed in Isaiah's prophetic movement, only Yhwh is "exalted" (רום; cf. Isa 6:1; 57:15). Whenever Israel "exalts" herself, these actions are perceived as pride or haughtiness with the result that Yhwh cuts her down (cf. Isaiah 2; 10).[25] Yhwh's judgment is a debasing of the pride and arrogance of "this people" that is demonstrated in the concrete conduct of vv. 1-2. The discerning of the times was a crucial aspect of the prophetic vocation. One recalls the prophetic debates taking place in Jeremiah regarding the discernment of the times (cf. Jeremiah 28). Micah makes clear that this is an "evil time" (2:3c) not only for those committing the crimes of

---

[24] Andersen and Freedman, 278.
[25] See the discussion in Mark Gignilliat, "Oaks of Righteousness for His Glory: Horticulture and Renewal in Isaiah 61, 1-4," *ZAW* 123 (2011): 391–405.

vv. 1-2 but for the whole of the nation (cf. Am 5:13).[26] The beneficence intended from top to bottom in Yhwh's social ordering of Zion also has the reverse effect that judgment directed at the actions of the top trickles down to effect the bottom as well.

The phrase "in that day" (ביום ההוא) continues the train of thought from the previous verse's announcement: "for it will be an evil time." A hopeful word of promise typically follows this phrase (though cf. Hos 1:5). Here, however, it serves to exacerbate the shame of the forthcoming humiliation. A "proverbial saying" (משל) is put on the lips of an unidentified and impersonal agent.[27] "He or they will raise a taunt song against you." The use of the adversative preposition (על) identifies the scene as hostile (cf. Hab 2:6; Deut 28:37), though the lamentation to follow functions as a true lamentation. The difficult phrase "and wail with bitter lamentation" makes concrete the character of the more abstract "proverb" or "taunt song" (משל).[28]

The force of v. 4, therefore, functions on two levels. In the first level, the mourning or lamentation reflects the genuine grief of the first-person voices (singular and plural) of the "taunt song." Jeremias identifies the change in voice as an important interpretive point. The "we" voices surround the "I" voice in the middle of the song and indicate the collective suffering of Judah. According to Jeremias, the plural voices are the guilty indicted in vv. 1-2, and the "I" voices are those for whom Micah is particularly concerned, namely, "my people" or those

---

[26] See Nogalski, 537, on the intertextual relation between Amos and Micah at this point. Nogalski identifies a similar thematic movement in both texts with Amos ending his focus on Israel and Micah on Judah.

[27] Waltke, 99. See DCH 5, 537.

[28] The phrase "and wail with bitter lamentations" poses textual problems. 4QXII has the first verb in the plural, though none of the translations follow. The primary textual difficulty is the third word of the phrase: היהנ יהב ההנו. None of the translations translate the word in its current form: the *niphal* of היה. If the *niphal* verb is intended, then one would gloss it as "It has happened." Gelston (*BHQ*, 98*) suggests the translations may understand היהנ as a noun in a cognate relationship with יהנ. If היהנ is a feminine form of יהנ, then a superlative genitive may be the syntactical solution: "a groan of groans" (see Waltke, 100). Alternatively, the translators may be guessing. Or with the editors of the BHS *dittography* may be the genetic explanation. Andersen and Freedman are right to note that whatever textual or syntactical solutions are offered, the effect of the collocation is the sharing of sounds (assonance). Such literary plays are expected in a משל and lean against the suggestion of the BHS to emend the text.

who suffer on account of the actions of others (Jeremias, 149–50). Collectively, they do experience utter ruination as in v. 3. Their portion or inheritance (חלק) by divine gift is now a forfeiture of covenant infidelity. As the lines of the taunt song continue, the nature of the loss becomes more clear. They are losing their fields, their land. A species of *lex talionis* takes place here in a moment of divine irony. The presenting cause of divine displeasure in vv. 1-2 becomes the mirror of their own forthcoming judgment. Apostates (שובב) now have ownership of what was once theirs. The term "apostates" or "backsliders" may refer to willful and stubborn Israel but can describe foreign enemies as well (cf. Jer 49:4).[29] The second level of the song, and perhaps the more sinister, is the use of this genuine dirge or lamentation by Judah's enemies as a jeer or a taunt. Judah's suffering and their songs of lamentation become the occasion for satire by her enemies. The dirge becomes derision. The double force of the dirge as genuine and derisive marks the devastation of the scene.

Verse 5 follows v. 4 with the logical connector "therefore" (לכן) linking the verses. The second-person address of v. 5 picks up from the second person of v. 3 with the oppressors and covetous of vv. 1-2 once again in view. This prophetic word opens itself to the future where those who oppress will no longer have a part in the distribution of the land. They will no longer share in the inheritance given by divine favor in the "assembly of the Lord" (בקהל יהוה)—the place where tribal boundaries are decided (cf. Deuteronomy 33).[30] Israel's memory of their past measurement of the land and the casting of lots for land distribution (cf. Josh 18:8-10; Num 26:55, 36:2) function now as an eschatological promise for Yhwh's future actions (cf. Ez 48).[31] A word of promise runs alongside the word of judgment for the oppressors. On the far side of the collective devastation experience by the first-person

---

[29] DCH 8, 298. Sweeney understands the term in relation to its basic lexical sense, "to return"—thus, "returners" or "one who restores." The opaque term, in Sweeney's reading, may reference conquerors who redistribute the land back to the rightful property owners (Sweeney, 361).

[30] Andersen and Freedman, 289.

[31] Jeremias describes the scene as "eine neue Josua-Zeit" (Jeremias, 150).

voices ("I" and "we") of v. 4, the inheritance of the land will be apportioned once again. The oppressors, however, will have no place in this future scene. Hillers is right to note the tame character of the language of v. 5 in comparison with the preceding indictments. Yet, he continues, "[I]n comparison to the preceding lament, this is the severest of the judgments" (Hillers, 33). The oppressors who cut off landowners from their divine inheritance will be cut off themselves in the future moment of restoration.

Micah 2:6-11: A different sermon, please

This section of Micah's prophecy is riddled with interpretive and textual challenges. Central to the presenting difficulties is the identification of the speaking voices, and the text provides little to no interpretive aids. Who is preaching or prophesying or "driveling" away in 2:6? Is the force of the utterances in 2:7 positive or negative? How do vv. 8-10 relate to the inclusio of the prophet against prophecy warnings in 2:6-7 and 2:11? If we have an interlocution between Micah and his opponents, where do the respective voices begin and end? Such questions reside at the interpretive center of this section and sorting through them is no mean task. In light of these challenges, Ben Zvi does well to remind us of the link between 2:6-11 and 2:1-5 lest rereaders lose the forest for the trees (Ben Zvi, 56). To continue Calvin's line of thought, the second table of the Law remains in view here as the prophet registers his complaint against a disordered prophetic office.

Our interpretive focus zeros in on the written character of the text, seeking to make sense of the MT. A quick glance at the critical apparatus of the BHS reveals the editors' proclivity to emend the text at almost every turn (*prp; prb l*). Ben Zvi rightly cautions readers against such instincts, suggesting our understanding of or desire for textual coherence may part company with the biblical texts concern for such matters. Moreover, if Micah went through a compositional process toward its final form, then the tradents of the material and initial readers register no obvious discomfort or misunderstanding (Ben Zvi, 58). Making such claims does not neutralize the interpretive challenges of this section. Rather, it keeps the focus of these difficulties clear: the text in its received form with the judicious use of text-critical analysis where requisite.

The threefold use of the term "to preach" (*hifil* of נטפ) in v. 6 brings the prophetic interlocutors into view.[32] A rough reading of the first two clauses may be rendered as follows: "Stop preaching, they preach; they will not preach concerning these things." The difficulties of identifying the speaking voices are apparent, not to mention that the opposing voices are never clearly identified. Van der Woude's identification of the opponents as representatives of "the established religious-political order of the day" brings clarity to the kind of debate taking place.[33] Micah is leveling a complaint against those who practice injustice as a forfeiture of their covenantal inheritance. The "pseudo-prophets" represent those in positions of leadership or power involved in the activities described in 2:1-5. The pseudo-prophets turn a blind eye toward their actions and their calamitous effects, and thus deny Micah's prophetic warnings. These pseudo-prophets base their "preaching" on a lopsided and faulty reliance on a half-baked Zion theology.[34] Here Micah joins company with his prophetic cobelligerents who stand against those in religious or political authority who rely on the Zion traditions to the denial of the covenantal claims Yhwh has on his people and their actions (cf. Jer 5:18-19; Am 7:16—note the use of נטפ).

The voices in 2:6 are proposed in the following table:

---

[32] The term נטפ remains a lexical challenge. Its basic sense is "to drip" (cf. Am 9:13). The association of "dripping" with prophecy or preaching may have to do with "driveling" or salivating either in the speaking moment or in an ecstatic experience (see Shalom, *Amos*, 250). The term does not require a pejorative sense (cf. Ez 21:2,7), though this sense in Micah cannot be ruled out (cf. Amaziah's opposition to Amos, Am 7:16). Rendering the term with the neutral "preaching" is a responsible reading given the lexical challenges.

[33] A. S. van der Woude, "Micah in Dispute with the Pseudo-Prophets," *VT* 19 (1969): 27.

[34] See Ollenburger, *Zion The City of the Great King*. See van der Woude, "Micah in Dispute," for further details of the opponents' Zion theology at work.

"Stop preaching"—voice of the pseudo-prophets
"They preach"—Micah's voice
"They will not preach concerning these things"³⁵—Micah's voice

There is no clear referent for the demonstrative pronoun "these things." It is possible for the pronoun to refer to the prophetic injunctions of 2:1-5. Or, and this seems a preferable reading, the demonstrative pronoun may come before the antecedent with "these things" referring to the next clause. "They will not preach concerning these things, namely, ... " In other words, the following clause identifies the content of the message that the pseudo-prophets are unwilling to preach. This reading leads in turn to another interpretive hurdle. How do we best understand the last clause of 2:6?

Most if not all English versions identify the term "disgrace" (כלמות) as the subject of the verb "overtake" or "turn away" (יסג, *niphal* from סוג): "Disgrace will not overtake us." The problem with such a rendering is the lack of verb-subject agreement. "Disgrace" is a feminine plural noun and "turn away" is a masculine singular verb. While it is not impossible for the Hebrew to yield the sense of the English translations, it is neither preferable nor necessary.³⁶ The phrase is best rendered: "He will not turn away or withdraw disgraces." Sweeney makes a compelling argument for Yhwh as the implied subject of the masculine verb. "Yhwh will not withdraw disgraces."³⁷ If such a rendering persuades, then it follows that

---

³⁵ "Concerning these things" renders לאלה. The use of the *lamed* before the demonstrative pronoun may suggest a personal agent: "to these persons." If personal agents are in view, then this clause could be put on the lips of Micah's opponents. The similar phrase in 2:11, however, does not require a personal agent and leans against this reading in 2:6. The LXX *epi autois* indicates an early understanding of the phrase as "concerning these things."

³⁶ For support of this reading, see GKC §145o, though not all the textual evidence persuades. See John T. Willis, "Micah 2: 6-8 and the 'People of God' in Micah," *BZ* 14 (1970): 74–75. Willis suggests emending the text so that "disgraces" is singular, for the sake of singular subject. Furthermore, he emends the verb to a feminine singular (תשׂיג) for the sake of gender agreement. The reading above avoids such textual straining by understanding the final clause as Micah's rehearsal of what the pseudo-prophets are unwilling to say. Yhwh is the implied subject of the 3ms verb and the text stands in its received form. Emendations are certainly possible and sometimes necessary. But such does not seem the case here.

³⁷ Sweeney, 363.

the final clause is Micah's report of what the pseudo-prophets are unwilling to preach, namely, "Yhwh will not withdraw disgraces."

Verse 7 continues Micah's engagement with the pseudo-prophets. They are unwilling to preach about forthcoming disgraces because of their confidence in the covenant.[38] Such confidences stem from the Zion traditions and are represented in the catchwords repeated in v. 7: "Is the Lord's patience exhausted?" "Are these his deeds?" "Do not my words do good to those who walk uprightly?" The verse begins with a lexical riddle because the phrase "should this be said?" is an unattested form (האמור). Various suggestions and emendations for this phrase are offered in the secondary literature: from changing the verb to "curse" (ארר, cf. BHS) to rendering it "he affirmed the House of Jacob" with covenantal overtones present (van der Woude).[39] Like v. 6 where every phrase begins with a negative particle, so too v. 7 begins every phrase with an interrogative particle, suggesting that the phrase be read as it is most often translated, "should it be said" or "is it said."[40] The first phrase, therefore, asks "the house of Jacob" whether or not certain questions are being asked. The questions they are asking then appear in the next three interrogative phrases.

The first two questions of v. 7 reveal the theological confidence of Micah's opponents. The questions the opponents raise are rhetorical in nature. "Is the spirit of the Lord shortened?" "Are these his deeds?" Answer: No. The experienced difficulties of the people of God are real, but Yhwh remains patient, so Micah's opponents claim. Our misfortunes are not deeds of judgment, but events requiring perseverance because Yhwh will come to our immediate rescue. After all, Zion cannot be shaken (cf. Pss. 46, 48). Readers may recall the prophetic squabble between Hananiah and Jeremiah regarding the length of the Babylonian

---

[38] Van der Woude, "Micah in Dispute," 27–28.
[39] See Waltke, 114, for the range of interpretive suggestions. See van der Woude, "Micah in Dispute," 27.
[40] There is no textual evidence for the BHS suggestion "to curse." See Willis, "Micah 2:6-8," 78–79, for various textual, lexical, and grammatical options. The scribal addition of the *waw matres lectionis* suggests the scribe intended to preserve the form as a *qal passive* from its previous defective form (see Andersen and Freedman, 309).

conquest (Jeremiah 28). For Hananiah, the tyranny would last for two years. For Jeremiah, it will last for seventy. The force and content of Jeremiah's debate resembles Micah's contest with the other prophets. As van der Woude clarifies, "In their [pseudo-prophets] opinion giving credence to Micah's prophecy of doom amounts to having no confidence in Yahweh and in what He does!"[41]

The speaking voice in the last question of v. 7 is ambiguous. The phrase reads, "Will not my words do good with the one walking uprightly?"[42] The phrase is syntactically parallel to the preceding phrases with its opening interrogative marker. Nevertheless, most commentators understand these words as Micah's.[43] If Micah's, the rhetorical force of the phrase relates to the positive character of God's word for those who walk uprightly, and this despite their character as words of doom. Moreover, Micah's call to arise and flee the comfort of their land (2:10) is a word of hope for those who have the ears to hear, to wit, those who walk uprightly. Those committing acts of injustice and the prophetic office that directly or indirectly lends them support are those without the ears to hear such an injunction. Their hopes are placed on one facet of their theological tradition to the exclusion of others.

On final analysis, however, the speaking voice of this phrase remains ambiguous. For it could also be Micah's rhetorical take on his opponents' sentiments. The grammatical parallel between the three questions leans in the direction of this reading, though this grammatical facet is not conclusive. On this reading, the pseudo-prophets' confidence is built on a faulty understanding of their own uprightness, marked by hope in Yhwh's eventual good on their behalf. They attend to religious and liturgical "righteousness" and the prophetic concerns of Micah cannot attenuate their overall "right walking." As Calvin comments, "We

---

[41] van der Woude, "Micah in Dispute," 28.
[42] The LXX renders "my words" with a 3ms pronominal suffix "his words." The more difficult MT is preferred.
[43] Ben Zvi links the 1cs pronominal suffix on "words" with the same suffix on "glory" in 2:9. This linkage clarifies whose words these are, viz., Yhwh (Ben Zvi, 59). The fluidity of Yhwh's voice and the prophet's voice is a standard and important trait of the prophetic literature.

indeed know that hypocrites ever hide themselves under their religious rites, and spread them forth as their shield whenever they are reproved. Hence the Prophet says, that they were not to be deemed the people of God for spending their labours on sacrifices, for they were at the same time robbers, and plundered innocent men" (Calvin, 203). The relating of Israel's liturgical life to her lived life remains a theme throughout the book (cf. 2:1-5; 6:1-8). Or in the words of Anglican Prayer Book tradition, "And, we beseech thee, give us that due sense of all they mercies, that our hearts may be unfeignedly thankful; and that we show for thy praise, not only with our lips, but in our lives."

Micah challenges the pseudo-prophets and their overly optimistic religious understanding in vv. 8-10. Their prophetic words are a sham with eyes blinded to the reality of the current and future religious situation. As the Book of the Twelve reveals, Yhwh is indeed gracious and patient—the leitmotif of the *middot* (attributes) of Ex 34:6-7 in the Twelve. Nevertheless, his patience has a limit and the dominant character trait of his mercy can and does elide into severity as the *middot* of Ex 34:6-7 attest. God's people are not "walking uprightly." In fact, they have become the enemies of God.

As readers might anticipate, interpretive difficulties present themselves in v. 8. If the verse begins with "Yesterday" or the more general "Recently" (אתמול) then the imperfective verb does not seem to work (*polel* יקומם). Moreover, the subject of the verb proves difficult to identify, especially if this particular verb is transitive elsewhere: "establish or erect something" (cf. Isa 44:26, 58:12, 61:4).[44] This lexical fact leads Sweeney to identify Yhwh as the subject of the verb with "my people" (עמי) as the object: "Recently, the Lord has established his people as an enemy" (Sweeney, 364). A reflexive sense of the verb is not beyond the pale, however, with the implied object as the subject: "My people have established themselves."[45] Also, the imperfective verbal form when linked with a temporal marker may, according to Waltke, have an

---

[44] See H. G. M. Williamson, "Marginalia in Micah," *VT* 47 (1997): 360.
[45] See *HALOT* and *DCH*, ad loc.

"incipient progressive force": "begin to rise up."[46] McKane's suggestion that the "my people" of v. 8 is incompatible with the "my people" of v. 9 is an overstatement. God's people as "my people" is predicated on those Micah seeks to protect and the nation as a whole in covenant infidelity (cf. 1:9; 2:3; 3:5; 6:3, 5).[47] Though other options are available, given the evidence it seems preferable to translate the first clause as follows: "Recently, my people have begun to establish themselves as an enemy."

Micah's rejoinder to the pseudo-prophets' message and religious discernment of the times comes as a jolt. The ringing comfort of the Zion traditions apart from covenant fidelity ("you are *my* people") is now a cracked bell. Micah again launches into a prophetic injunction against the injustices of "my people" against "my people" in vv. 8-9. The prophetic concerns of 2:1-5 appear again with a charge leveled against those in positions of power who exploit "my people." They take away the robes from those who in innocence are returning from war. A reference to garments given as a financial pledge may be present here (cf. Am 2:6). While the exact actions in v. 8 are difficult to identify, the sense is clear. Those seeking to live in peace, fleeing from war, are oppressed by those who have the power to do so. Women and children are driven from the comfort of their lives, simple as such comforts are: home, family, clothing, safety. These are not the actions of God's people as "my people." These are the actions of God's enemies.[48]

Micah levels his own prophetic word in v. 10 over against the pseudo-prophets who announce peace when there is none. Disgraces are

---

[46] Waltke, 117; cf. WO'C §31.3b. Waltke's grammatical window problematizes Andersen and Freedman's insistence that the imperfective form necessitates emendations to the clause as a whole (Andersen and Freedman, 315). Andersen and Freedman translate the clause as follows: "And yesterday (against) my people he stood up as an enemy." Though Waltke's readings seems the path of least resistance, Andersen and Freedman's reading has merit and is in accord with the overall sense of the text. "He stood up against my people as an enemy" or "My people have begun to establish themselves as an enemy" shares a similar semantic force.

[47] McKane, 84.

[48] The referent of "my splendor" is not clear. The possessive pronoun most likely refers to Yhwh. The term "splendor" (הדר) may have cultic connotations. Though human activity cannot diminish God's splendor, his glory can depart from a particular place (cf. Ezekiel, 10; see Andersen and Freedman, 322). For Waltke, "glory" is a metonymy for the physical benefits God gave to his people (Waltke, 120).

coming because of transgressions.⁴⁹ This is not a time or place for rest. This is a time to arise and flee. This is a time marked by travail or destruction, and the destruction is painful or grievous (וחבל נמרץ). What lends to the grievous nature of the destruction is the double entendre of the term "resting place" (מנוחה). This lexeme, located in the lexical field of "rest" (נוח ;שבת), is a technical term for the Promised Land. In most instances, the verb "rest" (נוח) emphasizes the cessation of wandering and the settling down in the Promised Land. Deuteronomy conceptually links the verbal form of "rest" (נוח) with the nominal form "Promised Land" (מנוחה). Promised "rest" is a cessation from wandering and an alleviation of threat from the surrounding enemies. This theme is picked up in the Deuteronomistic history as well with David in I Sam 26:19: "rest" (נוח) is the possibility of living in the promised land undisturbed. Yhwh identifies Zion as his habitation with the promised land (מנוחה) in parallel relation to his habitation (Ps 132:13ff.). Here, God's מנוחה is understood locally, as a place he inhabits. Micah's call to arise and flee is causally based on the reality that the promised land is no longer theirs. "This is not a promised land." The inheritance of the land as a covenantal blessing, as a gift of promise, is now forfeited.

The book of Hebrews makes the threat of lost rest or lost Sabbath central to its sermonic appeal (Heb 3:17-4:11).⁵⁰ Rest in Heb 4:1 is an eschatological concept. Here, the Numbers' narrative of entering into the land provides a proleptic or figural picture of the eschatological rest awaiting those in Christ. On this account, faith is understood as a confident expectation for future security based on the gospel promises of God. Hebrews frames the whole narrative in this eschatological vein. The warning, the perpetual plight threatening God's people, emanates from Heb 3:14: "For we share in Christ, if we hold on to our initial confidence/faith until the end."

Psalm 95 functions as an interpretive lens for the author to the Hebrews: "Today, if you hear his voice, do not harden your hearts" (Ps 95:11). The author displays this eschatological hermeneutic when he recognizes the Psalm as reorienting our conception of rest along eschatological lines. The promised rest of God for his people could not be achieved in the conquest of the land alone or Psalm 95 would become superfluous. Psalm 95's rereading of the Numbers' narrative highlights the symbolic/figural role this episode plays as an eschatological adumbration of a future day of coming rest. Hebrews follows this reading in

---

[49] The preposition בעבור would typically govern a noun. This leads to several suggestions to adjust the text accordingly (see BHS). Waltke provides a syntactical option with טמאה as an infinitive construct "with a nominal function" (Waltke, 121). It is "because of transgressions" that God's people are being destroyed/in travail.

[50] See especially, Jon Laansma, *I Will Give You Rest* (WUNT II/98; Tübingen: Mohr Siebeck, 1997).

suit. For the author to the Hebrews, Psalm 95's promised "Today" is in fact the eschatological "Today" shaped by the person and work of Jesus Christ, God's final word.

Genesis 2:2 and Ps 95:11 merge horizons so that God's seventh day of rest is itself an anticipation for a future reality, a reality made available Today because God's own space is a perpetual seventh day of rest or cessation: the location from which God providentially and redemptively governs his world. It is worth remembering the seventh day of creation is the crowning achievement of creation, not the sixth day. As von Rad reminds, "God's desisting from a continuation of his work of Creation and his resting are obviously to be taken and pondered as things in themselves."[51] God's rest or cessation exists now, alongside and in human history.

God's own sabbath rest, therefore, is the space prepared for those whose pilgrim existence awaits a future consummation and this awaiting takes place from the perspective of Today's assured promises. Thus, the warning: do not let the disobedience of unbelief keep you from entering the space of God's own cessation from his creative labors. The warning is real, as real for these first-century Christians as it was for those under the auspice of Psalm 95's backward look and future warning. The struggle, the pilgrimage, the holding fast with confidence to the saving promises of God entail the burden of faith and the promise of eventual cessation or rest. The loss of such rest in Micah's prophecy attests to the real dangers that remain for the people of God when the obedience of faith no longer marks the community of faith. Mere religiosity is no substitute for the obedience of faith in Micah and in Hebrews.

Micah resumes his invective against the pseudo-prophets in v. 11, rounding off this section with a lexical inclusio: "preach/ing" (נטף). In vv. 6-7 Micah rehearses what the pseudo-prophets are unwilling to preach. Now in v. 11, the prophet provides an outline of the kind of preaching more in tune with the pseudo-prophets' religious and social outlook. Their "going" is in a deceptive spirit. They lie.[52] The metaphoric reference to "wine" and "strong drink" gives a clear sense of the effect of the pseudo-prophets' preaching. Their preaching has an intoxicating effect on the hearers, dulling their senses and judgment regarding the reality of their precarious position and the truth of God's word. Micah's warning bears the marks of Paul's injunction to Timothy: "For the time is coming when people will not put up with sound doctrine, but having itching ears, they will accumulate for themselves teachers to suit their own desires, and will turn away from listening to the truth and wander

---

[51] von Rad, *OTT I*, 147 n.23.

[52] The sense of the first line of v. 11 is straightforward. The syntax, however, has some hurdles. The Masoretic accentuation separates "spirit" (רוח) and "deception" (שׁקר). Otherwise, a nominal hendiadys works handsomely as a modifier of "the man" walking: "a man walking in a deceiving spirit" (see Arnold and Choi, 148). The fact that "he lies" (כזב) is typically intransitive supports the linking together of "spirit" and "deception." Wolff understands "spirit" in the sense of "windy" or "unstable" (Wolff, 84). Mays references Hos 9:7 where "man of the spirit" is a title for the prophet, indicative of a prophet's ecstatic state.

away to myths. As for you, always be sober, endure suffering, do the work of an evangelist, carry out your ministry fully" (2 Tim 4:3-5). The conditional character of v. 11 runs as follows: *If* a person comes with a deceptive spirit, preaching intoxicating sermons that are a smoke screen to the truth, *then* this is the preaching of the people; this is the preaching "my people" listen to with open ears but with blind eyes to the truth.

Micah 2:12-13: Lead on, O King Eternal

With the last two verses of Micah 2, readers encounter the book's first words of hope. The exile spoken of in 2:6-11 is an antecedent reality from the viewpoint of 2:12-13. Salvific promises are given to Jacob that despite incurred and suffered judgment, Yhwh's saving arm is not too short that it cannot or will not redeem. Jeremias is right to describe these two verses as a contextual "surprise" (*überraschend*).[53] They catch the reader off guard given the preceding and forthcoming contextual themes. It may not come as a surprise, however, that the understanding of these verses are contested. Not all are persuaded by the hopeful character of these words.[54]

John Calvin and Marvin Sweeney, strange as the combination of those names might appear, concur on their reading of this text. Both believe the context of judgment leading to and following from these two verses is not broken. Rather than painting a picture of Jacob breaking free from their captivity and following after their Shepherd King, Calvin and Sweeney see Yhwh leading his people into their exile or judgment. While this reading is not followed by many in the secondary literature, it does have merit. The phrase "it will resound with people" (תהימנה מאדם) may carry a negative connotation: "they will be discomfited or confused with the

---

[53] Jeremias, 154.
[54] Ibn Ezra read these verses as the pseudo-prophets' continued words of false promise. Van der Woude also believes 2:12-13 continue as *Disputationswort*. He admits the case is harder to make for these verses, yet he remains convinced (van der Woude, "Micah in Dispute," 36-37.

people."⁵⁵ Also, the term "breaking out" (פרץ) tends to have a destructive sense (cf. 2 Ki 14:3; 2 Chr 25:23; Isa 5:5; Hos 4:2). The destructive sense of the term does not tip the interpretive balance because a positive reading of this text accounts for this sense: walls of captivity being torn down. Still, Sweeney believes the overall sense of this clause is the leading away from protective walls into the dangerous open.⁵⁶ For Sweeney, vv. 12-13 are the actualization of the "calamitous plan" Yhwh devices in 2:3.

Calvin agrees. After nodding in the direction of those who read this text as a word of hope, Calvin demurs, following in the interpretive direction of Sweeney. "[F]or I see not how the Prophet could pass so suddenly into a different strain."⁵⁷ In fairness to Calvin's logic, commentators who see this as a word of hope often do so on the basis of redaction-critical reconstruction.⁵⁸ They agree with Calvin regarding the disjointed nature of the text and provide a diachronic rationale for this disjunction. Such interpretive options are not available to Calvin nor can we assume Calvin would have taken them if offered.⁵⁹ Calvin's interpretive sensibilities range close to Sweeney's. It is the lexical character of the text that leads to his understanding of it.

> It follows, *Ascend shall a breaker before them*; that is, they shall be led in confusion; and the gate shall also be broken, that they may go forth together; for the passage would not be large enough, were they, as is usually done, to go forth in regular order; but the gates of cities shall be broken, that they may pass through in great numbers and in confusion.⁶⁰

---

⁵⁵ Sweeney, 366.
⁵⁶ Ibid.
⁵⁷ Calvin, 211.
⁵⁸ See Mays, 74.
⁵⁹ It is worth noting that van der Woude's understanding of these verses as Micah's retelling of the pseudo-prophets' message trades on the dating of this text. For those who see these words as words of hope, then the texts are typically dated to the exile. This redaction-critical instinct can be traced to Stade in the late nineteenth century. Van der Woude is not convinced 2:12-13 stems from the exile but is still operating with the standard redaction-critical logic. These are not words of hope. The warning of Benjamin Sommer addressed in the introduction speaks to this text as well. This text's dating should not trade on its positive or negative judgment. Such dating of texts becomes too brittle, or in Sommer's expression, a species of "pseudo-historicism."
⁶⁰ Calvin, 213.

For Calvin, like Sweeney, Yhwh is leading his people into the exile of his judgment.

While there is much to commend in the reading of Sweeney and Calvin, the scales do tip in the favor of a more positive or hope-filled interpretation. The language of "survivors" (שארית) suggests a positive construal with the view of judgment having already taken place.[61] It seems unlikely the survivors or remnant are targeted for further judgment: one recalls the redemptive movement of Isaiah into ch. 40. The imagery of a Shepherd also lends itself to the protective and redemptive character of vv. 12-13. The picture of a Shepherd gathering his lost flock—the survivors—and breaking them free from their captors seems more fitting than the Shepherd gathering his flock for judgment (cf. Ps 23).[62]

The language of "gathering" (קבץ), according to Wolff, "denotes the bringing together and reuniting of Israelites scattered across the nations (cf. Isa. 40:11; 43:5; Jer. 23:3; 31:10; Ezek. 34:13; Zeph. 3:19)."[63] These opening words of v. 12 are analogous to the words of comfort in Isa 40:1-2. They, like Isa 40:1-2, are untethered to a particular historical moment, though form-critical hypothesis are not wanting. Rather, these verses remain open to the future, witnessing to the character of God's covenant with his people. God's word of judgment remains open to his eventual word of comfort and redemption. He will surely gather Jacob, all of you. The awkward syntax "all of you" (כלך) speaks to the far-ranging scope of Yhwh's eventual salvation. He will gather them all.

---

[61] See Nogalski, 541.

[62] Andersen and Freedman believe it is possible that "Bozrah," the capital of Edom, may have been a center for sheep shearing (Andersen and Freedman, 339). Ben Zvi suggests that readers should not ignore the link between Edom and Babylon (cf. Ps 137:7-8; Ben Zvi, 66). Ben Zvi follows Wolff on this reading. Wolff believes the reference to Bozrah as a city speaks to the foreign captivity of God's people (Wolff, 85) and lends itself to furthering the redemptive character of these verses.

[63] Wolff, 85. See the discussion of יחד "together" as it was received by the Qumran community, i.e., God gathering the exiles into a community, in Richard Bauckham, *Gospel of Glory: Major Themes in Johannine Theology* (Grand Rapids: Baker Academic, 2015), 27. At the end of the day, Bauckham sees no connection between John's use of "one" and the Qumran community.

Admittedly, the last phrase of v. 12 is obscure. The following is a literal gloss: "they will be noisy or in turmoil from a man."[64] Understanding the phrase is a challenge: (1) a man (singular) may be responsible for the tumult of the community (causative reading); (2) the community may be in tumult because there is no man or men (privative reading); (3) the flock may be noisy because of men; in other words, the flock is bustling with the noise of people ready to break free; (4) "Man" or "Adam" might be a defective spelling of "Edom," especially given the reference to Bozrah in the preceding clause (Andersen and Freedman, 340). Waltke understands the phrase in its basic and straightforward sense. There is a tumult among the flock because of a lack of a man or a lack of a human shepherd.[65] This vacuum of leadership created by the judgment of God will in time be filled by that selfsame God. Waltke's reading fits the overall context well, especially given the character of Yhwh as providing the Shepherding they so desperately need and are without. Still, the phrase remains clouded in obscurity.

The metaphor of the Shepherd morphs in v. 13 to more militaristic imagery. The "one breaking through" will go up before them and lead them out of the gate, presumably the gate of their captivity.[66] The last line of v. 13 is striking. "Their king" travels before them, and Yhwh is at their head. "Their king" leading them from captivity is the unveiled identity of "the one breaking through" in the previous line. But how many figures are in view here? It is possible that two figures emerge in the last line: "their king" and Yhwh (cf. Hos 3:5). If two figures are in view, then the renewed Davidic figure as Yhwh's human agent and representative works in conjunction with the primary leadership of Yhwh, as the last clause intimates. Or one figure may be in view, namely, Yhwh. The poetic relation of the two lines may suggest the overlap of identities: "their King" is Yhwh. In the latter reading, Yhwh emerges in

---

[64] Andersen and Freedman describe the phrase "from a man" as "utterly baffling" (Andersen and Freedman, 340).

[65] Waltke, 135.

[66] Though see Mays, 75–76. The antecedent of בו could be "the gate." "And they will go out through it." Or the antecedent could be implied Yhwh. "And they will go out with him." Given the next clause, the latter is preferable.

these two verses as Israel's Shepherd, the One who breaks through, their King and Leader.[67]

Calvin's reading of this text is addressed above in conversation with Sweeney. Calvin demonstrates his willingness to swim in his own interpretive stream, though certain voices from the medieval Rabbinic stream of interpretation support his reading (e.g., Ibn Ezra). Whether Calvin is engaging this stream, we cannot be sure. Martin Luther's reading of these verses ranges closer to the reading on offer in this commentary. Micah is presenting his first words of redemptive hope on the far side of judgment. Or in Luther's terms, Micah moves from the "impious pontiffs and priests who were taking over everything" to "the eternal, spiritual kingdom of Christ" (Luther, 227). Luther's prophetic hermeneutic is on display in this text. The prophets, according to Luther, speak firstly about judgment and the external kingdom of Israel and then move to the spiritual and eternal kingdom of Christ. Luther's reading follows an empirical observation about ancient Israel, namely, the promises made and the encompassing language used therein—"all"—were never fully realized for the Kingdom of Israel per se. Luther's reading, in concert with most readings from this period of time, is supercessionist of the economic kind. The reference to Jacob is a reference to all humanity (Luther, 228). And while we may rightly challenge Luther's understanding of "Jacob" as a placeholder that in time becomes untethered to empirical Israel (cf. Rom 9-11), his relating of this text to the gospel is a step in the right interpretive direction.

From the vantage point of a two-testament canon, the blessing promised to all, the deliverance of Yhwh's people from judgment, and the forward glance of hope all relate substantially to the person and work of Jesus Christ. Jesus as "Son of God" relates on the level of shared substance to the history of the covenant between Yhwh and Israel, a history marked by election, rejection, and future promise. Luther's instinct to read 2:13 as a verse untethered to a particular historical phenomenon—viz., the Neo-Assyrian incursions of the late eighth century—allows him the space to understand the true captivity of Jacob and humanity: "Satan, sin, the Law, death, and the entire old Adam" (Luther, 229). For Luther, when Christ says, "Be of good cheer. I have overcome the world" (Jn 16:33), He speaks in terms of fulfilling the forward-looking hope of Mic 2:12-13. "In this way," claims Luther, "the Lord is our Head, that is, our Leader and Conqueror. As He Himself has broken through, so also we are going to break through through Him" (Luther, 229). Luther also follows the interpretive space created by the language of the last line of 2:13 when he claims, "From this text—although it appears to be vague—it is very clear that Christ is both God and man, that He died and rose again, that He ascended to the Father and now rules eternally, etc." (ibid.). As mentioned in the comments above, the relating of "their king" and Yhwh in 2:13 is open to a couple of syntactical options. Still, the reading Luther offers here with his Trinitarian metaphysic in full gear is a fair reading of the ontological space created by the verbal character of this text. In a sense, Luther has his syntactical cake and eats it too. "Their king" and Yhwh are indeed the same figure in essence but differ from one another in person. Therefore, "their king" and Yhwh are the same and distinct at the same time in Luther's reading, and such a reading is not at odds with the verbal character of the text in light of Scripture's theological metaphysic. After all, in a Christian hermeneutic the literal sense of Scripture resists separation from its Trinitarian subject matter.

---

[67] See Andersen and Freedman, 341. Yhwh as King on the far side of Israel's judgment is an important theme in the canonical shaping of the Psalter (cf. Pss 95-100).

3

Micah 3—Prophetic Recapitulation and Justification

Introduction

Micah 3 revisits the prophetic themes of ch. 2. The invectives against the disordered desires of the powerful and the self-serving nature of the prophetic office appear once again. The themes of ch. 3 are not new, though Micah's prophetic voice in ch. 3 draws on pointed metaphors that serve to enhance the malevolent character of the deeds performed by political and religious leaders. Though Micah has been fighting bare-knuckled from the beginning of this book, ch. 3 leaves little doubt that the gloves are on the ground. In a compare-and-contrast movement, Micah provides evidence for his own integrity and authenticity as Yhwh's prophet over against the pseudo-prophets introduced in ch. 2. He does so first and foremost by drawing attention to the effective power of the Spirit in his prophetic office. The evidence of the Spirit's power and presence is manifest in Micah's willingness to call a spade a spade regarding the transgressions of the political and religious halls of power. Eventually, Zion will come undone because of the failures of Judah's leadership. What was once the mountain of the Lord will in time become a wooded height whose memory boasts of a once thriving political and religious center.

3:1-4: Contra *injustice*

Chapter 3 begins with a contextual puzzle: "And or But I said" (ואמר). The puzzle relates to the kind of speech-reporting attested in the text's final form and the lack of surrounding narrative with which to link it. One would expect this kind of grammatical form (*wayyiqtol*) in a larger narrative context. Yet the current setting has none, despite whatever historical or diachronic contexts we might reconstruct. The answers to this puzzle are varied and sundry—from textual-critical suggestions that the text should be read as "And *he* said" (cf. LXX) to redaction-critical hypothesis that the phrase was added in order to link to the preceding material, to diachronic suggestions that the editors heisted this section from an original narrative when shaping Micah's corpus.[1] Whatever the diachronic history of this syntactical conundrum, there is little to no evidence that the current form of the text should be altered.[2]

As noted in the previous chapter, van der Woude understands 2:12-13 as a continuation of Micah's characterization of the pseudoprophets' message. Rather than a word of hope from Micah, 2:12-13 are false words of weal from those in prophetic office.[3] While having some contextual merit, this reading was found wanting. Nevertheless, van der Woude's suggestion that 3:1a begins with "And or But I said" as a contrast to the false words of hope outlined in ch. 2 provides a helpful handle on this grammatical form in its current literary setting. This reading does not rest on van der Woude's understanding of 2:12-13, reaching back as it does to the deceptive preaching practices on display in 2:11.[4] As 3:8 makes plain, Micah is unflinching when he compares and contrasts his own prophetic ministry and that of the pseudoprophets. In this contextual light, ch. 3 begins a sharp counterpoint to the message on offer by Micah's opponents in ch. 2.

---

[1] For an array of explanatory options, see John T. Willis, "A Note on ואמר in Micah 31," *ZAW* 80 (1969): 50–54. See also, Ben Zvi, 75–77; Wagenaar, *Judgement and Salvation*, 242–43. It is worth noting Wolff's redaction-critical suggestion that ואמר is a later insertion by Micah himself as early tradent of his own material. Wolff finds wanting Lescow's hypothesis that this section was originally included in a larger autobiographical narrative (*Ich-Bericht*) (Wolff, 95). Cf. Theodor Lescow, "Redaktionsgeschichtliche Analyse von Micha 1-5," *ZAW* 84 (1972): 47–48.

[2] The genetic history of the LXX's reading supports the move from the *wayyiqtol* form to the *weqatal*.

[3] Van der Woude, "Micah in Dispute," 36.

[4] Andersen and Freedman note this link, suggesting that it provides further evidence for 2:12-13 as a later interpolation (Andersen and Freedman, 349). See Jeremias, 160.

The connections between 2:12-13 and 3:1 tip and tuck into each other as, once again, "Jacob" and "Israel" come into view. As observed earlier, the eponyms "Jacob" and "Israel" emerge from the religious traditions of the preexilic world as the prophets of the eighth century applied them to the Southern Kingdom and its capital in Jerusalem.[5] Moreover, 2:13 ends with a hopeful and positive portrayal of Yhwh at the head (ראש) of the redemptive parade. The kingship of Yhwh as one who leads his people away from harm and into safety is set over against the "leaders of Jacob" (ראשי יעקב) in 3:1 who in point of fact lead in the opposition direction. These leaders are held to account as this section begins with summons "to hear" (שמע), a summons that resembles the beginning of Micah's prophecy (1:2) and indicates the coherence of chs 1–3.

These political leaders and the political office they hold remain in the abstract. Jeremias is right to note that the designations, "leaders" and "rulers," do not represent particular political offices per se.[6] Rather, for Jeremias, the language includes those in civil and military leadership. The description of the second group, "rulers of the house of Jacob," may have militaristic overtones. Elsewhere, the term "rulers" (קציני) indicates leadership in military matters (cf. Josh 10:24; Judg 11:6,11). In the Judges reference, the terms "leader" and "ruler" are applied together to Jephthah because of his role as military commander against the Ammonites.[7] While the term may refer to military leaders in this context, readers cannot be sure.[8]

---

[5] See Hillers, 43; Williamson, "Judah as Israel." Williamson does not believe the terminology "house of Jacob" is simply the application of an appellative for the Northern Kingdom to the Southern. In fact, such terminology is not found for the Northern Kingdom per se. Rather, the term indicates its source in the Zion traditions of the First Temple (Williamson, "Judah as Israel," 84–87). Williamson accounting of the evidence, scant as it is, differs from Jeremias who suggests that Israel language was applied to the Southern Kingdom after the fall of Samaria (Jeremias, 160).

[6] Jeremias, 160.

[7] See Sweeney, 369. See DCH, ad loc.

[8] Andersen and Freedman are hesitant to allow military connotations into this context. The military context of the term in Joshua and Judges is centuries removed from Isaiah and Micah. Andersen and Freedman see little reason to believe the term remains unchanged in referent during this period and most likely refers to political leaders with no necessary military overtones (Andersen and Freedman, 349).

Whatever the civil office occupied by these leaders, they were the gatekeepers of "justice" (מִשְׁפָּט).[9] It was within their civic responsibility to serve the cause of justice. Micah levels a heavy rhetorical question in their direction: "Should you not know justice?" Of all people, the leaders of Judah should know their responsibility and Yhwh's deep concern and care for justice. Their own leadership should be marked by this knowledge and concern.[10] Jeremias draws attention to an allusion to Hos 5:1 in Mic 3:1. In the Hosea text, the terms "house of Israel" and "justice" are brought together in service of an invective against the leaders of the Northern Kingdom. Jeremias points out that the sins of the Northern Kingdom have indeed reached the gates of Jerusalem as the Hosea text reaches now into a Judahite provenance (cf. 1:9).[11] Moreover, the description of these leaders in 3:2a as "haters of good and lovers of evil" harkens back to Am 5:15. There too the leaders of the Northern Kingdom are castigated for their lack of justice, the context of which breathes the same air as Micah 3. In Am 5:15, the leaders are called to a repentance marked by "loving good and hating evil." The opposite is the case for the Northern leaders in Amos's purview and the same sins of injustice in the ruling class have made their way to the Southern Kingdom as well (again, cf. 1:9).[12]

In Mic 3:1, the term "justice" is introduced for the first time, though the concerns of justice have been with readers since ch. 2. What is the "justice" civil leaders are to know? As mentioned before, much of the sociopolitical culture of Judah is based on the hierarchy of a Zion theology with Yhwh at the apex moving down to religious and political

---

[9] Readers may recall Jethro's advice to Moses regarding shared leadership in the judicial load of ancient Israel (Exodus 18). These leaders, as archetypes of the ideal leaders of Israel, were to be "able men among all the people, men who fear God, are trustworthy, and hate dishonest gain" (Ex 18:21).

[10] Waltke claims that "to know" (יָדַע) entails both intellectual and emotional knowledge. Citing Renaud, Waltke understands this "knowledge" to include personal concern and sympathy for those the law is meant to protect and not mere intellectualism in the application of the law (Waltke, 155).

[11] Jeremias, 160. Jeremias also draws attention to Hosea's preference for the term "to know" (*kennen*) and its presence here in Micah for further support of the intertextual allusion. See also, Andersen and Freedman, 351.

[12] See Nogalski, 546.

leaders and then to the common person. A chain of beneficence from top downs holds the sociopolitical/ethical culture in order and is based on the election and redemption of Israel by the loving initiative of Israel's God. This redemptive and electing logic and order will come into view again in Mic 6:1-8. Those in whose hands "justice" is held have forgotten this order. They lack knowledge. The ruling class, as explained by Andersen and Freedman, "had executive function, and his responsibilities were to secure the right for the offended party by making a just decision and by seeing that it was carried out."[13] These adjudicatory responsibilities should be based on knowledge, presumably knowledge of Torah and legal traditions. Yet, as Micah 6:1-8 will make plain, more than intellectual knowledge is in view here. This legal knowledge includes a theological rationale for just judgments, to wit, the electing and covenantal love of Yhwh for Israel.

The situation is worse, however, than a broken judicial system. The gatekeepers of justice are its worst offenders. The "haters of good and lovers of evil" are themselves purporting gross acts of injustice (cf. Ezek 34:2-3).[14] The scene is indeed gross, and Micah details a shocking metaphor to make his point. As more recent metaphor theory has made us aware, metaphors provide access to reality. Rather than mere rhetorical ornaments, metaphors are avenues by which a thing is discovered and without which the fullness of the thing remains attenuate.[15] It is one thing to say the leaders of Judah no longer broker justice and, in fact, purport acts of injustice themselves. Such a proposition claim is true and indicting, even if tame. It is quite another thing to say the following: "[They] tear the skin off my people, and the flesh off their bones; who eat the flesh of my people, flay their skin off them, break their bones in pieces, and chop them up like meat in a

---

[13] Andersen and Freedman, 351.
[14] Isaiah portrays the true successor of David as one who would establish the monarchy with "righteousness and justice" (Isa 16:5). Jeremiah speaks of Josiah in the same vein because of his concern for the poor and needy (Jer 22:15-16). See Moshe Weinfeld, *Deuteronomy and Deuteronomic School* (Winona Lake: Eisenbrauns, 1992), 155.
[15] Notably, George Lakoff and Mark Johnson, *Metaphors We Live By* (Chicago: University of Chicago Press, 2003). See also, Charles Taylor, *The Language Animal: The Full Shape of the Human Linguistic Capacity* (Cambridge: Belknap Press, 2016), 156–64.

kettle, like flesh in a caldron" (Mic 3:2b-3).[16] Micah's metaphor provides readers with a deeper sense of the reality of injustice. The metaphor evokes cruelty and indifference, a kind of banality of evil, to borrow a phrase from Hannah Arendt. Instead of protecting "my people," the civil leaders are eating them.

There are consequences to such cruelty and indifference. Verse 4 reveals the conditional character of this unit. Since the actions of vv. 1-3 remain, "then" (אז) the following divine response will occur.[17] Yhwh will not answer them when they "cry out" (זעק) to him. It was Israel's "cry" of oppression that drove Yhwh to redemptive action in Exodus (3:7). The remembrance of their ancient cry of oppression was the shared and lived memory meant to fuel the just actions of Judah's civil leaders.[18] Micah seems to play here on the ironic twist of fate for Judah's leaders, much like he does in Mic 2:1-3. They pay no heed to the oppressed and their cries for justice. So too Yhwh will not listen to them when they cry out to him, when they seek an answer in their moment of need.

Moreover, Yhwh will hide his face from them. Here the prophet draws from a rich and frightening Old Testament theme: the hidden face of God.[19] God hiding his face is the reversal of the life-giving promise of the Aaronic blessing (Num 6:24-26). We know from the Aaronic blessing of Number 6 that the shining face of God is Israel's only hope of security and peace. The shining face of God is our only place of safety or in the words of the Anglican Prayer Book tradition: "Only in Thee can we live in safety."

---

[16] The term for "tear" in 3:2b is the same for "stealing" in 2:2 (גזל). The linguistic layers here play into Micah's metaphor and real concern.

[17] Vv. 1-3 are a suppressed protasis made clear with the apodosis of v. 4 (see *HALOT*, ad loc).

[18] Wolterstorff makes the following claim: "The idea is that those with social power in Israel are to render justice to the vulnerable bottom ones *as a public remembrance, as a memorial,* of Yahweh's deliverance of Israel from Egypt" (Nicholas Wolterstorff, *Justice: Rights and Wrongs* [Princeton: Princeton University Press, 2008], 80); see also Gordon McConville, "Biblical Law and Human Formation," *Political Theology* 14 (2013): 633. He states, "The people's former condition as impoverished slaves who depended on deliverance by a compassionate God should govern their attitude both to themselves and to the poor among them (Deut. 24:18)."

[19] Cf. Deut 31:17, 18; 33:20; Isa 8:17; 54:8; 64:5 (64:4 MT); Jer 33:5; Ezek 39:23, 24, 29; Pss 13:1 (13:2 MT); 22:25; 27:9; 30:7 (30:8 MT); 69:17 (69:18 MT); 88:14 (88:15 MT); 102:2 (102:3 MT); 143:7; Job 13:24; 34:29. See Sweeney, 370.

Safety from what? Safety from ourselves. Safety from the Evil One. Safety from God. Hans Urs von Balthasar put the matter clearly. "When God hides his face everything created dies away, and when he again turns his face towards creation everything awakens to new life.[20]" The restoration of all things entails the turning of God's face toward his people (cf. Ps 80). The future moment Micah prophecies—"that time" (בעת ההיא)—is a moment of divine concealment, divine hiding. The day of the Lord in Mic 3:1-4 shares in the same imagery of the day of the Lord in Mic 2:3. This day is a day of disaster. As announced in Micah 1, so too the theme continues here in ch. 3 regarding the location of Judah's culpability. All of these harrowing moments will occur because of the evil deeds of Judah's leadership class. Judah's leaders had forgotten, and their forgetting was no benign oversight. The entirety of Judah's civil stability would come undone because of it.

> In Nicholas Wolterstorff's *Justice: Rights and Wrongs*, he draws attention to a distinction made by philosophers between two kinds of justice: *distributive/commutative* and *rectifying/corrective*.[21] The latter category speaks to the proper ordering of society by various civil and legal entities. *Rectifying justice* becomes necessary when *distributive justice* has broken down.[22] Wolterstorff's interest is to provide a philosophical and theological account for the primacy of *distributive/commutative justice* or what he refers to as *primary justice*. Justice understood in this way is independent of *rectifying justice* and speaks to the inherent rights of human beings as human beings. Those who attenuate this category in favor of *rectifying justice* often do so because, in their view, *distributive justice* is a modern phenomenon whose origins can be traced to the rise of Enlightenment ideals in the seventeenth century.[23] Wolterstorff finds this narrative wanting and makes his case for the primacy of *primary justice*, tracing its roots to the Hebrew Scriptures and New Testament. As one would expect, Wolterstorff gives ample attention to the prophets in his account of *primary justice* in the Old Testament. When he does so, Wolterstorff enters into an appreciative debate with Oliver O'Donovan's *The Desire of Nations*.[24] For O'Donovan, the Old Testament concept of justice (*mishpat*) is first and foremost *rectifying justice*.[25] Justice on this account is the making right of wrongs. And while this element is certainly present in the Old Testament concept of justice—Micah 3 is a case in point—Wolterstorff believes O'Donovan's thesis is a reduction. While affirming the etymological roots of *mishpat* as juridical in nature,

---

[20] Hans Urs von Balthasar, *The Glory of the Lord: A Theological Aesthetics*, Vol. VI, (trans. B. McNeil and E. Leiva-Merikakis; ed. J. Riches; Edinburgh: T&T Clark, 1991), 69.
[21] Wolterstorff, *Justice*, ix.
[22] Ibid.
[23] Ibid., xii.
[24] See the critical interaction between O'Donovan and Wolterstorff regarding the language of "rights" or "right" or justice as inherent justice or right order. Oliver O'Donovan, "The Language of Rights and Conceptual History," *JRE* 37 (2009): 193–207; Nicholas Wolterstorff, "Justice as Inherent Rights: A Response to My Commentators," *JRE* 37 (2009): 261–79.
[25] Ibid., 68–75.

Wolterstorff wonders if O'Donovan's understanding of the term is right to leave it there. Wolterstorff concludes his engagement with O'Donovan by engaging texts where *mishpat* has a *primary* sense as well that goes beyond those responsible for juridical judgments (e.g., Mic 6:8). Wolterstorff concludes, "My conclusion is that just as we use our word 'justice' to speak of both primary and rectifying justice, so Israel used its word "*mishpat*" to speak of both. Israel's writers move seamlessly back and forth between these two applications of the term, as we do. A second conclusion, more important because it goes beyond linguistic usage, is that one cannot think in terms of rectifying justice unless one recognizes the existence of primary justice and injustice."[26] Micah 3:1-3 operates well in the distinctions Wolterstorff provides. The legal mechanisms of rectifying justice given to those in positions of civil leadership are, as mentioned above, built on a Zion theology moving down from Yhwh at the apex to the common person. Yhwh's beneficence flows to all those under his protection as his face turns to shine on them. When Micah describes the cannibalistic patterns of Judah's leaders, he identifies those fileted as "my people." Such an appellation speaks to the necessity of *primary justice* as the governing concern of *rectifying justice*. Wrongs are to be righted because those under the purview of Judah's leadership are not their people but Yhwh's.

3:5-8: Prophetic comparing and contrasting or against the prophets

The movement of ch. 3 mirrors ch. 2—from civil leaders/the powerful to the corrupt prophetic office. After Micah addresses the crooked leaders in vv. 1-4, he then turns his attention once again to the prophets in vv. 5-8. Micah describes these prophets as "those who lead astray my people" (המתעים את־עמי). Readers observed a species of their preaching in 2:11, marked as it was by lies and deception with the result of a swooning audience. Once again, Micah describes their prophecies as causing "my people" to go into error. The term "leading astray" or "wandering" can also refer to a drunken stupor (cf. Isa 28:7). They are being misled and intoxicated by the prophets into error. The prophets' agency was intended to provide divine guidance, yet they abandon this vocational priority for baser things. Amos also renders his judgment against Judah because their lies "lead them astray" (cf. Hos 4:2). Jeremiah's jeremiad against the Shepherds and Prophets in Jeremiah 23 speaks repeatedly of their actions "leading astray" God's people (Jer 23:13-32). To lead God's people into error is a serious charge. As Calvin

[26] Ibid., 75.

remarks on this unit, "For anyone who flatters sinners and allows them to sleep in their filth, while at the same time encouraging them to believe that all is well, is a seducer of souls."[27] Micah charges the professional prophets of Judah as those who lead into error and whose concerns center on self-interest rather than divine address.

"[M]oney talks louder than God."[28] Mays characterizes the situation well when he describes the prophets in this way. It should be noted that payment for prophetic services rendered or a particular professional class of prophets is not Micah's explicit concern here.[29] Micah's stated concern is the malleable state of the prophets' message. The jejune translation "when they have something to eat" does get at the quid pro quo nature of the prophets' enterprise. When the prophets have something to eat or are paid properly for their services, then they give the kind of message the one paying wishes to hear: "Peace!"

The language, however, suggests a more sinister scene. As Anderson and Freedman observe, "to bite" (נשׁך) never refers to mere "mastication."[30] "Biting" carries with it the necessary image of teeth, rendering the activity of the prophets as snake-like in nature (cf. Gen 49:17; Num 21:8ff.).[31] The malleable nature of their message according to payment rendered and the desired result of the ones paying is biting and deadly. Readers would be remiss to forget the cannibalistic imagery of the leaders in the previous verses. In their efforts to maximize their profit margins, the prophets lead the people astray and show their fangs all along the way. Therefore, as long as the prophets are properly paid, they are happy to render the desired results for those who pay.

The opposite scenario is the case as well. When they do not have something in their mouth, they "sanctify war against him." This phrase is somewhat obscure, though we find the phraseology elsewhere to

---

[27] Calvin, *Sermons*, 155.
[28] Mays, 83.
[29] Cf. I Sam 9:6-10; Am 7:12. See Mays, 83; Sweeney, 371.
[30] Andersen and Freedman, 362.
[31] See *HALOT*, ad loc.

speak of preparations for war (Jer 6:4; Joel 4:9). Micah may have his tongue in his cheek at this moment. Those responsible for holy or sanctified actions in fidelity to Yhwh's word are making personal holy wars against those unwilling or unable to meet their demands. Wolff points out that these false prophets are willing to preach a message of doom as well.[32] In other words, they are not prophets of weal alone. Nevertheless, the content of their message—doom or salvation—rests on their own desired ends not on the will of Yhwh.

As readers descend their way into the heart of Dante's *Inferno*, they arrive at the eighth and next to last circle of hell: the Malebolge (evil ditches). Dante designates the eighth circle for the Fraudulent and Malicious. As this circle descends lower and lower, Dante and Virgil have to navigate a series of ditches (Bolgia), with each ditch assigned to a particular class of Fraudulent and Malicious persons. Readers in Dante's day, as in ours, are stunned with the people they find in this lowest region of hell, especially in the third ditch (Canto XIX). Therein Dante and Virgil encounter the Simoniacs, or "sellers of ecclesiastical favors and offices."[33] Prue Shaw describes Simoniacs with the following: "Those guilty of this sin are men of the church (priests, friars, cardinals, popes) who buy and sell things of the spirit (church sacraments and ministries), perverting their true meaning and value by treating them as an opportunity for personal material enrichment."[34] The term "Simoniac" stems from the narrative of Simon Magus and his offering of money to Peter for spiritual gifts (Acts 8:9-24). Peter rebukes Simon Magus for his offering and calls him to repentance for his actions.

> O Simon Magus! O you wretched crew
> who follow him, pandering silver and gold
> the things of God which should be wedded to
> love and righteousness! (Canto XIX, 1-4)

When Dante and Virgil descend into the third Bolgia, an arresting and awful scene opens before them. The ditch is speckled with holes, and from the holes the legs and feet of sinners are protruding as their bodies are hidden upside down. Shaw describes the scene: "As flames lick over the sinners' feet, they kick to alleviate the pain. The scene is as surreal and disturbing as any Dante has yet encountered."[35] As Dante approaches, he observes one set of protruding feet as in more agony than others. Dante presses closer to identify the man. When asked for his identity, the suffering man believes his questioner is Boniface, the pope. But it is not Boniface; it is Dante. When the man finally identifies himself, he does so with the following line: "that the Great Mantle was once hung upon me."[36] The suffering man was the previous pope, Pope Nicholas III. He then describes what is below him in the hole, namely, the previous popes who came before him, each one displacing the previous as they descend lower into the rocks.

---

[32] Wolff, 103.
[33] Dante Alighieri, *The Divine Comedy: The Inferno, The Purgatorio, and the Paradiso* (trans. J. Ciardi; New York: New American Library, 2003), 149.
[34] Prue Shaw, *Reading Dante: From Here to Eternity* (New York: Liveright Publishing Corporation, 2014), 43.
[35] Ibid., 44.
[36] Dante, *Divine Comedy*, 151 (Canto XIX, 66).

Ah Constantine, what evil marked the hour—
not of your conversion, but of the fee
the first rich Father took from you in dower! (Canto XIX, 109–11).

Dante is, of course, a poet and political writer whose portrayals are not absent his own political and personal vendettas. Nevertheless, the charge of simony from Dante in the thirteenth century shares in the material concern of Micah's prophetic worry in ch. 3. Similarly, much of the indulgence controversy in the late fifteenth and early sixteenth centuries had simony as the primary concern.[37] Again, payment for religious services rendered do not come under the prophet's critical scrutiny. As Paul reminds us, "muzzle not the ox" (1 Cor 9:9). Rather, the concern is the character of those in religious office whose ministry no longer operates under the authority of God and his authoritative word but under the auspices of personal self-interest and avarice.

As the leaders of vv. 1-4 had consequences commensurate with their actions, so too do the prophets in vv. 5-8. "Therefore" (לכן) connects v. 5 to vv. 6-7. Because of their simony, their visions and divinations will grow dark. The daytime will become nighttime as the sun sets on them. The exact referent of the metaphors here is open to debate. Sweeney believes Micah is being ironic because dreams and visions often took place at night or during a dream-like state (cf. 1 Samuel 3; Genesis 15).[38] Isaiah makes use of similar imagery to describe God's judgment against the soothsayers and diviners operating outside of Yhwh's word (Isa 8:22). On this reading, which appears as the standard one, the diviners and seers are thrown into confusion, into darkness and night, because their visions will cease.[39]

Andersen and Freedman offer another reading where the metaphors "darkness" and "setting sun" are apocalyptic in nature (cf. Ezek 32:7-8; Joel 2:10; Am 5:18-20; Zeph 1:15). In other words, Micah is not claiming that their visions will dry up, for as Andersen and Freedman remark, a diviner or seer could concoct a vision at any time with their mantric instruments. Remember, these figures are for hire. "Their system could never fail."[40] Rather, the "sun setting in the daytime" speaks of the ensuing

---

[37] See Scott H. Hendrix, *Martin Luther: Visionary Reformer* (New Haven: Yale University Press, 2015), chs 5–7; Heiko A. Oberman, *Luther: Man Between God and the Devil* (New Haven: Yale University Press, 2006), 187–92. Oberman is especially helpful, given the discussion of Dante above, for placing Luther's concerns about papal/clergy abuse in a medieval context. Luther's ideas did not emerge in a vacuum.
[38] Sweeney, 371–72.
[39] See Mays, 84.
[40] Andersen and Freedman, 373.

judgment God will unleash on Judah. Their shame in v. 7 relates to the failure of their prophetic office (cf. Jer 28:9). Their intoxicating message of peace was in fact a deception. Andersen and Freedman's reading should not be ruled out, though the last line of v. 7 provides support for the standard reading: "for there is no answer from God." The cause of their shame is the lack of divine revelation. God no longer speaks. The famine Amos warned of, a famine of the Word of God, was upon them (Am 8:11). The famine of God's Word leads these prophets to shame and the covering of their mouths (literally, "moustache"). Mouth covering was a sign of public grief (Ezek 24:17-22). The visible action was also associated with unclean lepers (Lev 13:45).[41] The force of their shame is public and a visible scourge to the community. Whatever religious power they levied before the darkness is now a faint memory for the prophets. Now they are a public embarrassment who have nothing to say.

Micah sets his own prophetic ministry in sharp distinction from the pseudo-prophets and their self-serving vocational objectives (v. 8). The opening word of Micah's retort indicates this antithesis and the sharp rhetoric he is using (אולם; cf. Job 2:5). Unlike the pseudo-prophets, Micah is filled with a strength that manifests itself through his courage to bring an unpopular and hard message (cf. Isa 58:1). Micah's message is not for hire, making Micah here and Peter in Acts 8 cobelligerents against those who believe God's Word and power can be bought. Yet, Micah's strength is derivative strength. It does not flow first and foremost from an internal quality of his being. Micah's strength and power come from the Holy Spirit.

The grammar of v. 8 is a challenge because it appears as if Micah is filled with two objects: strength, justice, and might and the Holy Spirit.[42] Despite the difficult grammar, readers do well to hold these two

---

[41] Waltke cites Allan who notes the irony that the covering of their mouths may also speak to the fact that they have nothing to say (Waltke, 165).

[42] Andersen and Freedman do well to challenge the editors of the BHS who dismiss the clause "with the Holy Spirit" because it breaks up the triad "strength, justice, and might" (Andersen and Freedman, 376). The verb "to fill" (מלא) is *qal*, rendering the phrase more stative in sense. If a *piel*, then the Spirit could be viewed as the filling agent, but the *qal* form may be predicated on the one filled or the filling substance. According to Andersen and Freedman, Yhwh should be viewed as the unstated filling agent (ibid., 377).

together. Micah's strength, justice, and might derive from his being filled with the Holy Spirit. Like the promise of Isa 40:25-31, Yhwh provides strength and power to the weary because of the greatness of His might (Isa 40:26). It is a pointed and direct claim for Micah to place his prophetic ministry in contradistinction from the civil and religious leaders he has just castigated in vv. 1-7. Over against the civil leaders, Micah's ministry is marked by "justice" (מִשְׁפָּט), and readers of the prophets know that Yhwh loves justice (cf. Isa 61:8). Moreover and *contra* the pseudo-prophets, Micah is willing and enabled to announce to the leaders of Judah their sin and their revolt against Yhwh. Micah's message is not his own. It is forever stamped as "the word of Yhwh" that has come to him (Mic 1:1).

In his reading of the debate between Jeremiah and Hananiah (Jeremiah 27), Childs makes clear that the problem of the false prophets was not one of "hermeneutics."[43] Or put in other terms, the challenge of true prophecy was not a psychological one but a theocentric challenge. "What is God's purpose?"[44] This is the prophetic question. Jeremiah remains open to God changing his stated purpose, but such a change will stem from God's revelation of his purposes and not a hermeneutical or psychological strategy of the prophet (Jer 28:6-9). Childs concludes, "This passage has nothing at all to do with Jeremiah's ability to time his prophecy correctly, nor does he differ with Hananiah merely in the practice of hermeneutics. No, the content of Hananiah's message is wrong ... The test of the truth lies in God who makes known his will through revelation."[45] So too with Micah. His prophetic office, marked as it is by strength, justice, and might, bears the marks of the power and filling of the Holy Spirit. "We can do nothing to advance the praise of God," Calvin reminds, "unless God grants us, first of all, the grace to do it."[46] Micah's message rings with authenticity because Micah is empowered and enabled by Yhwh and His Spirit.

---

[43] Brevard Childs, *Old Testament Theology in a Canonical Context* (Philadelphia: Fortress Press, 1989), 136–37.
[44] Ibid., 139.
[45] Ibid.
[46] Calvin, *Sermons*, 165.

For Micah, his being filled with justice flows from the power of the Spirit. Being filled with the Spirit and being given to primary and rectifying justice, to use Wolterstorff's terminology, are related to each other as cause and effect. The one flows necessarily into the other. Todd Billings speaks of the *duplex gratia* in Calvin's theology. On Calvin's account, justification and sanctification for the Christian both flow from the grace given in Christ. And this grace is made effective by the agency of the Holy Spirit. Participation in Christ is a participation in His righteousness as passive gift and the activity of new life in Him. As Billings summarizes,

> The new life received in Christ by the Spirit bears fruit in acts of justice in our lives, yet the new life is a gift. In ourselves, we are not the source of this good—our actions of justice are not the good news of the gospel. Rather, our actions that display love of God and neighbor reflect the gift of new life received in Christ through the Spirit.[47]

Reading this theological account onto Mic 3:8 is a figural reading of the tropological kind. There are certainly discontinuities between the prophetic office and Christian existence that need to be taken into account.[48] Still, the logic with which Micah operates does properly order the theological relation between human agency and the Spirit's effectual work. Faithful acts of justice require the antecedent work of the Spirit's power and effectual presence.

3:9-12: Trickle down divine displeasure

The final unit of ch. 3 is Janus-faced, looking back to conclude chs 1–3—observe the call to "hear" (שמע) at 3:9 as a linguistic inclusio with 1:2—and opening up to the promise of restoration in the following chapter.[49] Jerusalem's destruction will come. Yet in the synchronic form of the book, destruction is not Yhwh's final word (4:1-5). A silver lining of hope outlines the devastating promises of 3:9-12, though the cloud of forthcoming destruction looms large.

Again, the prophetic word takes into view the civil and religious leaders spoken of in the early verses of the chapter. Micah castigates Judah's "heads" and "rulers." We learned in vv. 1-3 of the cannibalizing activities of Judah's civil leaders. Those in whose hands the responsibility for justice rests are in fact its chief offenders. Micah

---

[47] J. Todd Billings, *Union with Christ: Reframing Theology and Ministry for the Church* (Grand Rapids: Baker Academic, 2011), 108.
[48] See Childs, *Old Testament Theology*, 137.
[49] See Jean M. Vincent, "Michas Gerichtswort gegen Zion (3,12) in seinem Kontext," *ZThK* 83 (1986): 169.

leans into these offenders as he describes them as *haters of justice* and *benders of uprightness* (3:9b; cf. Am 5:10). As Jeremias observes, vv. 9b-11 do not advance Micah's message (*Botschaft*) per se (Jeremias, 165). Readers already have a clear picture of the injustice policies and actions of the political and religious leaders of Judah. Rather, the characterization of the addressees comes more fully into view along with the concretization of their unjust acts (Jeremias, 165). The political and religious leaders are unjust in the following concrete ways: (1) they mistreat people; (2) they accept bribes; and (3) they affect a pious self-security.[50]

Micah describes the civic leader's mistreatment in relation to the building programs in Judah's capital: Zion. Zion and Zion-related themes run through this subunit, providing the location for Micah's invective and the misguided conceptual/theological framework of the addressees affected piety. Zion is built with blood.[51] This similar phraseology is found in Hab 2:12 and in Jeremiah's diatribe against Jehoiakim's oppressive building campaign (Jer 22:13-17). The term "bloodshed" or "built with blood" does not necessitate a literal flow of blood, though such cannot be ruled out. Rather, as Jeremias observes, the term "bloodshed" (*Blutschuld*) speaks of serious guilt (*schwerste Schuld*; Jeremias, 165). The shedding of blood is an offense against God who alone has the authority to give life ("blood") and take it away.[52]

---

[50] See Wolff, 106.
[51] The phrase in the MT contains a singular participle, "the one building" (בנה). If this is the case, then Micah has a particular figure in view, perhaps the unnamed king (see n. 49). The LXX renders the phrase with a plural participle, as do most translations. Andersen and Freedman are right to identify this move as an attempt to harmonize with the more difficult singular participle preferred. Jeremias understands the singular form of Hab 2:12 to have influenced Micah's phraseology (Jeremias, 165). Waltke makes a case for understanding "to build" (בנה) as an infinitive absolute in epexegetical relation to the verbs of v. 9. Waltke has his misgivings about "to build" as a participle because it would require the definite article if functioning as a substantive in a relative clause (Waltke, 178). If an infinitive absolute, then the subject is not a singular king per se but the general "heads" and "rulers" identified in v. 9. Waltke's suggestion is appealing and avoids speculating about the text's corruption.
[52] Jeremias, 165.

The historically particular events Micah has in view are not made clear.[53] Again, with Ben Zvi, the final form of the book leaves these events nondescript and thus open to future events in mimetic relation to them. Jeremias suggests the intertextual relation between Mic 2:10 and Hab 2:12 encourages the reciprocal reading of the two texts. "Bloodshed" in Mic 2:10 should be read in light of the various acts of "bloodshed" described in the near context of Hab 2:12 (2:6ff).[54] The civic leaders are not the only leaders in view, however. The prophets and, in their first appearance in Micah, the priests are all placed on level plain of leadership and culpability.

The civil leaders offer judgments according to a price. Prophets offer visions for hire, presumably with the outcome of the visions shaped according to the level of remuneration. Priests, whom Wolff describes as the stewards of the Torah (cf. Deut 33:10; Hos 4:6), adjust their sacred teachings in light of the lining of their pockets.[55] While their spheres of leadership and vocational responsibilities differ from one another in certain measures, the entirety of the political and religious spheres of leadership are guilty of *bribery* (cf. Isa 1:23; 5:23). When Jerusalem falls, and in time it will (cf. Jer 26:18), the responsibility will rest on the shoulders of these guilty leaders. Their sacred responsibilities can be bought.

Perhaps the most disconcerting charge Micah levels against the civic and religious leaders has to do with their feigned piety and religious confidence (v. 11b). While taking bribes, offending Yhwh's care for justice, and compromising their own divine office, they continue in

---

[53] Mays (89), et al. (106–07), see Micah the lowlander in conflict with the building programs of Hezekiah. The historical and biblical records attest to his aggressive building program. There is support for this understanding in Jer 26:18-19. See Ben Zvi who claims that not mentioning the king by name is standard practice in prophetic literature. This text is a case in point (Ben Zvi, 86–87). Ben Zvi also provides a rationale for why post-monarchic scribes might hesitate to name the king in the formation of the literature (ibid.). The quick move to identify Hezekiah as the culprit causes pause, though it is not beyond the pale. Andersen and Freedman provide compelling evidence for why Ahaz, also named in the superscription, is a more fitting historical referent (Andersen and Freedman, 382–83). Nevertheless, with Waltke from a grammatical standpoint and Ben Zvi from a redaction-critical standpoint, identifying a particular king as the historical referent of the building program appears unnecessary given the text's final literary form.

[54] Jeremias, 165.

[55] Wolff, 107. The verb "to teach" (ירה) relates to *Torah* and identifies the teaching of the priests with the interpretation and application of *Torah*.

liturgical acts of worship and lean confidently on their half-baked Zion theology. "Surely the Lord is with us!" Jeremiah chides such liturgical shortsightedness in his temple sermon. "Do not say, this is the temple of the Lord, the temple of the Lord, the temple of the Lord" (Jer 7:4). Liturgical language associated with temple worship became disassociated with the claims of the living God on their lives and actions.

The Zion theology of the civil and religious leaders was a feeble crutch and a blinding veil to the whole of Yhwh's covenantal claims on his people.[56] As Wolterstorff summarizes,

> The prophetic critique of the cult is grounded in the conviction that the point of the liturgy is to give symbolic expression to the commitment of our lives to God. The point of liturgy is not the performance of certain self-contained actions such as confession and praise, no matter how sincere and appropriate those actions … Liturgy is for giving voice to life oriented toward God. This we learn from the prophetic insistence that the words and gestures without the life disgust God.[57]

Micah joins the prophetic chorus as he speaks against religion or liturgy divorced from the totality of a worshipping life. For as Micah understands the situation, overweening religious confidence bred an ethical callousness among Judah's leadership class. With a biblical theological gesture, Wolff ends his comments on 3:9-12 with a reference to Jesus's disconcerting saying in Matt 7:21-23:

> Not everyone who says to me, "Lord, Lord," will enter the kingdom of heaven, but only the one who does the will of my Father in heaven. On that day many will say to me, "Lord, Lord, did we not prophesy in

---

[56] Steck makes the following interpretive claims: "[I]n the thematic unit of Mic 3:9-12, circulating around Zion/Jerusalem, the formulation that YHWH is in the midst (beqereb) of the inhabitants of Zion (3:11) points to the concept of the protective presence of YHWH on Zion (cf. the corresponding formulation and the context Ps 46:6; Jer 14:9; and Zeph 3:15,17)." Odil Steck, *Old Testament Exegesis*, 130 n. 159. On Zion in Isaiah and Micah, see especially Gerhard von Rad, *OTT II*, 155–69.

[57] Nicholas Wolterstorff, *Hearing the Call: Liturgy Justice Church and World* (ed. M. R. Gornik and G. Thompson; Grand Rapids: Eerdmans, 2011), 52–53. See also, R. W. L. Moberly, "'In God We Trust'?: The Challenge of the Prophets," *Ex Auditu* 24 (2008): 18–33.

your name, and cast out demons in your name, and do many deeds of power in your name?" Then I will declare to them, "I never knew you; go away from me, you evildoers."[58]

The interpretive instinct to highlight certain quarters of the canonical witness to the exclusion of others has a long history in the Church's interpretive tradition. Such instincts are analogous to the confident claims of Judah's rulers regarding Zion's indestructability. To use a modern, Christian colloquialism, they had Bible verses on their side (e.g., Pss 46 and 48). So too did Arius in the fourth century, along with just about every heterodox instinct in the Church's long struggle to identify God and His will for the church and humanity. The Scripture principle resides somewhere near the heart of Reformation thought. For Karl Barth, the Scripture principle is for Reformed confessional writings the *articulus stantis et cadentis ecclesiae* ("the article upon which the church stands or falls").[59] Barth defines the Scripture principle as follows: "The church recognizes the rule of its proclamation solely in the Word of God and finds the Word of God solely in Holy Scripture."[60] For the Reformed Orthodox theologians, Scripture was the *principium cognoscendi theologiae* or the locus of theology's rational exercise of seeking to order faith and life.[61] The Scripture principle therefore includes within its range the slogan *Sola Scriptura*, a term that does not entail the dismissing of tradition but its proper dogmatic location in relation to Scripture's priority and authority.[62] *Sola Scriptura* as a Reformation slogan is well known and well attested. Its counterpart, however, is not as well known, to wit, *Tota Scriptura*. As Fred Klooster reminds, "The Scriptural principle involves both *sola Scriptura* and *tota Scriptura*, and the complex question of hermeneutics is raised."[63] He further explains, "Thus the question of *sola Scriptura* calls for attention to *tota Scriptura* at the same time; not only 'Scripture alone' but also 'the whole of Scripture,' the entire canon, is at stake."[64] On this account, the Christian canon as Old and New Testaments is formally and materially sufficient. As Childs claims, "Canon functions to sketch the range of authoritative writings. It establishes parameters of the apostolic witness within which area there is freedom and flexibility. It does not restrict the witness to any single propositional formula."[65] The Reformation instinct to bring the whole of the canon into view is no *novum* in the church's life, taking its cue from a Pastristic instinct to seek the "mind" (*dianoia*) of Scripture or its "scope" (*skopos*) in the canon's entirety. Frances Young allows Cyril of Alexandria's interpretive techniques in his John commentary to model this Pastristic concern to hear the whole of the canon even when attending to particular texts.[66] Several "techniques" emerge from Cyril's commentary for Young, but for our purposes the third is worth highlighting. "Cross-references are

---

[58] Wolff, ad loc.
[59] Karl Barth, *The Theology of the Reformed Confessions* (Columbia Series in Reformed Theology; trans. D. L. Guder and J. J. Guder; Louisville: WJK, 2002), 41.
[60] Ibid.
[61] See Richard A. Muller, *Post-Reformation Reformed Dogmatics: The Rise and Development of Reformed Orthodoxy, ca. 1520 to ca. 1725; Volume Two, Holy Scripture: The Cognitive Foundation of Theology* (Grand Rapids: Baker Academic, 2003), ch. 3.
[62] See Webster, *Holy Scripture*, ch. 2.
[63] Fred H. Klooster, "The Uniqueness of Reformed Theology: A Preliminary Attempt at Description," *CTJ* 14 (1979): 39.
[64] Ibid.
[65] Brevard Childs, *Biblical Theology of the Old and New Testaments: Theological Reflection on the Christian Bible* (Minneapolis: Fortress Press, 1992), 724.
[66] Frances Young, "The 'Mind' of Scripture: Theological Readings of the Bible in the Fathers," *IJST* 7 (2005): 131–36. See also, Frances M. Young, *Biblical Exegesis and the*

made to discern the overall 'mind' or 'sense' intended by the biblical authors."[67] Such an interpretive instinct is pursuant to a confession of faith regarding Scripture's unity and divine author. "So Paul," says Young, "is used to interpret John without embarrassment, as is the Old Testament."[68] The canonical witness with all its diversity and breadth of range must come into view when the church seeks to order its faith and life in accord with God's revealed Word. Moreover, the kerygmatic content of Scripture as God's saving revelation of Himself in Jesus Christ by the Holy Spirit keeps clear the common goal and subject matter of Scripture's diverse voices in the Old and New Testaments.[69]

God does not remain motionless in the face of the religious platitudes and unjust actions of Jerusalem's civil and religious leaders (3:12). Judgment ensues. And Micah leaves no doubt as to its cause. Zion's destruction will occur because of "you (pl.)" (בגללכם). The leadership class is to blame. Micah 3:12 speaks of Zion being plowed as a field. With a play on words, Zion and Jerusalem will become a heap of stones (*Zion* ציון becomes *Eyeen* עיין). As Samaria became a heap of stones in 1:6, so too will Jerusalem become a pile of stones. The "wound from the north" is now indeed at Jerusalem's gates.

The "mountain of the house" (הר הבית) refers to the temple and is a pregnant reference because the leadership class has placed undue confidence on their Zion and Temple theology. The temple will in time become a high place of the forest. As Jeremias observes, temples are not normally found in the forest (*Wald*).[70] Zion will become an overgrown mountain with little to no indication of civilization. The imagery is hyperbolic, yet the hyperbole reveals the true extent of Jerusalem's forthcoming destruction. Readers observed Yhwh treading on the "high places" of the earth in 1:3 and now 3:12 reintroduces the "high places" (במות) once again at this critical juncture of the prophetic book. The reference to the high places in 1:3 served as a double entendre to reinforce the prophet's focus on idolatry. The high places were metonyms for the idolatrous worshipping practices Micah speaks of in the first chapter. Here, however, the term "high places" function

---

Formation of Christian Culture (Peabody: Hendrickson, 2002), ch. 2; John J. O'Keefe and Rusty Reno, *Sanctified Vision: An Introduction to Early Christian Interpretation of the Bible* (Baltimore: John Hopkins University Press, 2005).

[67] Ibid., 133.
[68] Ibid., 14.
[69] Childs, *Biblical Theology*, 725.
[70] Jeremias, 167.

more as a metaphor than metonym. In other words, idolatry per se is not the charge Micah brings against Judah's leadership class. Rather, the prophetic word speaks against their unjust practices, abuse of their divine office, and religious confidence and self-satisfaction. Given the manifest intertextual relation between the end of the Micah 3 and Micah 1, the referent to "high places" is no accident. In fact, it reinforces by means of a metaphoric rapier thrust that despite their temple worship—externally pure as it might have been—their actions betray that worship, rendering them as idolatrous as those in view in Micah 1.

A further word about the reception of this text is in order. Few of the so-called writing prophets refer to other prophets by name. A well-known exception to this general tendency is Jeremiah's reference to Micah in the closing arguments of his trial for treason (Jer 26:17-19). Jeremiah appeals to "Micah of Moresheth" who prophesied in the days of Hezekiah and then proceeds to offer a direct quote from Mic 3:12.[71] Jeremiah offers a historical commentary on Mic 3:12 in light of the redemptive effect Micah's words had on Hezekiah. Jeremiah's explanation illuminates the character of the prophetic word in the context of lived covenantal relations. Not only did Hezekiah not seek to take Micah's life—a lesson Jeremiah hopes Jehoiakim will heed—the prophetic word was effectual. It led Hezekiah to fear and repentance in the hopes that the disaster might be avoided. And indeed, it was. The prophetic word as it pertains to the plan of God is, in Jeremias's terms, "no iron law" (*kein ehernes Gesetz*).[72] Rather, the prophetic word is announced in all of its terror with unstated qualifications of reprieve attendant to it. God may relent and is predisposed to do so in the face of repentance. Such is his character (Exodus 32-34; Ezek 33:11). Jonah's prophetic book sits comfortably with Jeremiah's view of the prophetic word in the face of lived human/divine relations. Unfortunately for Jonah, Yhwh's relenting character of grace extends to all the nations.

---

[71] Holladay observes that the quotation is almost word for word. William L. Holladay, *Jeremiah 2* (Minneapolis: Fortress Press, 1989), 108.

[72] Jeremias, 167.

Though Micah's threat to King Hezekiah did not eventuate in that historical moment, Micah's prophetic word remained open to the future for kings, like Jehoiakim, who do not take Hezekiah's path of repentance. Jeremiah's closing arguments to King Jehoiakim include this tacit assumption about the reach of Micah's threat to the current moment.

Micah 3:12 marks the halfway point in the Book of the XII. The large note in the *Masorah Parva* identifies Mic 3:12 as "the half or mid-point of the book by verses" (חצי הספר בפסוקום).[73] This feature of the text seems to go unnoticed in most of the commentary literature but suggests the effort taken by those shaping the XII to accomplish this phenomenon. Christopher Seitz describes Mic 3:12 as the Good Friday of the XII, situated as it is before Micah 4 and its Easter Sunday hope.[74] In other words, the critical juncture at the end of Micah 3 and the beginning of Micah 4 speaks to the *heart* of the XII's literary achievement (both literally and figuratively). The space between death and life resides at the center of the XII's canonical shape, witnessing as it does to the character of the God to whom Micah and the XII witness. A striking portrait of God's severity and mercy is strategically located at this crucial juncture in the XII's final form.[75] For Yhwh is the One who does not allow death a final word, severe as such a word is, but opens the darkest of human experiences to the future of saving redemption. For Seitz, the location of Mic 3:12 also speaks to the prophetic books' bending of time according to an eschatological frame of reference. Events, figures, prophetic warnings, words of hope do not follow one another on a sequential and logical pattern of unfolding temporal moments, easily plotted and identified in the course of human history—see the discussion above regarding Jeremiah's reception of Mic 3:12. Instead, these words and events figure for us our own engagement with history as types and patterns by which faithful existence is measured and by which faithful existence understands God's judging and saving engagement with his world.

---

[73] See Page H. Kelly, Daniel S. Mynatt, and Timothy G. Crawford, *The Masorah of Biblia Hebraica Stuttgartensia: Introduction and Annotated Glossary* (Grand Rapids: Eerdmans, 1998), 86. The commentary on the *Masorah Parva* in the *BHQ* makes no reference to this note.

[74] Seitz's comments on Mic 3:12 are found in Christopher Seitz, *The Unique Achievement of the Book of the Twelve: Neither Redactional Unity or Anthology* (SBL Baltimore, 2013).

[75] Seitz, *Prophecy and Hermeneutics*, 237.

4

Micah 4—Between Then and Now

Introduction

As mentioned at the conclusion of the previous chapter, the ending of Micah 3 and the beginning of Micah 4 reside at the center of the Twelve both literarily and theologically. The severity of Yhwh's judgment leaves a stark impression on the reader in view of Zion's ruinous state. Yet as the *middot* of Exodus 34 assert, the acuity of Yhwh's severity is in an imbalanced relation to the generosity of His mercy. The former gives way in time to the latter with the literary movement from Micah 3 to 4 attesting to this gracious prerogative of Israel's God. Zion will not remain plowed as a field, a ruinous heap of stones echoing of a civilization long lost. In time, Zion will arise as the highest of mountains with the nations streaming to it in search of Yhwh's tutelage. The result of this moment is an era of universal peace where instruments of warfare become agrarian tools and the beauty of a simple life is affirmed.

The focus of Micah 4 is the first five verses, and the balance of the following comments will tip in favor of this unit. The latter two-thirds of the chapter (4:6-5:1 [4:14 MT]) move between the future moment witnessed to in the first five verses and the here and now. In sum, the move from the end of chapter three into chapter four mirrors in reverse the movement from a future focus in 4:6-7—"in that day"—to the present moment here and now in 4:8-5:4 (5:3 MT)—"but you" (ואתה; 4:8; 5:1 MT) and "now" (עתה; 4:9, 11; 5:1 [4:14 MT]). The hoped-for future promised by Yhwh does not resemble the current moment, the "now," Micah's prophecy addresses. Hence, Mic 4:8 is a central text in the move from future promise to current moment as the prophetic word addresses the reader in the here and now to look with hope for the then and there: "And you, O tower of the flock, hill of daughter Zion, to you it shall come, the former dominion shall come, the sovereignty of daughter Jerusalem."

Micah 4:1-5—Established Zion and streaming nations

The striking overlap between Mic 4:1-5 and Isa 2:1-4 has piqued interest for some time.[1] Even Martin Luther had an opinion on the diachronic relationship between the two. "We find this prophecy," says Luther, "almost to the word, in Is. 2 also. It definitely seems to me that Isaiah took his from Micah."[2] Luther's rationale is straightforward, even if simplistic: Micah was older than Isaiah (or so Luther suggests); therefore, material common to the two is probably borrowed from the younger Isaiah. Sorting out the diachronic problems did not bog Luther down nor did his opinion on the priority of Micah play any material role in his exegesis.

Matters are more complex now for those seeking to relate these two texts together and wishing to make sense of where Micah and Isaiah as prophetic books go their respective ways. The shared and divergent material between the prophetic corpi bearing these prophets' names has led some to identify a bona fide debate between Micah and Isaiah regarding the character of the era of universal peace promised by these prophetic words. The following question makes the interpretive differences plain: Does Mic 4:5 present the nations in the future reign of

---

[1] "There is no question that both texts record the same saying; they are so nearly identical that the minor differences hardly show in translation." James Luther Mays, *Micah*, Old Testament Library (Philadelphia: Westminster Press, 1976) 94.
[2] Martin Luther, "Micah," in *Luther's Works: American Edition* (ed. H. C. Oswald; Saint Louis: Concordia Publishing House, 1975), 18: 236.

Yhwh as continuing in the worship of their gods, while Judah recognizes the validity of Yhwh alone or not?[3]

Who's first; who's better?

The diachronic relationship between Micah 4 and Isaiah 2 has puzzled interpreters for some time. Enough has been said on this matter elsewhere so that I will not bog down the discussion with a detailed taxonomy.[4] Though not exhaustive, a sampling of diachronic viewpoints are as follows:

1. Micah borrowed from Isaiah, the eighth-century prophet (Wildberger).
2. Isaiah borrowed from Micah, the eighth-century prophet (Cannewurf).

---

[3] The "conflicted" reading of Mic 4:5 vis-à-vis Isa 2:1-4 is by no means a consensus reading. It is, however, gaining an ascendency within the secondary literature. Sweeney claims, "True inter-religious dialog comes not from the assertions that all religions—or any religion for that matter—are fundamentally the same; it comes from the recognition of the differences between them and affirming the right to differ while holding to the integrity of one's own viewpoint. Indeed, that principle is articulated in Mic 4:1-5" (Marvin A. Sweeney, *TANAK: A Theological and Critical Introduction to the Jewish Bible* [Minneapolis: Fortress Press, 2012]), 489. Sweeney's more detailed textual argument for the "debate" between Isaiah and Micah can be found in Marvin A. Sweeney, *Form and Intertextuality in Prophetic and Apocalyptic Literature*, FAT 45 (Tübingen: Mohr Siebeck, 2005), 210–21. Sweeney and Nogalski in their respective commentaries on Micah conceive of no other option. Yoram Hazony's recent *The Philosophy of the Hebrew Bible* states without reservation, "Nor can one harmonize Isaiah's claim that in the time of the king to come all the earth will have one God with the prophet Micha's vision, in which each nation will walk with its own god, and Israel will walk with theirs." Yoram Hazony, *The Philosophy of Hebrew Scripture* (Cambridge: Cambridge University Press, 2012), 41. The point is not to deny Hazony's larger concern, namely, there is a diversity of theological and political outlook within the Hebrew Bible. Different accounts for understanding this diversity are available. Nevertheless, the point here is more modest. The "discrepancy" between Micah and Isaiah may not provide the corroborating evidence Hazony assumes it does. Benjamin Sommer unreservedly affirms Sweeney's reading: "Even in the eschaton, the other nations will relate primarily to their own gods, turning to Yhwh only when conflicts among them necessitates recourse to a higher authority." Benjamin D. Sommer, *The Bodies of God and the World of Ancient Israel* (Cambridge: Cambridge University Press, 2009), 165.

[4] Andersen and Freedman give perhaps the best taxonomy. Andersen and Freedman, 2000, 413–27.

3. An earlier prophecy or tradition was borrowed by each prophet or circle of tradents independently of the other (Mays finds this option most promising).
4. An oracle not original with Isaiah but within the Isaianic tradition was later adapted into the book of Micah or vice versa: a redactional version of options 1 and 2 (Stade takes the postexilic view; likewise Wolff).
5. Related to 4, the shared material between Isaiah and Micah reveals these two books are products of the same tradents who were responsible for collecting, expanding, and shaping the material (Childs).[5]

A few comments regarding these options are in order. The first two are self-explanatory on the surface of things. After Wildberger, the eighth-century view has lost a hold in critical discussions. Isaiah's borrowing from Micah is a minority view with few supporters. Hillers describes the attempt to resolve the problem "fatuous" and settles that options 1–3 are all possible.[6] In the process of transmission, so Freedman and Anderson, Micah's poetic form remains more stable and less edited than Isaiah's and is, therefore, closer to the "original."[7] Andersen and Freedman's claim here does not answer the question of priority, as the compositional history itself may obfuscate the problem. Williamson likewise believes Micah's text is perhaps "superior" to Isaiah's but is quick to attenuate the statement's significance for drawing conclusions about the relative priority of either passage.[8]

Regarding option 3, it could be suggested Micah and Isaiah are borrowing from the liturgical tradition of the cult. It has long been noted that Zion theology exerted a pressure on Isaiah, the eighth-century prophet, and the book that bears his name. The Zion theology present in Psalms such as 46, 48, and 76 emerge from this cultic milieu, though care should

---

[5] Brevard S. Childs, *Introduction to the Old Testament as Christian Scripture* (Philadelphia: Fortress Press, 1979), 438–39. Christoph Levin suggests something similar in his "Das 'Vierprophetenbuch'."
[6] Delbert R. Hiller, *Micah; A Commentary on the Book of the Prophet Micah* (Hermeneia; Philadelphia: Fortress Press, 1984), 53.
[7] Andersen and Freedman, *Micah*, 420.
[8] H. G. M. Williamson, *Isaiah 1–5* (ICC; London: T&T Clark International, 2006), 166. Williamson argues for a late exilic or postexilic setting for the shared oracle of Isaiah and Micah (*Isaiah 1–5*, 176).

be taken once comparisons between these Psalms and Isaiah/Micah begin.[9] One glaring distinction between these Psalms and Isaiah 2/Micah 4 is the relationship of the nations to Zion. In the Psalms the nations are brought in by force, while they enter willingly and safely in Isaiah and Micah.

Moreover, dating the Psalms is tricky business. Few argue against the antiquity of the Zion traditions. The dating of the Psalms and the antiquity of the traditions are two related but distinct matters.[10] Day identifies the inviolability of Zion and the *Völkerkampf* motif of the Zion psalms as stemming from Canaanite/Jebusite traditions. He resists the notion of moving these Zion psalms, or at least an early form of them, to the Josianic period or later.[11] The differences between Isaiah 2/Micah 4 and the Zion psalms are not alleviated on this account, even though the Zion theology present in the Zion psalms was available to Isaiah and Micah, the prophetic personae.[12] Where differences are observed between Isaiah/Micah and the Zion psalms, however, the creative freedom of the prophets need not be underestimated. Is it not possible they are adapting certain aspects of the temple's liturgy to the concerns of the given moment much in the same way, say, that Reformation liturgies,

---

[9] Williamson challenges Wildberger's arguments for Isaianic authorship at this juncture. Williamson, *Isaiah 1–5*, 175–77. Wildberger's argument for the eighth-century date rests on the anteriority of the Zion psalm tradition. Williamson affirms the early dating of these Psalms but recognizes the difficulty of securing these dates. He also sees points of divergence between Isa 2:2-5 and the Zion psalm tableau.

[10] See Ollenburger, *Zion the City of the Great King*; Levenson, "Zion Traditions," *ABD* 6: 1098–1102; Hans-Joachim Kraus, *Theology of the Psalms* (Minneapolis: Fortress Press, 1992), 78–84; Hossfeld and Zenger identify the Zion theology "as an Israelite interpretation of the pre-Yahwist Jerusalem theology *and* an assimilation of common ancient Near Eastern ideas." Psalm 76, for example, could deploy this Zion theology within the "mythic complex" of an anti-Assyrian perspective. Frank-Lothar Hossfeld and Erich Zenger, *Psalms 2* (Hermeneia; Minneapolis: Fortress Press, 2005), 263. von Rad, *OTT II*, 157. Day, however, understands the *Völkerkampf* motif of the Zion psalms as a nonhistorical cultic motif whose source is Canaanite mythology—observed most notably in the reference to Zion as Zaphon in Ps 48:3. John Day, *God's Conflict with the Dragon and the Sea: Echoes of a Canaanite Myth in the Old Testament* (Cambridge: Cambridge University Press, 1985), 127.

[11] Day, *God's Conflict with the Dragon*, 125–40. Robert Miller offers a sociological understanding of the Zion psalms' *Sitz im Leben*: what function did these Psalms have in defining society. He concurs with Mowinckel et al., that the Zion psalms defy identification with a particular historical event. Robert D. II Miller, "The Origin of the Zion Hymns," in *The Composition of the Book of Psalms* (ed. Erich Zenger; Leuven: Peeters, 2010), 672.

[12] Stansell's tradition-critical work on Micah and Isaiah finds an "Isaianic" influence on Micah wanting. Where similarities are present, according to Stansell, it is due to the shared resources in Judah's traditions: theophanic and Zion traditions in particular. Stansell leans against any notion of Micah, the eighth-century prophet, as an epigone of Isaiah. Micah has his own distinct voice and concerns, despite substantial material overlap. Following the standard critical divisions, Stansell limits his investigation to "authentic" Isaiah and Micah material: Isaiah 1–39 and Micah 1–3. On the other hand, Stansell affirms Childs's earlier claim that Micah and Isaiah share a common redactional history. "Although we have attempted her to emphasize those elements which illustrate the contrasts in the message of Micah and Isaiah, it appears that, fairly early in the tradition and redaction of their sayings, their prophecy was understood as standing in the closest possible relationship." Gary Stansell, *Micah and Isaiah: A Form and Tradition Historical Comparison* (SBL Dissertation Series; Atlanta: Scholars Press, 1988), 133.

whether Lutheran or Anglican, reworked the Roman Catholic liturgical tradition in light of reformational doctrinal concerns? Though unprovable, this is surely possible.

Sorting out the diachronic issues is a complex matter because the editing and shaping of the biblical materials, in this case the prophets, is not necessarily unpacked in a tidy linear unfolding where discrete units of the prophetic literature can always be assigned to this or that particular period with confidence.[13] Cross-fertilization and a dynamic process of "back and forth" rather than "straight ahead" better characterize the shaping history of the prophets.[14] Related to Isaiah 2 and Micah 4, Williamson "complicates" the literary history of these two texts by bringing fragment 4QIsa^e to the table of evidence. Williamson reveals, as one would expect, the Qumran scroll agrees for the most part with MT Isaiah but in three crucial places it goes with Micah's rendering and "in one significant respect" it goes its own way irrespective of MT Isaiah and Micah.[15] Williamson concludes, "With such attested variety, it would be foolhardy in matters of detail to claim priority for one reading or the other: the degree of influence of each passage on the other throughout their early transmission puts any putative 'original' text beyond reach."[16] Given the textual evidence, it follows to allow each text, Micah's and Isaiah's, to retain their literary integrity without correction by an "original" or "better" rendering. Despite their origin or source, both texts have gone through the mill on the way to their current literary form.

As mentioned in the introduction, Benjamin Sommer challenges disciplinary instincts for dating Isaiah 2/Micah 4.[17] He questions the confidence biblical scholars often attach to their ability to link textual ideas with particular eras. He calls this overconfidence "pseudo-

---

[13] Again, Sommer, "Dating Pentateuchal Texts." See also Childs, "Retrospective Reading," 368–69. For description, analysis, and programmatic suggestions for engaging the prophetic literature as literature and the complexity of the redaction-critical project, see especially Kratz, *Prophetenstudien: Kleine Schriften II*.

[14] Childs, *Isaiah*, 4. See Odil Hannes Steck, *The Prophetic Books and Their Theological Witness* (trans. James D. Nogalski; St. Louis: Chalice Press, 2000).

[15] Williamson, *Isaiah 1–5*, 166.

[16] Ibid.

[17] For example, focusing on Zion as the goal of pilgrimages, the universal scope of the nations' journey to Zion, and lasting peace throughout the world are the three convergent themes in Isaiah 2 and Micah 4 that lead Wolff to push these texts into the postexilic period (*contra* Wildberger; Wolff, ad loc.). One must wait for Trito-Isaiah and Zechariah for comparable themes, both postexilic in character.

historicism" and makes a laudable attempt to bring some historical modesty into redaction-critical studies. As his argument pertains to Isaiah 2 and Micah 4, Sommer makes the following sagacious claim:

> Even if it is surprising to suggest that an eighth-century thinker might have hoped for peace in Israel and among the nations, this would not make the suggestion impossible. Micah and especially Isaiah conceived of notions that were unexpected, even bizarre. Therein lies the genius of any original thinker. To deny that an idea could have been thought of in a given age is to deny the possibility of intellectual creativity. Such a denial is a very odd position for a scholar of the humanities.[18]

Sommer's exhortation regarding the confident assigning of texts to particular periods makes a strong point, eliciting a fair amount of modesty when attending to the dating of texts.

A few examples to illustrate the milling of the two texts will suffice. The placement of "establish" נכון is difficult in each passage, though Micah's periphrastic use after the copulative verb is more attested and possibly "better." Micah 4:3b balances the line out with a defectively written feminine plural ending and an expanded form of the three masculine plural pronominal suffix (חַרְבֹתֵיהֶם), whereas Isaiah 2 has a plene form of the feminine plural and deploys the shortened pronominal suffix with no י link (חַרְבוֹתָם). Possibly in the shared logic of *lectio difficilior* it could be argued the tradents of Micah cleaned things up a bit for the sake of balancing out these lines (or possibly Micah is closer to the original because of the rhyme his line achieves?). Turning back to Freedman and Andersen's understanding of the purer shape of the oracle in Micah, it is worth recalling that this judgment does not sort out the diachronic matters; it only highlights the complexity of the compositional history of both texts.[19] As already noted, however, *allowing each text to do the particular work it sets out to do in the given literary contexts of their respective books is a better way forward than correcting one text in light of the putative "original" or "better" text.*[20]

---

[18] Sommer, "Dating Pentateuchal Texts," 96.
[19] For further details on points of divergence, e.g., Isaiah's "all nations" (2:2b) and Micah's "nations" (4:1) streaming, see the textual comments in Williamson, *Isaiah 1-5*, ad loc. These minor variations, while not to be glossed over, do not present a competing vision of the future. Micah 4:5 is the juggernaut pertaining to the diverging accounts of the future, universal reign.
[20] Freedman and Anderson, however, on the basis of their close examination of the poetics of Micah 4 and Isaiah 2 consider Micah to be closer to the original shared poem. The poetic language of Micah 4 puts it in contrast with the prose materials lending credence

An ancient illustration of the need to do justice to these two texts in light of each other is the LXX handling of Mic 4:1. As mentioned above, נכון is placed after הימים in Isa 2:2 and after בית יהוה in Mic 4:1. These differing locations of נכון are both taken into account in the LXX rendering of v. 1. A gloss is provided for נכון at the positions present in both Isaiah and Micah—ἐμφανες "revealed" in the Isaianic position and ἕτοιμον "made ready" in the Mican position. Anthony Gelston comments, "It seems therefore to reflect a conflation of the two passages, as well as a double interpretation of this word."[21] The LXX translator of Micah was aware of the differences between the two texts and sought to give an interpretive account of the matter in his translation. In other words, sorting out the relationship between these two texts is an old problem.

Canonical context and shared compositional history: Who's debating whom?

Given the stark overlap between these chapters in Micah and Isaiah, it does not seem adequate to pass by the question of their relationship to each other on the canonical level.[22] The evidence indicates that the prophecy of Isaiah played a formative role on the tradents of Micah. Or as Childs, Williamson, Steck, and Bosshard-Nepustil in their various ways have suggested, it is likely the tradents of Isaiah and Micah were the same.[23] This matter is of some import when we turn again to the supposed "debate" between Isaiah and Micah regarding the character of the universal era of peace described in these prophetic texts. Identifying the original form of the text vis-a-vis Micah versus Isaiah, a kind of comparing and contrasting of literary quality, etc., is a different enterprise than observing the mutual relativity of these two texts in their compositional history and the shaping influence of Isaiah on the final form of Micah (and the Twelve).[24]

---

to the "distinctive poetic character of this portion." It follows then that "Micah has preserved a version of the oracle closer to the original." Andersen and Freedman, *Micah*, 420. It does not follow, however, that Isaiah necessarily borrowed from Micah. Their claims are more modestly related to the poem's current form in Isaiah and Micah. Micah could still borrow from Isaiah or be shaped by the Isaianic traditions though the compositional history of Isaiah is still in media res.

[21] *BHQ*, 102*.

[22] E.g.,Waltke's very learned commentary on Micah skirts the diachronic/tradition-historical matters.

[23] Steck, *Der Abschluß der Prophetie Im Alten Testament*.

[24] Bosshard-Nepustil does not make a definitive claim regarding the priority of Isaiah 2 or Micah 4, though he is inclined (*neigen*) to consider Micah as stemming from Isaiah. He

An important and understated matter indicative of the Isaianic influence on Micah is the phrase "for the mouth of the LORD Sabaoth has spoken" (כי־פי יהוה צבאות דבר) in 4:4.[25] This collocation is only found in the Isaianic corpus. The language of Sabaoth, either adopted from Jebusite traditions or brought from Shiloh, has a firm location in the traditions of the temple cult.[26] As has been suggested elsewhere, terms such as Yhwh Sabaoth and the Holy One of Israel, so replete within Isaiah, are indicative of the liturgical influence on Isaiah's thought.[27] Therefore, the suggestion that the editors of the Isaian and Mican materials were the same is not beyond the pale given the linguistic and semantic overlap, with a nod in the direction of Isaianic influence on the shaping of Micah: "for the mouth of the Lord has spoken."

What is one to make of all this data? As mentioned in this commentary's introduction, Levin suggests that Hosea, Amos, and Micah were edited and shaped in light of the *Vorbild* of Isaiah in the *postexilic* period. These books existed without superscriptions before

---

also considers it a possibility that the redactor of the prophetic literature located within Isaianic circles could have simultaneously placed these texts in their current contexts. Furthermore, Bosshard-Nepustil sees a material and semantic overlap between Isaiah 1 and Mic 3:9-12. He locates this redaction (in conjunction with Obadiah, Zech 8:20-22, First Isaiah with Isaiah 60) within a Völker level of redaction particular to the Persian period's adapted Zion theology: a significant matter that needs to be taken into account if a "debate" is taking place. One need not follow the details of the redaction-critical reconstruction to appreciate the literary/canonical insights at play in the diachronic history, namely, the Isaianic influence on the redaction history of the Twelve, in particular for our purposes, Micah. Erich Bosshard-Nepustil, *Rezeptionen von Jesaia 1-39 im Zwölfprophetenbuch: Untersuchungen zur literarischen Verbindung von Prophetenbüchern in babylonischer und persischer Zeit* (OBO 154; Göttingen: Vandenhoeck & Ruprecht, 1997), 415-20.

[25] Williamson, *Isaiah 1-5*, 178-79. Williamson believes 4:4 original to the earlier form of this oracle in Isaiah as well. In the postexilic redaction of the book, 4:4 dropped from its current location. The presence of the *Schlussformel* in Micah may add additional support to the notion that Micah's current literary form is superior to Isaiah's.

[26] Miller believes the pre-Israelite Jebusite influence on Israel's Zion theology is overwrought. Miller, "Zion Hymns," 670.

[27] Wiliamson, "Judah as Israel in Eight-Century Prophecy," 81-95. For a competing religious-historical understanding of the history of "Israel" language in the Southern Kingdom, see Kratz, "Israel in the Book of Isaiah," 103-28; "Israel als Staat und als Volk," *ZTK* 97 (2000): 1-17. The nature of "Israel" language in the preexilic, Southern Kingdom is a matter of some contest at the current moment: Williamson and Kratz are respective representatives of differing trends. For Kratz, "Israel" language in the Southern Kingdom only makes sense on the far side of the Northern Kingdom's demise. Williamson is less reticent to locate the source of such language in the cult of the early monarchy.

this period but were later shaped in associative relation with the Isaianic materials. The details of Levin's arguments need further examination. For example, Williamson and others claim that Isa 2:1 with its second superscription is the titular head of an exilic edition of the book.[28] It begins with "the word which he saw, Isaiah son of Amon." Amos begins, "the words of Amos which he saw." One may not need to go as late as the postexilic period to see the beginning of the shaping of this material in light of the *Vorbild* of Isaiah. Nevertheless, that the Isaianic traditions have influenced Micah seems apparent. Despite the complex history of how we arrived at what we now have in Isaiah 2 and Micah 4, an intentional relationship between these prophetic books is observed on the level of the redactional shaping of the materials. If Levin's larger thesis is headed in the right direction, then the supposed "debate" between Micah and Isaiah at the precise point of their most substantive overlap raises questions about who is debating with whom (i.e., the same tradents)?[29]

Our attention turns at this point to the shared and discordant material between Isaiah 2 and Micah 4. There are detailed differences between Isaiah 2 and Micah 4 which need not slow us down at this point. As mentioned above, there are orthographic and syntactical differences: plene versus defective writing, swapping of word order, e.g., גוים and עמים in Isa 2:4 and Mic 4:3. The glaring matter, however, is the plus in Mic 4:4. The utopian future where Mt. Zion is established as the premier mountain because nations stream to it to be taught by Yhwh results in the end of learned warfare. Micah ends with a pastoral image. Everyone is sitting under their own vine and fig tree with fear now a faint memory from a bygone era. The conclusion to v. 4, as mentioned above, is the Isaianic *Schlussformel*, כי־פי יהוה צבאות דבר. Whereas in Isaiah, v. 4 of Micah is absent and the oracle concludes with a summons

---

[28] Williamson, *Isaiah 1–5*, 9.
[29] Sweeney and Levin concur on the postexilic location of Isaiah 2/Micah 4. Where Sweeney identifies a debate between a different circle of tradents, Levin and Childs understand these two texts in their current literary shaping as a product of the same circle of tradents.

to the house of Jacob, "Oh house of Jacob, come, let us walk in the light of the LORD" (בית יעקב לכו ונלכה באור יהוה).

The differences between the endings of these two shared oracles are highly suggestive, according to Sweeney. The supposed debate between Isaiah and Micah enters in at this point. Isaiah ends with a summons to follow in the light of Yhwh in view of His universal authority as judge and ruler. The result is an era of peace where all sit under the tutelage of Torah. Whereas for Micah, the fabric is quite different. Israel and the nations each enjoy an era of peace under Yhwh, *but* they do so by going their own ways religiously.[30] "The key difference," claims Sweeney, "between Micah 4:4-5 and Isaiah 2:5, however, appears in Micah 4:5, which emphasizes the difference between the nations and Israel with regard to the gods that each will follow."[31] Sweeney makes such a claim on the basis of his reading of Mic 4:5: "For all the peoples, each one, will walk in the name of his god, but we will walk in the name of the Lord our God forever." The כי clause of v. 5 is glossed with the same causal force of the כי clause in v. 4.[32] Sweeney argues that Mic 4:1-5 is a single literary unit on syntactical grounds: the one verse flows naturally into the other in a shared perspective of the *future* day. The resultant picture in Micah is, therefore, starkly contrasted with Isaiah's.[33]

---

[30] Sweeney, *Form and Intertextuality*, 214.

[31] Ibid.

[32] Sweeney states, "The functions of *kî* are not well understood, but it does function as a syntactical connector so that in the present instance it links verses 6ff to verse 5, i.e., 'for you have rejected your people, the house of Jacob.'" Sweeney, *Form and Intertextuality*, 214. For a very learned analysis of the complex history and polyvalent character of כי as this impinged on the Temple's Scroll rendering of conditional legal codes, see Bernard M. Levinson and Molly M. Zahn, "Revelation Regained: The Hermeneutics of כי and אם in the Temple Scroll," *DSD* 9 (2002): 296-34

[33] Sweeney's claim regarding the "debate" over the nature of the future reign of Yhwh has possible support in the LXX translation of v. 5. כי is translated with ὅτι and the following phrase is a paraphrastic rendering due to the translators' theological predisposition. Instead of "each one will walk in the name of his God," the LXX says, "each one will walk in his way" (τὴν ὁδὸν αὐτοῦ). The next phrase is not translated paraphrastically but literally, "but we walk in the name of the Lord our God for ever and ever." The uneven character of the translation, from paraphrastic to literal, indicates the possible discomfort the translator has with the claim made in the first clause of the Hebrew text. In fact, the BHQ has "theol" in brackets by this variant to indicate the theological motivation for the resignified or altered text. But care must be taken here because the exact theological issue at stake for the ancient translator might not be Sweeney's, e.g., in the era of Yhwh's rule of peace the nations continue to worship their Gods. Rather, it may simply be the growing discomfort of identifying the existence of other gods and lending credence to this notion.

A concessive account

A different reading than Sweeney's is on offer here. Micah 4:1-4 should be viewed as a literary unit. The concluding formula of 4:4 (*Schlussformel*), with its distinctly Isaianic phraseology, is exactly that, a conclusion formula. The phrase is original to the oracle, though in the editorial history of Isaiah it has either been dropped or moved elsewhere. The כי clause of v. 5 is not of necessity causal, though a causal understanding does not defeat this reading.[34] Rather, it is likely concessive and brings the reader back into the current moment in the divine economy, a moment it should be added where the promises of vv. 1-4 have not as of yet been realized.[35] Verse 5 is a commentary on vv. 1-4 that challenges the reader in the current moment to continue to walk in the name of Yhwh despite the fact that the nations continue with the worship of their gods. Such a temporal shift in this chapter does not catch the reader off guard. The fourfold use of עתה (4:9, 10, 11, 14) within this chapter moves the reader back and forth between future promise/reality and the current moment. The understanding of 4:5 within this particular temporal nexus balances out the literary movement of the chapter as a whole.[36] Instead of reading כי as "for" we read it as "although" and separate it from the literary unit 1-4 while still viewing it as materially linked to the

---

[34] See note 19.
[35] Stade's early redactional insights were in the right direction. "4,5 ist eine sehr ungeschickte Anknüpfung. v. 1-4 ist noch nicht eingetroffen. Noch verehrt jedes der fremden Völker seinem Gott. Da dem so ist (כי), so soll Israel erst recht den seinigen verehren." Bernard Stade, "Bermerkungen Über das Buch Micha," *ZAW* 1 (1881): 166. Stade's observation affirms the causal reading of כי while still understanding v. 5 as a redactional commentary on 4:1-4. McKane's "skeptical" understanding of the redaction history of v. 5 is not self-evident (McKane, 126). Mignon Jacobs identifies the כי clause of v. 5 as a logical connector to 4:1-4 while at the same time maintaining the distinction in time frame between "then" and "now." Jacobs, *The Conceptual Coherence of Micah*, 147. Within English translations, e.g., KJV, RSV, NRSV, the כי is translated causally ("for"). The NIV leaves the כי untranslated but does render ילכו as a modal verb ("may") rather than the typical present indicative. Notably, the JPS TANAKH and NASB are the minority translations that translate the כי as a concessive ("though").
[36] Nogalski describes Mic 4:1-5:15 as a "complex message of promise for the distant future, though the current generation will experience threats to its existence that must be endured." James D. Nogalski, *The Book of the Twelve: Micah-Malachi*, Smyth & Helwys Bible Commentary (Macon: Smyth & Helwys, 2011), 515. The forward-looking character of faith is a shared motif between Isaiah and Micah. What von Rad said of Isaiah's

preceding unit because of the eschatological tension faced by the reader: such a structure is suggested by the *sedarim* liturgical marker as well, though the *petuḥa* comes at the end of v. 5. Micah 4:5 brings us back into the current moment as commentary on the implications of the future for the here and now.

Though not in dialogue with Sweeney, several commentators on Micah offer this reading as well, so much so that this reading could be viewed as the "traditional" reading. The medieval Rabbinic commentator David Kimchi suggests such by assigning v. 5 to a different period than 1-4. Verses 1-4 anticipate the Messianic era and v. 5 brings the reader back into the current moment. Jeremias says of v. 5, "Der noch einmal jüngere V.5 sprichts allerdings Menschen im Gottesvolk an, denen das Warten auf die Vollendung der Geschichte lang wird und die die Völker ihrer Zeit sehr anders erleben als in jener Endzeitperspektive" (p. 174). James Mays makes a similar comment, "The time of pilgrimage to the 'city set on a hill' is not yet. In the meantime faith in the fulfillment of the vision means faithful enactment of it in their life."[37] Kessler says, "Aber jetzt wird zwischen dem Gehen der Nationen und dem des Wir unterschieden. Das, was am Ende der Tage Wirklichkeit sein wird, ist es jetzt noch nicht. Denn noch geht jedes Volk im Namen seines eigenen Gottes."[38] Freedman and Andersen offer this reading as a possibility but do not argue strongly for it. Ben Zvi believes on syntactical grounds both options are equally possible and does not land one way or the other.

In light of the reading of Mic 4:5 on offer here, the differences between the concluding comments of v. 5 in Micah and the final call in Isaiah 2 might not be as contentious as some suggest.[39] Isaiah 2:5 heralds, "Oh house of Jacob, come, let us walk in the light of the LORD."

---

prophecy applies to Micah as well (esp. ch. 4): "The 'object' upon which this faith should be based did not, however, as yet exist for his contemporaries; it lay in the future. The astonishing thing was therefore this: Isaiah demanded of his contemporaries that they should now make their existence rest on a future action of God." Von Rad, *OTT II*, 161.

[37] Mays, *Micah*, 99.
[38] Rainer Kessler, *Micha* (Herders Theologischer Kommentar Zum Alten Testament; Freiburg: Herder, 1999), 187.
[39] Sweeney, *Form and Intertextuality*, 213–14. The "very different scenario[s]" between Isaiah 2 and Micah 4 in their respective appeals to הלך trade on Sweeney's particular reading of Mic 4:5.

The vocative address to the house of Jacob is a call to walk in the light of Yhwh because the future promises are true. Perhaps Mic 4:5 is an expansion on this theme. Readers of Micah are also called to continue on in the name of Yhwh despite the fact that the promise of a raised Zion and streaming nations has not yet occurred. Such a reading is not to say Micah and Isaiah always speak the same idiom or that traces of a debate might not be found. Nor is it to flatten these prophetic voices into a monotone choir with no sensitivity to their given literary contexts. Nevertheless, it is not clear that a debate regarding the nature of Yhwh's future reign is taking place between the prophetic books of Micah and Isaiah. The opposite in fact appears to be the case.

Micah 4:5 in the Book of the Twelve: Brief reflections

A few concluding comments are in order about Mic 4:5 in light of the Book of the Twelve. In a programmatic article on the shaping of the Twelve, Raymond van Leeuwen identifies a redaction-history of the Twelve in the postexilic period dealing particularly with the theodicy question raised by the cataclysmic events of Israel and Judah in the Neo-Assyrian and Neo-Babylonian periods.[40] This redaction has a sapiential character as is observed in the ending of Hosea: מִי חָכָם וְיָבֵן אֵלֶּה נָבוֹן וְיֵדָעֵם (Hos 14:10a). The readers of the Twelve are forced to reckon with the complex history of God's dealing with Israel and Judah, i.e., the theodicy question, and exhorted to live faithfully *and* see wisely beyond the surface historical events to the future eschatological hope of Yhwh's promises: כִּי־יְשָׁרִים דַּרְכֵי יְהוָה וְצַדִּקִים יֵלְכוּ בָם וּפֹשְׁעִים יִכָּשְׁלוּ בָם (Hos 14:10b). In particular, the *middot* of Ex 34:6-7 are located at key junctures in the eighth-century prophets as a redactional guide for putting the prophecies in their proper theological context, an internal *regula fidei* if you will. Micah ends מִי־אֵל כָּמוֹךָ and then elaborates on the rhetorical question with an intertextual appeal to Ex 34:6-7.

A great deal more needs to be said here about the Twelve, but Mic 4:5 is situated quite well within this sapiential context in the overall intention of the Twelve: an account of the character of God is given in hopes for an eschatological coming day of the Lord, along with an exhortation to continue in faithfulness despite the complexity of the current moment.[41] If one accepts an intentional shaping of the Twelve over a longer period of time up until the postexilic period (whether or not we can sort this out neatly), then Mic 4.5 functions within this broader redactional history as an internal commentary on Mic 4:1-4 in light of the larger concerns within the Twelve. The promise of Zion's prominence and streaming nations to be taught Torah by Yhwh is not responded to cynically in v. 5 with a distressed, "Well, look how bad things are despite this promise."[42] Rather, it is an invitation to live in

---

[40] Van Leeuwen, "Scribal Wisdom and Theodicy in the Book of the Twelve," 31–49.
[41] The term "eschatology" is used loosely here. These are not necessarily events outside time and space nor the "end of the world." See Talmon, "The Signification," 795–810.
[42] *Contra* McKane.

the eschatological tension of God's promises and their unrealized status: a major theme scholars have identified in the redaction history of the Twelve.

Finally, and more tenuously, the phrase "each one walks in the name of his God" may allude to the collective use of איש in Jon 1:5, "each one cried to his God."[43] By the end of this well-known chapter in Jonah, the pagan sailors are crying out to Yhwh as well as sacrificing and making vows to him. The tale is cryptic enough to keep us from specifying whether these sailors actually went to the temple to fulfill these vows. Ben Zvi identifies the differences between the pagans in Jonah and the Yehudites, namely, temple, Torah, and exclusive worship of Adonai.[44] But such desire for details obscures the narrative's stark portrayal. Within Jonah we see in proleptic fashion the promise of Mic 4:1-4 realized on a small scale, an adumbration of what will be a future reality in full. The book of Nahum, on the other hand, reminds us of the unfulfilled character of Micah's promise: the proper location of Mic 4:5 within the redemptive economy. Perhaps in the final shaping of the Twelve, Mic 4:1-5 and Jonah's interaction with the pagans relate to one another in a reciprocal and illuminating fashion regarding the eschatological hope for the nations and the call to faithfulness in the time of anticipation: Jonah did not fair very well in the face of this. This matter could also provide some support for why Micah is located where it is in the Twelve, a matter of some dispute and a subject in need of further exploration.[45]

Micah 4:1-5 speaks of the future exaltation of Zion as the pinnacle of Yhwh's encounter with the whole of His world. The idyllic picture of Mic 4:1-4 is made possible and actual by the self-revealing of Israel's God and His teaching office. Nations stream to learn from Yhwh. Torah or divine instruction resulting in the knowledge of God and His ways leads to a rightly ordered world. By means of comparison and contrast, Hos 4:1-2 reveals a society marked by unfaithfulness, swearing, lying, cheating, and adultery. How could Israel be described in such a way? Because there is "no knowledge of God in the land" (4:1).

It is worth highlighting that this era of peace is marked by lack of military hostility and agrarian simplicity: "sitting under vines and fig trees." The effect of Torah has as its final aim human flourishing in all spheres of life. As McConville claims, "[B]iblical law aims ultimately to realize a society in which human beings experience freedom and may flourish in all parts of their lives."[46] Because the Torah has this kind of totalizing view as its telos, it is little wonder the prophets place Torah's

---

[43] Kessler offers a parenthetical comment in this direction: "[M]an vergleiche dazu die Szene auf dem Schiff, mit dem Jona vor Gott fliehen will; in Seenot schreit 'ein jeder zu seinem Gott', Jona 1, 5." Kessler, *Micha*, 187.

[44] Ehud Ben Zvi, *Signs of Jonah: Reading and Rereading in Ancient Yehud* (JSOTSupp 367; Sheffield: Sheffield Academic Press, 2003), 124-25.

[45] See Zapff, "The Book of Micah," 129-46.

[46] McConville, "Biblical Law," 632.

reach within an eschatological frame: "in the latter days."[47] For what provides a more moving vision of eschatological hope than the beauty and simplicity of basic human existence as both free and flourishing. Perhaps Zechariah says it best:

> Thus says the LORD: I will return to Zion, and will dwell in the midst of Jerusalem; Jerusalem shall be called the faithful city, and the mountain of the LORD of hosts shall be called the holy mountain. Thus says the LORD of hosts: Old men and old women shall again sit in the streets of Jerusalem, each with staff in hand because of their great age. And the streets of the city shall be full of boys and girls playing in its streets. (Zech 8:3-5)

For Athanasius, the Torah's eschatological reach is actualized in the person and work of Jesus Christ. After quoting Isa 2:4, Athanasius describes the barbarians of his day as marked by savagery and infighting. "But when they hear the teaching of Christ, forthwith they turn from fighting to farming, and instead of arming themselves with swords extend their hands in prayer."[48] For Athanasius, the effects of the gospel on the barbarians are proof positive for the Godhead of the Savior and the in-breaking of the eschatological moment promised by Isaiah and Micah taking place in the middle of time. "In the latter days" does not speak necessarily of the suspension of time but a future moment when God's kingdom breaks in on the world. For Athanasius and the apostolic witness, that eschatological promise is now actualized in the resurrection of our Lord as guarantee of the future resurrection of the dead and the life of the world to come.

Theodoret of Cyrus characterizes those who read Micah 4 as a promise of Judah's return from exile with less than flattering language: such a reading is "stupid" (Theodoret, 159–60). "I mean, which nations nearby or living at a distance betook themselves to the Jewish Temple after the return, embracing their Law and attracted to the preaching issuing from there?" Rather, Theodoret understands Micah 4 as a prophecy of the Great Commission in Matt 28:19-20 where the spread of the gospel to the nations comes into view. From Zion, the evangelical witness streams to the nations, aided by the *Pax Romana* as a providential vehicle in aid of the gospel's dissemination (ibid., 160–61). In a similar vein, Cyril of Alexandria also sees the Great Commission of Matthew's Gospel as the fulfillment of Micah's future promise. Cyril offers his reading not as a counterfactual reading against poor Jewish ones, a'la Theodoret, but on the basis of the grammar of Mic 4:2. Who are the plural voices among the nations urging them to "come" and "go up" to Mt. Zion? "Who would be the ones to introduce them to it?" (Cyril, 222). For Cyril, "[c]learly the disciples of the Savior" answer the question.

---

[47] Ibid., 631–32.
[48] St. Athanasius, *On the Incarnation* (Popular Patristic Series; Crestwood: St. Vladimir's Seminary Press, 1996), 90–91.

Micah 4:6-7

The phrase "in that day" introduces a new subunit, though the introductory formula links the unit to the forward-looking frame of vv. 1-4. This unit is Yhwh's speech ("says the Lord") and speaks to the character of His judgment. As divine communicative address, the divine word itself is the agent of healing. The force of its promise is guaranteed by the nature and source of the address. For Yhwh's hand of judgment wounds: it makes lame; it drives away; it afflicts. Yet Yhwh's judgment has restoration as its telos. In a similar vein, Hos 6:1 calls for communal repentance—"Come, let us return unto the LORD"— because Yhwh's judgment strikes in order that he might heal. And while Hosea's call to repentance and the content of Micah's divine speech need not be viewed in tension with each other, Micah's oracle lays claim to the repentance of God toward his people. Yhwh's will is resolved—note the cohortative verbs of v. 6—to gather the very people he dispersed because of his wounding judgment. He wounds in order to heal.

Commenting on this text, Cyril of Alexandria brings to memory the following: "Blessed Paul said, remember, 'Godly grief produces a repentance that leads to salvation and brings no regret.' It is therefore out of love that he punishes them, and out of his concern that they should not willingly descend to a point of experiencing anything that distressed them" (Cyril, 228).

Strong verbal links tie this unit with 2:12-13—another factor in favor of reading 2:12-13 as a word of promise. The same sets of verbs are deployed in a shared collocation: "gathering" (אסף), "gather" (קבץ), and "placing" (שׂים). As Jeremias states, "Es steht daher außer Frage, dass der Leser von 4, 6f an 2, 12f erinnert werden soll" (Jeremias, 175). There are points of divergence, however, between 2:12-13 and 4:6-7. Micah presents the flock in 2:12-13 as in need of protection with the working assumption that the "remnant" are the ones remaining at the end of the catastrophe (Jeremias, 176).[49] Whereas Mic 4:6-7 focuses on the strengthening (*Erstarken*) and numerical advancement (*Zahlreichwerden*) of the people

---

[49] On the gathering of the flock as an eschatological image, cf. Isa 54:7; 56:8; Jer 23:3; 29:14; 31:8, 10; Ez 11:17, see esp. Zeph 3:18-20 and the intertextual relation between Mic 4:6-7.

of Israel in fulfillment of the Abrahamic promise in Gen 12:2 (ibid.). The key point of differentiation between these two intentionally related texts is the eschatological focus of ch. 4. The gathering of the stricken and the lame represents the hope of the latter days or, in Jeremias's terms, the emerging of the currently concealed promise of the coming kingdom of God whose scope ranges beyond a mere hope for survivors on the far side of Judah's exile (ibid.). For Jeremias, the shaping of Micah in the Persian period indicates the "eschatologizing" of the concepts of "remnant" (*Rest*) and kingdom of God as an end-time expectation (*endzeitlicher Erwartung*, ibid.).[50] The future "remnant" or "survivors" are those gathered by God at the end of days as fulfillment of his promise to save and establish his kingdom on earth. From Mount Zion, Yhwh will rule and reign over His people, a people who have grown strong in numbers and in their identity as partakers in the kingdom of God. For Luther, Mic 4:7b is as good as saying, "And I look for the resurrection of the dead, and the life of the world to come" (Luther, 241).

The object of God's saving action in 4:6-7 is twice identified as "lame" (צֹלֵעַ).[51] The lexical allusion to the narrative of Jacob at the Jabbok in Gen 32:32 is not lost on several commentators. Jeremias makes a passing comment to the allusion (*Anspielung*), as does Ben Zvi (Jeremias, 175; Ben Zvi, 109). Sweeney provides more substantial engagement with the Jacob tradition, suggesting that the narrative of Jacob and his own exile from Judah to Aram in search of a bride (Gen 25-35) typifies Judah's own exile and return. For Sweeney, the subtle reference to Judah as "lame" brings the whole of the Jacob traditions into view, including the "lame" and "outcast" as Yhwh's "cast-off bride" in mimetic relation to Jacob and Rachel in their wilderness sojourn (Sweeney, 382). Whether the whole of the Jacob narrative is in view here is up for interpretive debate with much depending on the eye of the beholder. Nevertheless, the allusion to the narrative of Jacob at Penuel (Gen 32:22-32) appears on surer ground because of the lexical link "lame" (צֹלֵעַ, cf. Gen 32:32). The allusion

---

[50] See the comments above from Theodoret of Cyrus on such a reading. His logic is in line with Jeremias's understanding of the eschatological view of the tradents of the XII in the Persian period who also recognize the limited reach of these prophecies for Yehud on the far side of exile.

[51] A textual difficulty emerges in 4:7 in the second colon of line 1. The participle translated in the NRSV as "those who were cast off" follows the suggestion of the BHS that the lexeme should be read as a denominative form of the adverb "cast off." This textual solution has its genesis with Wellhausen. Williamson provides a convincing alternative to this reading, providing a helpful way forward with an admittedly difficult textual matter. He finds Wellhausen's account "dubious" because this denominalized verb is found nowhere else in the Hebrew canon. Rather, Williamson suggests, the term חלא from 2 Chr 16:12 may provide the solution. For the scribal error of replacing a *hey* (ה) with a *cheyt* (ח) is "easy to accept" and keeps the second phrase in semantic parallel with the first ("lame" and "diseased"). Williamson, "Marginalia," 364-65.

to Jacob at the Jabbok River does not make its first appearance here in the Twelve. Hosea deploys the tradition as a type for Israel's repentance (Hos 12:2-6). Israel's progenitor and eponym provides a figured account of the long-term identity of Yhwh's people. They strive with God, marked by the wounds of his judgment, yet persistently and tenaciously holding on to the redemptive promises of God despite current circumstances of despair.

Micah 4:8-5:1 (4:14 MT)

Micah moves from the forward-looking prospects of 4:1-7 to addressing his readers in their current moment of distress. This prophetic unit is structurally organized by the lexical markers "but you" (ואתה; 4:8; 5:2 [5:1 MT]) and "now/but now" (ועתה/עתה; 4:9, 11, 14). Comments on Mic 5:2 (5:1 MT) will appear in the next chapter; however, the grammatical inclusio of 4:8 and 5:2 (5:1 MT) places the promises of 5:2 (5:1 MT)—"But you Bethlehem Ephrathah"—within the contextual frame shaped by the current distress of 4:8-5:1 (4:14 MT). Moreover, 4:8 and 5:2 (5:1 MT) address the current distress by placing Judah's hope on the enduring character of the Davidic promises. The former dominion will come, though the way in which the Davidic kingdom will appear signals something new in the divine economy of redemption as will be seen in the next chapter (5:2 [5:1 MT]).

Verse 8 begins with a disjunctive clause—"but you" (ואתה)—bringing the prophetic word back into the present moment. The overall force of the prophetic word emerges prima facie: the former Davidic dominion and kingdom (cf. 2 Samuel 7) is given as a future promise. What was lost or what will be lost in time will again be restored. Ambiguity exists regarding the first phrase of v. 8 (a *casus pendens* whose presence resumes in the next line, "unto you ... "). What exactly is *Migdal Eder* or "tower of the flock"? And what is the referent of *opel* (עפל) or "hill of the daughter of Zion"? Reading this verse backwards helps to orient readers as to these terms referent, namely, Jerusalem. However, more than a mere reference to Jerusalem appears in view here.

The pastoral imagery is not new to Micah (cf. Mic 2:12-13). Yhwh and His king function as shepherds leading their people from danger to safety. An allusion to the Jacob narrative of Genesis 35 may take place here as well, suggesting to readers that a return to this narrative may aid in the reading of Micah.[52] Such an allusion to the Jacob narratives do not surprise as indicated by the allusion to Jacob at the Jabbok in vv. 6-7. In Gen 35:21, Jacob camps at *Migdal Eder* after the death of his mother Rachel. The exact location of *Migdal Eder* is up for debate, though it lies in relative proximity to *Ephrathah* (Gen 35:16). The precise location of this unknown citadel appears beyond the point for Micah. On the other hand, the forging of a relationship between Mic 4:8 and 5:2 (5:1 MT) on the basis of these place names is more to the prophetic concern. The "hill" (עֹפֶל) of Daughter Zion is the location of the Davidic palace (cf. 2 Chr 27:3; Neh 3:26). Jacob's narrative and the Davidic dominion both past and future are being fitted together in Mic 4:8-10. The future Davidic promises are assured because of the mimetic nature of the Jacob narratives as a plot already written.

Zion appears in feminine form in vv. 8-10—daughter of Zion—and is in the death throes of delivery in vv. 9-10. The narrative of Genesis 35 presents Jacob's mother Rachel in the shared suffering of Daughter Zion. Rachel is to be delivered of Benjamin only to lose her life in the process. Rachel is buried at Bethlehem; Jacob camps at *Midgal Eder*. The promises Micah gives in the "now" moments of vv. 8-10 require a figural participation in the narrative of Israel's patronym, Jacob, and his suffering mother, Rachel. Rachel suffered in labor even unto death resulting in Benjamin, the progenitor of David's ancestral tribe. Likewise, Judah must suffer in labor's throes, even to death, in the full hopes of a future Davidic moment. The narratives of Judah's patriarch are no mere rehearsal of events long lost and lapsed. Rather, the narratives are present and inhabitable memories in the figural patterns set out by Scripture's traditions and narratives. When Judah enters into exile, her labor pains are mimetically related to Rachel's, devastating as they are. Yet Judah enters into this frown of providence in the assured hope of a future promise. "There the Lord will redeem them."

---

[52] See Sweeney especially on the presence of the Jacob narratives (Sweeney, 383–84).

The second "but now" section, vv. 11-13, places the religious perspective of Judah onto the nations. They gather in order to see Zion defiled (cf Isa 10:6; Jer 3:1, 9; Num 35:33).[53] The defiling of the land thus demonstrated in Micah 1-3 leaves Zion vulnerable to the attack of her enemies. But on final analysis within the economy of redemption, the nations are subject to a divine ruse. The nations gather themselves against Yhwh and his people only to have the tables turned. From apparent defeat, Zion will emerge in strength and splendor. From death there emerges life. The very nations looking to exploit Lady Zion will in turn bring their wealth to Israel's God. Again, the move from despair to salvation is on display in these texts.

> Calvin's pastoral insight from this text is fitted to the particularity of its verbal sense. Yhwh calls on Zion in v. 13 to "arise" (קוּמִי). The affliction endured by God's people made Zion differ "nothing from a dead man" (Calvin, 288). Calvin requires little to no heavy hermeneutical lifting as he moves from God's speech to ancient Israel to God's current speech to the Church. These two entities share in the same divine economy and thus share in an overlap of substantial identities. When the Church suffers, even because of its own doing, the character of God on display in Mic 4:13 gives heart to the weary. For Israel's God "rouse[s] the dead" (ibid.). Calvin continues,

> [T]here is no reason for the faithful to wholly despair, when they find themselves cast down, for their restoration is in the hand and power of God, as it is the peculiar office of God to raise the dead. And this same truth ought to be applied for our use, whenever we are so cast down, that no strength, no vigour, remains in us. How then can we rise again? By the power of God, who by his voice alone can restore us to life, which seemed to be wholly extinct. (Calvin, 289)

The final "but now" unit (5:1; 4:14 MT) brings with it challenges regarding contextual place and purpose.[54] Given the high notes of 4:13 and 5:2 (5:1 MT), why the word of despair here? This commentary's sympathies are with those who understand 4:14 MT within the larger structural frame of 4:8-5:5 MT.[55] The future promises of 4:13 are juxtaposed to the present moment of suffering as Judah incurs

---

[53] Hillers is correct to reject the BHS suggestion to emend this verb to תֶּחֱשֹׁף (Hillers, 60-61). This commentary follows Hillers in his understanding of the projection of an Israelite attitude on their attackers.

[54] For the range of explanations, see esp. Andersen and Freedman, 458-59. Willis (1968) argues that v. 14 begins a new unit; Hillers believes the verse is a fragment to be dealt with on its own (Hillers, 62); Beyerlin argues that 4:14 was originally located after 1:16.

[55] See Wolff, 133-36, though Wolff does not include 4:8 within this unit. The inclusio of "but you" (וְאַתָּה) at 4:8 and 5:1 MT suggests otherwise, especially given the shared outlook of 4:8 and 5:1 MT regarding the future Davidic kingdom.

divine judgment at the hands of her national aggressors. In turn, the current moment of crisis will open to the future of God's redemptive promises: "But you, Bethlehem Ephrathah." For now, however, siege and destruction mark the providential moment.

Micah 4:14 is riddled with lexical ambiguities. The initial phrase is rendered in various ways: "Now you are walled around with a wall" (NRSV); "Marshal your troops now, city of troops" (New International Version, NIV); "Now you gash yourself in grief" (Jewish Publication Society, JPS). There is little to no lexical evidence in support of the NRSV's following of the LXX. (It often comes as a personal relief for teachers and students alike when we recognize that the Septuagint translators struggled with the Hebrew text like we do.) The semantic issue trades on the lexeme *gdd* (גדד). Waltke favors reading *bath gedud* (בת־גדוד) as the congeneric noun "troops" (daughter of troops), clarifying the preceding verb (תתגדדי) as from its secondary sense of troop gathering (Waltke, 262–63). The NIV represents this reading of the lexical conundrum.

The verbal form, however, of the first verb (*hithpolel*) refers most often to lacerating oneself (cf. I Ki 18:22; Hos 7;14; Deut 14:1; Jer 16:16; 41:5; 47:5). Though this practice is forbidden (Deut 14:1), the JPS reading appears to do better justice to the lexical and contextual sense of 4:14. In other words, it solves more problems. While it is possible that the text is calling on Judah to gather for battle even though defeat is inevitable, such a reading strains in light of its lexical sense. Moreover, as Andersen and Freedman remind, if *gedud* refers to troop gathering, the associations of this noun are with "small roving bands of brigands, which is not the way a city under siege would organize her defenders" (Andersen and Freedman, 460). "Daughter of gashing" in 4:14 parallels "daughter of Zion" in 4:8. In 4:9-10 Lady Zion is in the pains of delivery. Here in 4:14 Lady Zion gashes herself in mourning because she is under siege. Zion is in great pains because her enemies strike the judge of Israel on the cheek. Jeremias describes the custom as associated with "extreme mourning" (*extremer Trauerritus*; Jeremias 183). The structural linkage of 4:14 MT and 4:9 suggests the judge of Israel is

Israel's king (Andersen and Freedman, 461). Assyria, in Isa 10:5, 24, is the rod (שֵׁבֶט) of Yhwh's anger. According to Wolff, striking on the cheek is an insult (cf. I Ki 22:24). Striking with a staff on the cheek "intensifies the shame" (Wolff, 143). Micah 4:14 portrays the horror and shame of Yhwh's judgment on Israel. But as the whole of 4:8-5:5 attests, weeping endures for the night but joy emerges in the morning. "But you, Bethlehem Ephrathah."

Micah 5

As observed in the previous chapter, Mic 4:8 and 5:2 (5:1 MT) both begin with "and you" (וְאַתָּה). They also deal with the same subject matter: the Davidic promise as eschatological hope. This grammatical and thematic inclusio offers a sharp point of focus for readers. From the ruins of current distress a future moment of promise remains, fixed as it is to the redemptive figures and patterns of Israel's history with God.

5:2-4 (1-3 MT): Fresh beginnings and Davidic hope

A stark juxtaposition exists between Mic 5:1 (4:14 MT) and Mic 5:2 (5:1 MT). The enemies of Zion stand against Judah's king. They submit him to public humiliation and disgrace by striking him on the face. The very institution God promised to uphold in perpetuity is now the object of scorn. The scene is bleak. Yet the move made by the prophet is now a familiar one (cf. 2:11-2:12-13; 3:12-4:1-5). The location of despair becomes the catalyst for promise and hope. It is possible that the labor metaphor of 5:3 (5:2 MT) echoes Isaiah 7 and the promise of Emmanuel.[1] Isaiah's promise of a future king and his description of this coming child share much in common with the substance of Micah's claims in 5:2-4 (1-3 MT). At the same time, the picture of labor indicates a time of duress, a season from which to be delivered. Readers of Micah

---

[1] Sweeney, 388. Mowinckel claims, "It is not impossible, as has been maintained, that in Mic. V, 1-3 the prophet bases his message directly on a 'Messianic' interpretation of Isa. vii." Sigmund Mowinckel, *He That Cometh: The Messiah Concept in the Old Testament & Later Judaism* (trans. G. A. Anderson; Grand Rapids: Eerdmans, 2005), 185.

have already met this metaphor in 4:9. Judah's suffering moment will in time deliver to her a future redeeming king.

Israel's God promises a new beginning with a new king from David's line. This forthcoming king, in contrast to those under Micah's invective in chs 1-3, will shepherd in the strength of Yhwh. The future promise of "secure dwelling" portrayed in Mic 4:1-4 includes within its frame the promise of the coming king in Mic 5:2-4 (1-3 MT). "And they will live securely" provides the focal point of hope for these three verses (5:4 [3 MT]). Life lived under kings who shepherd in their own strength, with god in their hands (2:1), is chaotic, disordered, and lacking security. The future king who operates in the strength of Yhwh leads his people to security and peace.

Jeremias, among others, makes much of the location of Bethlehem Ephrathah as the localized source of Judah's king of promise.[2] Bethlehem signals something new in the divine economy (cf. Isaiah 11). The reference to Bethlehem suggests that God is taking up his Messianic work from the beginning, "in that he again starts at the very same place as he began in the past, namely in Bethlehem."[3] Jeremias concurs with von Rad's account, providing two further implications of Bethlehem's significance. First, Bethlehem is removed from the guilt associated with the current iteration of David's line in Jerusalem.[4] The future Davidic king is *ad fontes*, a fresh start absent the aggregate guilt of the current Davidic line located in Jerusalem (cf. Mic 1:5). Second, Bethlehem as a place befits the modesty Yhwh desires of His leaders: "though you are small among the clans of Judah." Jeremias demonstrates how the future king's birth in Bethlehem accords with a figural pattern of God's call on various leaders in Scripture: Moses cannot speak (Exodus 3); Jeremiah is too young (Jeremiah 1); Gideon's tribe is the smallest in Manasseh (Judges 6); Saul comes from a miniscule tribe (I Samuel 9); Israel is the least of all nations (Deuteronomy 7).[5] In other words, the future king's

---

[2] On the complex history of the relation between Ephrathah and Bethlehem, see Sweeney, 387–88.
[3] Von Rad, *OTT II*, 170.
[4] Jeremias, 184.
[5] Jeremias, 186.

modest origins are of consequence for his ability to shepherd in Yhwh's strength.[6]

Within Christian liturgical and interpretive traditions, Mic 5:2 (5:1 MT) is an Advent text (cf. Matt 2:6). Except for Isa 7:14, few texts share Mic 5:2's signal status within Advent liturgical readings. Christians shaped wittingly or unwittingly by the hermeneutical implications of their liturgical contexts will have a difficult time reading this text as something other than a promise of Christ's incarnation. But is such a reading warranted by the verbal character of the text itself? A few interpretive points are worth highlighting in an attempt to answer this question.

First, the syntactical phrase, from you to me (לי), remains a challenge simply because the first-person referent derives from nowhere. The form is odd. Nevertheless, despite efforts to correct the text in various ways, there are no textual variants that allow emendation: except perhaps the Micah fragment at Qumran which has a לא after the לי. The LXX and Vulgate read the text as "to me," *moi* or *mihi*. In sum, the figure who will emerge as a ruler in Zion is *from you to me*, with the first-person referent implicitly understood as Yhwh.[7]

It is, however, the next line of the prophetic utterance that receives the spotlight in the history of this text's interpretation. "And his going forth is from of old, even from days of eternity or days long ago." The term "going forths" or "origins" מוצאות is in effect a hapax legomenon. The only other use is 2 Ki 10:27, and there it means "latrine." Readers are safe to assume this is not the sense here. Wolff suggests the plural "going forths" or "origins" gives the expression a heightened sense of feeling.[8] A great deal depends on settling the meaning of "going forth." Mays describes this term in the following suggestive way: "Origin echoes the verb 'come forth' and thinks of children originating in the

---

[6] "Alle diese Texte wollen verdeutlichen, dass Heil nicht von menschlichen Qualitäten abhängt, sondern allein von Gott" (Jeremias, 186).
[7] Wolff understands the strange syntax as stemming for the use of a Davidic tradition and its preference for the verbal phrase יצא, cf. Isa 11:1 and 2 Sam 7:13.
[8] Wolff, ad loc.

loins of their father."⁹ This phraseology is unique in the Old Testament, and as such, our philological instincts should be on guard about making immodest claims about what the rest of the text can or cannot mean.

Can "from of old" (מקדם) refer to a distant time in the past, thus limiting its potential? Yes it can (cf Am 9:11).¹⁰ Can a similar claim regarding "from days of eternity" (עולם) be made, especially given the fact that it is preceded by a temporal absolute noun, days?¹¹ Yes. And many, if not most, modern commentators go this route. But must it? Are readers forced to nod in the affirmative with *NIDOTTE*'s lexical conclusion regarding Mic 5:2? "While it is tempting to see here a reference to the eternal preexistence of the Messiah, no such an idea is found in biblical or postbiblical Jewish literature before the Similitudes of Enoch (I En 48:2-6)." Does such a philological instinct make good on a historical referent or potentially even the intention of the author/tradents (however such is conceived) while at the same time divorcing the linguistic character of Scripture from its divine referent in a two-testament frame?

It is worth recalling the following: the terms "from of old" and "days of eternity" are deployed in reference to the eternal character of God (Deut 33:27—"The eternal God (אלהי קדם) is your refuge, and underneath are the everlasting arms (עולם)"; Ps 90:2—"from everlasting to everlasting").¹² Hillers suggests that "from of old" has a mythical quality to it, "primeval, from the beginning, as an order of creation."¹³ Jeremias believes the connotative force of "from of old" refers to "mythische Urzeit," a time properly referred to as "Gottes Zeit." Why is this God's time? Because in it, claims Jeremias, the primeval saving will of God (*Heilswille*) originates.¹⁴ As already mentioned, *the highlighting*

---

⁹ Mays, 115–16.
¹⁰ See Mowinckel, *He That Cometh*, 163–63.
¹¹ See Waltke, ad loc.
¹² Richard Hays makes note of the LXX rendering of מקדם as ἀπ' ἀρχῆς, suggesting the phrase echoes in John's gospel at Jn 1:1 and more laconically at Jn 7:42 in association with the reference to Bethlehem. Richard Hays, *Echoes of Scripture in the Gospels* (Waco: Baylor University Press, 2016), 293–94.
¹³ Hillers, 66.
¹⁴ Jeremias, 185. This reading shares much in common with Calvin who places "going forth" in the divine will. Again, speculative theology helps here because the divine will is one with the various personae of the Trinity sharing in it.

of Bethlehem and not Jerusalem is itself significant because God makes clear his future purposes will begin with something new regarding the Davidic line rather than the current Davidic line in place in Jerusalem. Moreover, the use of "days" does not necessarily limit "eternity" as we see in Dan 7:9—the ancient of Days (or the long of days). In other words, a strictly governed historical account of this text's philological sense may attenuate its canonical intentionality. The fog and smoke of eternity wafts alongside the verbal dimension of this text.

The question here is a modest one. Given the unique character of this text, should its referent be limited to its undeniable, Davidic context in the historical moment of ancient Judah or Yehud? Given its verbal character and shared subject matter with a two-testament canon, the answer appears in the negative. Commenting on this text, Anderson and Freedman claim,

> At the least the language suggests that the birth of the Messiah has been determined, or predicted in the divine council, in primal days … Even if *mosaʾot* means no more than an oracle expressing the divine determination, it does not require a great shift in conceptuality to move to the Son of Man figure of the later apocalypses—the *Urmensch*.

They conclude, "So Christians did not abuse the text when they found Jesus in it."[15] This commentary will press the matter further and suggest the following: not only have Christians not abused this text when allowing it a substantive role in the doctrine of the eternal generation of the Son, but they in fact are reading the text well in light of the Trinitarian subject of Scripture. The Trinitarian subject matter of Scripture provides a ruled reading, setting expectations and alerting interpreting sensibilities regarding the text's referential nature. As such, the Trinitarian context of Scripture not only provides a hermeneutic for all of Scripture but is in fact the retina that allow us to see the text's ontological relation to its subject matter. Can Mic 5:1(2) be read in different ways than the traditional, Christian reading that links this text

---

[15] Andersen and Freedman, 468.

to the eternal generation of the Son? Certainly. Nevertheless, given the subject matter of Scripture and its canonical function as a continued means by which the Father reveals himself in the Son by the Spirit, must it be read in this overly historicist fashion? Not if the text of Mic 5:1(2) and the New Testament canon share in the same subject matter. His processions are from eternity, emerging from the eternal counsel of God's own inner-Trinitarian communication and a singular divine will given to the creation and redemption of the world.

Micah 5:2 in the tradition: John Owen as exemplar

Socinianism made its tyrannical march from Italy in the late sixteenth century into Poland during the early seventeenth century. There its roots settled deeply. The Racovian Catechism emerged from Poland's Socinian movement, and, in time, Socinian doctrine made its way into England via an Oxford don by the name of Mr. John Biddle—a Dickensian name if there ever was one. Mr. Biddle translated the Racovian Catechism into English, and the publication of this non-Trinitarian form of Christianity prompted Owen the polemicist into action. Mr. Owen produced a counterattack to Biddle's catechism, line by line, in his *Vindiciae Evangeliae (Defense of the Gospel)*. Some 589 pages of English prose later, Mr. Owen completed his rejoinder. The denial of Trinitarian faith was of massive moral consequence for Owen. Nothing less than humanity's salvation hung in the balance.

As one might anticipate, Owen's counter to Mr. Biddle's Socinian views focuses much on the relation of the Logos to the Father in an attempt to provide biblical and theological support for Nicene orthodoxy. Central to the concerns are the full divinity of the Son with attention given to the notion of the Son's eternal generation by means of the Father's eternal act of generating, language familiar to fourth-century Trinitarian debates.

Mr. Biddle's catechism denies the eternal generation of the Son because, in his terms, "if Christ were begotten of the essence of his Father, either he took his whole essence or but part. Part of his essence he could not take, for the divine essence is impartible; nor the whole, for it being one in number is incommunicable."[16] Owen's immediate comment after quoting Biddle cuts straight, "And this is the fruit of measuring spiritual things by carnal, infinite by finite, God by ourselves, the object of faith by corrupted rules of corrupted reason."[17]

What fascinates about this section in Owen, and for that matter Mr. Biddle's catechism too, relates to the location of the exegetical debate—the Old Testament. Mr. Biddle raises the question, Where do they argue for the eternal generation of the Son? Answer: "From these chiefly, Mic v. 2; Ps. ii. 7; cx. 3; Prov. viii. 23." From the identification of these texts, Mr. Biddle argues against their validity concerning the eternal generation of the Son by various and sundry means. Micah 5:2, for example, does not refer to the eternal generation of the Son. This is a misunderstanding of the lexical data, according to Mr. Biddle. The language refers quite simply to days of antiquity, and the use of the term "day" removes us from the sphere of eternity. The reference to days of antiquity conjoined with the identification of

---

[16] John Owen, *The Gospel Defended, The Works of John Owen*, Vol 12 (Edinburgh: Banner of Truth, 1966), 237.
[17] Ibid., 237.

Bethlehem as the place of nativity refers simply to David and his progeny, the line from which Christ would come—a reading conspicuously like most current approaches to the selfsame text. And Mr. Owen counters with his theological/exegetical armor strapped on for battle. The whole of chapter 9 in Owen's *Defense of the Gospel* is an exegetical debate regarding the eternal generation of the son and the Old Testament. Micah 5:2 registers as the first text under critical scrutiny.

The exchange between Owen and Biddle remains instructive, especially in the realm of evangelical hermeneutics, because Owen and Biddle formally agree when it comes to their doctrine of Scripture. In fact, Owen says little against Biddle's catechetical statements concerning Scripture, a point of some interest. Carl Trueman's work on John Owen explains,

> When Owen tackles Biddle's text proper, he starts with a surprisingly brief comment on the *Twofold Catechism*'s doctrine of scripture, with which he has little disagreement. The very brevity of the chapter, along with its somewhat petulant *ad hominem* nature, indicates the problem: the Socinians appear to hold to a basic scripture principle in a formally similar manner to the orthodox. The differences, in fact, are significant, and go straight to the heart of why Owen can see scripture as teaching the doctrine of the Trinity and the Socinians reject such a conclusion: the point at issue is not simply whether scripture is the authoritative noetic foundation for theology, but how that scripture is to be interpreted, a point which draws in matters of logic, of metaphysics, and of how individual passages of scripture are mutually related in the act of interpretation.[18]

Biddle's claim is a claim that strikes at the heart of an evangelical sensibility, a sensibility marked by an "I am only interested in what the Bible claims and nothing more" attitude. And while this kind of appeal has a pedestrian cache, with interpretive instincts heading in the right direction—we seek to order our thoughts and prayers in accord with Scripture's norming voice—the surreptitious character of the statement remains. For Biddle is working with metaphysic commitments as well, namely, it is logically impossible to hold to a sharing in the divine essence between a plurality of personae in the Godhead. The divine essence is indivisible and the eternal generation of the Son from the Father's divine essence does not follow this indivisibility. This a priori notion of the divine essence functions as a hermeneutical cipher for Biddle. Owen identifies this Socinian metaphysic as "rationalistic reductionism."[19]

As an aside, Spinoza's interpretive outline in his *Tractatus* makes similar claims. He too displays an "I am only interested in coming to terms with what Scripture claims and nothing more."[20] Starting afresh with a Cartesian mode of inquiry, Spinoza sets to the task of allowing Scripture to speak for itself. But the indubitable foundation of Spinoza's hermeneutic was the natural light of reason, a claim he repeats enough to register it as a central leitmotif in the *Tractatus*. This "neutral" hermeneutic led to the necessary sequestering of metaphysical truth claims from Scripture into the specialized world of philosophy. Owen's response to Spinoza would mirror his to Biddle: "rationalistic reductionism."

Why? Because Owen is steeped enough in the church's exegetical tradition to recognize the necessary two-way street between the engagement with the biblical texts themselves and

---

[18] Carl R. Trueman, *John Owen: Reformed Catholic, Renaissance Man* (Great Theologians Series; Aldershot: Ashgate, 2007), 48.

[19] Op cit., Richard Muller, *Post-Reformation Reformed Dogmatics: The Rise and Development of Reformed Orthodoxy*, ca. 1520 to ca. 1725, Vol. Four, *The Triunity of God* (Grand Rapids: Baker Academic, 2003), 283.

[20] Benedict de Spinoza, *Theological-Political Treatise* (Cambridge Texts in the History of Philosophy; trans. J. Israel; Cambridge: Cambridge University Press, 2007), 8, *et passim*.

the confession regarding the identity of the one God witnessed to therein. In David Yeago's formulation, Trinitarian language, while extra-biblical, is deployed as an act of *hermeneia* for the sake of coming to terms with Scripture's total witness regarding its naming of the persons of the Trinity: naming related to the divine essence at times and to eternal relations or processions at others. Owen strives to give a rational and ordered account of Christian orthodoxy, and he does so in an effort to come to terms with Scripture's total witness. For Mr. Biddle, the distinction between *essence* and *person* is patently false, unallowable by the assumptions of his metaphysic. For Owen, on the other hand, this distinction maintains Scripture's unity while at the same time comes to terms with Scripture's diverse modes of expression concerning divine unity and plurality. Again, the Bible's own self-witness demands such an account.

As far as Mic 5:2 is concerned, Owen finds Biddle's philological analysis lacking. For Owen, the מוצאת refers unquestionably to the Son's eternal generation. He complains Biddle takes no account of מקדם, which for Owen refers to eternity. And despite the temporal *nomen regens* (construct noun), given the subject matter, Owen understands מימי עולם as a reference to pre-temporal eternity as well, much in the same way as the Aramaic ancient of days in Dan 7:9 makes use of days with reference to eternity.

Owen overreaches perhaps in his downplaying of the Davidic context. He finds Hugo Grotius's identification of Zerubbabel as the immediate fulfillment of this text problematic. Owen appeals to the Targum's paraphrastic rendering of the text as a reference to the coming Messiah, undercutting Grotius's reading—not to mention Zerubbabel is born in Babylon, not Bethlehem. Of interest, Theodore of Mopsuestia understands this text as having an immediate reference to Zerubbabel, though not at the expense of its ultimate Christological referent: a double-literal fulfillment one might say or perhaps a figural reading that takes into account multiple referents?

What are readers to make of all of this? One, Biddle's (and Grotius's) reading of this text shares much in common with current scholarship on Mic 5:2, as observed above. Two, Owen's reading of the text is a close philological analysis of the words themselves. Yet, the words of Scripture do not operate apart from the subject matter of Christian Scripture: a subject matter whose character remains an article of faith. As his snarky response to Grotius intimates, "That it [Mic 5:2] properly belongs to Christ we have a better interpreter to be sure than Grotius or any of his rabbins, Matt. ii. 4-6" (240). For Owen, the exegetical deck is stacked because Scripture itself speaks clearly about this text's final referent. And because this is so, the literal sense of the text can only be made sense of in a close reading of the verbal/grammatical character of the text in shared relation with its Triune subject matter. Owen's reading is standard fare in the tradition.

Glosses from the Christian interpretive tradition

- Cyril of Alexandria: understands the "going forth" of Mic 5:2 as either (1) eternal generation or (2) the emergence in time of the Logos's incarnation (*logos incarnatus*).
- Theodoret of Cyrus: Micah 5:2 relates substantially to the prologue of John's gospel and resists reduction to immediate fulfillment in Zerubbabel.
- Aquinas, *Summa Theologiae*, Pt 1, Q 42, Art 5 (Whether the Son is in the Father, and Conversely): Obj. 2 states, "Further, nothing that has come out from another is within it. But the sone from eternity came out from the Father, according to Micheas v. 2 ... Therefore the Son and the Father are not in each other." Aquinas replies, "The Son's going forth from the Father is by mode of the interior procession whereby the word emerges from the heart and remains therein. Hence this going forth in God is only by the distinction of the relations, not by any kind of essential separation." Again, Aquinas is drawing on the metaphysical tradition of the church fathers in

distinguishing between essence and persons. As Gilles Emery clarifies, "The sole distinction in the Godhead is between the persons, but there is no distinction between the persons and the divine nature."[21]

- Luther too sees the correspondence between Mic 5:2 and John's prologue regarding the eternal generation of the Son from the Father.
- Melanchthon states, "Although this testimony is brief, yet it asserts that the Messiah existed before the creation of the world. Therefore He is eternal and God" (Melanchthon, Loci Communes, p. 26).
- In his sermons on Micah, Calvin's exegetical instincts are similar to the tradition, but he follows a pastoral path encouraging hearers in their suffering to recognize the eternal character of Christ's kingdom. His commentary on Micah makes the strange statement that though he is willing to grant this text refers to the eternal generation of the Son, he prefers reading the text more simply as a reference to the long-before determination of God to bring Christ into the world. Why the simple reading? Because the traditional Christian reading "will never be allowed by the Jews."[22]

While the chord may be struck with a different cadence and emphasis in the tradition, by and large, the Trinitarian referent of Mic 5:2 is assumed. The phrase "[W]hose origin is from of old, from ancient days" refers not simply to the eternal plan of God to perpetuate David's throne, though it should be added the text does not say less than this. Rather, the text, whose theological referent is God's Triune revelation of himself in the redemption of humankind, refers to the coming Davidic ruler who does indeed perpetuate David's throne but does so as one whose eternal identity is in procession from the Father in a shared divine essence.

Micah 5:5-9 (5:4-8 MT)

Micah 5:5 (5:4 MT) begins with the temporal marker "and it will be" (והיה). This marker shapes the rest of ch. 5 as it begins v. 7 (v. 6 MT) and v. 10 (v. 9 MT). The future indicators fill out for readers the forward-looking hope associated with the promised leader of 5:2-4 (1-3 MT). Identifying the antecedent of the demonstrative pronoun "this" (זה) in 5:5a (5:4a MT) remains a challenge. The NRSV, as with most English translations, understands the referent as the announced king of 5:2-4 (1-3 MT): "and *he* shall be the one of peace."[23] Both Nogalski and

---

[21] Gilles Emery, O. P., *The Trinity: An Introduction to the Catholic Doctrine on the Triune God* (trans. M. Levering; Washington, DC: The Catholic University of America Press, 2011), 106. See Lewis Ayres, *Nicea and Its Legacy: An Approach to Fourth-Century Trinitarian Theology* (Oxford: Oxford University Press, 2004), 236.

[22] Calvin, 299.

[23] See Mays, 119. Waltke supports the traditional reading, leaning on the Vulgate for support (Waltke, 286). He also nods in the comparative philological direction with those who understand the phrase זה שלום as a divine title based on Arabic and Ugaritic *du*, "the one of." In this light, the phrase reads, "and he will be The One of Peace." Hillers also makes

Sweeney lean against the traditional reading because "this" tends to refer to something new with "that" as the pronoun of choice when looking backwards.[24] On this account, the formula, "and it will be," introduces a moment in the future when Judah endures and survives the onslaught of the Assyrians. The antecedent of "this," therefore, is the future scene on display in vv. 5-6 (4-5 MT).

The Masoretic Text collects vv. 1-5 within one paragraph (*parashiyya*).[25] Such a delimitation does intimate the thematic unity of this section, despite a clear understanding of the particular referent of the demonstrative pronoun. Whether "this" looks forward, so Nogalski and Sweeney, or backwards to the promised king with "this" translated as "he" or "this one," the promised peace of 5:5 (5:4 MT) resists detachment from the promised king of 5:2-4 (1-3 MT). Jeremias cuts the Gordian knot of this ambiguous phrase by claiming that the coming king is either the mediator (*Vermittler*) of this coming salvation or the personification (*Verkörperung*) of it: *he is peace*.[26] Both are grammatically possible. As Jeremias claims, "The salvation of the community (and of the world) is unthinkable without the new David according to this text."[27]

> As observed in preceding chapters, van der Woude advances a trenchant argument for the presence of the pseudo-prophet's voice in passages of Micah often associated with the prophet himself or prophetic tradents. While this commentary has not followed van der Woude at every turn because of the subtle nature of the argument and the problems posed for future generations of readers, it is of interpretive interest to note Luther's agreement with van der Woude at this juncture of Micah's prophecy. For Luther, the phrase "and this shall be peace" is Micah's strident account of the false prophets' overly confident Zion theology. In other words, this is the kind of peace they promise, to wit, the terrorizing presence of the Assyrians trampling through our villages and cities (Luther, 250). Luther continues his account by identifying a future spiritual peace that will indeed come but not the kind of false peace promised by the pseudo-prophets.

such a claim about this phrase as a divine title (cf. Isa 9:6; Hillers, 65). Andersen and Freedman offer support for this reading as well based on the comparative philological arguments of Cathcart. For Andersen and Freedman, the title "the One of Peace" alludes to Solomon and his era of peace (Andersen and Freedman, 476). Wolff believes "this" refers to the Messianic figure of 5:1-3 MT and finds the arguments weak that read זה שלום as a construct or title, i.e., all of the above (Wolff, 147).

[24] Nogalski, 563; Sweeney, 389-90.
[25] Waltke and O'Connor, §38.1c. See Andersen and Freedman, 473.
[26] Jeremias, 186-87.
[27] Jeremias, 187. "Das Heil der Gemeinschaft (und der Welt) ist für den Text undenkbar ohne den neuen David."

The promised peace associated with the coming king manifests itself in the endurance and salvation of Judah from the threatening advances of the Assyrians. The peace promised herein is of the salvific kind as described in the verses to follow. The sequence of events is straightforward: Assyrian incursion, the defense of Judah by its leader/ shepherds, and a counteroffensive attack against Assyria. The presentation of the events, however, do not follow a linear temporal frame. Nogalski's suggestion of reading the *ki* (כי) clauses of 5:5-6 (4-5 MT) as concessive ("though") rather than the standard temporal rendering ("when") has much to commend it. He understands the A B B A pattern of these verses (*ki weki* [כי ... וכי]) as conditional clauses (A) enveloping two consequential elements (B).[28] In brief, *though* Assyria enters the land in hostility, Judah will take measures of defense resulting in their endurance. The resultant endurance and redemption from Assyrian onslaught is the promised peace of v. 5 (v. 4 MT).

The first conditional clause (5:4b MT) describes the Assyrians entering the land and treading upon the palaces of Judah.[29] The consequence of this action is the appointment by the community ("we will raise") of seven shepherds and eight tribal leaders. The phrase is riddled with ambiguities. The identification of Judah's leaders as shepherds is a standard feature of the prophetic literature (cf. Jeremiah 23). The archaic term "tribal leader" recalls the pre-monarchical Transjordan.[30] Andersen and Freedman suggest that if this were the allusion, then the number twelve would be expected rather than eight. They make the interesting suggestion that an etymological relation exists between *nsk* ("to appoint as a leader"; cf. Ps. 2:6; Prov 8:26) and *msch* ("to anoint"). In other words, the term "tribal leaders" (נסיך) could

---

[28] Nogalski, 563.
[29] The phrase "our palaces" (בארמנתינו) is rendered "our soil" in the NRSV. It follows the suggestion of the BHS to emend "our palaces" with באדמתנו ("our land"). There is some support for this reading in the LXX ("our land" or "our region"). See Williamson who argues for the MT against the suggested emendation. Williamson understands the corruption of the next verse "in her doorways" (בפתחיה) as making best sense against the MT rendering of "our palaces" over against the emendation to "our land." Williamson, "Marginalia," 365-67.
[30] See Andersen and Freedman, 479.

be in synonymous relation to "messiah."[31] Yet the plural character of these appointed leaders problematizes a following of this reading too far.

What is more perplexing is the use of the numbers "seven" and "eight" to modify the "shepherds" and "leaders" of the people. Solving this riddle definitively will remain elusive.[32] As with Amos, the sequence of numbers, 3 + 4 or 7 + 8, may have no specific numeric reference, simply referring to a multiplicity of entities.[33] The Assyrians will, according to Sweeney, "have their hands full" when dealing with Judah's revolt.[34] On the other hand, the numerical pattern may draw attention to the second number as the real number (cf. Prov 30:18-31).[35] Nogalski displays a preference for an "apocalyptic" understanding with the number eight in view, especially if read from the perspective of the eighth century. From Hezekiah to the fall of Jerusalem under King Zedekiah, there were eight kings of Judah. Andersen and Freedman continue their Messianic line of interpretation suggesting that the number eight relates to David as the eighth son of Jesse, though they are quick to point out that there is no tradition where David holds a position of primary leadership in some shared capacity with his seven brothers.[36] Waltke provides a helpful path to make sense of the relation between the singularity of the promised coming king and the multiplicity of leaders announced here. For Waltke, the seven/eight phraseology does draw attention to the number eight in order to demonstrate the going beyond perfection that the number seven indicates. Seven, according to Waltke, symbolizes totality and sacredness. Therefore, the sons of Israel appointed to shepherd and lead in the midst of Assyria's incursion will do so in "more than full cooperation" with the Messianic ruler appointed in vv. 2-4 (1-3 MT).

---

[31] Andersen and Freedman, 479.
[32] The reading of these leaders as Assyrian rather than Judean (e.g., Wolff and Ben Zvi) does not persuade. See Nogalski, 564.
[33] See Duane Garret who does see a significance in the numbers 3 + 4 in Amos as collectively 7.
[34] Sweeney, 390. Interestingly, Calvin follows the same interpretive line. "By *seven* and *eight*, the Prophet no doubt meant a great number" (Calvin, 310).
[35] Waltke, 289-90.
[36] Andersen and Freedman, 478.

The text is ironic when it describes these leaders of Judah "shepherding" Assyria with the sword and the "drawn sword."[37] While there is no historical evidence that Judah in the eighth century made offensive incursions into Assyria, such hyperbole is fair game when describing God's providential redemption of his people against such a tyrannical force as Assyria. Moreover, the eschatological shaping of the prophetic literature makes possible the tropic nature of Assyria in Micah's final form. Assyria on this reading is a figure whose referential potential exceeds the moment of the eighth century per se. Such is the reading offered by Cyril of Alexandria as he follows the text's literal sense to its spiritual or figural sense. For Cyril, Assyria represents the very inventor of sin himself, namely, Satan.[38] Assyria on this reading is "the implacable and warlike mass of demons which oppose everything holy and fight against the holy city, the spiritual Zion."[39]

> Calvin follows Cyril's figural instincts at this interpretive juncture. Calvin pursues a more pastoral line of thought as he thinks through the difficult juxtaposition of promised peace and Assyrian onslaught in the text's literal sense. This is a commendable interpretive move made by Calvin. The verbal character of text and the tensions present therein are allowed to stand as he provides a pastoral and theological point of entry for textual sense making. In brief, Calvin raises the question "Why?" Why would God allow the Assyrians violent entrance to the land after the remarkable announcement of Christ's coming? For Calvin, this prophetic word is not hemmed in to the moment of its literary genesis or redactional finality. The prophets speak to the preservation of Christ's church before and after his incarnation. Here the figural pattern is observed as the temporal moment of Assyrian's incursion plays a transhistorical role in providing a prophetic pattern for God's dealings with his Church *ante* and *post Christum natum*. The answer to the "Why?" question for Calvin is straightforward. "The Prophet intimates that the Church of God would not be free from troubles, even after the coming of Christ."[40] As the prophets indicate, often God humbles his people even in the form of discipline and chastisement in order to deliver them.

Yhwh's providential oversight and protection of His people spill over the borders of Judah (vv. 5-6 [4-5 MT]) to the scattered remnant of the diaspora throughout the nations (vv. 7-9 [6-8 MT]). Yhwh's power and sovereign reach is not limited to the national borders of those who worship Him. Yhwh is powerful to preserve and protect wherever land and sea exist.

---

[37] On following the emendation "drawn sword" over "its doorways," see Williamson, "Marginalia," 366; cf. Wolff, ad loc.
[38] Cyril of Alexandria, 237.
[39] Ibid.
[40] Calvin, 307–08.

The nature of the similes in vv. 7-8 (6-7 MT) is the subject of some discussion. As is often noted, a grammatical parallelism exists between vv. 7-8. Both verses begin with the same future formula, "and it will be" (והיה), followed by the phrase "a remnant of Jacob in the midst of many peoples." Following this formula, the similes of dew (טל)/showers (רביבים) appear in v. 7 and lion (אריה) in v. 8. The difficulty comes in relating the two metaphors that prima facie appear incompatible: dew as blessing and lion as predator.

The image of the remnant (שארית) appears in Micah already at 2:12 and 4:7. At both locations, the remnant exist as a testimony to the saving hand of Yhwh to shepherd and protect his people despite the egregious circumstances having led to their dispersion. Jeremias believes 5:7-8 refers the reader back to these two texts in Micah yet from a different standpoint. Whereas 2:12 and 4:7 speak to the future (*Endzeit*), 5:7 addresses the current circumstances of the reader, where the "now" (*jetzt*, עתה) of 4:9 and 5:1 (4:14 MT) has turned to a new moment, namely, the postexilic period.[41] Whether or not the initial audience was postexilic (see Willis for an eighth-century reading), a new situation is at hand, one that stands in continuity with the promises for the remnant in 2:12 and 4:7ff.

Heidelberg Catechism Q & A 27

Q. What do you understand by the providence of God?
A. The almighty and ever present power of God by which God upholds, as with his hand, heaven and earth and all creatures, and so rules them that leaf and blade, rain and drought, fruitful and lean years, food and drink, health and sickness, prosperity and poverty—all things, in fact, come to us, not by chance but by his fatherly hand.

The relation of vv. 7-8 is an antithetical one, and this despite attempts to flatten out the contrast.[42] In the future moment of God's dealings with his dispersed remnant, they will either bless the nations like dew or curse

---

[41] Jeremias, 189.
[42] See Wolff who argues impressively for the simile of "dew" as an indication of something only God can do, thus the clarifying end of v. 7: "which do not depend upon people or

the nations as predators of God's judgment. Jeremias points back to the Abrahamic covenant in Gen 12:3 where such a contrast is already on offer: Abraham's offspring as either a blessing or a curse to the nations.[43] Moreover, Hosea has already set the tone with these two metaphors: dew and lion. Yhwh acts like a lion in vengeance against his rebellious children (Hos 5:14) and will also be like the dew when He redeems and forgives sins (Hos 14:5). These metaphors stand in specific relation to the actions of Yhwh; Hosea prepares us for this understanding. Here in Mic 5:7-8, the remnant act as the human agents through whom Yhwh executes his blessings of forgiveness and his ferocious judgment for and against the nations. Micah's prophecy has already prepared readers for the juxtaposition of these seemingly incompatible metaphors. In Mic 4:1-4, the nations stream to Mt. Zion in order to receive instruction and blessing from Yhwh. While in Mic 4:11-13, the nations are portrayed as those who in time will experience Yhwh's wrath by means of his agent Zion. As mentioned in the previous chapter, neat and clean categories like "universalism" or "particularism" are problematized by the prophetic literature when seeking to relate Israel and the nations. Yet, Israel's unique role as mediators of Yhwh's salvation to the nations remains an unassailable affirmation of the prophets in general and Micah here in ch. 5.

Micah 5:10-15 (9-14 MT)

The final "and it will be" (והיה) section of ch. 5 turns to Yhwh's purging of Jacob.[44] The grammatical structure of the text (MT) is striking as a series of first person, future verbs (*waw-consecutives*) begin each line of the

---

wait for any mortal." The discordance between the two similes is in large measure the rationale for Wolff's resistance to allow "dew" to function in its typical way as a positive image of the blessing of God. Rather, for Wolff "dew" speaks to the doings of God and God alone apart from human achievement. The existence of the remnant is like the existence of dew, inexplicable apart from the powerful activity of God (Wolff, 156–57).

[43] Jeremias, 190.
[44] The standard defense of the "authenticity" of Mic 5:9-14 remains. John T. Willis, "The Authenticity and Meaning of Micah 5:9-14," *ZAW* 81 (1969): 353–68.

section. The first-person speaking voice of each verb except one is Yhwh. The only verb attributed to Judah's action is a negation, a nonaction. They will no longer worship the work of their hands (the second line v. 13 [v. 12 MT]). The juxtaposition of divine action and human nonaction speaks to the nature of the situation at hand. The section displays the resolution of Yhwh's singular will: to rid Judah of her military reliance and idolatry. Yhwh is pruning, cutting off the cancer of Judah's infidelity. Both idolatry and a reliance on arms turn on the self-confidence of Judah to rely on itself for national and religious security. As in Isa 2:6ff, such actions reveal the pride and arrogance of God's people. Moreover, as Isaiah 2 ends with Yhwh shearing and pruning, so too does God cut away at Judah's national and religious self-reliance.

The phrase "in that day" (ביום־ההוא) following the future indicator "and it will be" in v. 10 (9 MT) links this final section of Micah 5 to the beginning of Micah 4. The "in the latter days" of Mic 4:1 and the future "in that day" of 5:10 reveal the multifaceted character of the Day of the Lord theme within these two chapters. The future entails nations streaming to Zion in order to hear Yhwh's teaching, and the fifth chapter ends with a view to the future day where a cleansing of God's people from their self-reliance occurs. As within the Twelve as a whole, the Day of the Lord is a varied thing, able to be viewed from multiple perspective depending on the nature of the audience in view. Here, the future day is a day of reckoning for God's people, and Mic 5:10-14 (9-13 MT) makes clear why this day will be darkness (cf Am 5:18).

The first two verses speak to Judah's reliance on the machinations of their military strength: horses and chariots, cities, and strongholds (cf. Isa 2:7, 15; Deut 17:16-17).[45] Whereas vv. 12-14 (11-13 MT) reveal religious self-confidence as a plethora of humanly crafted approaches to control and steer the divine are identified: sorceries, diviners, idolatrous images, and the Asherah or female consort of the Canaanite god El.[46]

---

[45] See Andersen and Freedman, 493, on the intertextual association of these verses with Zech 9:9-10.
[46] See "Asherah" in *Dictionary of Deities and Demons in the Bible, Second Edition* (ed. K. van der Toorn, B. Becking and P. van der Horst; Leiden: Brill, 1999), 99–105.

These are all listed in concert because they all attest to a single act of religious infidelity, namely, a rejection of the revealed will of Yhwh as to his identity, singularity, and sovereignty. In this light, military reliance absent the leading light of Yhwh and religious ingenuity apart from revealed religion are flip sides of the same coin of human pride.

The surprising element of 5:10-15 remains the final verse. It follows the same grammatical structure of the verses preceding it, beginning with a future verb (*waw consecutive*). Readers would naturally assume the subject matter and identity of the addressees would remain the same. Yet, v. 15 reads as follows: "And in anger and wrath I will execute vengeance on *the nations* that did not obey." The use of the term "nations" (גוים) comes as a surprise given the identity of Judah as the addressees of this unit. As readers might imagine, several interpretive options are offered in the secondary literature to make sense of this conundrum. Wagenaar is representative of a redaction-critical explanation. On this account, 5:15 (14 MT) is the work of a later editor who added it to 5:10-14 (9-13 MT) in order to frame the whole of this unit as an oracle of judgment against the nations. In other words, the surprise ending functions as a redactional gloss for interpreting the whole unit as not against Judah per se but against the nations.[47]

Ben Zvi makes note of the redaction-critical argument, suggesting there are two approaches to understanding 5:15 (14 MT) in its current literary setting. The first approach places 5:15 (14 MT) in temporal relation to the preceding verses according to the following logic: after the pruning of Judah, God will turn his judging efforts toward the nations. As noted elsewhere, Ben Zvi understands the *Sitz im Buch* of Micah as postexilic Yehud. In this location, Judah has already suffered vv. 10-14 (9-13 MT), and they now await the execution of v. 15 (14 MT).[48] Sweeney offers this temporal reading with the judgment of Zion leading to the judgment of the nations for the sake of restoring Judah.[49]

---

[47] Wagenaar, *Judgement and Salvation*, 310–11. See also Nogalski who follows this reading, ad loc.
[48] Ben Zvi, 138.
[49] Sweeney, 393.

The second approach, according to Ben Zvi, is to follow the logic of Micah 1 where the summons to the nations and the identification of Jerusalem and Samaria as the targets of God's judgment blur into each other (Mic 1:5). The textual intention of this blurring results in two interpretive options—one, readers read from the beginning to end with the conclusion that Judah is listed as part of the nations under God's judgment or two, readers read from back to front where, as with Wagenaar, the whole of this section is targeted at the nations and not Judah per se.[50]

Jeremias, along with Mays, Wolff, and others, recognizes the editorial function of 5:15 (14 MT) as well, though he goes in a different interpretive direction than Wagenaar. Jeremias accepts the depth dimension of Micah's prophecy as an editorial whole but does so in order to come to terms with the text's in its final, canonical form. Jeremias identifies the link of 5:15 (14 MT) to ch. 1 with its summons to hear (שמע; 1:2). The editorial shaping of this unit suggests that 5:15 (14 MT) and 1:2 relate to each other as bookends of chs 1–5. The nations experience God's vengeance (נקם) because they did not "hear" or "obey" (שמעו) the summons (cf. 1:2). There is a theological integrity and unity to chs 1–5 in the text's final form. Jeremias also draws attention to the arch (*Bogen*) from 5:10-15 (9-14 MT) to 4:1-4 where a distinction is made in the final days between those who stream to hear and listen and those who refuse to hear.[51] The faithful community is a community marked by loyalty and attendance to Yhwh's teaching, whereas the community under judgment bears the faithless marks of 5:10-14 (9-14 MT).[52] Like the surprising list of nations in Amos 1-2, so too here in the final form of Micah's prophetic book, faithless Israel is identified and linked with the nations who did not hear.[53]

---

[50] Ibid., 138–39.
[51] Jeremias, 195.
[52] Wolff (160–61) draws attention to the significance of "wrath and anger" in Deut 29:21-27.
[53] As indicated in Am 5:18, there was an expectation that the Day of the Lord would bring only light, not darkness. Such is indicative of the overweening Zion theology at play among political and religious leaders.

As mentioned above, Isaiah 2 provides an interpretive and canonical aid for the internal logic of Micah 4-5. The vision of "the latter days" where the nations stream to Mt. Zion follows with a summons to Judah to walk in the light of the LORD (Isa 2:5). The future promise of Yhwh's universal reign and resultant era of peace is intended to elicit self-scrutiny among Yhwh's elect as to their own actions in the present. Yet, as in Micah 5, Jacob follows the paths of the nations, adopting their political and religious practices and sensibilities (Isa 2:6-8). As ch. 2 continues its unsettling line of thought, the pride of Jacob is wrapped up with the pride of the nations such that the terrible day of God's forthcoming vengeance will be equally meted out to arrogant Judah and lofty Lebanon, Bashan, and Tarshish. The canonical effect of Isaiah 2 and Micah 4-5 is a summons to repentance for God's people because God's judgment against human arrogance does not discriminate according to national boundary lines.

Calvin is quick to bring the material force of the prophetic word into the life of the church in its current existence. His comments on the sins of self-reliance are poignant and worthy of reproducing in toto:

> This truth ought to be carefully contemplated by us. Whenever we see that the Church of God, though not possessing any great power, is yet diminished daily, yea, and becomes, so to speak, like a naked land, without any defenses, it so happens, in order that the protection of God may be alone sufficient for us, and that he may wholly tear away from our hearts all haughtiness and pride, and dissipate all those vain confidences by which we not only obscure the glory of God, but, as far as we can, entirely cover it over. In short, as there is nothing better for us than to be preserved by the hand of God, we ought to bear patiently the removal of all those impediments which close up the way against God, and, in a manner, keep off his hand from us, when he is ready to extend it for the purpose of delivering us. For when our minds are inflated with foolish self-confidence, we neglect God; and thus a wall intervenes, which prevents him to help us. Who would not wish, seeing himself in extreme danger and help not far distant, that an intercepting wall should immediately fall down? Thus God is near at hand, as he

has promised; but there are many walls and many obstacles, from the ruin of which, if we would be safe, we must desire and seek, that God may find an open and free way, in order that he may be able to afford us aid.[54]

---

[54] Calvin, 321–22.

6

Micah 6

Introduction

Up unto this point in its literary movement, the prophecy of Micah reflects a series of intentionally shaped markers of coherence and continuity. The move from doom to hope is found at critical junctures, the razing of Zion at the end of ch. 3 opens to the future exaltation of Zion at the beginning of ch. 4, the humiliation of Judah's king at the break of ch. 4 leads to the promised coming king in 5:1: These all reveal a unified movement and shape to Micah's prophetic legacy in the first five chapters. The final section of Micah's prophecy—chs 6–7—dips back into the themes of the first three chapters with little to no internal references to chs 4–5. Jeremias claims that if readers of Micah read only chs 4–5 and then move to chs 6–7 they will experience "another world" (*einer anderen Welt*).[1] Andersen and Freedman identify the interlocking themes of "condemnation and conciliation" making their way through chs 6–7, yet they conclude that "it is hard to find any overarching structure" to these chapters.[2] From a synchronic perspective, Sweeney suggests chs 6–7 function as a call to repentance in order to actualize the future promises of chs 1–5.[3] While such a reading has promise, one is hard-pressed to locate it in the material of these chapters. The strong intertextual connections between 6–7 and 1–3 suggest that Micah's prophecy ends with an address to the reader's current moment in a

---

[1] Jeremias, 196.
[2] Andersen and Freedman, 500.
[3] Sweeney, 394. Sweeney sees no reason to date Micah 6-7 in the postexilic community. Jeremias and Kessler both understand Micah 6-7 as a prophetic *Fortschreibung* of chs 1–3 on the basis of the nature and subject matter of the literature.

move from the future forecast of chs 4–5 back to the current situation of distress and disorder.

Micah 6:1-8—He has shown you

The beginning of Micah 6 mirrors the beginning of the book at 1:2. The summons to "hear" (שמע) sets the stage for the legal dispute to follow between Yhwh and his people (עמי, "my people"; 6:2, 3). Unlike ch. 1, Micah 6 summons the creation itself as witnesses to the case at hand. There in ch. 1, the hills and the mountains endure the effects of Yhwh's judgment. Here, they are called on as witnesses in a cosmic legal dispute Yhwh has with his people (cf. Isa 1:2; Deut 4:26; 30:19; 31:28; 32:1).[4] Micah 6:2 identifies creation's witnesses as the "mountains" (ההרים) and the "enduring foundations of the earth" (האתנים מסדי ארץ). In Deut 32:22, the foundations of the earth range in proximity to Sheol, functioning as the underworld foundation for creation's highest members: the mountains. The extremity of mountains and their underworld foundation suggest a merism of the material creation in its entirety, from its highest heights to lowest depths (cf. Isa 24:18).[5] The enduring character of the mountains and their foundations stand in stark contrast to the ephemeral nature of the human agents with whom Yhwh is contending.[6]

Micah 6:1-2 is the subject of much reflection because it appears to lack clarity in its forward movement.[7] The first verse introduces the

---

[4] Hillers draws attention to Hittite treaties where the gods and created order as part of a "fundamental cosmic framework" are called as witnesses to covenant lawsuits (Hillers, 77). The gods and cosmic order brought judgment on the vassals if they failed to honor the covenant. Hillers concludes that it is difficult to decide whether the calling on the mountains, hills, and streams served more than a rhetorical device in Israel's religion. He does suggest that these entities are associated with "permanence and numinous age" (ibid.). Nevertheless, according to Hillers, there does not appear to be any biblical validation of the cosmic framework executing judgment.

[5] See Wolff, 173; Waltke, 347.

[6] Kessler makes note of the "foundations" (יסד) of Samaria being exposed attest to her destruction and end, while the foundations of the earth summoned as witnesses in 6:2 are perennial and always ready to be summoned (Kessler, 262).

[7] Jeremias describes Mic 6:1-8 as "in mehrfacher Hinsicht ungewöhnlich" (Jeremias, 198).

section as "that which Yhwh says" only to find Yhwh presented in the third person thereafter. Moreover, it is possible that the syntax of the first summons in v. 1 indicates a dispute with the mountains and hills, while the second summons in v. 2 calls on the same entities as jurors/witnesses to the case Yhwh has against his people.[8] Similarly, the identity of the speaking agent and the addressees of the imperatives are not prima facie clear. Mays, for example, understands 6:1b as the speech of Yhwh to Israel despite the use of the third person for Yhwh. Israel is summoned to present her case in 1b with Yhwh beginning His arguments in 6:2.[9] Ben Zvi believes these verses are intentionally polysemous, resisting quick or facile identification of the speaking voices (Yhwh, the prophet, or Israel).[10] This commentary shares Ben Zvi's resistance to pit 6:1 over against 6:2 as in redactional conflict, though his arguments for the polysemous character of these verses appear unnecessarily complex. There seems little textual reason to avoid the straightforward reading of 6:1-2 as unified in presentation: the prophet who announces the forthcoming speech of Yhwh in 1a calls on Yhwh in vv. 1b-2 to bring his case before the mountains, hills, and foundations of the world.[11] The prophet functions as a master of ceremonies for the forthcoming disputation, calling the actors to the legal stage before the looming and enduring presence of the mountains

---

[8] Wolff sets v. 1 off from v. 2 by identifying the speaking voice as a plaintiff, perhaps the prophet, standing in Yhwh's stead with the mountains and the hills as the legal opponents. Wolff's suggestion that "mountains and hills" may be ciphers for the nations has not found many followers (Wolff, 166–67). Jeremias makes an argument for 6:1 as an insertion by a redactor to serve as a bridge into the new material from the preceding (Jeremias, 199–200).

[9] Mays, 131.

[10] Ben Zvi, 143–44.

[11] See, e.g., Sweeney, Waltke, and Andersen and Freedman. Kessler's insistence, among others, on understanding the את preposition of 6:1b as a contestation "against" or "with" the mountains is overwrought (Kessler, 257; see note 7 on Wolff). Waltke affirms the usual syntactic function of this preposition following ריב as "with" or "against" (cf. Gen 31:36; Judg 6:32; and Hos 2:4 [2]; Waltke, 345). But these instances have to do with human agents and the preposition does mean "before" elsewhere (cf. Gen 20:16; Isa 30:8). Limburg's essay affirms Waltke's understanding of the preposition (J. Limburg, "The Root ריב and Prophetic Lawsuit Speeches," *JBL* 88 [1969]: 301). Limburg believes את in this context "clearly" means "before" (ibid.). The LXX translates the preposition as *pros*.

and their foundations. The wizened and aged stability of Treebeard from Tolkien's *The Lord of the Rings* serves as an illustration of creation's witnesses in 6:1-2.

After the prophet sets the stage in vv. 1-2 for the juridical arguments to follow, the first-person arguments of Yhwh ensue (vv. 3-5). The characters in the courtroom have already been introduced: Yhwh, creation's witnesses, and "my people" (עמי). The nature of Yhwh's argument, however, comes as a surprise. The LORD presents himself as the defendant rather than the prosecutor. Yhwh raises questions that appear defensive in nature. "How have I wearied you?" This is no voice of accusation but of self-defense in the face of a wearied people. The verb "to weary" (לאה) is found in Job 16:7 where Job laments God's making him weary or exhausted. The connotative force of the causal verb is weary by excessive toil and exhaustion.[12] Readers need not strain to feel the pathos of this cosmic courtroom as Yhwh pleads his own case before his beleaguered people. What is the exact cause of your annoyance and exhaustion with your God? Yhwh demands an answer: "answer me!."[13]

In the face of weariness and relational exhaustion, Yhwh paints with broad brushstrokes a portrait of his redemptive history with Israel from the Exodus to entry into the promised land.[14] The rhetorical force of this portrait does not escape the reader. Much like a parent reminding a complaining child of the many benefits and goods they enjoy in the home, Yhwh brings needed perspective to the complaint at hand. Was it when I redeemed you from your slavery in Egypt? Is this the cause of your complaint? Or was it when I appointed and gifted you with leaders to navigate the difficulties of your wilderness wandering? Moses, Aaron, and Miriam.[15] Perhaps my redemptive intervention on

---

[12] See "לאה" in *DCH*.

[13] Wolff notes the phrase as a "fixed expression" of the Old Testament law court (cf. I Sam 12:3f.; 2 Sam 1:16; Isa 3:9; Job 9:14; Wolff, 175).

[14] Weinfeld identifies "to ransom" פדה and "house of bondage" בית עבדים as typical of Deuteronomic phraseology (Weinfeld, *Deuteronomy and the Deuteronomic School*), 326-27.

[15] The collocation Moses, Aaron, and Miriam is unique to Micah (cf. Num 26:59).

the plains of Moab is the source of your frustration? Do you recall when Balak the king of Moab sought to hire the prophet Balaam to curse you (Numbers 22-24)? Balaam rejected the king's initial offers, only to concede in time. Yet, Balaam was unable to provide Balak with his desired end because Yhwh instructed Balaam that the Israelites were blessed by him. To Balak's dismay, Balaam could only provide words of blessing, not cursing. The drama on the plains of Moab is a central narrative in Numbers.

Dozemann provides an important insight into the Balaam narrative when he mentions Israel's passive role in the whole affair. In fact, Israel remained unaware of the threat, while Yhwh was working on their redemptive behalf unbeknownst.[16] The rhetorical force of this rehearsal manifests itself. Was it on the plains of Moab where you grew wearied? Was it when I protected you from the threat of Moab's king, though you remained ignorant of your impending danger? Did this weary you? Israel camped at Shittim during the Balak crisis (Num 25:1). Gilgal was the first encampment of the Israelites in the promised land (Josh 2). The redemptive movement from Egypt to the promised land was riddled with difficulties and troubles. Yet, the providential oversight of Yhwh for his people remained intact and gracious, through and through. Again, the force of this clipped redemptive rehearsal is to shed light on the nature of Judah's complaint. You were a no-people before I redeemed you and gave myself to you. My "righteous acts" or "saving acts" are on display in your cultic and narrative traditions (cf. Judg 5:11). You "know" these righteous acts. Your memory of them is an active participation in them. Your current existence is an existence in the present character of these redemptive historical moments. You are because of them, and because of them you know your God. "How again have I wearied you?"

In due course our attention will turn to Micah's most oft-repeated verse, "He has shown you, O man, ... " (6:8). While we need not attenuate the instructive force of Micah's claim to fame, it does bear highlighting that Yhwh begins with a rehearsal of Israel's redemptive history before moving to the paraenetic reminder. There is a *theo-logic* at play in this move

---

[16] Thomas B. Dozemann, *The Pentateuch: Introducing the Torah* (Minneapolis: Fortress Press, 2017), 457. See also Dozemann's comments in "Numbers," in *The New Interpreter's Bible Commentary* (Nashville: Abingdon Press, 1998), 177–96.

where Israel's election and redemption provide warrant for the call to moral agency. Put in other terms, Israel's being or essence as elect or recipients of divine grace resists any divorce from Israel's activity or moral agency. In terms quite familiar to Christian discourse, the *gospel* plays a primary role in its relationship to the law. The *gospel* precedes. Thus, the *gospel* is both temporally and theologically prior to the law. While the distinction between *gospel* and *law* is an important one, a division between the two is fatal. Such a logic flows from the internal claims of the Christian canon—e.g., Deut 6:20-25 and Romans 12— where a division between Law and Gospel as two distinct words of God does not stand.[17] In Karl Barth's terms, "The one Word of God is both Gospel *and* Law."[18] It is the *gospel* that envelops, shapes, and provides the motivation for the *law's* place in the community of the redeemed. Continuing with Barth, "It is the Gospel which contains and encloses the Law as the ark of the covenant the tables of Sinai."[19] When *gospel* and *law* either come apart or lose their proper ordering the one to the other, species of antinomianism or legalism lurk in earnest around the corner of Christian practice.[20] John Webster beautifully summarizes the relationship between the gospel as promise and command:

> Standing beneath the gospel's *promise* means hearing the joyful declaration: "Behold your God." In such hearing the Church is once again faced with the gospel's affirmation that God is one who comes, one who is *with* us as saviour, renewing and preserving his people and fulfilling with final authority the divine commitment: I will be your God ... But to stand beneath that promise of the gospel is already to stand beneath the gospel's *commandment*: the end of God's work of purification is active zeal for good deeds. Thus the Church is also holy as it stands beneath the gospel's commandment. As commandment the gospel is the declaration of law, the shape or direction for the life of God's holy people. Hearing the gospel's summons to obedience, the Church is holy, submitting to the gospel's judgment of sin, and setting itself to govern its life by God's commands. In this way, the Church is holy as it stands beneath the final promulgation of the summons to that holiness which

---

[17] Christopher Wright comments, "Certainly, in Deuteronomy 6:20-25, when an Israelite son asked his father about the meaning of, or reason for, all the law his family was observing, the answer was not a curt 'Because God commands it.' Rather, the father was to tell the story, the old, old story of the LORD and his love in action, the story of exodus. The meaning of law was to be found in the 'gospel'—the historical events of redemption." Christopher J. H. Wright, *Old Testament Ethics for the People of God* (Downers Grove: IVP, 2004), 28-29. See also J. G. McConville, *Deuteronomy* (Apollos Old Testament Commentary; Downers Grove: IVP, 2002), 144-47; Ronald Clements, "Deuteronomy," in *The New Interpreter's Bible, Vol. 2* (Nashville: Abingdon Press, 1998), 345-46.

[18] Karl Barth, *Church Dogmatics II.2* (trans. G. W. Bromiley, J. C. Campbell, I. Wilson, J. S. McNab, H. Knight, and R. A. Stewart; Edinburgh: T&T Clark, 1957), 511. Barth responded to some of his "Lutheran" detractors in *CD IV.3*. Of his responses, two are particularly germane to the discussion at hand: (1) If Law and Gospel are two distinct Words of God, Barth queries after what sort of Christology will allow for such a schema; and (2) If Paul is working with a strict Law/Gospel separation, then Paul remains at odds with the Old Testament's plain sense on the matter. Barth is loath to force Paul and the Old Testament into a repugnant relationship. Karl Barth, *Church Dogmatics IV.3* (trans. G.W. Bromiley; Edinburgh: T&T Clark, 1961), 370.

[19] Ibid. See also the penetrating essay by David S. Yeago, "Gnosticism, Antinomianism, and Reformation Theology," *Pro Ecclesia II* (1993): 37-49.

[20] O'Donovan speaks of the dangers of moralism and antinominianism. Moralism is the detachment of moral convictions from the good news of the gospel, while antinominianism is a holding of the Christian faith apart from moral questions. O'Donovan, *Resurrection and Moral Order*, 11-12.

corresponds to the divine commitment of election: You shall be my people. How, then, is the Church holy? By attention and submission to the gospel as the indicative of election and imperative of obedience.[21]

Micah 6 begins with a stated conflict between God and his people. The nature of the conflict will turn to the question of moral agency, but it begins here with Yhwh's rehearsal of the good news of Israel's election and redemption from Egypt, a rehearsal of Israel's covenant ontology. Such a reading corresponds in figural relation to the Christian understanding of the covenant relation between Christ and His people. I am who I am on the basis of the self-determination of God to be in covenant with me because of the active and passive obedience of Jesus Christ, my Savior and Lord. Such is a Christian's understanding of their own covenant ontology. McCormack relates the priority of our covenant ontology to human agency in our current moment of the divine economy. "We are what we truly are (and what we will be in the eschaton) in those moments when our humanity is conformed on the level of lived existence to the humanity inaugurated in time by Christ's life of obedience."[22] In other words, as Christians we are called into conformity with the essence of who we already are in Christ. When we live in accord with the humanity established by Christ's lived obedience, we do so as an act of correspondence between our existence and current essence in Christ. Commenting on this text, Luther reminds Christian readers of the external signs we enjoy on analogy to those of ancient Israel, namely, their deliverance from Egypt. Luther clarifies, "He has given us, too, those external signs of grace, Baptism and the Eucharist, by which He encourages us to remember those things which have happened to us through the Gospel and which never fail to happen to those who believe" (Luther, 258).

The response of vv. 6-7 indicates the exoneration of Yhwh before his people. Whatever the source of their wearied relation with Yhwh, the counterarguments of vv. 3-5 reveal the anemic cause of their frustrations. The people have nothing to say in rebuttal except to raise questions about how best to restore the fractured relation. "With what shall I come before the LORD?" This question before the litany of sacrifices resembles the Temple Entrance Liturgy where questions about proper entrance to the presence of Yhwh are raised (cf. Ps 15; 24), though the identification of 6:6-7 according to this particular genre is problematic.[23] The sacrifices listed correspond to sacrifices from Exodus, Leviticus, and Numbers, though the hyperbolic character of the references is not easily missed.[24] The building hyperbole bolsters

---

[21] John Webster, *Holiness* (Grand Rapids: Eerdmans, 2003), 72–73.
[22] Bruce McCormack, "What's at Stake in Current Debates over Justification," in *Justification: What's at Stake in the Current Debate* (ed. M. Husbands and D. J. Treier; Downers Grove: IVP, 2004), 115.
[23] See Sweeney, 399; Ben Zvi finds the Temple Entrance Liturgy genre wanting here (Ben Zvi, 151).
[24] Whole burnt offerings are daily sacrifices consumed in their entirety (Leviticus 2). The reference to a year-old calf reflects the requirement of certain sacrifices, e.g., sin offerings (Lev 9:3).

the rhetorical force of the litany: from typical "burnt offerings" to "thousands" to "ten thousands" to "child sacrifice."[25] Child sacrifice was prohibited in Israel's worship and viewed as an abhorrent practice of Canaanite worship (cf. Lev 18:21: Deut 12:32), though there are instances where the practice occurs in extreme moments (cf. the King of Moab in 2 Ki 3:27). Climaxing with child sacrifice whether as a hyperbole by the prophet or a sincere offer of a vexed people reveals the religious desperation of vv. 6-7.

Yet, the prophet responds in 6:8 with what appears as measured incredulity. External religious rituals are not the answer to their vexing question: "How shall I come before the Lord?" Placed in the larger contextual frame of the preceding seven verses, the prophet in v. 8 is calling Judah to an existence grounded in her election where her actions are commensurate with and in extension of her true identity: loved by God; rescued and liberated by Yhwh. Religious rituals apart from this communal self-understanding and absent the love of God are meaningless (cf. Am 5:21-24).[26] God's redemptive actions, actions of love and self-giving, are intended to yield in return human actions of gratitude in keeping with God's own love and self-giving.[27] As Wolterstorff reminds, cultic action apart from justice do not serve the

---

[25] Though see Andersen and Freedman who understand the suggestion of child sacrifice as sincere (Andersen and Freedman, 534–45). See also Jon D. Levenson, *The Death and Resurrection of the Beloved Son: The Transformation of Child Sacrifice in Judaism and Christianity* (New Haven: Yale University Press, 1993), 10–12. Levenson cites George Heider who understands Mic 6:6-7 in a "contrary-to-fact mood" where none of the sacrifices are accepted absent the virtues of 6:8 (ibid., 11). Levenson counters, however, by stating his own misgivings about an "abominated" sacrifice listed along with acceptable ones. Why would Micah mix and match in this way? Levenson concludes that Micah is reflecting an accepted part of the cultus at Micah's moment. Levenson appears to overstate his case with Mic 6:6-7. For it makes good sense for Micah to mix and match the accepted with the abominable when all are viewed from the same standpoint of the ethical injunction of v. 8. The rhetorical logic is in effect as follows: whether you offer prescribed or proscribed offerings, absent the reflective justice and piety of v. 8, they are all the same.

[26] Spieckermann clarifies the relationship between righteousness and worship, "Instead, he will not allow himself to be served in worship and will not serve people when commandment and life become detached from one another" (Reinhard Feldmeier and Hermann Spieckermann, *God of the Living: A Biblical Theology* [trans. M. Biddle; Waco: Baylor University Press, 2011], 290).

[27] See Kessler (272) on the potential reduction of the relationship with God to ethics or cultic observance. Both are requisite and related to each other.

shalom or human flourishing God intends for his redeemed people.²⁸ Religious lip service apart from the infusion of God's goodness and lordship in all spheres of the faithful's existence is a clashing gong.

"He has shown you, O man." The direct address "man" (אדם) raises the curiosity of almost every interpreter. Some understand "man" as a term of universal applicability, unlike vv. 1-7 where Judah is in view. Other interpreters, e.g., Hillers, Wolff, and Waltke, rightly deny this reading. "Justice" and "loyalty/loving mercy" are attributes of covenant keeping, not general universal maxims. Hillers suggests that "man" highlights the distinction between God and human creatures.²⁹ This connotation may be at play. Wolff's references to Deuteronomy (5:24; 8:3) where "man" denotes the person who hears the proclamation of Yhwh provide clarity regarding the term.³⁰ The prophet is addressing the covenant people of God as recipients of divine instruction. Moreover, the prophet is reminding the covenant people of that which has already been revealed to them (hifil נגד).

Addressing "The Content of the Divine Claim," Barth makes the following comment on Mic 6:8:

> The man who, according to Mic. 6:8, has been told what is good, is not man as such and in general, but Israelite man, the people of Israel.³¹ That which is required of him—to do justly, and love mercy, and walk humbly before his God—is not, therefore, the compendium of a natural duty incumbent on men generally, but, as in the case of the Ten Commandments, a condensation of the demand which is proclaimed and established and enforced by the fact that God has chosen this people of Israel to be His people, and Himself to be the God of this people.³²

---

[28] Wolterstorff, *Hearing the Call*, 50–52. Wolterstorff continues, "The prophetic critique of the cult is grounded in the conviction that the point of the liturgy is to give symbolic expression to the commitment of our lives to God. The point of liturgy is not the performance of certain self-contained actions such as confession and praise, no matter how sincere and appropriate those actions. Liturgy is for giving voice to life, to lives of faith. In our lives we seek to obey God; in the liturgy we praise the one whom we seek to obey and confess our failings" (ibid., 52). In the words of the BCP, we seek to praise Him with our lips and our lives.

[29] Hillers, 79.

[30] See the lexical discussion in Waltke, 362–63.

[31] Barth begins section 2 of The Command of God, "The Content of the Divine Claim," by quoting Mic 6:8. Micah 6:8 is a compendium of the content of the divine claim. If one is "claimed by God" then such a person is not left to himself or herself to decipher the material content of that claim. The Scriptures, e.g., Mic 6:8, provide for claimed persons such content. Karl Barth, *Church Dogmatics II.2*, 566.

[32] Ibid., 572.

For Barth, Jesus Christ is the telos of Israel's history and the fulfillment of the Law's promises and threats. The history of Israel's disobedience and judgment becomes Jesus's own history, experiencing as he does the curses of the covenant in his place-taking work on the cross. The continuing validity of Mic 6:8 or the Decalogue for the Christian community takes as its basic premise and presupposition that the Law of God has been kept and fulfilled by Jesus Christ.[33] "It is as such," Barth clarifies, "that it is now valid and authoritative."[34] The thanksgiving of men and women in the church is a genuine thanksgiving because Christians know they are marked by disobedience and unfaithfulness. Within the Book of Common Prayer, the announcement of the Law in the Eucharist liturgy—Love God and Love Your Neighbor—is always followed with *Kyrie Eleison*. It is this self-recognition in view of the completed work of Jesus Christ where sincere keeping of the Law resides. Regarding the material content of the Law, however, the Old Testament Law retains its validity, especially in the compendium forms of it found in Mic 6:8 and the Decalogue. Yet the relationship of the Christian to the Law is one formed by Jesus Christ, his death and resurrection. As Barth concludes, "The new thing is Jesus Himself. But Jesus Himself is also the Old. For He is the promised One for whose sake the Law was given to Israel."[35]

It is not without significance that the term "reported" or "communicated" (hifil נגד) appears in Mic 3:8. There Micah places his own prophetic ministry over against the false prophets who hesitate to "report" or "communicate" to Judah their sin. Within the confines of the book, the source of the reporting or communicating of the good over against the evil stems from Micah's own prophetic legacy.[36] Therefore, when the question is raised, "Where did Yhwh tell us what he seeks from us?" an immediate answer is, "Micah the prophet." Yet the answer to the source-question ranges beyond Micah per se. One finds the call to "justice" (משפט) and "loyal love" (חסד) in Hos 12:6. There the move toward "justice" and "loyal love" is indicative of the repentance of God's people. Moving beyond the Prophets, the Psalms share a similar concern for "loving with our lips and lives" (cf. Psalm 24). Deuteronomy (4:13 and 5:5) introduces the Decalogue with the verb "to report" (hifil נגד). Commentators often note the similarities in language between Mic 6:8 and Deut 10:12-22.[37] From a canonical perspective, the reporting of

---

[33] Ibid., 574.
[34] Ibid.
[35] Ibid., 575. See also, John B. Webster, "The Imitation of Christ," *TynBull* (1985): 95–120.
[36] Reflecting on the opening of 6:8, Kessler comments, "Es erhebt sich die Frage: Wer hat 'gesagt' oder: Wo ist es 'gesagt'?" (Kessler, 269).
[37] McConville, *Deuteronomy*, 199. Comparing Deut 10:12-22 to Mic 6:8, McConville concludes, "This requirement of a heartfelt love of what is right, based on loyalty to Yahweh, is the stuff of Deuteronomy too." See Jon Levenson, *The Love of God: Divine Gift, Human Gratitude, and Mutual Faithfulness in Judaism* (Princeton: Princeton University Press, 2016), 30.

what God seeks and identifies as good is found in the broad sweep of the Old Testament's tripartite witness.[38] It is not hidden under rocks and trees but emerges from the cross-associative range of the entire witness.

Micah 6:8 is not the first call to justice in Micah's oeuvre. It is the principle concern of chs 2–3 where, in Calvin's terms, Micah focuses his attention on the breach of the Law's second table. The litany of "the good" in 6:8 take the form of three infinitives: to do, to love, and to walk. All three infinitives are related to each other in necessary and mutual reciprocity. The parts of the triad are taken whole or not taken at all. For the call to do justice apart from "loving loyalty" and "walking circumspectly" becomes moral self-actualization of the kind that is not sustainable. Though a familiar triad, Micah's phraseology and concrete thought are in beautiful proportion and relation.

1. "To do justice (משפט)" (equity, care, concern). Here is the love of neighbor where the direction of our good works flow from faith: not for ourselves but for the good of our neighbor. Herein lies the gracious control of power so that it is directed toward care and concern for the other and not self-aggrandizing promotion and advancement. It is the preceding grace of Christ, our union with him in salvation by faith, that moves us outside of ourselves for the sake of the other. Or in Hoang and Johnson's terms, justice is the love of God gone public.[39] To do justice is to act in accord with who we already are in Christ by faith.
2. "To love loving loyalty (חסד)" or "the loving of loyal faithfulness" (genitive construction).[40] This phrase is unique in the Old Testament. By the nature of this fact, the phrase arouses interest. It calls attention to itself. Within the XII, Hos 6:6 already

---

[38] See Andersen and Freedman, 528, where they contrast the practical and concrete explication of "the good" in Mic 6:8 over against the more hypothetical and philosophical question within classical literature, viz, "What is the *summum bonum*?"

[39] Bethany Hanke Hoang and Kristen Deede Johnson, *The Justice Calling: Where Passion Meets Perseverance* (Grand Rapids: Brazos Press, 2016).

[40] See Wolff, 181, and Andersen and Freedman, 528–29, on the presence of this phrase in the Qumran documents.

witnesses to the principle concern of Mic 6:1-8: "For I desire steadfast love (חסד) and not sacrifice." Within the Psalter, steadfast love (חסד) is predicated on God, indicating the assurance and confidence the community has in Yhwh's loyalty and commitment to them. The term, often translated anemically as "kindness," has a broad semantic range: loyalty, faithfulness, kindness, love, mercy, devotion.[41] The summons here to the "loving of loyal faithfulness" speaks to the disposition of the will *and* affections toward communal concerns, toward a mode of being marked by love. Understanding the second phrase of the triad as an extension of the first—"to do justice"—is a step in the right interpretive direction.[42] Micah's call to justice is not an appeal to our stripped-down wills apart from the government of our affections.

The potential for actualization in the call to "justice" and "loyal faithfulness" resides in the disposition of the heart or the affections. Put in Christian theological terms, to "love loyal faithfulness" is to walk in the existence of the preceding love shown to us. Commenting on Deuteronomy 6, McConville claims that "loyalty" (חסד) "is expressed in heartfelt adherence to Yahweh … For this reason it can be said that the love of God has a cash value in love of neighbor …, since the commands of God aim at a society in which each promotes the good of the other."[43] The love *of* God (objective and subjective genitive) yields the affections and dispositions of our own hearts and minds toward a concomitant kind of existence: an existence in the love and favor of the resurrected Christ. Faithfulness, love, mercy, grace, and kindness, all of these words are connoted in "loyal faithfulness." Micah's call is not directed merely to the human will but is directed at a will

---

[41] See "חסד" in DCH.
[42] Andersen and Freedman believe there is an intentional change of the typical idioms with the first two phrases for the sake of reading them in relation: the typical phraseology is "to love justice" (Andersen and Freedman, 529).
[43] McConville, *Deuteronomy*, 147.

shaped by the affections and dispositions of the heart: loving loyal faithfulness as an indication of the gratitude of humility shown to us in God's own love.[44]

3. "To walk circumspectly, reflectively, wisely, humbly with your God." A verse as familiar as Mic 6:8 becomes part of the liturgical culture of the believing community. Many who learned the King James Version of John 3:16 as a child find other translations jarring. The triad of Mic 6:8 is standard fare as well: "to do justice, to love mercy, and to walk humbly with your God." Yet, the last phrase, oft-repeated as it is, does run the danger of limiting the connotative force of the text's lexical dimension to one facet. Put in other terms, when readers read "to walk humbly with your God" the English terms are familiar enough to portend straightforward connotative associations. "Micah 6:8 ends with a call to a humble walk with God." The phrase is more obscure than the traditional rendering, however. The infinitive "to walk" indicates communion. If the modifier "humbly" were removed, the phrase "to walk with your God" by itself would indicate a life lived in communion with God (cf. Deut 10:12).[45]

The challenge of the phrase arises with its adverbial modifier—"humbly" according to the standard translations (עֲנֻ). After referencing the ancient translations—LXX ("to be ready to walk"); Pesh ("to be ready"); Theodotion ("to be careful"); Quinta ("to be prudent"); Vulg ("to go around anxiously"), HALOT makes the following statement: "[T]hus the exact translation equivalent of עִנְצֵה is difficult."[46] As is often pointed out, the only other place where one finds this term in the Old Testament is Prov 11:2. There the word stands in opposition to "pride" and, thus, recommends itself as "humility." Yet, this appears as a prima facie conclusion.[47] Giving a definitive answer to the lexical question

---

[44] See Levenson, *The Love of God*, 48ff.
[45] See Hillers, 79.
[46] *KBL*, 1039.
[47] Wolff, 182.

will remain difficult.[48] Yet a contextual reading of the phrase in its current literary setting, along with its wisdom associations elsewhere, may point readers in a good semantic direction.

Von Rad, leaning on a seminal study by H.J. Stoebe, suggests the term's wisdom context leads toward the following semantic associations: "measured," "discerning," or "circumspect."[49] The call to a reflective or measured or circumspect walk with God in the literary setting of 6:8 leads readers back to the rehearsal of Yhwh's redemptive history with His people in 6:3-5.[50] Such a discerning and circumspect "going with God" takes into account the basis of the believing community's very existence in the redemptive grace of God.[51]

The triad of 6:8 fits together, seemingly working backwards to indicate how "justice" is possible. It is possible when the community walks reflectively with God, understanding her history of undeserving election and grace. Such a walk yields the affections and devotion called for in the second phrase: "to love loyal lovingkindness." This affection grounded on a discerning and reflective walk with God in turn leads to concrete actions of equity: "to do justice." "Humility" certainly shares in the connotative space of the adverb but does so in a derivate way. As Jon Levenson says elsewhere, "The virtue of gratitude ... is closely associated with that of humility."[52] And gratitude is the natural consequence of covenant love when one walks with God in reflective consideration of God's redemptive grace. The opposite of humility from a biblical perspective is ingratitude. And a state of ingratitude is a perilous state for the believing community; it is an idolatrous state.

---

[48] See esp. the lexical discussion and rehearsal of scholarship in Waltke, 364–66.
[49] Von Rad, *OTT II*, 186, n. 18. So too Waltke, see above.
[50] Kessler makes this suggestion as well, 271.
[51] In discussing biblical law in the context of the divine/human relationship, McConville claims the following: "Biblically speaking, right human understanding of anything is inseparable from the knowledge of God (Hos. 4:1-2). The kind of wisdom, therefore, that makes for good decision-making in the realm of law and ethics, is cultivated within the divine-human relationship" (McConville,"Biblical Law and Human Formation," 637–38).
[52] Levenson, *The Love of God*, 48.

Little wonder the Apostle Paul often commends the churches to be thankful. As Levenson concludes, "If, moreover, the benefactor wishes the best for his beneficiary, he will discourage him from persisting in the ungrateful behavior that has disrupted the relationship."[53] Micah 6:1-8 is Yhwh's best wish for His people as a benefactor who desires the good for those whom He loves.

The sober warnings of Hannah Arendts's moral and journalistic account of the Adolf Eichmann trials retain its instructive power. Though stirring significant backlash when first published in 1963, Arendt's *New Yorker* articles turned book, *Eichmann in Jerusalem: A Report on the Banality of Evil*, provide a chilling account of Eichmann not as a mad and murderous monster but as a banal bureaucrat.[54] Eichmann insisted in the trial that he was not *innerer Schweinehund* (an inner dirty bastard), harboring no deep hatred of Jews.[55] He simply would have failed his conscience if he did not follow through on his superior's directives: the calculated deportation of millions of women, children, and men to their orchestrated deaths. As Arendt reported, psychologists diagnosed Eichmann as "normal" with enviable familial affections. This was the horror. Eichmann was an ambitious man, prone to braggadocio, who desired the advancement of his career.[56] This "normal" man could be transformed into the abhorrent perpetrator of humanity's grossest crimes because his banality kept him, in Micah's terms, from a reflective or circumspect mode of being. The enduring contribution of Arendt's reporting coordinates with Micah's backward movement with his famed triad. Absent reflection, a recognition of God and humanity's creation in His image, "normal" citizens are capable of the grossest actions of injustice. Such a potential state is not cause for self-righteous finger pointing but for the grace of repentance to walk circumspectly and reflectively in the face of our natural proclivities to banality.

Perhaps standing opposite the banality of evil, yet sharing in its culpability and skewed view of God and the self, is the smugness and self-congratulation of self-righteousness. Luther understands Micah's triad as in proper proportion and balance to ward off this danger:

> In fact, there is a danger that after we have been justified we become lukewarm, that we become proud, that our gifts of the Spirit tickle us because in them we surpass others, that we please ourselves. It is as if he were saying: "When you have done what I say, when you have developed a concern for your neighbor, see to it that you do not become smug, that you do not have an eye for mischief, that you do not please yourself and go around looking for praise and glory that is owed to God alone." (Luther, 262)

A circumspect walk with God, marked as it is by the humility that stems from knowledge of God and the self, keeps what Luther calls "self-love" at bay or as an impossible possibility. Both the banality of evil and the pride of self-congratulation in the doing of good are outside the house of a circumspect walk with God.

---

[53] Ibid., 52.
[54] Hanna Arendt, *Eichmann in Jerusalem: A Report on the Banality of Evil* (London: Penguin, 2006). See Daniel Maier-Katkin and Nathan Stoltzfuss, "Hannah Arendt on Trial," *The American Scholar* (2013): 98–103.
[55] Arendt, *Eichmann*, 30.
[56] Ibid., 46–48.

Micah 6:9-16—Hear the rod

Within the canonical shape of Micah's final form, this unit stands in relation to the one preceding it.[57] The Masoretic paragraph marking ends at 6:8 with 6:9 opening a new unit ending at the chapter's end. The relational logic between the two units appears on the text's surface level. The good Yhwh has shown to his people—justice, loving faithfulness, and a circumspect walk with God—stands in antipodal relation to the actual state of affairs in Judah. Though Yhwh revealed the good, Judah exists in a state of being contrary to it. The themes of chs 2–3 make their appearance again as the prophet calls Judah to account for the rampant injustice marking the community of faith.[58] In these verses, God describes Israel's unjust actions and renders her guilty in the face of them.

Yhwh's voice (קול) cries out to the city, with city standing in metonymic relation to its leaders and inhabitants.[59] Micah 6:8 ends with wisdom terminology—to walk "prudently" or "circumspectly" with God—and 6:9 borrows from the same linguistic pool. Though the etymology of the term "sound wisdom" (תושיה) is uncertain—HALOT suggests the lexeme's etymology relates to "being" (יש) with a basic notion of "promotion of being" or "elevation of skill"—the term's wisdom connotation is secure.[60] The fear of Yhwh's name marks the path of the successful, prudent, and shrewd. Love and circumspection walk hand in hand in Mic 6:8. Here too, the path of wisdom entails a reverential and circumspect view of Israel's God, to wit, the fear of Yhwh's name.

As Levenson states in his comments on Deut 10:12-13 (there too "love" and "fear" comingle),

---

[57] See Jeremias, 206ff., for a redaction-critical argument for the diachronic relation of the two units.
[58] As observed in the commentary's introduction, Jeremias understands the second and third sections of Micah as *Fortschreibungen* of chs 1–3.
[59] Ben Zvi (157) suggests the use of קול and קרא ("cry out") rather than the typical verb of direct speech "to say" (אמר) indicates a distance needing to be overcome.
[60] Wolff notes the term as in synonymous relation to "counsel" (עצה) in Prov 8:14 and Isa 28:29.

There surely is a tinge of fear in the negative sense, even in the reverence, the awe, or the sense of being overwhelmed that one has in the presence of a superior. And if the description of God in the Bible is at all accurate, there would be something gravely wrong with someone in whom the thought of God and the sense of his immediate presence did not evoke those very feelings.[61]

The wise and successful person walks in the fear of Yhwh, in a recognition of his character as merciful and severe. Yes, his predisposition is to mercy, with mercy tipping the balances in its direction: as observed in the proportion of the *middoth* in Ex 34:6-7. Yet his severity is serious and threatening when his people persist in a direction opposite His revealed will. As the Book of the Twelve reminds readers, Yhwh's patience is longsuffering but has a limit. It is unwise to make a trifle of Yhwh's severity. "Listen to the rod."[62] Or in paraphrastic form, "take heed to the instrument of God's judgment."[63] More importantly, reminds Micah, take heed to the One wielding the rod. Yhwh's character remains merciful and severe. Micah 6:9 is Yhwh's rousing call to attention in light of His name or his character. The wise take note and walk in accordance with Yhwh's revealed person and will.

After the arousing call to attention, vv. 10-12 follow with Yhwh's accusation. There are various suggestions for emending v. 10 because of its textual difficulties, notably the lack of prepositions. Most translations follow Wellhausen's suggestion to read the verse's second word (האש) as an interrogative preceding the verb "to forget" (אשא from נשא; this reading follows the BHS). This commentary follows the *BHQ* where the

---

[61] Levenson, *The Love of God*, 30.
[62] Cf., Deut 4:36; 5:25 where the "hearing" (שמע) of God's voice is the instrument of Yhwh's judgment.
[63] The end of v. 9 and beginning of v. 10 are notoriously difficult. Those who follow the LXX and amend the first word of v. 10 עוד to עיר are apt to read "rod" מטה as "tribe" (e.g., NRSV (see Hillers and Waltke, ad loc.)). This reading is as follows: "hear, oh tribe and assembly of the city." Andersen and Freedman observe the textual problem, glossing the verses as follows: "Hear oh Tribe, and who appointed her still!" (Andersen and Freedman, 539, 547). The trouble is with the term "yet" עוד at the beginning of v. 10 and the lexical hurdles of מטה as "rod" or "tribe." Final solutions to the textual conundrums will remain elusive, though this commentary edges in the direction of those who see the summons in relation to forthcoming judgment: the rod.

particle (אִשׁ) is equivalent to the particle for being (יֵשׁ; cf. 2 Sam 14:19; Prov 18:24; see KJV). When read in this light, the first word of the verse "yet, still" (עוֹד) does not require emendation. The reading of v. 10 is as follows: "Is there yet in the house of wickedness, treasures of wickedness and scant measures that are accursed."

Nogalski does well to show the intertextual links Mic 6:10-11 has with Amos and Hosea (Am 3:14; 4:4; 5:5-6; Hos 10:15; 12:4).[64] In these texts, the prophets link Bethel ("house of God") with wickedness. Where just interactions within the community are Yhwh's assumed standard, his house has become a house of wickedness. Both Am 8:5 and Hos 12:7 condemn the use of false scales where those who handle the purse strings exploit patrons by the use of deceptive balances and false weights. As Shalom Paul comments on Am 8:5, "Even the very scales themselves were tampered and rigged ... The buyer was always deceived—he received too little and paid too much."[65] As in Micah 3, rather than love of neighbor following love of God, the powerful are eating their neighbors in acts of exploitation, violence, and deception (6:10-12). The very fabric of the community whose ideal and shared goal was the rest and human flourishing of the promised land has broken down. They have been shown *the good* but exist (אִשׁ) in its very opposite: the house of wickedness.

After the accusation follows Yhwh's verdict, a verdict correlative to Judah's acts of wickedness (גַּם). Yhwh will strike with a heavy blow.[66] The city will be made desolate (שָׁמֵם) on account of her sin (cf. Isa 1:7; 6:11; Mic 1:7). Hillers describes the curses to follow as "futility curses" (cf. Deut 28:30-31).[67] The more they put their hand to a task with a

---

[64] Nogalski, 574–75.
[65] Paul, *Amos*, 258. Cf. Lev 19:35-36; Deut 25:13-15; Ezek 45:10-11; Prov 16:11 where honest balances and weights are demanded in Scripture.
[66] Again, the text and syntax are difficult. The LXX reads "and I will begin to strike" and the BHS suggests revocalizing חלה (to make sick) to חלל (to begin). Wolff overstates the matter when he says the infinitive (to strike, נכה) cannot follow חלה (Wolff, 187). BHQ affirms the attractiveness of revocalizing the text, though the more difficult reading might find a parallel in Isa 53:10. Waltke provides a literal reading of the MT: "I will strike you sorely" (Waltke, 401).
[67] Hillers, 82.

desired end, the less return they have on their labors. They will eat and not be satisfied. They will plant a hedge but not make it secure.[68] Or perhaps, you will reap but your labors will not come to fruition.[69] In fact, your agricultural labors will miscarry as they are delivered to the sword. You will sow but not reap. Treading on olives will yield no oil for anointing. Grapes will produce no wine. This dystopic account of Judah's future reverses the positive images of Judah's future in Mic 4:1-4. There, the future is marked by an absence of violence and the enjoyment of one's agricultural labors—figs and wine. Here, however, Judah's future of judgment entails the sword and the frustrations of their agricultural efforts coming to no fruitful end. A diachronic account of Judah's future might understand the relation of this text to Mic 4:1-4 as judgment preceding restoration. A synchronic account would place Mic 4:1-4 and 6:13-15 within the same vein of the eschatological tensions faced by the nations when looking toward their future with Yhwh. Two options emerge, a faithful move of repentance to Israel's God (4:1-4) or the experience of his judgment (4:11-13; 5:8-15). Both options are on the eschatological horizon of possibilities.

Cyril of Alexandria reads these futility curses as spiritual in nature. When the prophet says they will eat but not be satisfied, he speaks of their "dabbling" in the Scriptures only to gain no satisfaction from the teaching. "[T]hough seeming to eat, they die of hunger" (Cyril, 256). Cyril concludes, "[T]hough crushing the spiritual *olive*, the sacred Scripture, they are in no way enriched with the grace of the Spirit; and though expecting to harvest *wine*, they will be deprived of spiritual good cheer" (ibid.).

Micah's sixth chapter ends with an abbreviated form of the preceding six verses: an accusation is followed by a verdict. Yhwh castigates Judah

---

[68] Such is the reading Williamson suggests in Williamson, "Marginalia," 369. The difficulty rests with the verb סוג where the primary definition is "to remove." Williamson finds this wanting because it does not stand in relation to the negative counterpart to follow. Instead, Williamson suggests a secondary meaning of סוג that means "to hedge" or "build a fence" (ibid.). Williamson's reading is compelling, though attention should be drawn to Hos 5:9-10 where the terms "destruction" (שׁמם) and "removing" (סוג) are in proximity to each other with the removal of the boundary markers indicating neighborly dishonesty: a practice condemned in, e.g., Deut 19:14; 27:17; Prov 22:28.

[69] Another possible reading, following the *DCH*, is to read סוג in its primary sense—"remove" or "set aside"—with פלט as "bring forth" or "deliver." Following this lexical path, the two phrases would read: "You will set aside but you will not deliver" or your agricultural efforts will miscarry. Given the context, there is much to commend this reading as well.

for keeping the statutes of Omri and the deeds of the house of Ahab. While the Omride dynasty was *the* political powerhouse of the ninth century BC, its religious practices were excoriated in the Old Testament's prophetic books (the former and latter prophets).[70] For example, King Manasseh is condemned as a godless king because he followed the policies of Ahab, Omri's son, and the paragon of infidelity to Israel's God within the Deuteronomistic history (cf. 1 Ki 16:33).[71] The keeping of the Northern Kingdom's statutes reminds readers of Mic 1:9 where the incurable wound of the Northern Kingdom makes its way to the gates of Jerusalem—Ahab worshipped Baal and Asherah (cf. 1 Ki 16:31-33). Within Micah 6, the phrase "walking in the counsel"—the counsel of Ahab and his father Omri (6:16)—stands in direct opposition to *the good* of Mic 6:8 and its call *to walk* circumspectly with God. The result of walking in Ahab's path is destruction, scorn, and humiliation.[72] Kessler describes Mic 6:9-16 as a dramatic highpoint (*dramatischer Höhepunkt*) in the synchronic shape of Micah's prophecy.[73] As in ch. 1, Jerusalem and Samaria parallel one another on the same religious plane. They are idolaters. As idolaters, they share in the same fate of divine judgment.[74]

---

[70] For an account of how a negative view of the political implications of the Omride dynasty in the traditions of Monarchic Judah in time became viewed as negative religious implications in the Deuteronomistic History, see Omer Sergi, "The Omride Dynasty and the Reshaping of the Judahite Historical Memory," *Biblica* 97 (2016): 503-26; see also Kuhrt, *The Ancient Near East: c. 3000-330 BC, Volume Two*, 464-66; Jeremias understands the reference to Omri and Ahab relating primarily to their religious activities as idolaters. The religious concerns are in intertextual relation to Micah 1 (Jeremias, 211).

[71] On the tendency of the Omride kings to unjust regulations and exploitation of their subjects, see J. Maxwell Miller and John H. Hayes, *A History of Ancient Israel and Judah, Second Edition* (Louisville: Westminster John Knox Press, 2006), 315.

[72] On "hissing" cf. Deut 28:25, 27.

[73] Kessler, 283.

[74] Ibid. From a structural perspective, Kessler believes Micah shares much in common with Isaiah where the end of Micah brings a social/religious critique following a vision of salvation much like Third Isaiah as it follows Second Isaiah (ibid.).

7

Micah 7—Lamenting in Hope

Introduction

The final chapter of Micah's prophecy brings the book to its fitting conclusion. The judgment announced and promised in the first three chapters will have its day. Zion will suffer the blow of Yhwh's wrath and will suffer it for her covenantal infidelity. The scope and concrete character of her infidelity is outlined in the first three chapters and expounded and expanded again in 6:1-7:7. Yet, the character of God as One whose mercy outweighs his severity will not allow his judgment to be the final word. From the embers of judgment, Zion will arise in the face of the nations who scorn her and her God. Micah's prophecy ends with a reminder of Yhwh's name and faithfulness.

Micah 7:1-7—A faithful lamentation amid Judah's sorry state of affairs

The first seven verses of Micah's final chapter begin with a lamentation in v. 1 and end with a reaffirmation of trust in Yhwh and his salvation. Within the bookends of lamentation and trust readers find the cause for lamentation, namely, a complete breakdown in the social and familial order. Justice and faithfulness are nowhere to be found; they are like absent fruit after the gleaning of trees. This unit is riddled with literary plays and metaphors as the prophetic word makes its forceful presence known.[1]

"Woe to me" cries the first-person voice of 7:1. Identifying the speaking agent is a matter of some contest. Chapter 6 ends with the first-person voice of Yhwh, moving as it does into ch. 7 without any clarification regarding the change of subject. The affirmation of faith in v. 7 makes clear Yhwh is no longer the "I" in view.[2] Moreover, the term for "woe" is suggestive (אללי). It is not the typical expression for lamentation as one finds in Isa 6:5 (אוי). The only other location for the term is Jb 10:15 where the term is part of a conditional clause. "If I am guilty, *then* woe to me."[3] If the lexeme's use in Job sheds light on Micah, then the woe suggests the guilt of the one lamenting in his state of helplessness. From a lexical standpoint, therefore, reading Yhwh as the continued first-person voice of 7:1-7 becomes strained. Who is speaking then?

From a literary/contextual vantage point, the identification of the voice has two options. The first and well-worn path is the identification of the "I" as the prophet (e.g., Hillers, Jeremias, Wolff, Waltke, Sweeney). What prophet is a matter of dispute. Standard redaction-critical readings locate ch. 7 in the postexilic period. Mays, for example, sees the "tone and attitude" of the unit as incongruent with Micah during the reign of Hezekiah.[4] Sweeney, on the other hand, believes the "tone and attitude" fits well the period of Sennacherib's incursion in 701 BC. The breakdown of societal and familial order often mark periods of extreme duress.[5] The scene in Mic 7:1-7 is ambiguous and broad enough to "fit" several moments in time. Reading with canonical lenses, it seems unnecessary to pinpoint a singular moment in time as the key to

---

[1] See especially Ben Zvi, 166–67, on the literary features of this pericope.
[2] Ben Zvi understands the contextual ambiguity of the "I" as opening several possible reading strategies, including Yhwh as the speaking voice (Ben Zvi, 168). This commentary agrees that the ambiguity makes the referent of the "I" open, though reading Yhwh as the "I" is not compelling.
[3] The form אללי is followed by לי in both Job and Micah (WO'C, 40.2.4b).
[4] Mays, 150.
[5] Sweeney, 406.

unlocking this unit. Rather, the text, emerging as it does from some moment in time, remains present for future times as well when lamentations and affirmations of faith are requisite in dire moments of distress. Reading the "I" of Mic 7:1-7 as the prophet gains support from the affirmation of faith in v. 7 (ואני). The prophet's faithfulness stands over against his faithless surroundings. This contrastive move mirrors a similar affirmation in Mic 3:8 where the prophet places his own actions over against his opponents.

The second option is a road less traveled, though compelling. On this reading, the "I" of 7:1-7 is kept in contextual continuity with the "I" of 7:8-10.[6] The feminine pronouns of the latter unit make clear that the first-person voice is Lady Zion or personified Jerusalem. It is possible that v. 8 introduces a new first-person voice much like 7:1 did, though the contextual clues are not as strong as they are at the juncture between 6:16 and 7:1. Much trades on the literary relation between 7:7 and 7:8ff. At the literary level, therefore, there appears little compelling rationale—beyond form-critical arguments about the liturgical character of 7:8-20 (more of this anon)—for a hard division between these two units. Ben Zvi's suggestion that 7:7 might serve double duty as both the concluding verse of 7:1-7 and the introductory verse of 7:7-20 is compelling and followed in this commentary.[7] If 7:7, like Mic 5:1 (MT), is a bridge verse linking the two units of Micah's final chapter, then the identification of the "I" as Lady Zion commends itself. The city itself laments the lack of faithfulness among its inhabitants. As the personification of the ideal Judah, the city also confesses its faith in the future salvation of her God. Any hard and fast conclusion regarding the identification of the "I" remains "tentative."[8] On final analysis, the two options need not be played over against each other. Both the prophet and the idealized and faithful city witness to the presence of faith and repentance amid faithlessness and social/familial insecurity.

---

[6] See Hagstrom, *Coherence*, 98–99.
[7] Ben Zvi, 166.
[8] Hagstrom, *Coherence*, 98–99.

The lament of v. 1 makes use of a simile drawn from harvest metaphors. The one lamenting here experiences the deprivation of one searching for something to eat after the gleaning of the fruit trees. A similar metaphor is used to describe apocalyptic deprivation in Isa 24:12-13 (cf. Jer 9:13). The trees are bare. No fruit is found; no summer delicacies like figs or grapes are for the taking. Instead, there are only cravings with no possibility of satisfaction. The metaphors remind readers of Am 8:1ff and the paranomastic play on the words "summer fruit" (קיץ) and "end" (קץ). The "end" has come upon my people, declares Yhwh in Am 8:2. Hosea makes use of the metaphor of "figs" and "grapes" to describe Yhwh's election of Israel when he first saw them (Hos 9:10). Now, however, the grapes and figs are gone (cf. Isa 5:1-7). Only deprivation and lamentation remain.

Micah 7:2 makes clear the referent of the metaphors in v. 1. The "clusters" and "figs" now gleaned and gone are "piety/faithfulness" (חסיד) and "uprightness" (ישר). What was at one time an indictment focused first and foremost on the political and religious leaders—"Should you not know justice?" (Mic 3:1)—now lands on all within the land: from princes and judges to simple folk in their domestic setting (7:3-6).[9] The use of the term "faithful" (חסיד) draws attention to "loving faithfulness" in Mic 6:8. The literary proximity reveals the radical distinction between what Yhwh has revealed as *the good* and communal life in the real. Instead of a faithful and a conscientious community, there is bloodshed and violence accomplished by acts of cunning and deception—the use of "net" (חרם) recalls a huntsman or fisherman. It is of note that "piety" or "faithfulness" within the frame of Mic 6:1-7:7 speaks to communal relations and the exercise of justice and equity within these relations. Again, readers of the prophets note the necessary correlation between the expression of faith in worship and devotion and the expression of faithfulness in deed.

A general tendency within Micah's rhetorical strategy is to begin an indictment with a broad brush and then move to the particular or

---

[9] See Jeremias, 214.

concrete actions involved (cf. Mic 2; Mic 3). Micah 7:1-7 follows the same course with v. 3 revealing the actions lacking faithfulness and honesty. Micah 7:3 is a recapitulation of themes already present in Mic 3:10-11. Those in positions of authority and power are for hire. The execution of justice flows from the whim or desires (הות) of the "great man" (most likely referring to court officials with access to the king).[10] The "great man," the "judge," and the "prince" all weave together or distort the justice they are authorized to execute. The term "weaving" (*piel* עבת) also makes playful reference to the "nets" these figures use in hunting their prey (7:2). In today's terminology, the magistrates are involved in a racket. As observed in ch. 3, the top-down beneficence intended within Zion's covenantal relation with Yhwh has broken down. Rather than bearers of justice and guardians of covenantal order, government officials seek their own personal advancement with little to no regard for *the good* (6:8).

The beginning of 7:4 makes use of another set of metaphors: the briar and the thorn bush. The best of them, with "them" referring to the stated officials of 7:3, are like briars and thorn bushes. Wolff cites Prov 15:19 where the thorn bush functions "to obstruct."[11] Like a thorn bush, so too do the government officials obstruct the justice they are meant to serve. Waltke understands pain as the suggestive referent of the metaphors. Like thorn bushes and briars, the magistrates are best left untouched.[12] Justice and its proper execution are left a tangled and painful mess by those whose hold the keys of power. As is often noted, there exists a wordplay between "thorn bush" (מסוכה) and "confusion" (מבוכה), the last word of 7:4. The paranomasia suggests an interplay between the actions of the officials and the result of Yhwh's forthcoming judgment, viz., confusion and disorder.

Micah 7:4b appears as a surprise given its contextual setting. Jeremias draws attention to the change of style at this juncture where

---

[10] See Wolff, 206.
[11] Ibid., 207.
[12] Waltke, 420.

for a short time the reader is addressed in the singular: "you."[13] The move from the injustice of "them" to the direct address of "you" heightens the tension for those addressed. Given this shift in style as it opens to the domestic disturbance of vv. 5-6, v. 7b may be viewed as the rhetorical center of this unit. It links together the guilt of the magistrates and commoner and places the whole of the community under the selfsame threat of impending judgment (cf. Jer 6:13). *Them* is *you*.

Moreover, the prophet makes use of the theological vocabulary of Hosea at this point. The collocation of "watchmen" (צפה) and day of "visitation" (פקודה from פקד) mirrors Hos 9:7-8. There the prophet identifies himself as the "watchman of Ephraim." This description of the prophet as a "watchman," as one who looks out for impending doom and announces immediate dangers (cf. 1 Sam 13:34; 2 Sam 13:34; 18:24-27; 2 Kgs 9:17-20), has an afterlife in later prophetic descriptions as well (cf. Jer 6:17; Ez 3:17). Hosea 9:8 portrays the prophet as a watchman "with my God" (עם אלהי).[14] Such language resembles descriptions of Moses as he received the Torah; he was "with Yhwh" (Ex 34:28). Samuel grew up "with Yhwh" in 1 Sam 2:21, a portrayal standing in counterpoint to the sons of Eli.[15] Here in Mic 7:1-7, the prophet places his own actions and outlook over against the corruption surrounding him (7:7). Like Hos 9:8, the watchman of Micah 7, the prophet, is *with God*. "But as for me ... "

Continuing with Hosea, Mic 7:4b makes use of the term "day of visitation" (nominal form of פקד; cf. Jer 6:6). The phrase "day of visitation" has its place within the larger tableau of the Day of the Lord theme in the Twelve.[16] Yet, the language of "visitation" is particularly

---

[13] Jeremias, 216.
[14] This reading follows Wolff's understanding of the syntax of Hos 9:8 (see Wolff, *Hosea*, ad loc.). For other interpretative options of an admittedly difficult text, see J. Andrew Dearman, *The Book of Hosea* (NICOT; Grand Rapids: Eerdmans, 2010), 244–48.
[15] See Stephen B. Chapman, *1 Samuel as Christian Scripture: A Theological Commentary* (Grand Rapids: Eerdmans, 2016), 82–83.
[16] See Rendtorff, "How to Read," 75–87. On the Day of the Lord in Joel, with Joel's theological account of the Day of the Lord as present and coming, see Seitz, *Joel*, 65–83, esp. 72.

Hoseanic.[17] Like Hosea and Amos, the day of visitation is a day of darkness, not light (Am 5:18). The product of Yhwh's visitation will be confusion: disorder and disarray (cf. Isa 22:5). It will be *their* confusion with the referent as both the magistrates of the preceding verses and the domicile disturbers of the following. Confusion and disorder mark the community from top to bottom. When Yhwh *visits* his people in judgment, their cosmos will turn to chaos. Jeremias draws attention to the fact that the actual timing of the "day of visitation" remains somewhat ambiguous in its relation to the disordered events described in 7:1-6. The question remains open as to whether the events described are in fact indications that the "day of visitation" is a realized event or an indication of what is yet to be.[18] Read within the frame of the Twelve, this ambiguity speaks to the *now* and *yet to be* character of the Day of the Lord (cf. esp. Joel). For example, Romans 1 describes the wrath of God as an event unwittingly experienced in the now by those who exchange Creator for creature. Yet, God's wrath is still open to the future. According to Jeremias, Micah read within the Twelve speaks to the wide range of the "day of visitation" beyond the event of the exile. The end of the exile in no way (*keineswegs*) brings an end to the strife between Yhwh and his people.

Verses 5-6 are particularly disturbing because of their gross depiction of neighborly and familial distrust. If love of God and love of neighbor are flip sides of the same coin, then the whole of the religious and social fabric is bankrupt. It is one thing to experience the injustice of the powerful magistrates. It is quite another to experience such betrayal and cruelty from those who share our blood.

---

[17] Jeremias cites Am 3:2, 14 and its use of *pqd* (only places in Amos where the term is used for "punishment") as further evidence of the influence of Hosea on the canonical shaping of Amos. For the term *pqd* is deployed with some frequency in Hosea as a term for punishment (1:4; 2:15; 4:9,14; 8:13, 9:9; 12:3). Jörg Jeremias, "The Interrelationship between Amos and Hosea," in *Forming Prophetic Literature: Essays on Isaiah and the Twelve in Honor of John D.W. Watts* (JSOTSupp 235; ed. J. W. Watts; P. R. House; Sheffield: University of Sheffield Press, 1996), 182. See Gunnel André, *Determining the Destiny: PQD in the Old Testament* (Lund: CWK Gleerup, 1980). André's full-length lexical and form-critical investigation of the term *pqd* places the nominal form in Hos 9:8 and Mic 7:4 under the category of "conditional act of the disfavor of Yhwh" (André, *Determining*, 184, esp. 234).

[18] Jeremias, 216.

In an essay entitled "Family," Marilynne Robinson offers a beautiful account of the matrimony of love and loyalty in family life:

> Imagine this: some morning we awake to the cultural consensus that a family, however else defined, is a sort of compact of mutual loyalty, organized around the hope of giving rich, human meaning to the lives of its members. Toward this end they do what people do—play with their babies, comfort their sick, keep their holidays, commemorate their occasions, sing songs, tell jokes, fight and reconcile, teach and learn what they know about what is right and wrong, about what is beautiful and what is to be valued. They enjoy each other and make themselves enjoyable. They are kind and receive kindness, they are generous and are sustained and enriched by others' generosity. The antidote to fear, distrust, self-interest is always loyalty. The balm for failure or weakness, or even for disloyalty, is always loyalty.

Robinson continues, "'Love is not love/Which alters when it alteration finds,' in the words of the sonnet, which I can only interpret to mean, love is loyalty."[19] Micah 7:5-6 provides a startling portrayal of the admixture of familial life, disloyalty, and confusion. Much like the Sophoclean tragedies, familial strife and discord are distinctive marks of a setting turned tragic.[20]

The prophetic voice of confidence in 7:7 need not leave behind the voice of despair in 7:1. Both confessions proceed from the same faithful mouth. In the face of confusion and breakdown—legitimate causes for prophetic lamentation—the prophet offers a confession of faith set over against the prevailing tendencies of covenantal disloyalty. The prophet also sets his hope on the future deliverance of Yhwh, and this despite the fait accompli of present/forthcoming judgment. At this critical juncture, the prophet enters the glorious company of the apostles and the goodly fellowship of the prophets (cf. Isa 8:16-18). Like the Psalmists who express their lamentations before God only to turn in time to confession of faith and renewal of hope, so too does the prophet here enter the selfsame pattern.[21] The prophet's residing in the tension of lamentation and future hope bears the marks of Habakkuk's prophetic existence—Hab 1:2-4 yields in time the confession of faith

---

[19] Marilynne Robinson, "Family," in *The Death of Adam: Essays on Modern Thought* (New York: Picador, 2005), 88–89.
[20] See the introduction to Sophocles, *Antigone, Oedipus the King, and Electra* (Oxford World Classics; Oxford: Oxford University Press, 1998), xi.
[21] The *waw disjunctive* marks the turning point in the Psalms of Lament when the Psalmist moves to renewed hope in the face of current circumstance (e.g., Ps. 13:5). A similar syntactical pattern is found here in 7:7—"But as for me."

in Hab 3:17-19.[22] The prophet's existence as lamenting and hopeful figures and anticipates Jesus Christ who suffers in the hope of future vindication/salvation (Heb 12:1-3). The "but as for me" mode of being is a call to prophetic existence, an existence that witnesses to a faithful hope in the future promises of God amid and despite the most difficult of current circumstances.

Micah 7:7-20—Zion's hope

The final unit of Micah's prophecy is divided into four subunits: 7:7-10; 7:11-13; 7:14-17; 7:18-20. The first subunit functions as a bridge, linking together 7:1-7 to 7:7-20. The final subunit brings ch. 7 to end; it also serves as a conclusion to the whole of Micah's prophetic book. It is fitting for the final chapter of Micah to bear the same marks of the book's overall structure, namely, the oscillation between judgment and future hope. Micah 7:1-7 affirms the cause and necessity for forthcoming judgment, while 7:7-20 offers hope for the future, a confident hope based on the identity and character of Israel's God (7:18-20).

As mentioned in the previous section, the identity of the first-person subject introduced in 7:1 is not immediately self-evident. From a synchronic viewpoint, there appears no compelling reasons to make a distinction between the first-person voice of 7:1-7 and 7:8-10. As mentioned in the previous section, the contrastive "but I" of v. 7 does bear a resemblance to 3:8, lending support to the identification of the "I" as the prophet. Nevertheless, the move from 7:7 to 7:8-10 is a natural response to the confession of faith in v. 7, providing support for the identification of the "I" as Lady Zion or Daughter Jerusalem (note the feminine pronouns in 7:8-10). This textual tension is in large measure the rationale for identifying v. 7 as a bridge verses linking that which precedes with the forthcoming. There may be redaction or form-critical

---

[22] On the relation of Habakkuk to the unit, see Nogalski, 579.

reasons for separating 7:8-20 from 7:1-7—more of this below—but these fade at the level of the book's final form. In other words, the text's prehistory may shed light on the final form of the text, but it does not transcend the text's final form and logic.

A theological point emerges amid this textual tension where the identification of the prophet and Lady Zion overlaps with one another. Much is made of Calvin's biblical Christology where the threefold office of the mediator derives its substance from the Old Testament witness: prophet, priest, and king.[23] And rightly so, for these charisms of Old Testament political and religious leadership converge in the singular figure Jesus Christ. Moreover, Jesus Christ's person and work elevates these offices in continuity and discontinuity with those figures in the Old Testament who held such offices. For example, Jesus is a prophet in the sense that he brings the Word of God, but unlike the prophets of old, Jesus not only brings the Word but *is* the Word (Jn 1:1). A figural pattern of the prophetic office in relation to the covenant people emerges here in Micah 7 as well. We observe the prophet in solidarity with his people, representative of them in their guilt and punishment: lamenting in anguish; admitting of guilt (v. 9); bearing Zion's punishment. At the same time, the prophetic voice represents the faithful hopes and actions of a people unable and unwilling to enter into the same mode of being (vv. 7-10).[24] The prophet may be understood as a vicarious figure who offers faithful hope, obedience, and patience (vv. 7-10) amid a scene marked by the decay and disorder of 7:1-7. The textual tensions and overlap of the identity of the "I" in 7:1-10 provide the grounds for a figural extension of these two units in relation to a Christological pattern rooted in the Scripture's total witness. The prophet is himself and representative other at the same time: in the suffering of Zion's guilt and in the presentation of Zion's faith.

The tendency to separate 7:8-20 from 7:1-7 has its roots in the form-critical identification of 7:8-20 as a "prophetical liturgy." Gunkel provides the full-length treatment of the form-critical approach.[25] He makes a case for the prophet applying motifs of the Individual Dirge to Lady Zion (vv. 8-10; 14-17) along with an oracle (vv. 11-13) and a hymn (vv. 18-20). Reference to Gunkel's "prophetic liturgy" is standard fare in the secondary literature on Micah as commentators rehearse Gunkel's line of thought: (1) A: vv. 8-1—the voice of the suffering people; (2) vv. 11-13—the announcement of a glorious future; (3) B: vv. 14-17—a

---

[23] *The Institutes of Religion*, II. xv.

[24] Gunkel made a similar observation along form-critical lines. "The prophets were so accustomed to personify Jerusalem and Zion that they occasionally went so far as to put words in their mouths." He continues, "The Hebrew poets and prophets thus carried over into the national religion forms of expression which had been originally used to express personal religious experience." Herman Gunkel, "The Close of Micah: A Prophetical Liturgy; A Study in Literary History," in *What Remains of the Old Testament* (trans. A. K. Dallas; New York: Macmillan Company, 1928), 126. The figural extension of this prophetic instinct is not a line Gunkel would follow. For Gunkel texts move back to religious moments rather than forward in figural anticipation.

[25] Ibid.

communal prayer for the return of the Divine Shepherd; (4) vv. 18-20—a hymnic confession of faith.[26] The combining of the Dirge and the Oracle are formal markers of "such liturgies," and Micah resembles this kind of "artistic composition" (cf. Ps 94 where national and individual dirges are found).[27] Gunkel aims to prove that, despite the differences in "mood and thoughts," the whole of 7:8-20 forms an artistic whole.[28] Gunkel argues in the affirmative because the Dirge of B, though similar in content to the first Dirge of A, is more passionate and comprehensive, building as it does on its relation to the preceding Dirge.[29] Gunkel goes so far as to imagine the liturgical setting where two choristers sing Dirge A, while the whole choir responds in antiphon with Dirge B.[30] With standard form-critical instincts in gear, Gunkel allows the form of the text to provide an imaginative and reconstructive avenue to the actual cultic events themselves.

The initial form-critical suggestions from Stade (a Psalm) and Gunkel (a prophetic liturgy) entailed the notion that 7:8-20 existed independently from its setting in the book as a performed liturgy—recall Gunkel's choristers. For Gunkel, only later in the postexilic period was the prophetic liturgy inserted as a conclusion to the whole of Micah without much contextual linkage to its new literary setting. This particular facet of the form-critical project is no longer found persuasive, though the Psalm-like quality of Micah's final unit retains its force.[31] Ben Zvi prioritizes the Psalm's *Sitz im Buch* over against its form-critical prehistory, whether or not the Psalm's genesis was in fact a cultic setting.[32] The recognition of the liturgical or Psalm-like character

---

[26] E.g., Hiller, Wolff, Ben Zvi. See Hillers, 89–90, on the theory of the Northern provenance of 7:8-20 (Ewald's early suggestion). Gunkel located the "prophetic liturgy" in the time of Trito-Isaiah. See the discussion in Andersen and Freedman, 576. See the range of social settings for this unit in Willis, "A Reapplied Prophetic Hope Oracle," 64–76.
[27] Gunkel, "Close of Micah," 143, 144.
[28] Ibid., 146.
[29] Ibid., 147.
[30] Ibid., 148. See also J. T. Willis, "A Reapplied Prophetic Hope Oracle," *VT* 26 (1974): 64–76.
[31] See the critical response of Zapff, "The Book of Micah," 135.
[32] Ben Zvi, 180.

of Micah's ending aids in understanding this final section as a fitting response to the hard passage leading to the book's end.

Jeremias believes the Psalm was created for the sake of concluding Micah's prophetic book, bringing together its various parts (*Teilen*).[33] He first provides an excursus on the diachronic history of 7:8-20— Jeremias understands vv. 14-17 as a later extension and interpretation of vv. 8-10; the view of the nations is milder in 14-17 (*ashamed*) than 8-10 (*enemies*) with the door of hope opened to them in vv. 14-17 when they embrace the fear of the LORD; 14-17 expands on the nations motif (*Völkerthemas*) of chs 4–5. After the excurses, Jeremias allows his understanding of Micah's depth dimension to provide an interpretive point of entry to Micah's final unit. Lady Zion's affirmation of her guilt in v. 9 takes the view that with the exile's coming to an end, so too does her guilt.[34] However, the view of the hymn in vv. 18-20 takes the continuing guilt of the people beyond the exile into account (e.g., Mic 6:1-7:7). Why does Judah continue to exist in its continued state of guilt, irrespective of the exile's coming to a beginning or an end? For the prophetic book of Micah, there is but one answer to this question. Because Yhwh is quick to forgive and make good on his promises to the patriarchs despite the continuing guilt of his people.[35] Micah's prophecy ends with a clarion call to future hope because of Yhwh's past dealings with the fathers and the enduring character of his being: Yhwh is quick to forgive. Borrowing New Testament capital from the Apostle Paul, the canonical shape of Micah's prophecy lends credence to Paul's claim that it is the goodness of God that leads to repentance (Rom 2:4).

In vv. 8-10, Lady Zion via the voice of the prophet acknowledges her guilt, submits to Yhwh's judgment, and opens herself to Yhwh's eventual vindication. Drawing on creation imagery from Genesis 1, the light of Yhwh's redemption will engulf the darkness of Judah's momentary judgment. The legal dispute Yhwh has against his people in 6:1-8 (ריב) is now Yhwh's legal defense of his people (ריב; 7:9). The

---

[33] Jeremias, 219.
[34] Jeremias, 223–24. See Zapff, "Book of Micah," 136, for a counter reading to Jeremias's.
[35] Ibid., 224.

prosecutor is now Zion's defense. The patriarchal themes of Jacob and Abraham will appear at the chapter's end (7:20). Here too, the Jacob/Esau drama makes its presence known when the nations are challenged not to rejoice over Zion (7:8). Such a question mirrors the charge against the Edomites, Esau's progeny, in Obadiah 12ff.[36] The long-term tension between Judah and her enemies will end in Judah's vindication. The scoffing nations will be trampled down.[37]

The promises of restoration in vv. 11-13 are set against the backdrop of the day of visitation in 7:4. In final view, the promised day of judgment is not Judah's destined end but a necessary destination point along the way. Walls once destroyed are now being rebuilt (cf. Isa 5:5). Boundary lines once restricted will extend exponentially (cf. Isa 54:1-3). The day of visitation yields to the day of restoration. The challenge of this subunit is the depiction of the nations in vv. 12-13 and the identification of the "he/they" returning in v. 12. In brief, are the *Israelites* of the diaspora returning back to Judah from the nations and the farthest reaches of the earth? Or do we have a parallel text with Mic 4:1-4 where the *nations* are streaming to Yhwh to be taught? The answer to this question of identification is not mitigated by the description of the "earth" (ארץ) as desolated in v. 13. The use of the term "desolate" (שמם) predicated now on the whole earth might be viewed in counter distinction to Zion's desolation in 6:16. What was once Zion's lot has now come to an end. Now the earth surrounding Zion is in desolation and only Zion's inhabitants enjoy the safety of its walls (v. 11). But the desolation of the "earth" does not mean the earth's inhabitants in toto are destroyed. This tension of the nations in Mic 4-5 makes its appearance here in the final chapter as well.

---

[36] Hillers (90) makes mention of another intertextual referent to Ob: "my eye will see" (Ob 10/Mic 7:10).

[37] Kaminsky's categories of Elect, Non-Elect, and Anti-Elect provide helpful distinctions when navigating the different accounts of the nations in the prophets in general and Micah in particular. The identity of the nations who scoff at Israel's God, placing themselves in hostile relation to Yhwh and his people, is properly deemed anti-elect. The Day of the Lord will be night to them. Yet, those who are not Israelite (non-elect) yet turn to Israel's God will enjoy the benefits of Yhwh's universal reign (cf. Mic 4:1-4).

Returning to the textual difficulty mentioned in the preceding paragraph, an ambiguity exists regarding the identity of the "he/they" of v. 12. Who is "coming" or "entering"? If the referent is Israel in its diaspora, then the text accords with the outlook of Isa 27:13.[38] If, with Dillers and others, the referent is the nations, then the portrait of 7:12 parallels Mic 4:1-4 (cf. Isa 66:18-21; Zech 14:16-19).[39] Ben Zvi believes the literary setting lends itself to seeing the nations as in view (cf. 7:13, 17), though on final analysis the ambiguity cannot be finally resolved.[40] Perhaps polyvalency is the order of the day where the textual ambiguity allows for both readings: the turning nations and the Israelites in diaspora are coming back to restored Zion.[41] The collective "he" includes the streaming nations of Mic 4:1-4 and the scattered diaspora of Mic 2:12-13.

The third subunit of 7:7-20 takes the form of a prayer addressed to Yhwh (7:14-17). The prayer mirrors the Psalm-like quality of looking to Yhwh's marvelous deeds in the past for the sake of current comfort and future hope (cf. Pss 77-78). Again, the speaking voice is Zion in direct address to Yhwh. The call for Yhwh to "shepherd" his flock entails the royal image of the shepherd-king (cf. Jeremiah 23). Within the frame of Micah's final form, Zion's petition calls for the actualization of Micah's first word of redemptive promise (2:12-13). In earnest, Zion cries out for Yhwh to make good on his promises to lead them from danger to pastures of safety. Yhwh's rod (שבט; cf. Ps 23:4) performs double duty as an instrument of protection and guidance. Zion reminds Yhwh of his own electing promises and their identity has "his" ("*your* inheritance"). The use of the second-person possessive pronoun (*your*) recalls Moses's not so subtle reminder to Yhwh in his moment of intercession. In the

---

[38] See Zapff, "The Book of Micah," 137. Andersen and Freedman raise it as a possibility that the singular "he will enter" may refer to the coming Messianic hero, tucking back to Mic 5:1 (Andersen and Freedman, 587).

[39] See Hiller, 91. Luther reads the text as the nations streaming (Luther, 273-74). So too does Calvin with a more sophisticated set of exegetical arguments (Calvin, 385-86).

[40] Williamson's suggested emendation does not convince because the singular verb is apposite to a collective subject. Williamson, "Marginalia," 370-72. Waltke understands the subject of "to enter" as "your people" of v. 14 (Waltke, 439).

[41] So too Sweeney (411) and Ben Zvi (177).

midst of the gold calf debacle, Moses prays, "O LORD, why does your wrath burn hot against *your* people, whom *you* brought out of the land of Egypt with great power and with a mighty hand?" (Ex 34:11). As Yhwh's inheritance, Judah is Yhwh's privileged and prized possession (cf. Deut 4:20; 9:26, 29; Ex 19:6). The logic of election is at work in the prayer of Zion. Zion's only status and leverage for intercession is their identity as Yhwh's very own, his inheritance.

Jesus's description of himself as shepherd and gatekeeper inhabits the contours of Micah's shepherd imagery (Jn 10:1-18). Raymond Brown takes umbrage with Bultmann's dismissal of the Old Testament background for the shepherd metaphor in John 10.[42] For Bultmann, the Old Testament links the shepherd motif with the ideal king. Such a link appears absent in the Johannine context. Yet Brown believes Bultmann has overshot in his assessment. The presence of the Old Testament background and the originality of Jesus's use of it need not be played over against each other. Brown believes Ezekiel's portrayal of God (or the Messiah) as the true shepherd over against wicked shepherds who plunder the sheep is present in John 10. The linking of gatekeeping and shepherding in Jn 10:3 squares with Micah's portrayal in 2:12-13. Moreover, the redemptive context of the divine shepherd here in Mic 7:14 serves the redemptive portrayal of Jesus the Good Shepherd in Jn 10:14-18 (along with Isa 40:11; Jer 23:3-4; Ezek 34:11-16; Zech 10:3).[43] The Davidic portrayal as a shepherd of the sheep who belong to God elicits Messianic and future hope in the prophetic witness. Jesus's self-description as the Good Shepherd embraces the figuration of the Shepherd, whose kingly identity is unmistakable within John's overall narrative scheme (Jn 19:19).

The imagery in the second and third line of 7:14 leads interpreters down two opposing interpretive tracks. Wolff, e.g., understands the image of *forest* (יער) in opposition to *garden land* (כרמל).[44] Therefore, when Zion describes herself as *alone* (לבדד) in a forest (cf. 3:12), this reveals the difficult existence of Judah in their exilic and postexilic setting. In other words, Judah resides in a forest without recourse to the *garden lands* of her ancestral heritage.[45] The other interpretive option, and the one preferred here, is to view the whole of 7:14 as a hopeful look at Judah's future restoration. The *forest* and *garden land* are in relation to one another as fertile fields of pasture. And the term *alone* marks Judah as distinct among the nations: Yhwh's inheritance. The scales tip in this

---

[42] Raymond Brown, *The Gospel according to John i-xii* (AB; Garden City: Doubleday & Company, 1966), 397.

[43] See the helpful discussion in Marianne Meye Thompson, *John* (NTL; Louisville: WJK, 2015), 224-27.

[44] While reference to Carmel as a place name is a possibility (see Ben Zvi, 177), its parallel relationship to *forest* suggests otherwise.

[45] See Mays, ad loc.

interpretive direction because the same verb for *dwelling* (שׁכן) appears in Num 23:9 where it is in association with the term *alone* (לבדד): the same syntactical feature of Mic 7:14. The Numbers text appears in the first of Balaam's oracles to King Balak. According to Balaam, Israel's status as *alone* speaks to her uniqueness among the nations as favored by Yhwh.[46] The allusion to Numbers here is not Micah's first reference to the Balaam traditions (6:5).

Zion appeals to Yhwh on the basis of his own gracious favor and election of her. The references to Bashan and Gilead perform a double function. Both places were known for their fertile pastures (cf. Ps 22:12; Num 32:1): Bashan in the Southwest region of Syria overlooking the Sea of Galilee (the Golan Heights) and Gilead in the Transjordan region just south of Bashan and north of the Dead Sea.[47] While known for their pastureland, these two regions also refer to territories lost to the Assyrians (2 Kgs 15:29).[48] Zion's prayer here entails the fulfillment of the prophetic promise in 7:11 regarding the expansion of Judah's territories. With the restoration of these territories comes the restoration of Israel's boundaries from the *days of old*.[49]

The petition continues with the *days of old* theme in v. 15. Reference is now made to the Exodus, that paradigmatic redemptive moment of Israel's covenantal history. While it may be tempting to read the referent of *your* in *your coming out* as the people, a second glance prefers the identification of Yhwh as the referent (cf. Ex 33:14). Yhwh goes out before his people to lead them and deliver them. The Exodus of Israel's past is in mimetic relation to his future deliverance of his people. In those future moments, tethered as they are to the wondrous deeds of the past, Yhwh will go before them (2 Sam 5:24; Mic 2:12-13). The NRSV renders the final phrase of 7:15 as an imperative: "show us marvelous thing." While such a reading gets at the text's sense, it does,

---

[46] See Jeremias, 227–28.
[47] See Miller and Hayes, *History*, 20.
[48] See Oded Lipschits, *The Fall and Rise of Jerusalem* (Winona Lake: Eisenbrauns, 2005), 2.
[49] The clan of Machir as a branch of the tribe of Manasseh may have dwelt in Bashan and Gilead (cf. Josh 12:1-6; 13: 29-31; 17:1); see Miller and Hayes, *History*, 89.

nevertheless, attenuate its rhetorical force. The phrase is best read as the first-person speech of Yhwh, the One who is going out of Egypt in triumphal procession of his people. "I will show them marvelous things." Yhwh is flexing his redemptive arms before his people—in demonstration of their redemption—and the nations—for the sake of their own humiliation before him (cf. Ex 3:20; Isa 29:14; Ps 78:4). The final verses of this subunit witness to the devastating effects of Yhwh's redemptive power on the arrogance of the nations (cf. Isa 2:9-22). Nations who once mocked with "where is your God?" (7:10) now stand mouths covered and in shame before Yhwh's awe-inspiring redemption. As in the Song of Moses, the nations tremble in dread and awe before the "greatness of Yhwh's arm" (Ex 15:13-16).

As Jeremias observes, the nations here are no longer described as "enemies" but as those who are overwhelmed by the fear of Yhwh, turning to Him in such a state. The terrifying imagery of 7:17 entails a silver lining of hope for the nations. For though shamed, their continued existence remains possible as they dwell in a continued state of the fear of Yhwh. As Jeremias claims, "The true might of their life is fear before God."[50] The intertextual links to Jonah, along with Micah's proximity to Jonah in the XII's canonical shape, suggest reading Jonah 1 as an illustrative and substantive narratival construal of Micah's prophetic word.[51] As the storm ceases and the great fish appears, the pagan sailors stand gobsmacked before the wondrous deeds of Yhwh. The narrator describes the effect of this dramatic moment on the sailors as follows: "Then the men feared the LORD even more" (וייראו האנשים יראה גדולה; Jon 1:16). The intertextual association of the nations *fearing* in Mic 7:17b and Jon 1:16 suggests reading the two texts in relation to each other. If so, then Jeremias's understanding of the silver lining for the nations is affirmed. In Jonah 1, the fear of Yhwh leads to the worship of Yhwh, however laconic the narrative is about the long-term effects of

---

[50] "Diese Bewegung führt die Besiegten und ihrer vormaligen Macht Beraubten zu einem positiven Aspekt des 'Schreckens', nämlich zur Ehrfurcht vor Gott als der wahren Macht ihres Lebens;" (Jeremias, 229).
[51] See Zapff, "The Book of Micah," 141–42.

the sailors' repentance.[52] Similarly, the locust plagues in Joel represent the Day of the Lord as a time experienced and a time to come. Drawing from the Exodus traditions (Ex 10:2), Joel clarifies the purposes of the wondrous deeds of Yhwh, namely, the knowledge of the LORD (Joel 1:2-3; Joel 2:27).[53] As the experience of the locust plague in Egypt resulted in the knowledge of Yhwh, so too will his current and future wondrous deeds yield the same for both Israel and the nations. Micah 7:7-17 is an expansion on the variegated depiction of the nations observed in chs 4–5. As with the books surrounding Micah—Jonah and Nahum—the future remains open for the nations regarding their relation with and posture before Israel's God. Fear leading to repentance and worship (Jonah; Mic 4:1-4; 7:17b) or continued hostility, arrogance, and rejection leading to doomed consequences (Nahum; Mic 4:13; 7:10) remains open to the future.

Micah's prophecy ends with a hymn of praise exulting in the character of Israel's God (7:18-20).[54] As observed above in the introduction to this unit, the prophetic book ends by providing the only grounds for Judah's future hope, viz., the name and character of Yhwh. As the plagues in Exodus and the Day of the Lord in Joel lead to the proper knowledge of God, so too here in Micah's prophecy does the display of Yhwh's judgment and mercy lead to a proper understanding of God's identity. The question "Who is a God like you" plays on the prophet's name, Micah (*who is like Yhwh*). At the same time, the Exodus traditions hover near the surface of this question. The Song of Moses asks, "Who is God like you, O LORD, among the gods?" (Ex 15:11). The display of God's glory and wonder (Ex 15:11b) is inextricably linked to the revelation of the divine name: "I will be who I will be" (Ex 3:14; 6:2).[55] As the Exodus

---

[52] See Ben Zvi, *Signs of Jonah*, 123–26. For Ben Zvi, the sailors of Jonah 1 "adumbrate a future world in which all the nations will consist of pious people who will follow many of the divine teachings held now by the Israelites" (ibid., 124). The distinction between Israel and the nations remains, though the theological differences between the two blur (cf. Isa 56:3-7).

[53] See Seitz, *Joel*, 47–48; Ronald L. Troxel, *Joel: Scope, Genre(s), and Meaning* (Critical Studies in the Hebrew Bible 6; Winona Lake: Eisenbrauns, 2015), 42–43, 46.

[54] See Introduction.

[55] Ibid.

narrative unfolds, the golden calf fiasco leads to the pinnacle moment of divine self-revelation as Yhwh provides Moses with a display of his glory by the revelation of his name (Ex 34:6-7). The character traits (*middoth*) of Yhwh's name describe him as merciful and severe, with his mercy far outweighing Yhwh's severity. "How can I give you up, Ephraim?" (Hos 11:8).

Thus ends the prophetic book of Micah with a rehearsal of the merciful character of Yhwh as derived from the *middoth* of Ex 34:6-7. Yhwh pardons and forgives sins. He holds fast to his people as his inheritance (cf. 7:14). Though his people lack faithfulness (חסד; 7:2), Yhwh delights in maintaining his own faithful love (חסד) to the object of his affections. His anger endures for a moment while his mercy extends in perpetuity. Though Israel's hands were dripping with guilt before the golden calves, Yhwh's wrath elided into his mercy and favor (Exodus 32-34). As Calvin comments, "This passage teaches us, as I have already reminded you, that the glory of God principally shines in this,—that he is reconcilable, and that he forgives our sins."[56] Have forgiven our sins and having cast them into the depths of the sea, sin as a pernicious and material force is removed from God's view. The result of such removal is Yhwh's reconciliation with his people.[57]

> Martin Luther on *into the depths of the sea*: "That is, He will put our sins far away from us so that they never again trouble our conscience. He will give us peace of conscience and a very free conscience, for indeed, peace follows the forgiveness of sins—a peace where the heart feels the sweetness of divine goodness, now that its sin has been forgiven, etc."[58]

John Calvin on 7:18-20 and authentic worship:

> Hence the fear of God, and the true worship of him, depend on a perception of his goodness and favour; for we cannot from the heart worship God, and there will be, as I have already said, no genuine religion in us, except this persuasion be really and deeply seated in our hearts,—that he is ever ready to forgive, whenever we flee to him.[59]

Francis Watson's *Paul and the Hermeneutics of Faith* provides a prolonged engagement with the XII's canonical history and reception in the Qumran texts and Paul. The canonical shaping of the XII entails a thorough eschatological reception of these prophetic voices as a witness to God's continued dealings with his people. Their "non-fulfillment" opens these

---

[56] Calvin, 400.
[57] See Gary A. Anderson, *Sin: A History* (New Haven: Yale University Press, 2009), 23.
[58] Luther, 277.
[59] Calvin, 401.

texts to the future and places future readers at "the intersection between a past dominated by the divine judgment and a future characterized by the hope of salvation."[60] As mentioned elsewhere in this commentary, Ben Zvi shares a similar logic regarding Micah's intended audience, namely, those rereaders who find in Micah a word from times past yet open to and shaping of the rereader's present and future. For Watson, the canonical shape of the Twelve provides a hermeneutic by which to read the corpus. He concludes, "[T]he hermeneutic entailed in the canonical form of the Book of the Twelve is above all a hermeneutic of hope."[61] The conclusion of Micah lends material support to Watson's thesis.

Joel Kaminsky's *Yet I Loved Jacob: Reclaiming the Biblical Concept of Election* makes the following claim: "Nearly every book among the fifteen canonical Latter Prophets ends on a note of hope for future restoration."[62] While aware of the dangers of a kind of naïve Biblicism where the practice of biblical authors becomes normative—e.g., the New Testament authors' Bible was the Septuagint therefore Christians today should use the Septuagint—nevertheless, the prophetic pattern of ending prophetic words with hope is suggestive for the form and shape of Christian preaching. Gospel hope is the telos of Christian preaching on analogy to the prophetic books of the Old Testament. The burden of preaching entails an honest appraisal of the human condition under the scrutiny of God's Word. Yet, as Paul reminds, God shuts up humanity in their disobedience so that he might have mercy on all. The balance of the *middoth* (Ex 34:6-7) where mercy tips the scales speaks to the character of God and the hope of Christian proclamation. "A bruised reed he will not break" (Isa 42:3).

The covenant pledge Yhwh made to Judah's ancestors, Abraham and Jacob, will sustain the relationship with his people, leveraging his severity with his mercy and love.[63] In fact, the community of faith is the present iteration of Abraham and Jacob in this moment of the divine economy. These figures relate in figural fashion to the community of faith both as representatives who went before and as extended identities of the elect in the present moment of the divine economy.[64] God's promises to Abraham and Jacob are as solid and faithful as God's promises to the current community. For to speak of the one requires the presence of the other. What is the basis for hope in the community of faith? The answer from Micah—as in Exodus and many Psalms—is none other than the enduring, gracious character of God. Weeping may endure for the night but joy comes in the morning.

---

[60] Watson, *Paul and the Hermeneutics of Faith*, 138.
[61] Ibid., 137. Watson's reading of Deuteronomy in the same volume is not as compelling. See the critical interaction in Seitz, *The Character of Christian Scripture*, 56-58, 60-62, and esp. 152-53.
[62] Joel S. Kaminsky, *Yet I have Loved Jacob: Reclaiming the Biblical Concept of Election* (Nashville: Abingdon Press, 2007), 156.
[63] Wolff observes an association between the last verse of the Magnificat (Lk 1:55) and Mic 7:20 (Wolff, 234).
[64] Such is the logic of Hosea's reference to Jacob's wrestling with God as an exemplar of the repentance Israel was to embrace (Hos 12:2-6).

Index

Note: Locators with letter 'n' refer to notes.

a priori 179
Aaron 196
Aaronic blessing 132
Abraham 166, 187, 225, 232
abstraction 11, 26 n.61, 27 n.65, 88, 92, 104, 110, 129
Achaemenid period 43
Achan 104
actualization 38, 102, 122, 164, 193, 203, 204, 226
Adam 85, 124, 125
Adonai 83, 85, 163
Adullam 99
adultery 105 n.15, 163
Advent 26, 175
Ahab 105, 106, 212
Ahaz 71, 76, 142
Albertz, Rainer 74, 75
allegory 27 n.65, 30
Allen, Michael 47
alliteration 94 n.72, 97
Ambrose, Bishop of Milan 71
Ammonites 129
Amon 158
Amos 37 n.9, 53, 54, 55, 67, 73–6, 79–80, 84, 85 n.39, 89, 94, 108, 110, 113, 118, 130, 134, 137, 138, 141, 157, 158, 176, 184 n.33, 188, 190 n.53, 200, 210, 216, 219
analogy 26 n.61, 41, 46, 100, 106, 123, 144, 199, 232
Anatolios, Khaled 23–4
ancient of Days 177, 180
Andersen, Francis I. 39, 48–9, 80–1, 83, 95 n.75, 96 n.79, 97, 102 n.5, 103, 104 n.10, 108 n.23, 110 n.28, 115 n.40, 118 n.46, 123 n.62, 124, 129 n.8, 131, 137, 138, 141 n.50, 142 n.53, 151 n.4, 152, 155, 156 n.20, 161, 169 n.54, 170–1, 182 n.23, 183, 184, 193, 195 n.11, 200 n.25, 203 n.40, 204 n.42, 209 n.63, 226 n.38
André, Gunnel 219 n.17
anger. *See* wrath
Anglican Prayer Book tradition 117, 132–3
antinomianism 198
apostates/backsliders 111
Aquinas, Thomas 25–6, 28, 76, 180–1
Aram 166
Aramaic 20, 97, 180
archaeology 9, 90
Arendt, Hannah 207
Aristotle 107
arrogance 109, 188, 191, 229, 230
Asherah 188, 212
"assembly of the Lord" 111, 209 n.63
associative field-mappings 27, 28
Assyria/Assyrians 15, 16, 76, 84, 125, 162, 171, 182–5, 228
Athanasius 24, 164
atonement 87–8
Augustine 24, 26, 27 n.65, 71, 93 n.67, 107–8
authenticity 5, 9, 33, 34, 42, 45, 127, 139, 153, 187 n.44, 231
authorship 4, 8, 13, 19–23, 28, 36 n.9, 43, 44–50, 68, 69, 72, 73–9, 119–20, 137, 144–5, 153 n.9, 179, 232
Ayres, Lewis 14 n.32

Baal 212
Babel 86 n.44
Babylon/Babylonians 16, 66 n.26, 109, 115–16, 123 n.62, 162, 180
Balaam 197, 228
Balak 197, 228
Balserak, Jon 94 n.74
Baptism 71, 199
Barth, Karl 7, 20–1, 22–3, 25, 26 n.61, 68, 87–8, 92, 93 n.67, 94–5, 144, 198, 201–2
Bashan 191, 228
Bathsheba 105 n.15
Baumgartner, Walther 20–1
Bavinck, Herman 4 n.8, 5
Becker, Uwe 5, 6
"becoming" 76, 77
Being 36
Beiser, Frederick 10–11, 12
belief 11, 17, 18, 19, 22, 23, 100
Benjamin 82 n.28
Ben Zvi, Ehud 43–5, 52 n.1, 74–5, 77–9, 91–2, 99, 100, 109, 112–13, 116 n.43, 123 n.62, 142, 161, 163, 166, 189–90, 195, 199 n.23, 208 n.59, 214 nn.1–2, 215, 223, 226, 230 n.52, 232
Bethel 210
Bethlehem 167, 168, 170, 171, 173–7, 179, 180
BHS *(Biblia Hebraica Stuttgartensia)* 94 n.72, 98, 108 n.23, 110 n.28, 112, 115, 119 n.49, 138 n.41, 166 n.51, 169 n.53, 183 n.29, 209, 210 n.66
Biblicism 232
bibliology 8
Biddle, John 178–80
"biting" 135
bitterness 98, 110
blind eye 21, 29, 113, 117, 121
blood/bloodshed 61, 67, 141–2, 216, 219

Boda, Mark 99 n.84
bones 131
Book of Common Prayer 202
Book of the Four 52 n.2, 53 n.3, 55 n.6, 73–5
Book of the Twelve 4 n.6, 16, 51–69, 75–6, 117, 147, 162–4, 166, 203–4, 209, 229, 231–2
Bosshard, Nupestil 37 n.10, 44, 156–7 n.24
Bozrah 123 n.62, 124
break through 125
briars 216
bribery 141, 142
burnt offerings 199 n.24, 200

Calvin, John 12–13, 23, 25, 37, 77, 79, 88, 91, 94, 101, 103–4, 112, 116–17, 121–3, 125, 134–5, 139–40, 169, 176 n.14, 181, 184 n.34, 185, 191, 203, 222, 226 n.39, 231
Cameron, Michael 26 n.62
Canaanite tradition 153, 188, 200
canon consciousness 2
Carson, D. A. 24 n.55
casting lots 111
Catholicism 25, 104 n.11, 154
cessation. *See* rest
Chapman, Stephen 69 n.29
cheating 163
Childs, Brevard 2, 5 n.9, 12 n.29, 13, 20 nn.45–6, 35, 40–1, 44, 53 n.3, 68–9 n.29, 79 n.23, 100, 104 n.12, 105, 139, 144, 152, 153 n.12, 156, 158 n.29
child sacrifice 200
Chladenius, Johann Martin 12
Christology 26 n.62, 29, 85, 94–5, 180, 198 n.18, 222
2 Chronicles 122, 166 n.51, 168
Church Dogmatics IV.1 (Barth) 22, 87, 198 n.18
church fathers 24, 180–1

Church's existence 84–5
Clements, Ronald 36
Colossians 7
comfort 116, 118, 123, 220, 226
"coming" 76, 77, 86 n.44, 99, 226
commandments. *See* Law
comparative religion 9
compositional history 1–31, 34, 35, 37, 38, 44, 46, 49, 50 n.35, 51 n.1, 52, 56, 72, 83, 152, 155, 156–9
conceptual incoherence 41
confession 7, 14–15, 18, 20, 21, 28, 143, 144, 145, 180, 201 n.28, 220–1, 223
confidence 115, 116, 119, 120, 142–3, 145, 146, 188, 204, 220, 221. *See also* faith
1 Corinthians 137
2 Corinthians 3
cosmology 9 n.24
covenant formula 109
covetousness 104–5, 106 n.20, 111
creation 66, 120, 133, 176, 178, 181, 194, 196, 207, 224
Creator 66, 67, 108, 219
creed 30
Cross, Richard 11
Cross, the 87, 202
cross-reference 2, 144–5
crucifixion 87
cruelty 131–2, 219
curse 115, 186–7, 197, 202, 210–11
Cyril of Alexandria 144, 164, 165, 180, 185, 211
Cyrus Cylinder 5 n.9

Damascus 15
Dante 136–7
darkness 137, 138, 188, 219, 224
Daughter of Zion 63, 95 n.76, 98, 99, 100, 167, 168–70
David 37 n.9, 82 n.28, 85, 98–9, 105 n.15, 119, 124, 131 n.14, 167, 168, 169 n.55, 173–81, 182, 184, 227
Dawson, John David 27 n.65
Day of the Lord 37 n.9, 133, 162, 188, 190 n.53, 218, 219, 225 n.37, 230
Dead Sea 228
death 87 n.47, 99, 101, 125, 147, 168, 169, 202, 207
Decalogue 59, 104 n.11, 202. *See also* Law
deception/deceptive spirit 98, 120–1, 128, 134, 138, 210, 216
De Doctrina (Augustine) 26, 107
deliverance 125, 132 n.18, 199, 220, 228
desire 93 n.67, 103–5, 107, 108, 109, 120, 127, 192, 204, 207
Desire of Nations, The (O'Donovan) 133–4
despair 167, 169, 173, 220
destruction/doom 34, 81, 90–2, 95, 119, 140, 145, 170, 194 n.6, 211 n.68, 212
"deuteronomistic" influence 35, 53, 55 n.6, 74, 75, 76, 106 n.20, 119
Deuteronomy 86 n.41, 91, 93, 101, 103, 105, 110, 111, 119, 132 n.18, 142, 170, 174, 176, 188, 190 n.52, 194, 196 n.14, 198, 200, 201, 202, 204, 205, 208, 210, 211 n.68, 212 n.72, 227, 232 n.61
dew 186, 187
de Wette, Wilhelm Martin Leberecht 13
dialectics 26, 53–4, 63, 65, 69
Diblaim 100
Dillers 34, 48, 226
dirge 111, 222–3
discernment 37, 47, 68, 109, 118, 145, 206
discourse 6, 24 n.55, 28, 71, 99, 198

disgrace 114–15, 118–19, 173
dishonesty 105 n.15, 130 n.9, 211 n.68
disobedience 23, 87, 92, 120, 202, 232
distancing 58 n.11, 109
divinations/diviners 137, 188
Divine Comedy (Dante) 136
divine favor 111, 204, 219 n.17, 228, 231
divine knowledge 26 n.61, 86
Dorrien, Gary 9 n.24
dowry 98
Dozeman, Thomas 59, 104 n.12, 197
dreams 137
drunkenness 134
duplex gratia 140
Durham, John 104–5

ears, open/itching/deaf 17 n.38, 116, 120, 121
ecclesiology 84–5
Edom 123 n.62, 124, 225
Egypt 15, 64, 83 n.31, 132 n.18, 196, 197, 199, 227, 229, 230
Eichmann, Adolf 207
El 188
elect 191, 198, 225 n.37, 232
election 92–3, 100, 125, 131, 198, 199, 200, 206, 216, 227, 228, 232
Eli, sons of 218
Elliott, Mark 30–1
Elohim 63
Emery, Gilles 25, 26 n.61, 181
Emmanuel 173
emptiness 108
enjoyment *vs.* use 107–8
Enlightenment 10–11, 18–19, 133
Ephraim 15, 218, 231
Ephrathah 167, 168, 170, 171, 174
Epigonen 45
epistemology 22, 23, 24, 41
Esau 225
eschatology 24, 60–7, 100, 106 n.18, 111, 119–20, 147, 161, 162–6, 173, 185, 211, 231
eternity 8 n.19, 27 n.65, 175, 176–8, 180
Eucharist 199, 202
evil 98, 102–4, 108–10, 130–3, 136–7, 202, 207
Ewald, Heinrich 33 n.3
"Exegetical Obituary, An" (Levin) 75
exile 41, 82 n.28, 99, 100, 121–3, 164, 166, 168, 219, 224
Exodus 16, 53–4 nn.3–4, 55–60, 64–5, 66, 68, 98, 104 nn.11–12, 105 n.14, 117, 130 n.9, 132, 146, 149, 162, 174, 196, 198 n.17, 199, 209, 218, 227–32
exploitation 92, 118, 169, 210, 212 n.71
Ezekiel 5–6, 85, 94, 111, 113 n.32, 118 n.48, 123, 165 n.49, 218, 227

Fabry, Heinz-Joseph 66, 84
face of God 132–3
faith 7, 9 n.24, 13, 18, 20 n.46, 22, 23, 24, 45, 62, 67, 78, 85, 119, 120, 144, 145, 160 n.36, 161, 178, 180, 201 n.28, 203, 208, 214, 215, 216, 220–1, 222, 223, 232
faithfulness 16, 57, 69, 91, 101, 140, 147, 161, 162, 163, 164, 169, 190, 203, 204–5, 208, 211, 213–22, 231, 232
false weights/scales 210
family 108–9, 118, 198 n.17, 214, 215, 220
famine, of God's Word 138
favor 111, 228, 231
fear of Yhwh 208–9, 224, 229–30, 231
fidelity 59, 92, 118, 136
fields (land) 105, 111, 145, 149, 227
fig tree/figs 62, 106 n.18, 158, 163, 211, 216
Fishbane, Michael 2
flesh 47, 77, 131–2

forgiveness 41, 57, 58, 65, 67, 85, 86, 187, 224, 231
form-critical approach 5–6, 33, 44, 45, 46, 78, 102 n.5, 123, 215, 219 n.17, 221–3
Fortschreibung 1, 6, 34, 35, 36, 38 n.12, 40, 46, 49, 193 n.3, 208 n.58
Freedman, David Noel 3, 39, 48–9, 80–1, 83, 95 n.75, 96 n.79, 97, 102 n.5, 103, 104 n.10, 108 n.23, 110 n.28, 115 n.40, 118 n.46, 123 n.62, 124, 129 n.8, 131, 137, 138, 141 n.50, 142 n.53, 151 n.4, 152, 155, 156 n.20, 161, 169 n.54, 170–1, 182 n.23, 183, 184, 193, 195 n.11, 200 n.25, 203 n.40, 204 n.42, 209 n.63, 226 n.38
fundamentalism 19
fury. *See* wrath

Gadamer, Hans-Georg 12 n.29
Galilee 228
Gath 97, 98, 99
Gelston, Anthony 110 n.28, 156
Genesis 30 n.71, 86 n.44, 120, 137, 167–8, 224
Geneva 79
German Historicist Tradition, The (Beiser) 11, 12
Geschichte Israels (Noth) 21
Gideon 174
Gilead 228
Gilgal 197
Gilkey, Langdon 9 n.24
glory 59, 99, 107, 116 n.43, 118 n.48, 191, 207, 230–1
Godly grief 165. *See also* repentance
gold 104, 136
golden calf 58, 59–60, 67, 227, 231
Goldingay, John 80 n.25
Gomer 100
Good Friday 87, 147

goods *vs.* preferables 107
gospel 17, 23, 46, 79, 87, 94–5, 119, 125, 140, 164, 176 n.12, 180, 198–9, 232
Gowen, Donald 58
grace/gracious 9, 26 n.62, 54 n.4, 56–60, 63, 64, 68, 79, 87, 92–3, 97, 117, 139, 140, 146, 149, 173, 197, 198, 199, 203, 204, 206, 207, 211, 228, 232
grapes 211, 216
gratitude 200, 205, 206
Great Commission 164
greatest commandment 101
Gregory of Nyssa 24
Grotius, Hugo 180
guilt 57, 65–6, 108, 110, 136, 142, 174, 208, 214, 218, 222, 224, 231
Gunkel, Hermann 13, 45, 57 n.9, 222–3
Gunneweg, A. J. 14
Gunton, Colin 87

Habakkuk 53 n.3, 66, 110, 141, 142, 220–1
Hagstrom, David Gerald 48–9
Hananiah 115–16, 139
happiness *(eudaimonia),* pursuit of 107–8
harvest 211, 216
haughtiness 109, 191
Hays, Richard 176 n.12
Hazony, Yoram 151 n.3
healing 165
Hebrews 77, 119–20, 221
Hegel, Georg Wilhelm Friedrich 10
Heidelberg Catechism 186–7
Helmer, Christine 8 n.19
Herder, Johann Gottfried 12
heritage 90, 95, 227
hermeneutics 7, 8, 9, 13, 14–15, 17, 22–7, 29, 30, 43, 44, 45, 71, 79, 85 n.34, 119, 125, 139, 144, 169, 175, 177, 179, 232

Hermisson, H. J. 41, 53
ḥesed 57
Hezekiah 15, 71, 76, 142 n.53, 146, 147, 184, 214
hierarchy. *See* social structure
high places 86–7, 88, 145–6
historicism 2, 4, 10–12, 13, 18–19, 21, 39, 122 n.59, 155, 178
Holy Spirit 4 n.8, 5, 6, 7, 8 n.19, 23, 25, 46, 73, 96, 107–8, 138–40, 145
hope 4 n.8, 17, 23, 24, 33, 38 n.12, 39, 43 n.22, 47, 48, 49, 62, 63, 65, 67, 69, 100, 110, 116, 121, 122–3, 125, 128–9, 132, 140, 146, 147, 149–50, 155, 162, 163, 164, 166, 167, 168, 173–92, 213–32
Hosea 4 n.6, 52, 53, 54, 55, 68, 73–6, 80 n.24, 85, 89 n.57, 91, 100, 130, 157, 162, 165, 167, 187, 210, 216, 218–19, 232 n.64
Hossfeld, Frank-Lothar 153 n.10
House, Paul R. 56
Hübner, Hans 3
Hugh of St. Victor 25 n.59
humiliation 110, 173, 193, 212, 229
humility 93, 101, 185, 205, 206, 207
hunger 107, 108, 211
Hunsinger, George 26 n.61
hymn 66, 222–3, 224, 230
hypocrisy 117

Ibn Ezra 121 n.54, 125
idioms 8 n.19, 62, 103, 162, 204 n.42
idolatry 58–9, 66, 86–7, 91–3, 94 n.74, 108, 145–6, 188–9, 206, 212
imagery 65, 80–1, 86–90, 91, 94 n.71, 100, 109, 123, 124, 133, 135, 137, 145, 167, 224, 227, 229
images. *See* idolatry
incarnation 27 n.65, 77, 175, 180, 185
indifference 132

Inferno (Dante) 136–7
infidelity 16, 86, 89, 92, 100, 111, 118, 188, 189, 212, 213
inheritance 82 n.28, 105–6, 111–12, 113, 119, 226, 227, 231
iniquity 57
integrity 33 n.3, 68, 127, 151 n.3, 154, 190
intercession 94 n.70, 226–7
intertextuality 1–2, 16, 35, 38, 43, 50, 56, 62, 64, 65, 66, 68, 73, 86 n.41, 98, 110 n.26, 130 n.11, 142, 146, 162, 165 n.49, 188 n.45, 193, 210, 212 n.70, 225 n.36, 229
Irenaeus 30, 31, 85
Isaiah 5, 17, 20, 33–9, 41, 42 n.21, 46, 53, 61 nn.19–20, 66 n.25, 71, 74, 75, 80, 82 n.28, 88, 90, 99, 109, 123, 129 n.8, 131 n.14, 137, 143 n.56, 173–4, 188, 191, 212 n.74, 223 n.26
and Micah, diachronic/shared oracle 150–71
Israel 2, 4 n.8, 5, 8 n.19, 9, 15, 16, 20–1, 36–9, 41, 47, 51, 59–61, 63–8, 72, 76, 78, 79, 80, 82, 84–6, 88–9, 92–3, 98, 99, 102, 105–6, 108–9, 110 n.26, 111, 117, 123, 125, 129, 130–4, 149, 151 n.3, 153 n.10, 155, 157, 159, 162, 163, 166, 167, 168, 169, 170–1, 173, 174, 184, 187, 190, 194 n.4, 195, 196, 197–202, 208, 211, 212, 216, 221, 225 n.37, 226, 228, 230, 231, 232 n.64
Issachar 105

Jabbok 166–7, 168
jackel 94
Jacob (patriarch) 83, 84, 88, 89, 121, 166–8, 225, 232
Jacob, Benno 57, 60 n.16

Jacobs, Mignon 47–8, 160 n.35
jealousy 58, 60
Jebusites 153, 157
Jehoiakim 141, 146, 147
Jehoshaphat 62
Jephthah 129
Jepsen, A. 89 n.57, 91
Jeremiah 20, 33, 34, 35, 36, 38 n.12, 74, 75, 95 n.77, 108, 109, 115–16, 131 n.14, 134, 139, 141, 143, 146–7, 174, 183, 226
Jeremias, Jörg 34–5, 38, 44, 46 n.25, 49–50, 61 n.18, 73–5, 82, 86, 91, 94, 110–11, 121, 129–30, 141–2, 145, 146, 161, 165, 166, 170, 174, 176, 182, 186, 190, 193, 195 n.8, 208 n.58, 212 n.70, 214, 217–19, 224, 229
Jeroboam II 55
Jerome 96
Jerusalem 34, 36, 38 n.12, 43 n.22, 66 n.26, 71, 74, 79–91, 95–8, 102 n.4, 129, 130, 140, 142, 143 n.56, 145, 150, 153 n.10, 164, 167, 174, 177, 184, 190, 207, 212, 215, 221, 222 n.24
Jesse 184
Jethro 130 n.9
Jews 79, 101, 181, 207
Job 94, 138, 196, 214
Joel 37 n.9, 55, 62, 63, 64, 65, 75, 76, 136, 137, 218 n.16, 219, 230, 232
John 25, 76, 123 n.63, 144, 145, 176 n.12, 227
Jonah 52, 53–8, 60–9, 84, 108, 146, 163, 229–30
Jonathan 99
Joshua 13, 104, 129 n.8
Josiah 131 n.14
Jotham 71, 76
Judah 15, 16, 38 n.12, 39–40, 52, 53 n.3, 60–1, 65–9, 71, 72, 74, 75, 76, 78, 79, 81, 82, 84, 88, 89, 93, 95–6, 98, 99 n.84, 100–11, 127, 130, 131, 132, 133, 134, 135, 138, 139, 140–1, 143, 144, 146, 151, 153 n.12, 162, 164, 166, 167, 168–9, 170, 173, 174, 177, 182, 183, 184–5, 188, 189–91, 193, 197, 200, 201, 202, 208, 210, 211, 212 n.70, 213–21, 224–5, 227, 228, 230, 232
judge 17, 76, 86, 87, 95, 159, 170–1, 216, 217
Judges 86, 129, 174
judgment 13, 16–17, 24, 34, 37, 47, 48, 49, 58, 62, 65, 67, 72, 76, 78, 81, 83–90, 92, 94–7, 99 n.84, 100, 108–12, 115, 120–1, 122 n.59, 123, 124, 125, 131, 134, 137, 138, 142, 145, 149, 155, 165, 167, 170–1, 186–7, 189–91, 194, 198, 202, 208–12, 213, 217–19, 221, 224–5, 230, 232
Jüngel, Eberhard 87, 101
justice/injustice 9, 28, 47, 58, 67, 78, 87, 103, 106 n.20, 113, 116, 118, 127–47, 156, 170, 200–8, 213, 216–19
justification 19, 56, 127, 140

Kaminsky, Joel 225 n.37, 232
Kessler, Rainer 34, 66 n.26, 81 n.26, 95, 103 n.8, 161, 163 n.43, 193 n.3, 194 n.6, 195 n.11, 200 n.27, 212 n.74
Kimchi, David 161
kindness 204, 206, 220
1 Kings 98, 105–6, 170–1, 212
2 Kings 55, 122, 175, 200
Klassiker 45
Klooster, Fred 144
Knierim, Rolf P. 89
knowledge 26 n.61, 77, 86, 130–1, 163, 206 n.51, 207, 224, 230

Index

Kratz, Reinhard 41, 53 n.3, 82 n.28, 89, 157 n.27
Kugel, James L. 90
Kuhrt, Amélie 15
Kyrie Eleison 202

labor 40 n.15, 168, 173–4
Lachish 16, 98
lamentation 60, 81, 93–6, 99 n.84, 100, 110, 111, 112, 213–32
Lamentations 94
land, as inheritance 105–6, 111–12, 119
Law 82–93, 101–5, 112, 125, 164, 198, 202, 203
leader/ruler, description of 129–30, 141
Lebanon 191
legalism 198
Legaspi, Michael 18
leitmotif 102, 117, 179
lepers 138
Lescow, Theodor 128 n.1
Levin, Christoph 52–3 nn.2–3, 55 n.6, 75, 157–8
Levinson, Bernard 2 n.3
Levinson, Jon 14
Leviticus 105
Limburg, J. 195 n.11
lion 62, 64, 186, 187
lip service 201
litany of "the good" 203–4
literal exposition, levels of 25 n.59
literary devices 97
literary form 12 n.29, 20 n.46, 25, 26, 28, 29, 30 n.71, 34–5, 38, 41, 42–7, 50 n.35, 61 n.19, 64, 72, 75, 77, 78, 80, 83, 94 n.72, 102, 113, 117–19, 128, 140, 142, 147, 152, 154–6, 157 n.25, 170, 185, 190, 203, 208, 209, 211, 215, 222, 226, 232
literary structure 38, 47–9, 71, 84, 105, 161, 187, 189, 193, 221

liturgy 38, 82 n.28, 143, 153, 201 n.28, 202, 222, 223
Logos 178, 180
Lohfink, Norbert 74
Lord of the Rings, The (Tolkien) 196
love
  God's 57, 60, 102, 140, 200, 203–7, 210, 219, 232
  of neighbor 88, 101–25
lust 105 n.15
Luther, Martin 8 n.19, 12, 69, 79, 101, 104 n.11, 125, 137 n.37, 150, 154, 166, 181, 182, 198 n.18, 199, 207, 226 n.39, 231
lying/lies 120, 134, 163

MacDonald, Neil 16
Malachi 4 n.6, 37 n.10, 52, 53 n.3, 54 n.5
Manasseh 174, 212, 228 n.49
Mark 102
marriage 100
Marshall, Bruce 17 n.38
Masorah Parva 147
Masoretic Text (MT) 52, 54–5, 73, 84, 98, 112, 116 n.42, 120 n.52, 141 n.50, 149, 154, 167–71, 173–8, 181–92, 208, 210 n.66, 215
Matthew 3, 143–4, 164, 175
Mays, James Luther 35 n.5, 47, 48 n.33, 92, 97, 98, 108, 120 n.52, 124 n.66, 135, 142 n.53, 150 n.1, 152, 161, 175, 190, 195, 214
McConville, Gordon 163, 202 n.37, 204, 206 n.51
McKane, William 38 n.11, 103, 118, 160 n.35
Melugin, Roy 78 n.21
mercy 47, 55, 56–60, 61, 64, 65, 67, 69, 85, 117, 147, 149, 201, 204, 205, 209, 213, 230, 231, 232

Merleau-Ponty, Maurice 28
Messianic prophecy 33, 161, 173–92, 226 n.38, 227
metaphors 23, 30, 61, 68, 86, 87, 88, 94, 95, 99, 104 n.10, 109, 120, 124, 127, 131, 132, 137, 146, 173, 174, 186, 187, 214, 216, 217, 227
metaphysics 8, 10–11, 12, 17–29, 125, 179–81
metonym 96 n.78, 89, 99, 118 n.48, 145–6, 208
Micah (prophet), persona and prophetic role 76, 81
Micah (Ben Zvi) 43
Michaelis, Johann David 18
middot (attributes) 56–8, 60, 61, 117, 149, 162, 209, 231, 232
midrash 3
Migdal Eder 166–8
military reliance 188–9
Miriam 196
Moab 197, 200
modernity 9–17, 12, 18, 19, 71
money 136
monotheism 51
moralism 198 n.20
Moresheth 15, 71, 76, 98, 146
Moses 58–9, 130 n.9, 174, 196, 218, 226–7, 229, 230–1
Moses's song 86 n.41, 230
mountains 65, 83 n.30, 86, 127, 145, 149, 158, 164, 194–6
mourning. *See* lamentation
mouth of the Lord 157, 222 n.24
mouths, covering of 64–5, 138, 229
Mowinckel, Sigmund 153 n.11, 173 n.1
mystery 8 n.19, 26 n.61, 96

Na'aman, Nadav 82 n.28
Naboth 105–6
Nachgeschichte 33
Nahum 52, 53–4, 57, 58, 60–7, 68, 69, 84, 163, 230

nakedness 94, 97, 191
natural law 19
Near East 9, 20, 21, 106 n.20, 153 n.10
neck(s) 109
neighbor, love of 88, 89, 101–25
Neo-Assyrian Empire 15, 76, 125, 162
new beginnings 173–92
Nicene orthodoxy 178
Nichomachean Ethics (Aristotle) 107
Nineveh 60–1, 64, 65, 66, 67, 108
NIV (New International Version) 160 n.35, 170
Nogalski, James D. 47, 53, 55, 56, 74, 81, 110 n.26, 151, 160 n.36, 181–2, 183, 184, 210
noise 124
nominalism 11, 18
Northern Kingdom 89 n.57, 95, 129 n.5, 130, 157 n.27, 212
Noth, Martin 21
NRSV (New Revised Standard Version) 43, 109, 166 n.51, 170, 181, 183 n.29, 209 n.63, 228
Numbers 119, 197, 199, 228
numbers, significance of 183–4

Obadiah 96 n.78, 157 n.24
obedience 59, 120
Oberman, Heiko A. 137 n.37
O'Donovan, Oliver 107 n.22, 133–4, 198 n.20
omnipotence 11 n.27
omniscience 86
Omri 212
ontology 2, 7–8, 23, 29, 85, 107 n.22, 125, 177, 199
oppositional ethos 4 n.6
oppression 106
oracle 35 n.5, 42 n.21, 66, 67, 78, 82–3, 87, 100, 102, 152 n.8, 155, 156 n.20, 157 n.25, 158–9, 160, 165, 177, 189, 222–3, 228

Origen 27 n.65, 29–30
original utterance 28
ostrich 94
Owen, John 178–80
owl 94

pain, of loss 99 n.84
paleography 9
parallelism 90, 186
parents, mistreatment of 105 n.15
paronomasia 97
particularism 47, 67, 84, 187
Passion 87
pasture/pastoral imagery 21, 158, 167–9, 181, 185, 226, 227, 228
patience 51, 57, 58, 59, 64, 66, 115, 117, 191, 209, 222
Paul 3, 5, 26, 120–1, 137, 145, 165, 198 n.18, 207, 224, 231–2
Paul, Shalom 210
Paul and the Hermeneutics of Faith (Watson) 231–2
peace 39, 61, 118, 132, 135, 138, 149, 150, 154 n.17, 155, 156, 159, 163, 174, 181, 182–3, 185, 191, 231
peasants 102 n.4
Pentateuch 39, 86
Penuel 166
perseverance 115
perversion 93 n.67, 106, 136
pesher 3
Peter 136, 138
2 Peter 13, 73
Pharisees 13, 73, 101
Philistia 99
philology 9, 13, 20, 21, 28, 30 n.71, 97, 176, 177, 180, 181 n.23, 182 n.23
phonetics 26, 27, 98
piety 37 n.9, 141, 142, 200 n.25, 216
pilgrimage 120, 154 n.17, 161
pleasure 107–8

pride 92, 93, 101, 109, 188, 189, 191, 205, 207
priests 88, 94, 106 n.20, 125, 136, 142, 222
Promised Land 119, 196, 197, 210
prophet, role of 142, 218
prophetic books 5–6
prostitution 90, 91–2, 100. *See also* idolatry
Protestantism 25, 69
Proverbs 37 n.9, 110, 183, 184
proverb/taunt song 110–11
providence 12 n.29, 19, 46, 168, 186
Psalms 37 n.9, 38 n.11, 66 n.26, 86, 94 n.74, 104, 119–20, 125 n.67, 133, 152–3, 202, 220, 220 n.21, 223–4, 226, 232
pseudo-historicism 39, 41 n.18
pseudo-prophets
 characterization of 113–18, 120–1
 vs. Yhwh's prophets, contradistinction 127–47
purging/cleansing 187–8
purpose 11, 25, 73, 139
puzzle 127–8

Qumran 3, 4 n.6, 52, 123 n.63, 154, 175, 203 n.40, 231

Racovian Catechism 178–80
Radner, Ephraim 11 n.27, 84, 85
reception/reception history 2–5, 12 n.29, 16, 40, 42, 73, 75, 77, 78, 80, 146, 147, 231
redaction/redaction criticism 1–2, 16, 33, 35, 36 n.9, 37, 38–44, 47, 48 n.33, 49, 52–4 nn.2–4, 64 n.24, 66, 71, 73, 74, 75, 83 n.32, 122, 128, 142 n.53, 152, 153 n.12, 154 n.13, 155, 157 nn.24–5, 158, 160, 160 n.35, 162–3, 185, 189, 195, 208 n.57, 214, 221–2

redemption 16–17, 19, 29, 34, 73, 82, 86, 92–3, 100, 120, 123, 125, 129, 131, 132, 146, 147, 163, 167, 169, 170, 173, 178, 181, 183, 185, 196–200, 206, 224, 226, 227–9
reductionism 12, 19, 21, 34, 87, 133, 179, 180, 200
Reformation 20, 69., 144, 153–4
refuge 62–5, 67, 176
rejection 100, 125, 189, 230
religiosity 120
remnant 52, 123, 165–6, 185, 186, 187
Renaud, Bernard 35 n.5, 130 n.10
Rendtorff, Rolf 51 n.1, 60, 61 n.18, 63
renewal 67, 85, 220
Reno, R. R. 30 n.71
repentance 60, 61, 63, 64, 65, 66, 67, 79, 85, 108, 130, 136, 146, 147, 165, 166–7, 191, 193, 202, 207, 211, 215, 224, 230, 232 n.64
rescue 115, 200
rest 119–20, 142, 166, 176
restoration 67, 111–12, 133, 140, 165, 167, 169, 189, 199, 211, 225, 226, 227, 228, 232
resurrection 164, 166, 202, 204
revelation 4 n.8, 8, 26 n.61, 59, 67, 68, 85, 106 n.20, 138, 139, 145, 181, 230–1
revenge 66
rhetoric 2, 68, 97, 98, 103, 115, 116, 130, 131, 138, 162, 194 n.4, 196, 197, 200 n.25, 216, 218, 229
Ricouer, Paul 59
righteousness 101, 103, 116, 131 n.14, 136, 140, 200 n.26, 207
robbers. *See* pseudo-prophets
Roberts, J. J. M. 42 n.21
Robinson, Marilynne 220
Rosenzweig, Franz 2 n.3
ruins 90, 111, 149, 173, 192
rupture 87, 109
Ruth 96 n.78

Sabbath 119, 120
sacraments 26, 136
sacrifices 63, 117, 199–200, 204
sailors 61, 63, 84, 163, 229–30
salt 108
salvation 47, 48, 49, 53 n.3, 73, 93, 99 n.84, 100, 121, 123, 136, 165, 169, 178, 182, 183, 187, 203, 212 n.74, 213, 215, 221, 232
Samaria 15, 34, 71, 79–84, 87, 88, 89, 90–2, 95–7, 100, 129 n.5, 145, 190, 194 n.6, 212
Samuel 218
1 Samuel 99, 105 n.15, 119, 137, 218
2 Samuel 86, 91, 98–9, 167, 175 n.7, 196 n.13, 210, 218, 228
sanctification 73, 135–6, 140
Sargon II 15
Satan/devil 96–7, 125, 185
Saul 82 n.28, 99, 174
Sauter, Gerhard 23
saving arm 121
Schart, Aaron 52 n.2, 53, 54 n.4, 55 n.6, 56, 61 nn.18–19, 66 n.26, 74, 75
Schleiermacher, Friedrich 23
Schmid, Konrad 37 n.10
Schopenhauer, Arthur 10
Scripture, compositional history 1–2
Scripture principle 144–5, 179
secular approaches 14 n.32
security 119, 132, 141, 174, 188
Seitz, Christopher 46, 76, 147
self-determination 59, 93, 199
self-giving 87, 101, 200
self-reliance 93, 188–9, 191
semantics 8 n.19, 27–8, 80, 91, 97–8, 104, 105 n.14, 157 n.24, 166 n.51, 170, 204, 206
Sennacherib 15–16, 81, 100, 214
Septuagint 170, 232
severity 55, 58–60, 61, 64, 65, 67, 68, 69, 112, 115, 117, 147 n.73, 149, 209, 213, 231, 232

244

Shalmaneser V 15
shalom 201
shame 64, 97, 110, 138, 171, 229
shaved head 100
Shaw, Prue 136
Shema 101
Sheol 194
Shephaleh region 76, 96–7, 100
Shepherd 121–5, 134, 167, 174–5, 183, 184–6, 223, 226–7
Sheppard, Gerald T. 36 n.9
Shiloh 157
silver 136, 140, 229
Simoniacs 136
Simon Magus 136
sin 16, 17, 57, 59–60, 86, 88–90, 92, 93 n.67, 100, 101, 108, 125, 136, 139, 185, 198, 199 n.24, 202, 210, 231. *See also* transgression
Sinai 58, 86, 198
sinner 87, 135, 136
skin 131
slavery 106 n.18, 109, 132 n.18, 196
Smith, Ralph L. 47
social justice 106 n.20
social structure 106, 109
Socinianism 178–80
Sola Scriptura 144
Sommer, Benjamin 2 n.3, 4, 39, 41, 41 n.18, 53 n.3, 122 n.59, 151 n.3, 154, 155
Son of Man 177
soothsayers 137
Southern Kingdom 15, 82, 88, 89 n.57, 100, 129, 130, 157 n.27
sovereignty 150, 185, 189
Spinoza, Benedict de 10, 13, 29, 179
spirit of the Lord 115. *See also* Holy Spirit
splendor 118 n.48, 169. *See also* glory
Spronk, Klaas 53 n.3
Stade, Bernard 33–4

Stansell, Gary 153 n.12
"state of sin" 92 n.64
steal(ing) 104 n.10, 105
Steck, Odil 37 n.10, 41, 44, 53 n.3, 143 n.56, 156
Steiner, George 26–7
Stoebe, H.J. 206
Stoics 107
stones, heap of 90, 145, 149
stubbornness 111
suffering. *See* lamentation
survivors. *See* remnant
swearing 163
Sweeney, Marvin 66 n.25, 89, 94 n.71, 95 n.76, 105, 111 n.29, 114, 117, 121, 122–3, 125, 137, 151 n.3, 158 n.29, 159, 159 nn.32–3, 160, 161, 166, 182, 184, 189, 193 n.3, 195 n.11, 214
symbolism 27 n.65, 93, 109, 119, 143, 184, 201 n.28. *See also* metaphor
syntax 15–16, 59, 82 n.29, 96, 97, 120 n.52, 123, 175 n.7, 195, 210 n.66, 218 n.14
Syria 228
Syro-Ephraimite war 15

Talmud 57
Tarshish 56, 191
"tearing away" 104 n.10, 132
temple 63, 85, 143, 145, 146, 153, 157, 163, 164. *See also* worship
Temple Entrance Liturgy 199
temporality 12 n.29, 65, 79, 147, 160, 176, 180, 181, 183, 185, 189, 198
text-critical analysis 50 n.35, 113
theodicy 55
Theodore of Mopsuestia 180
Theodoret of Cyrus 164, 166 n.50, 180
theological commentary, characteristics 1–8

theophany 65, 66 n.26, 83, 86, 87, 88, 93, 153 n.12
thirst 108
Thiselton, Anthony C. 93 n.67
thorn bush 217
Tiglath-pileser III 15
Timothy 120–1
2 Timothy 120–1
Tolkien, J.R.R. 196
Torah 61, 74, 77, 103, 106 n.20, 131, 142, 159, 162, 163–4, 218
Tota Scriptura 144
Tractatus (Spinoza) 179
traditio vs. traditum 2
transgression 88–90, 92, 98, 100, 119, 127
Transjordan region 183, 228
tribes 105, 111, 141, 168, 174, 209 n.63, 228 n.49
Trinity 6–7, 8 n.19, 13–14, 17–29, 76–7, 87, 107, 125, 176 n.14, 177–81
triumph 69, 229
Trueman, Carl 179
truth 17 n.39, 25, 69 n.29, 120–1, 139, 169, 179, 191
Truth and Method (Gadamer) 12 n.29
Tucker, G. M. 80 n.24

unbelief 92, 120
unfaithfulness 163, 202
universalism 67, 84, 187
uprightness, walking in 115, 116–17, 216

Van der Toorn, Karel 40 n.15
van der Woude, A. S. 113, 115, 116, 122 n.59, 128, 182
van Leeuwen, Raymond 55–6
Vatke, Wilhelm 13
vengeance 66, 187, 189, 190, 191
Vergegenwärtigung 2
vine 62, 106 n.18, 158, 163
vineyard 90, 105

vision 23, 63, 77, 79, 137, 142, 151 n.3, 155 n.19, 161, 164, 191, 212 n.74
visitation 218–19, 225
vocation 72, 81, 109, 134, 138, 142
Völkerkampf 153
von Balthasar, Hans Urs 133
von Rad, Gerhard 2, 5 n.10, 6, 17 n.38, 30 n.71, 40, 120, 160–1 n.36, 174, 206
Vorbild 157, 158
vow 63, 163

Wagenaar, Jan A. 38–9 n.12, 189, 190
wailing 94, 110
walk with God 205–9
Waltke, Bruce 47, 50 n.35, 92, 97, 104 nn.9–10, 117–18, 124, 130 n.10, 138 n.41, 141 n.50, 142 n.53, 156 n.22, 170, 181 n.23, 184, 195 n.11, 201, 209 n.63, 210 n.66, 214, 217, 226 n.40
Warfield, B. B. 20
warnings 23, 42, 64, 79, 81, 85, 87, 91, 92, 95, 97, 112, 113, 119, 120, 122 n.59, 147 n.73
wasteland 90
water 63, 86, 108
Watson, Francis 4 n.6, 231–2
Weber, Max 12
Webster, John 7–8, 73, 198
weeping 98, 171, 232
Westermann, Claus 30 n.71
wickedness. *See* evil deeds
wilderness 166, 196
will, God's 36, 61 n.18, 136, 139, 143, 176, 189
Williams, Rowan 27–8
Williamson, Hugh 20 n.45, 40, 80 nn.24–5, 82 n.28, 89 n.57, 99, 106 n.20, 129 n.5, 152–3 nn.8–9, 154, 156, 157 n.25, 157 n.27, 158, 166 n.51, 183 n.29, 211 n.68, 226 n.40

Willis, John T. 47, 83 n.32, 114 n.36, 115 n.40, 169 n.54, 186, 223 n.26
wine 120, 211
wisdom 68, 94, 206, 208
Wissenschaftliche 18
witness 9, 13, 17, 22, 43, 51–69, 73, 79, 83, 85–6, 93, 101, 123, 144–5, 147, 164, 180, 194–6, 203, 215, 221, 222, 227, 229, 231
woe oracle 102–3, 214
Wöhrle, Jakob 52–4 nn.3–4, 55 n.6, 56
Wolff, Hans Walter 38 n.12, 108 n.23, 120 n.52, 123, 128 n.1, 136, 142, 143, 152, 154 n.17, 169 n.55, 171, 175, 182 n.23, 186–7 n.42, 190, 195 n.8, 196 n.13, 201, 210 n.66, 214, 217, 218 n.14, 227, 232 n.63
Wolterstorff, Nicholas 132 n.18, 133–4, 140, 143, 200–1
"word of the LORD"
 linguistic feature of the prophetic expression 76–8
 prophetic word as 76, 79
 sending agency of Yhwh 76–8
 visions and 79–82
wordplays 97–8
"wound" 81, 95–7, 100, 145, 165, 167, 212

wrath, God's 58–60, 65, 87, 187, 189, 190 n.52, 213, 219, 227, 231
Wright, Christopher 198 n.17

Yeago, David 180
Yehud 43–4, 68 n.29, 78, 100, 163, 166 n.50, 177, 189
Yet I Loved Jacob (Kaminsky) 232
yoke imagery 109
Young, Frances 144–5

Zapff, Burkardt 54 n.4, 61 n.19
Zechariah 46, 154 n.17, 164
Zedekiah 184
Zenger, Erich 153 n.10
Zephaniah 4 n.6, 55 n.6, 73, 74, 75, 76
Zerubbabel 180
Zimmerli, Walther 5–6
Zion 39 n.12, 61, 63, 66, 67, 82 n.28, 95 n.76, 98, 99, 100, 105 n.14, 106, 110, 113, 115, 118, 119, 127, 129 n.5, 130, 134, 141, 143, 144, 145, 149, 150–3, 154 n.17, 157 n.24, 157 n.26, 158, 162, 163, 164, 166–70, 173, 175, 182, 185, 187–9, 190 n.53, 191, 193, 213, 215, 217, 221–32

Scripture Index

Old Testament

Genesis
1 224
2:2 120
2:9 104
12:2 166
12:3 187
20:16 195 n.11
24 30 n.71
31:29 103
31:36 195 n.11
32:22-32 166
32:32 166
35:16 168
35:21 168
49:17 135

Exodus
3 59, 174
3:7 132
3:14 230
3:20 229
6:2 230
10:2 230
15:11 230
15:11b 230
15:13-16 229
18 130 n.9
18:2 98
19:6 227
20:17 104
20:17a 104, 104 n.11
20:17b 104, 104 n.11
32 58
32-34 146, 231
33:14 228
34:6-7 53–4 nn.3–4, 55–60, 64–6, 64 n.24, 68, 117, 162, 209, 231–2
34:11 227
34 16, 149
34:28 218
98 18:2

Leviticus
9:3 199 n.24
13:45 138
18:21 200
25:23 105

Numbers
6:24-26 132
21:8ff 134
22:24 197
23:9 228
25:1 197
26:55 111
26:59 196 n.15
32:1 228
35:33 169
36:2 111

Deuteronomy
4:13 202
4:20 227
4:26 194
4:36 209 n.62
5:5 202
5:21 105, 105 n.14
5:24 201
5:25 209 n.62
6:4 101
6:4ff 93
6:20-25 198, 198 n.17
7 174
7:5 91
8.3 201
9:26, 29 227
10:12 205
10:12-13 208
10:12-22 202, 202 n.37
12:32 200
14:1 170
17:16-17 188
18 132 n.19
19:14 211 n.68
21 86 n.41
24:18 132 n.16
26 86 n.41
27:17 211 n.68
28:25, 27 212 n.72
28:30-31 210
28:32 103
28:37 110
29:21-27 190 n.52
30:19 194
31:16 86 n.41
31:17, 18 132 n.19
31:28 194
31 86 n.41
32:1 194
33 111
33:10 142
33:20 132 n.19
33:27 176

Joshua
1:7 37 n.10
1:18 41, 43
2 197
7:21 104
10:24 129
12:1-6 228 n.49
18:8-10 111

##Scripture Index

Judges
  4:4-5 86
  5:11 197
  6 174
  6:32 195 n.11
  11:6 129
  11:11 129

Ruth
  3:11 96 n.78

1 Samuel
  2:21 218
  3 137
  9:6-10 135 n.29
  11 105 n.15
  12:3f 196 n.13
  13:34 218
  22:1 99
  23:13 99
  26:19 119

2 Samuel
  1:16 196 n.13
  1:20 98
  5:24 228
  7 167
  7:13 175 n.7
  13:34 218
  14:19 210
  18:24-27 218
  21:19 86
  23:13 99

1 Kings
  9:16 98
  16:31-33 212
  18:22 170
  21:4 106
  22:24 171

2 Kings
  3:27 200
  9:17-20 218

  10:27 175
  14:3 122
  14:25 55
  15:29 228

2 Chronicles
  16:12 166 n.51
  25:23 122
  27:3 168

Nehemiah
  3:26 168

Job
  2:5 138
  9:14 196 n.13
  10:15 214
  13:24 132 n.19
  16:7 196
  30:29 94
  34:29 132 n.19

Psalms
  2:6 183
  13:1 132 n.19
  13:5 220
  15 199
  19:10 104
  22:12 228
  22:25 132 n.19
  23 123
  23:4 226
  27:9 132 n.19
  30:7 132 n.19
  46 82 n.28, 115, 144, 152
  46:6 143 n.56
  48 115, 144, 152
  48:3 153 n.10
  50:1-7 86 n.42
  68:7-8 86
  68:19 105 n.14
  69:17 132 n.19
  76 152, 153 n.10

  77-78 226
  78:4 229
  80 133
  88:14 132 n.19
  90:2 176
  94 223
  95 119-20
  95:11 119, 120
  132:13f 105 n.14, 119
  137:7-8 123 n.62
  143:7 132 n.19

Proverbs
  3:27 103
  8:14 205, 208 n.60
  8:26 183
  11:2 205
  15:19 217
  16:11 210
  18:24 210
  22:28 211 n.68
  30:18-31 184

Isaiah
  1:1 80, 81
  1:2 194
  1:7 210
  1-12 35
  1:23 142
  2:1 80 n.24, 158
  2:1-4 150, 151 n.3
  2:2 156
  2:2-5 35, 153 n.9
  2:2b 155 n.19
  2:3 77
  2:4 158, 164
  2:5 159, 161, 191
  2:6ff 188
  2:6-8 35, 191
  2:7 188
  2:9-22 229
  3:9 196 n.13
  5:1-3 90
  5:1-7 90, 216

Scripture Index

5:5 122, 225
5:8 102 n.5, 105
5:11 102 n.5
5:13 99
5:18 102 n.5
5:20 102 n.5
5:23 142
6:1 109
6:10 109
6:11 210
7:14 35, 175
7:20 94 n.71
8:16 5
8:16-18 220
8:17 132 n.19
8:22 137
9:6 182
10:5 171
10:6 169
10:10-11 91
10:11 95, 96
11:1 35, 175 n.7
13:1 80 n.24
13:21-22 94
16:5 131 n.14
20:1-6 94 n.71
20:2 94
22:5 219
24:12-13 216
24:18 194
27:13 226
28:7 134
28:29 208
29:14 229
30:8 5, 195 n.11
30:26 95 n.77
40:1-2 123
40:4 86
40:8 22
40:11 227
40:25-31 139
40:26 139
42:3 232
43:5 123
54:1-3 225
54:7 165 n.49
54:8 132 n.19
56:8 165 n.49
56-66 34
57:15 109
58:1 89, 138
58:12 117
61:4 117
61:8 139
64:5 132 n.19
66:18-21 226

Jeremiah
1:2 with 1:4 77
3:1 169
3:9 169
5:15 190
5:18-19 113
6:4 136
6:6 218
6:13 218
6:17 218
7:4 143
8:3 108
9:13 216
10:19 95 n.77
14:9 143 n.56
15:11 94
15:18 95 n.77
16:16 170
17:16 94
18:11 102 n.5
18:20 94
22:13-17 141
22:15-16 131 n.14
23:3 123, 165 n.49
23:3-4 227
23:13-32 134
26:17-19 146
26:18 33, 142
26:18-19 142 n.53
28 109
28:6-9 139
28:9 138
29:14 165 n.49
29:23 86
31:8 165 n.49
31:10 123, 165 n.49
33:5 132 n.19
41:5 170
42:5 86
47:5 170
49:4 111
116 34
118-19 34
119-20 35

Lamentations
4:3 94

Ezekiel
1-24 6 n.11
3:17 218
10 118 n.48
11:17 165 n.49
16 85
21:2 113 n.32
21:7 113 n.32
24:17-22 138
24:17-23 94
32:7-8 137
33:11 146
34:2-3 131
34:11-16 227
34:13 123
39:23 132 n.19
39:24 132 n.19
39:29 132 n.19
45:10-11 210 n.65
48 111

Daniel
7:9 177, 180 n.20

Hosea
1:3 100
1:4 218

1:5 110
1:7 91
1:9 109
2:4:(2) 195 n.11
2:12 90
2:15 218
3:5 124
4:1-2 163, 206 n.51
4:2 122, 134
4:6 142
4:9 219 n.17
4:14 91, 219 n.17
5:1 130
5:9-10 211
5:14 187
6:1 165
6:6 203
7;14 170
8:4 91
8:13 218
8:14 85, 91
9:1 91
9:7 120 n.52
9:7-8 218
9:8 218, 218 n.14, 219 n.17
9:9 218
9:10 216
10:15 210
11:8 231
12:2-6 167, 232 n.64
12:3 218
12:4 210
12:6 202
12:7 210
13:2 91
14 170
14:5 187
14:9 37, 91
14:10 43
14:10a 162
14:10b 162

Joel
1:2-3 230
2 65
2:10 137
2:27 230
4 62–3
4:9 136
4:10 62

Amos
1:1 79, 79 n.23
1:2 67, 190
1:3 89
2:6 118
3:1-4 210
3:2 14, 108, 219 n.17
3:8 85.n 39, 108
4:4 210
5:5-6 210
5:10 141
5:12 89
5:13 110
5:15 130
5:18 188, 190 n.53, 219
5:18-20 137
5:21-24 200
7 184 n.33
7:1-6 94
7:12 135 n.29
7:16 113, 113 n.32
8:1ff 216
8:2 216
8:5 210
8:11 138
9:11 176
9:13 113 n.32

Jonah
1 63, 229

Micah
1:1 71, 78 n.21, 79, 82, 139

1:2 83, 83 n.30, 84, 102 n.5, 129
1:2-4 83, 88
1:2-5 84
1:2-7 81, 82, 85, 88, 92
1:2-9 74, 81
1:2b 85, 86
1:3 35, 83
1:3-4 86
1-4 187
1:5 83, 88, 174, 190
1:5-7 88, 89 n.57
1:5a 88
1:5b 88
1:5c 88
1:6-7 81
1:7 91, 210
1:8-9 100
1:9 118
1:10 99
1:10-16 76, 100
1:12 98
1:13 98
1:14a 98
1:14b 98
1:15 98, 99
2:1-2 107
2:1-3 102 n.5, 132
2:1-5 78, 101, 102, 114
2:2 105, 132 n.16
2:3 118, 133
2:3c 109
2:6 112
2:6-7 112
2:6-8 114 n.36, 115 n.40
2:6-11 112
2:10 116, 142
2:12-13 121, 121 n.54, 122 n.59, 125, 128, 165, 167, 226–8

Scripture Index

2:13 125
3 210
3:1 106, 129, 130, 131, 216
3:1a 128
3:1-3 134
3:1-4 127, 133
3:2 104 n.10
3:2b 132 n.16
3:2b-3 132
3:5 118
3:5-8 134
3:8 202, 215
3:9 140
3:9-10 82 n.28
3:9-12 140, 143, 157 n.24
3:10-11 217
3:12 90, 145, 146, 147, 147 n.74
4:1 156
4:1-4 160, 162, 163, 174, 211, 225, 225 n.37, 226, 230
4:1-5 35, 150, 151 n.3, 159, 163
4:1-5:15 160 n.36
4:2 77
4:3 158
4:3b 155
4:4 106 n.18, 157, 158
4:4-5 159
4:5 150, 151 n.3, 155 n.19, 159, 161, 161 n.39, 162, 163
4:6-5:1 [4:14 MT] 149
4:6-7 165, 165 n.49
4:7b 166
4:8 150, 168, 170, 173

4:8-5:1 167
4:8-5:1 (4:14 MT) 167
4:8-5:4 (5:3 MT) 149
4:8-5:5 MT 169
4:9 186
4:9-10 170
4:11-13 187, 211
4:13 83 n.31, 169, 230
4:14 170, 171
5 118
5:1 173, 215, 226
5:1 (4:14 MT) 149, 186
5:1(2) 177, 178
5:2 35, 175, 178, 179, 180
5:2 (5:1 MT) 167, 168, 169, 173, 175
5:2-4 173
5:2-4 (1-3 MT) 174, 181, 182
5:3 (5:2 MT) 173
5:4b 183
5:5 (5:4 MT) 181
5:5-9 (5:4-8 MT) 181
5:7-8 186, 187
5:8-15 211
5:9-13 35
5:9-13 MT 84
5:9-14 187 n.44
5:10-15 187
5:14 84
6:1 83, 83 n.30, 84
6:1-2 194
6:1-7:7 35, 213, 216, 224
6:1-8 131, 194, 194 n.7, 204, 207
6:10-11 210
6:10-12 210
6:13-15 211
6:16 215

7:1 214–15, 220–1
7:1-6 219
7:1-7 213–15, 217–18, 221–2
7:2 216–17
7:3 217
7:3-6 216
7:4 217, 219 n.17
7:4b 217–18
7:5-6 220
7:7 215, 218, 220, 220 n.21
7:7-10 221
7:7-17 230
7:7-20 221, 226
7:8 215
7:8-10 215, 221
7:8-20 215, 222–3, 223 n.26
7:10 222, 230
7:11 228
7:11-13 221
7:12 226
7:14 227–8
7:14-17 221
7:17 229
7:17b 229, 230
7:18-20 221–2, 230
7:20 232 n.63
8-9 93
8-10 168
Judah
  1:8-9 81
  vv. 1-2 102, 108–11, 196
  vv. 1-3 132, 132 n.17, 140
  vv. 1-4 160, 165
  vv. 1-5 182
  vv. 1-7 139, 201
  vv. 1b-2 195
  vv. 2-4 83, 88
  vv. 2-4 and v. 5 83
  vv. 2-4 (1-3 MT) 184

vv. 3-4 86
vv. 3-5 108, 196, 199
vv. 5-6 (4-5 MT) 182, 185
vv. 5-6, v. 7b 218
vv. 5-7 88–90
vv. 5-8 134, 137
vv. 6-7 91, 93, 120, 137, 168, 199–200
vv. 7-8 (6-7 MT) 186
vv. 7-9 [6-8 MT] 185
vv. 7-10 222
vv. 8-1 222
vv. 8-9 93, 118
vv. 8-10 112, 117, 168, 224
vv. 8-10; 14-17 222
vv. 9-10 168
vv. 9b-11 141
vv. 10-12 96, 209
vv. 10-14 (9-13 MT) 183
vv. 11-13 222, 225
vv. 12-13 122–3, 225
vv. 12-14 (11-13 MT) 188
vv. 14-17 222, 224
vv. 18-20 222–4

Nahum
1:2:8 64, 66
1:3 57, 64 n.24, 65, 67
1:6 65
1:6a 67, 84 n.33
1:7 62
1:7b 62
1:9 62
3:19 95 n.77

Habakkuk
1:2-4 220
2:6 110
2:12 141, 141 n.51, 142
2:12 (2:6ff) 142
3:17-19 221

Zephaniah
1:15 137
3:8 86
3:15 143 n.56
3:17 143 n.56
3:18-20 165 n.49
3:19 123

Zechariah
1:1-6 46
8:3-5 164
8:20-22 157 n.24
9:9-10 188 n.45
10:3 227
14:16-19 226

Malachi
3:22-24 37 n.10

New Testament

Matthew
2:6 175
7:21-23 143
28:19-20 164

Mark
12:28-31 102

John
1:1 176 n.12, 222
1:5 163
1:14 77
1:16 229
1:18 76
3:16 205

7:42 176 n.12
10 227
10:1-18 227
10:3 227
10:14-18 227
16:33 125
19:19 227

Acts of the Apostles
8 138
8:9-24 136

Romans
1 219
2:4 224
9:11 125
12 198
15:4 4–5

1 Corinthians
9:9 137

2 Corinthians
6:2 3

Colossians
1:17 7

2 Timothy
4:3-5 121

Hebrews
1:1 77
3:14 119
3:17-4:11 119
4:1 119
12:1-3 221

2 Peter
1:20-21 73

Revelation
2–3 85

www.ingramcontent.com/pod-product-compliance
Lightning Source LLC
Chambersburg PA
CBHW051519230426
43668CB00012B/1662